# THE ENIGMA OF CHILDHOOD

# THE ENIGMA OF CHILDHOOD

## The Profound Impact of the First Years of Life on Adults as Couples and Parents

*Ronnie Solan*

Translated and edited by Ian Dreyer

Scientific editing by Ruth Shidlo

**KARNAC**

*The Enigma of Childhood* was originally published in Hebrew by Modan in 2007.

First published in English in 2015 by
Karnac Books Ltd
118 Finchley Road
London NW3 5HT

British Library Cataloguing in Publication Data

A C.I.P. for this book is available from the British Library

ISBN-13: 978-1-78220-211-0

Typeset by V Publishing Solutions Pvt Ltd., Chennai, India

Printed in Great Britain by TJ International Ltd, Padstow, Cornwall

www.karnacbooks.com

*Dedicated to my beloved husband and life partner*
*Dr. Haim Solan who inspired my writing*

*Note regarding the use of gender-specific pronouns*

Throughout the text, the use of gender-specific pronouns (e.g., him/her; his/hers) in situations where an infant, child, or adult is being referred to generally, rather than as a specific, named person, the pronouns used are universally male. This is to ensure consistency and prevent the reader wondering to whom the text is referring. Where a particular gender is being referred to (e.g., mother, father), or a clinical vignette is being related, the appropriate gender-specific pronoun is used.

# CONTENTS

# ABOUT THE AUTHOR

**Dr. Ronnie Solan** trained as a clinical psychologist and psychoanalyst in Switzerland and in Israel, where she became a training and supervising analyst. She works in Tel Aviv, with children, adults, and couples. For many years, she taught at the Israel Psychoanalytic Society in Jerusalem and the Psychotherapy Program of the Sackler School of Medicine's Continuing Education Program, Tel Aviv University. *The Enigma of Childhood* is her first book in English. The original Hebrew version of the book was widely acclaimed.

*The love which founded the family continues to operate in civilization ... it continues to carry on its function of binding together considerable numbers of people ... and create[s] new bonds with people who before were strangers.*

*Freud, Civilization and its Discontents*

# PREFACE

*Moshe Halevi Spero*

The interpretation of child development that clinical psychologist and psychoanalyst Ronnie Solan lays before us in the chapters to follow significantly enhances the vast literature with a fresh and intriguing perspective on the dynamics of the unfolding of the ego, and self, and its relationship to other selves. Bringing to the workbench the special sensitivities of a participant-observer trained in psychoanalysis and personally and professionally influenced by Jean Piaget, Solan's approach deepens and expands our understanding of the challenge of human relationship between parent and child, couples and the partners in a psychotherapeutic relationship (clinical or supervisory).

There have been a few efforts to enlarge and update the post-Freudian psychosexual model of the early stages of child development—Irene Josselyn's classic work, *The Psychosocial Development of Children* (1978) springs first to mind, followed in more recent times by the empirical turn represented by the work of Daniel N. Stern (1985) and the essays collected by Joseph Masling and Robert Bornstein (1996). Each of these has emphasised a crucially new piece of the pie, though none in recent times has attempted an organised redeployment of the original Freudian stage theory. Even Margaret S. Mahler's watershed outline of the phases of early separation-individuation (Mahler, Pine & Bergman, 1975) begs for realignment with the revised insights into the microcosms of psychosexual development that have emerged in recent years. I have in mind especially the unique influence of the work of the various French schools of psychoanalysis and the post-Kleinians. Indeed, in the decades that have passed since the publication of these earlier works, we have experienced a significant change in our comprehension of preverbal mental experience, the role of mirroring and the aesthetic domain, pre-object relatedness, the *anlage* of early sensory mapping and rudimentary psychic envelopes, the pathways of internalisation and symbolisation, and other subtle dimensions of budding mentalization and the representation of self-other experience. These areas of advance have broadened the "reach" or tensile strength of our clinical capacities; in turn, the clinical yield has sharpened our theories. And yet there has been lacking a scholarly and clinically-sensitive outline that would gather and align, and further refine, these developments, and present us with a suitably augmented model of the developing mind that might guide the psychoanalytically-informed student of childhood.

The *enigma* of childhood that Ronnie Solan wishes to illuminate in this important book is one that emerges essentially from a paradoxical dimension that is inherent to human development. This enigma is not always experienced as such (that is to say, we tend to experience an inchoate kind of anxiety regarding childhood without being able to localize or objectify the experience); the enigma cannot be always spoken of as such except when problematized and refracted through the eyes of philosophers, poets and psychotherapists. Yet whether or not we apprehend this enigma as such, it quite literally churns within us— motivating our development, rendering it complex or conflictual, or stymieing us completely—as children growing up, as speaking beings (who must internalise the preexisting linguistic patterns which drench us in otherness and yet through which we must articulate our selves), and as partners in relationships. The same applies to the work of psychoanalysts and psychotherapists who struggle to navigate and articulate the unique and often contradictory qualities of relationship that unfold during the therapeutic process, and for whom the enigmatic quality of intrapsychic and intersubjective dynamics is the hub of the work. Given our pragmatic goals, we as psychotherapists have considerably less leeway for allowing the enigma of childhood to remain unexplored or merely metaphoric.

I was fortunate to notice the stirrings of Ronnie Solan's thinking on this matter that were first published in the most suitable format for such observations, *The Psychoanalytic Study of the Child* (1991). It became immediately clear that she had grasped something fundamentally healthy in the role that narcissism can serve as a kind of necessary psychic buffer for the painful divide that exists within the constant movement of the self between its own separateness and joinedness (Solan refers to this as "jointness"). Despite Heinz Kohut's revolutionary writing on narcissism during the late 1970's, the prevailing view of narcissism was as an expression of pathology, and thus Solan's notions were still novel. It is ironic that the capacity for joining that Ronnie Solan herself expressed through her writing lingered in my mind and work, and magically encouraged me to invite her to explore her work further for a collection I was editing, resulting in the exposition of her concept of "befriending the unfamiliar" (Solan, 1998).

As stated, the *enigma* of childhood refers to a disturbing paradox that arguably characterises human nature and the experience of being human; hence, this sense of enigma dare not be ignored. The paradoxical dimension Solan focuses upon is, in fact, a double or bifurcated phenomenon. The first dimension—which we might conceive of as outer-oriented—is that our sense of self is predicated upon otherness, modeled upon the others or "not-ourselves" around us, and remains sensitive, throughout life and all relationship, to the amount of other-than-self that can be enjoyed. The second dimension—initially inner-oriented—derives from the fact that the self also emerges from a state of narcissism, total non-otherness, what we colloquially refer to as selfishness. To a large degree, we could not have a sense of self adequately distinguished from other without a complement of narcissistic investment.

These separate but interrelated tensions confront the soon-to-become-ego immediately, though they cannot yet be conceptualised. The ego must ask itself, we can imagine: how much narcissism is required to protect the self, and how much narcissism must be sacrificed or submitted to some other kind of mental operation so that we might welcome, acknowledge, befriend others, otherhood? Or, in the query of the ancient Jewish sage Hillel (*Pirkei Avot*, 1:14): "If I am not for myself, then who will be for me; and when I am only for myself, who am I?"

This paradox effloresces the moment the infant (if not the fetus) opens his or her mouth, experiences a gap and foreign entities that enter this gap, and becomes responsive to stimuli from the sensory surround, especially through the Janus-faced barrier known as our skin—primarily definatory of the oral stage. The paradox is experienced again, relentlessly as the child becomes more aware (as oral-stage achievements disposed the child to be) of the presence of food and stool within the alimentary canal and the meaning of even more portals of the body—definatory of the anal stage. And this double-valenced tension increases exponentially as the multifaceted signifiers of gender and competitive sexual aims and objects further complicate and sexualise the achievements of the earlier stages—definatory of the Oedipal stage and its precursors. Here I must point out that Solan emphasises primarily the oral and anal phases of separateness-jointness, and at times the reader sorely feels the underemphasis of the role of Oedipus; we must anticipate a further work from her which would complete her outline in light of the latter phases of development.

This perspective of double paradox is exceedingly important. For our contemporary theoretical formulations and clinical experiences have taught us that narcissism—that is, a kind of "sound" or normative, secondary narcissism in contrast to the more limited use of the term to refer to pathological (narcissistic) states of mind—does not stand *opposed* to healthy selfhood or relationships with others. Rather, and most significantly, narcissism serves to cloak, envelope (to envelope, metaphorically, and also serving as a kind of "envelop" within which the self is contained) and protect the self, regulating the wear-and-tear of intercourse with others.

The pleasure of self-experience is thus linked directly to our capacity to tolerate, seek out and enjoy, or embrace, enigma ("paradox" as such is not an affect state), *as well as to be able to accurately attend to signals that indicate that the intensity or quantity of enigma might soon exceed some baseline of safety.* In articulating her unique approach to how the ego contends with this dilemma, Solan speaks of the self "befriending" otherness, creating a sense of familiarity about otherness, about itself in its relations with others. Her use of the term is apt since the root of the term *friend* is powerfully linked to love and joy.[1] If I correctly appreciate her ideas here, it must be said that Solan is describing a protective apparatus that constantly *replenishes* the inner sanctity, subtlety and privacy of the self while restoring the capacity to engage others. In one of the many applications of her theory, Solan generously picks up one of my own areas of research and underscores how jokes and a sense of humor might be designed, at root, to maintain a protective envelope around our earliest perceptions of the enigma of otherness.

In Solan's view—and I consider this novel and crucial—narcissism is reconceived as a veritable immune system for the self, elaborating upon Freud's most fruitful notion of the stimulus barrier (or protective barrier). This enables her to further hypothesise a broader narcissistic autoimmune system that continues to operate throughout life, and she is able to distinguish eleven functions of this system. Health and pathology in the domain of comfortable and efficient self-other relationships—chiefly: the capacity to maintain a sense of *familiarity* in a world of non-self stimuli, entities, and processes—can now be more accurately conceptualised in terms of different levels and qualities of narcissistic immune functioning, that depends, among other things, upon the degree of internalisation that has been achieved by the subcomponents of this system.

As the book unfolds, Ronnie Solan details several of the most significant and until now only partially delineated components of this fascinating paradox in order to reduce the sense of puzzlement that the enigma of childhood/selfhood tends to evoke within us. I am not thinking here of a dry, intellectual riddle that we would prefer to see finally resolved. Rather, I am referring to a deep existential knot that straddles the core of the psychological experience—the experience of self and of other—over which we stumble, or learn to enjoy, at every moment.

Hell, then, is not *merely* "other people," the typical misinterpretation of Sartre's important phrase in his play *No Exit* (1944). Hell is not the other as such, it is not "out there"; hell is the otherness that is indelibly part of self. This principle psychic anxiety stems from the fact that *self*

---

[1] The Old English *frēond* connotes friend, lover, or relative, and is cognate with the Old Saxon *friund* and Old High German *friunt* (German *freund*), and the Gothic infinite *frēogan*, to love.

will always enigmatically signify *other*; that we inevitably come to see ourselves as an object in the world of other persons' consciousness and by virtue of enigmatic qualities within the language spoken to us that we cannot entirely identify or decipher (Laplanche, 1999).[2] This enigma is at once alien and familiar, and the task of the narcissistic processes as conceived by Solan is to help maintain a balance.

The enigma of childhood, of the self in relation to narcissism and otherhood, might rightly be compared to a similar range of experience that captured Freud's attention long ago, and has preoccupied us since. I am thinking of the experience of the uncanny, *Das Unheimlich*, un-hominess, the sense of *fremde*, strangeness, the antonym of *freund* … that odd, or enigmatic sense that someone or some experience is simultaneously known and unknown, familiar and unfamiliar. We are generally aware of the fact that we cannot conveniently dilute the peculiar discomfort and sense of apprehension and expectation that the uncanny evokes by insisting upon a decision: "Which is it?" It would distort the true value of the uncanny if one were to force the experience into an overly dichotomous frame, just as Donald Winnicott brilliantly admonished us to not compel the child to declare whether he or she *found* the transitional object or *created* it. To do so would destroy all that is special about transitional experience and to ultimately impede the development of symbolization. Moreover, any effort to prematurely or unnaturally modify the experience of uncanniness or enigma that comprises specific dimensions of psychic development would result in diminishment, numbness or schizoid compromise. The narcissistic immune system, as Solan defines it, safeguards the lambent quality of enigma.

---

[2]Similar to Solan's approach to the enigmatic quality of self, and of the role of narcissism, Jean Laplanche proposed the elevation of *seduction* from the purely pathological sphere so that we might better appreciate its fundamental role in the early architecture of essential psychic development. While a detailed discussion of this matter cannot be taken up here, suffice it to say that, differently than Freud's original or classic "general theory of seduction," Laplanche emphasised the crucial role of the adult other, and the other's unconscious, in the very formation of the child's (*qua* subject) psychical apparatus. In Laplanche's view, powerfully redolent of Lacan, the basic intrapsychic agencies—ego, unconscious and superego—can to some degree be viewed as secondary to the primal, enigmatic inscriptions of the other (conveyed by language and ploysemy), and as deriving their specificity from the partial successes and necessary failures of the infant's attempts to master, symbolise and "translate" those inscriptions. The overlap of Laplanche's ideas and Solan's concept of befriending the enigma of self-other/separation-jointness merits further exploration.

I will end my words with the following thought. It is refreshing to note, with indirect but inescapable relevance to the enigma of self, narcissism and the other, the following delightfully acidic personal episode offered by Freud, a gem that has been inexplicably (uncannily!) ignored in the vast psychoanalytic literature (1919, p. 248n):

> Since the uncanny effect of a 'double' also belongs to [the study of the uncanny], it is interesting to observe what the effect is of meeting one's own image unbidden and unexpected … I was sitting alone in my *wagon-lit* compartment when a more than usually violent jolt of the train swung back the door of the adjoining washing-cabinet, and an elderly gentleman in a dressing-gown and a traveling cap came in. I assumed that in leaving the washing-cabinet, which lay between the two compartments, he had taken the wrong direction and come into my compartment by mistake. Jumping up with the intention of putting him right, I at once realized to my dismay that the intruder was nothing but my own reflection in the looking-glass on the open door. I can still recollect that I thoroughly disliked his appearance. Instead, therefore, of being frightened by our 'double,' … I simply failed to recognize [it] as such. Is it not possible, though, that [my] dislike of the double was a vestigial trace of the archaic reaction which feels the 'double' to be something uncanny?

I believe that Freud offers us a compelling portrait of an enigma of childhood—if not *the* enigma of childhood!—that has lingered into adulthood. A deeply archaic, incompletely resolved sense of unfamiliarity or dislikeability that had managed to lie dormant (perhaps it is an anal one), hidden within a sense of self generally viewed as cohesive, known, predictable, and familiar, suddenly emerges—jolted, violently—(*einen heftingeren Ruck*)—as if dislodged by accident, temporarily distorting the sense of reality. That there is a "higher" oedipal connotation to the painfulness of the pseudo-encounter (the paternal "elderly gentleman") does not fully mask the deeper reverberations of *sheer otherhood*.

As I ponder Freud's intricate example it seems that he has also offered us a condensed isomorphism for the workings of the mind in analysis! That is, we can perhaps reconceptualize the private compartment—this suspended non-space shuttling along in a dreamlike mode between mental states and across borders—the looking-glass on the open door of the train *within* compartment, and the remarkably delineated *threshold* between mental spaces, as a simulacrum of the concept of the analytic frame. Momentarily distracted from convention and the etiquette of polite looking, the distracted mind, the mind in reverie, becomes more capable of gazing, or apprehending. The frame, through its magical involution of the dynamics of normative development, is designed to allow for the repetition of the 'vestiges' of an 'archaic' un-friendliness of the self toward some other, toward some sense of otherness. In the case of Freud, the other is temporarily experienced as an uncanny double; at other times in the form of mildly dissociative experiences of *jamais vu* and *déjà vu*, and at still other times in the sharply psychotic experience of an imaginary twin (Bion, 1950). Our customary 'night clothing' or envelopes cannot always conceal this enigma, or they congeal it to the point where all we can handle emotionally are dichotomies, splitting, black and white values and formalities. Whatever inner conflicts caused Freud to suffer a derealised (*Entfremdungsgefühl*) and intrusive self-other experience, Ronnie Solan would hope we could *befriend*. The challenge for the analyst and patient is to gradually learn anew how to contain and befriend these experiences and restore a more hospitable attitude toward enigma.

*Moshe Halevi Spero, Ph.D*
*Professor and Director,*
*The Postgraduate Program of Psychoanalytic*
*Psychotherapy; School of Social Work,*
*Bar-Ilan University; Editor-in-Chief,*
*Ma'arag: The Israel Annual of Psychoanalysis*

## References

Bion, W. R. (1950). The imaginary twin. In *Second Thoughts*. London: W. Heinemann, 1967, pp. 3–12.

Freud, S. (1919). The uncanny. In *The Standard Edition of the Complete Psychological Works of Sigmund Freud*, vol. 17. London: Hogarth, 1964, pp. 219–253.

Josselyn, M. I. (1978). *The Psychosocial Development of Children*. Second Edition. New York: Family Service Association of American/Jason Aronson, 1982.

Laplanche, J. (1999). *Essays on Otherness*. J. Fletcher, trans. London: Routledge.

Mahler, M. S., Pine, F. & Bergman, A. (1975). *The Psychological Birth of the Human Infant: Symbiosis and Individuation*. New York: Basic.

Masling, J. M. & Bornstein, R. F. eds. (1996). *Psychoanalytic Perspectives on Developmental Psychology*. Washington, D.C.: American Psychological Association.

Solan, R. (1991). Jointness as integration of merging and separateness in object relations and narcissism. In A. J. Solnit, P. B. Neubauer, S. Abrams & A. S. Dowling. *The Psychoanalytic Study of the Child*. Vol. 46. New Haven, Conn.: Yale University Press, pp. 337–52.

Solan, R. (1998). Narcisssitic fragility in the process of befriending the unfamiliar. *American Journal of Psychoanalysis*, 58: 163–86.

Stern, D. N. (1985). *The Interpersonal World of the Infant: A View from Psychoanalysis and Developmental Psychology*. New York: Basic.

# INTRODUCTION AND ACKNOWLEDGEMENTS

My aim in writing this book is to familiarise the reader with the child concealed in every adult, believed to represent the sum of memory traces of early life experiences. Each of us contains within him or herself layers of memory traces of various object-relation narratives from different stages of development. The concealed child reverberates within us in present situations, and affects our physical sensations and emotional reactions to them. This has an impact on the new relationships we create, on the way we relate as parents to our own children, and as partners in couplehood in its various forms.

The idea of writing a book arose from my wish to share with others the child's emotional development processes from birth; a stimulating subject that I was involved with over many years in seminars that I conducted. The seminars were part of a continuing education psychotherapy program at Tel Aviv University for psychologists, psychiatrists, and social workers. For me, this is a fitting opportunity to thank the hundreds of participants in the seminars for their personal contribution to shaping my new theoretical approach to the child's dynamic development—an approach I will elucidate in this book. Some of my ideas have been previously elaborated and presented in various professional articles and in the Hebrew precursor to this book.

My basic view, using Winnicott's terminology, is that most parents are "good enough" and do the best they can for their child, depending on their personality, their understanding, and the kind of love they feel for their offspring.

> ... in any case you will make mistakes and these mistakes will be seen and felt to be disastrous, and your children will try to make you feel responsible for setbacks even when you are not in fact responsible .... You will feel rewarded if one day your daughter asks you to do some baby-sitting for her, indicating thereby that she thinks you may be able to do this satisfactorily; or if your son wants to be like you in some way .... (Winnicott, 1971, p. 143)

*The Enigma of Childhood* sheds light on early psychic development in the oral and anal stages, its impact on the baby's evolution along a normal or pathological developmental course and the parents' influence on their baby's emotional development. The ages referred to in the context of the stages of emotional development are the average accepted age, deviations from which may be considered normative. The separation among different aspects of development is to some extent arbitrary and is done with the didactic intention of clarifying the processes described. It is done for the book to be accessible also to a readership that is not proficient in the analysis of emotional processes or familiar with clinical work. It is important to note that in daily life these aspects are intertwined and difficult to separate objectively.

Examples taken from clinical observations and treatments are presented to enable readers to improve their understanding of early developmental processes, and to familiarise them with the child hidden within themselves.

*The Enigma of Childhood* focuses on four major themes: narcissism, the ego, object-relations, and separation-individuation. These familiar basic concepts in emotional development are integrated and conceptualised in new theoretical and clinical terms.

My main contribution relates to the conceptualisation of the functioning of *healthy narcissism* as an emotional immune system for safeguarding the familiar sense of the self and for resisting any strangeness or otherness challenging this familiar sense. This conceptualisation will be examined in the context of the biological immune system. Moreover, I propose taking a fresh look at the functioning of the ego, including the distinction between the regulatory characteristics of adaptation mechanisms and defence mechanisms, and their operational modes at the oral and anal stages. This distinction will clarify how, through the functioning of the ego's adaptation, we improve and actualise our intelligence potential (psychomotor, cognitive and emotional) and cope with reality, as well as how we defend our self against strangeness, and the attendant fears and anxieties that may undermine our stability.

I suggest a new elaboration of normative object relations, defined as "jointness-separateness," which progress from birth along the lifespan, and are characterised during the oral stage by intimacy and in the anal stage by negotiation. This elaboration will clarify why I consider symbiosis in the context of the primary infant–mother relationship as an impairment in object relations.

Taken together, these concepts facilitate a better understanding of the foundations of normative emotional development. They also provide possible insights into impairments in narcissistic functioning and object relations that may lead to fragility and vulnerability of the self, immature individuation, narcissistic disorders, and pathological phenomena.

The innovative theoretical definitions that I propose are a continuation of the conceptualisation of development processes that first germinated in the greenhouse of my psychoanalytic forefathers and were nurtured by my mentors. I am aware that any theoretical innovation initially arouses a sense of strangeness and resistance; this, after all, is the subject of my book. At the same time, I hope that the way I will present my theoretical approach is sufficiently accessible and that it will facilitate the opening of emotional channels for absorbing the familiar and befriending the novel, without my having to resort to a review of well-known theoretical positions.

Many babies, children, and adults will populate the pages of my book. Some of them demonstrate normative developmental processes, others, emotional disabilities. The descriptions and the quotes from the therapies presented throughout this book are based on observations that I conducted of infants and children, as well as on my clinical and diagnostic work with children, adolescents, adults, and couples. I have selected the more salient examples (admittedly a small sample), in order to demonstrate my approach, based on many years of experience, against the backdrop of psychoanalytic and psychodynamic theory.

Identifying patient details have been deliberately obscured in order to maintain confidentiality. Nevertheless, the description of the emotional processes and the sequences of the personal narrative and of the events are authentic, so that the essence and the relevance of the processes are maintained. I wish to take this opportunity to thank my patients, from whom I have learned so much.

It has been my privilege to have studied under some of the foremost psychologists and psychoanalysts of our generation, including Jean Piaget at Geneva University, René Spitz at the Swiss Psychoanalytic Institute, René Henny at the Mental Health Center in Lausanne, and Erich Gumbel at the Israeli Psychoanalytic Institute in Jerusalem, all of whom opened the gates to reveal the wonderful world of the mind. I am deeply grateful to Marcel Roch from Lausanne, my personal mentor, under whose guidance, which I cherish, I chose psychoanalysis as my life's work. I am deeply moved that I am able to present in this book my own theoretical contribution to the understanding of the emotional development of the child that draws on the heritage of my teachers. This is my way of thanking all my teachers, including those whose names I have not mentioned, for their considerable investment in imparting to me their treasures of knowledge.

Many thanks to my dear ones: My husband, Haim Solan, for his considerable and challenging contribution to the linguistic processing, conceptualisation and transformation of my handwriting into an accessible book, a contribution that enabled us to reach new heights of creative partnership in our relationship. To my daughter, Anat Ben-Artsy Solan, whose critical, dynamic-developmental and integrative psychological thinking contributed so much to the professional editing of this book; to my other children, Zach Solan and Shira Solan-Shoham—as well as to their spouses, Shay, Maly, and Avishai—for their warm and loving encouragement and constant support. My love and thanks to all my grandchildren for the privilege of being a close participant in their experiences and for allowing me a fascinating look into the wonders of their development. I am deeply thankful to Dr. Ruth Shidlo for helping to conceptualise the book and for her scientific editing assistance. Finally, my grateful thanks to Ian Dreyer, my translator and editor, for his ability to effortlessly handle the Hebrew text.

In addition, I would like to thank Oliver Rathbone and the staff at Karnac, including Constance Govindin, Rod Tweedy, Tom Hawking, and especially, Cecily Blench, for their unwavering and most professional assistance throughout the publishing process. It has been a pleasure to work with them.

# PERMISSIONS

The author would like to thank the following publishing houses for permission to quote from these texts:

"Dulcinea" theme by Dale Wasserman.
*Man of La Mancha. A Musical Play.*
Lyrics by Joe Darion
Music by Mitch Leigh
Copyright © 1966 by Dale Wasserman
Copyright © 1965 by Andrew Scott Music, Helena Music Company.
Alan S. Honig, Administrator "Man of La Mancha" Rights. All rights reserved. Reprinted by permission.

*The Rosebush Murders* by Ruth Shidlo
Copyright © 2012 by Ruth Shidlo
Published by Hoopoe Publishing.
Reprinted by permission of the author.

Excerpt from *The Little Prince* by Antoine de Saint-Exupery, translated from the French by Richard Howard. Copyright 1943 by Houghton Mifflin Harcourt Publishing Company. Copyright © renewed 1971

# PART I

## THE ORAL STAGE—THE STAGE OF INTIMACY

### FROM BIRTH TO EIGHTEEN MONTHS

*Homo sum, humani nihil a me alienum puto*
I am a man: nothing human is alien to me (Terence)

# CHAPTER ONE

# Beginnings

I n the early morning hours, Sean makes his way from his mother's familiar womb into a new world: an unfamiliar space filled with light, in which all the living conditions are different from those he was used to. The sensory stimuli from his mother's womb and from the moments of his birth are engraved in him forever as memory traces of initial life experiences, providing him with a basis for differentiating the familiar from that which is strange and novel in his new world.

## *The beginning of emotional life*

We are amazed by the development of the foetus in its mother's womb, created by the merging of two separate and different cells, a creation that has similar characteristics to its two progenitors but also differs from them. The mother and the foetus, two separate entities sharing a common space, the womb, are connected to each other by the umbilical cord and the placenta. At times, the foetus is asleep and the mother is awake, anxious as to why it does not move; at other times, she sleeps and the foetus, now awake, disturbs her sleep. Sometimes, however, she tends to deny the foetus's separateness and tries to experience its existence within her as if they were unique entities. This flowing between people, from being separated to joining together, continues throughout life.

A mother is attentive to the tempo of her foetus's movements and reactions, and tries to interpret them and to make contact with the foetus by touching her belly or singing to it. She observes the foetus's movements on the walls of her abdomen as its form changes, and can view the movement on an ultrasound. She gets to know the foetus and tries to imagine how it will look when it emerges. In this way, as she "imagines the real", to borrow Buber's (1947) phrase, she transforms her unfamiliar foetus into a more familiar object, and longs for the moment she can hold her baby to her bosom. Feelings of love for it begin to surge in her.

The foetus in the womb is affected by its physiological conditions in the uterus and by the mother's emotional states, but it has no way of understanding them. Nevertheless, the womb is its familiar place, and by surviving while moving in this enclosed space, a sense of familiarity and well-being is aroused in the foetus, until the moment arrives when it is sufficiently equipped to emerge into the world.

Now, the newborn enters a totally different and strange world, one in which he is forced to breathe by himself. Crying is released from his throat. Possibly, he experiences himself as unfamiliar and encounters his mother from a new and unfamiliar perspective. Without doubt, this is a dramatic and traumatic moment for the newborn baby, and he needs all the help his parents can give him in order to survive and to maintain his sense of self-familiarity in confronting the new, strange world.

In the mother's eyes, the severe labour pains and progressive contractions represent a process of separation: the emergence of her foetus from within her, the separation from her foetus, and finally, an encounter with her newborn. His new presence is different from anything she has previously imagined. She can no longer rely on sensing his movements within her, which, by their vitality, provided security. Now she has to be attentive to him and to how he conducts himself when outside her womb. She sees her offspring from a new perspective, no longer as a foetus "inside", but rather as a baby "outside". This is an encounter filled with uncertainty, apprehension and happiness as well as physical aches and pains, emotional, and hormonal outbursts.

The mother and the father, with all their life experience, vigilantly keep watch over their newborn, who requires constant surveillance. Despite preparations for the baby's arrival, the encounter with the unfamiliar is complex. In order to experience greater familiarity, confidence, and control in the new emotional situation, the parents seek guiding figures, and also recall similar past experiences. The connection with their personal emotional history and their roots give each of the parents a feeling of direct continuity with their unique past, of partnership with their spouse and with their baby, and of a shared future. In this way, the baby continues the intergenerational historical legacy, in addition to the genetic heritage he has inherited from his parents.

Natalie's birth is the first delivery her parents experience, and she confers a new title upon them—Mummy and Daddy. They feel the weight of responsibility imposed on them in light of the dramatic changes in their lives. Together with their great happiness, they are sensitive and vulnerable, and sometimes overwhelmed by feelings of fatigue and anxiety. Will they manage to cope with the task at hand, identify their baby's needs, respond to them, and protect her from all harm?

At three days old, Natalie leaves the maternity ward for home, which is familiar to her parents but strange for her. During the first days of her life Natalie had come to know the taste of the colostrum that she imbibed, but since then the milk flows abundantly from her mother's breasts, and its taste and consistency have changed. Natalie refuses to suckle and "escapes" into protracted sleep. Meanwhile, congestion is created in the breast, and Natalie, who wakes up as her hunger intensifies, finds it difficult to attach herself to the nipple in order to suck. As an act of survival, Natalie bursts into heart-breaking crying. The parents try to calm her, but are unsuccessful and may come to feel helpless. They find it difficult to grasp that the minor differences in the consistency of the milk and its taste can arouse in Natalie a feeling of strangeness.

From the moment of birth onwards, the baby is very vulnerable and sensitive to any change from the familiar that she may experience, both around and within herself. We now know that physical contact—such as hugging and kissing, the rhythmic rocking of the cradle, speaking and singing, smelling and seeing, as well as regular massages[1]—all contribute to improving the baby's immune functioning and creating an emotional bond between baby and parent. Gradually, the baby's sense of his familiar self begins to crystallise, accompanied by a sense of sensory self-identity, self-continuity, self-constancy, and object constancy—all of which culminate in self-security. The baby therefore identifies himself as familiar within his changing environment, and differentiates himself from anything that feels strange to him ("non-self").

Fortunately, we are born with an emotional "survival kit" (part of our biological survival system) that consists of innate sensory-emotional potential for development as well as mechanisms for control and regulation. This kit, which accompanies us throughout life, becomes increasingly more sophisticated under the influence of the relationship with our parents and our environment. The emotional survival kit is supported by three emotional systems:

a. The *emotional immune system*—representing the functioning of healthy narcissism—whose function is to safeguard the familiarity and the well-being of the self against invasion by foreign sensations. The immunisation vacillates between attraction to the familiar and rejection of that which is strange or novel, in other words, between well-being in the presence of the familiar and alertness upon facing strangeness.

b. The *emotional self-regulation system*—representing the functioning of the ego—whose function is to regulate drives and emotions by exploiting the potential of intelligence (with its psychomotor, affective, and cognitive components) for the management of adaptation or defence mechanisms. The regulatory process vacillates between two opposite poles: emotional turmoil and emotional restraint.

c. The *emotional attachment system*—representing the progression of object relations—whose function is to create an attachment characterised by emotional contact and interpersonal communication, and to maintain relationships with others despite their otherness and inevitable conflicts of interest with them. The attachment process vacillates between two opposing states: individuation and attachment.

These three systems operate harmoniously and interdependently, so that it is sometimes difficult to trace or distinguish each one's unique influence. The distinction, although somewhat arbitrary, is for didactic purposes. In the two parts of this book I will survey the functioning of the three emotional systems in each of the two pre-genital stages of development: the oral and the anal.

## *A review of several psychoanalytic conceptualisations concerning narcissism and object relations*

The innovative theoretical conceptualisations that I propose are a continuation and extension of existing psychoanalytic developmental concepts. I would like to emphasise at the outset that while the narcissism I refer to is essentially no different from the concept we are familiar with, it does highlight new aspects that I propose we distinguish as healthy narcissism. Drawing from earlier works, I will illuminate the main aspects of these fascinating subjects, that is to say, the expressions of narcissism and object relations that have emerged in my clinical work and provided the links and continuity between previous conceptualisations and the theory I propose.

Four aspects of narcissism and object relations seem to me significant in the theoretical development of my psychoanalytic thinking:

a. the concept of narcissism
b. the need to defend the self against alien stimulation
c. narcissism, the self, and object relations
d. healthy versus pathological narcissism.

Following a discussion of some significant works pertaining to these four topics, I will present a summary of how this theoretical background contributes to my conceptualisations. I have chosen some of the works that most influenced my psychoanalytic thinking.

### *The concept of narcissism*

The concept of narcissism is borrowed from Greek mythology, in which the young Narcissus falls in love with his image as reflected in a pool. Ever since Freud stressed the importance of narcissism in his theory (1950 [1887–1902], 1905d, 1914c), the concept of narcissism has become linked to self-love. Havelock Ellis (1898) was the first to connect mythological narcissism to psychological narcissism and used the term "narcissus-like". Nacke (1899) coined the phrase "love of the self" and used the term narcissism in a study of sexual perversions. In 1910, Freud discussed narcissism in the context of his clinical experience of sexual perversion and homosexuality. Rank (1911) viewed narcissism as the normal development of love toward one's body and as vanity and self-admiration. Freud (1914c) added a genetic (developmental) aspect to narcissism, proposing it as a stage of libidinal development (a stage in which the boundaries between self and object are not yet clear), as well as a dynamic aspect (in which the ego is experienced as a libidinal object and the individual might thus be proud of, and even love himself).

From 1899 to 1914 the central thesis regarding narcissism revolved around *primary narcissism*, the libidinal investment in the ego and in the ideal ego (the ego had not yet been differentiated from the self). "Narcissism in this sense", said Freud, "would not be a perversion, but the libidinal complement to the egoism of the instinct of self-preservation, a measure of which may justifiably be attributed to every living creature" (1914c, pp. 73–74). In the course of emotional development the libido is also directed toward the object (*secondary narcissism*), and Freud suggested that the libidinal withdrawal from the investment in the object to the ego/self constitutes the basis for pathology. The common denominator for all forms of narcissism (normal and pathological) is the love of oneself and the reference to one's own body or to oneself as a sexual object.

Freud's concepts of primary and secondary narcissism (1914c) are related to three phenomena: choice of an object, relationship pattern, and ego ideal (from which the concept of self-esteem has evolved as being virtually synonymous with narcissism). Libidinal investment directed solely to the ego/self or to the object might, in this sense, evoke a supreme experience of elation in the realm between idealisation, omnipotence, and infatuation. It might also arouse the blissful state defined as happiness when there is ostensibly no longer a need for external objects.

As early as 1908b, Freud claimed that nobody gives up anything, but rather, only replaces it with something else. Later he even added that man "is not willing to forgo the narcissistic perfection of his childhood" (1914c, p. 94).

Duruz (1981) suggests that "there is no psychic life without the formation of narcissistic ideals" (p. 35) and that "the goal of ideals is the restoration of an alleged stage of primary blissful narcissism" (p. 37). The source of narcissism, this absolute blissful state, the "oceanic feelings" and feelings of elation, Freud (1930a) located in the uterine phase ("monad"), which he sees as continuing in normal development.

## The need to defend the self against alien stimulation

In 1950 [1887–1902], Freud was preoccupied with questions of the permeability and impermeability of stimuli in the nervous system and their relation to perception and memory. He coined the concept of a "protective shield against stimuli" (1920g, 1926d [1925]) and recognised its objective of filtering stimuli as an instinct of self-preservation (1914c).

After Freud, many psychoanalysts proposed various terms to express this need for self-protection, such as the "container object" (Bion, 1962), the "mother as a protective shield" (Khan, 1963), the "holding mother" (Winnicott, 1962), "psychic skin and second skin" (Bick, 1968), the "screening mechanism" (Esman, 1983), "ego-skin" and "psychic enve-lopes" (Anzieu, 1985, 1987), the "protective shell" (Tustin, 1990), and the "membrane, the family envelope, and structural stability" (Houzel, 1990, 1996). Symington (1993) assumes that narcissism embodies the characteristics of a protection against acute mental pain.

In *On Narcissism,* one of his most insightful essays, Freud discloses: "It is universally known … that a person who is tormented by organic pain and discomfort gives up his interest in the things of the external world … and sends them out again when he recovers …" (1914c, p. 82). Similar observations are described by Mahler when the baby's mother leaves the room: "the child withdraws into himself, apparently concen-trating on the memory of the previous state of oneness or closeness with his mother, exhibits diminishing interest in his surroundings, and tries to maintain his emotional balance" (1968, p. 9).

Anzieu (1985, 1987) conceptualises the psychic protective envelopes and ego-skin on which external and internal stimuli leave memory traces, producing via their interconnections a kind of sensory map of proprioception[2] and of sensations. This sensory map serves as a frame of reference for differentiating the outside from the inside, and the familiar from the alien. The ego-skin thus contributes to the secure boundaries of the self. Moreover, Anzieu claims that within the ego-skin, that is aimed to protect the self, there is also a destructive component impacted by the child's death instinct, and often influenced by the mother's defects, which are seen as pathogenic in relation to the child's narcissistic integrity.

In this respect, Klein (1957) considers narcissistic situations as resulting from aggressive and destructive impulses linked to the death instinct. This destructive activity leads the baby (and any narcissistic personality) to project his or her hatred. When this occurs, the other is experienced as a threat, and the baby internalises threatening object representations. Developing Klein's ideas, Hanna Segal (1983) specifies that "narcissistic structure is an expression of, and a defence against, the death instinct and envy" (p. 275).

Freud (1950 [1887–1902]) attempted to find a common denominator between biological (neurological) and mental processes. Pally (1997a) relates to the reigning doctrine of neuroscience and emphasises that "mental phenomena are derived from biological ... events in neuronal circuits" (p. 587). Neural circuits in a constant state of high arousal create constant network schemata that represent the memory of sensory stimuli, external or internal (Kandel, Siegelbaum & Schwartz, 1991). Associative links between neural circuits and the different brain centres together arouse a "sense of familiarity" (Tulving & Thomson, 1973) and of a familiar historical continuity (Pally, 1997a, 1997b).

These researchers claim that memories are encoded and stored in the neuronal network and are shaped into an index of imprints that provides a comparable basis for the recognition of a new stimulus as familiar. Martin (1991) indicates a special neuron receptor that converts the energy of the constant stimulation into neural codes that represent a "common language" for all the sensory systems. Familiar meaning is thus attributed to self-experiencing (Bollas, 1992; Modell, 1993; Ogden, 1989). The organising activity of sensory integration represents "an attempt to add meaning to incoming excitation ... in terms of past experience and future activity ... [that] constitutes an internal frame of reference by which the outside world is assessed" (Sandler, 1987, p. 3). Additionally, "the brain automatically and continually processes sensory stimuli, matches patterns and generates perceptions" (Pally, 1997b, p. 1025). Thus, pattern matching has special relevance for psychoanalysis, particularly transference. If a current situation activates a pattern that is similar to one stored in memory, because the brain only looks for a good-enough match, the brain may conclude that two different situations are the same. For this reason, we tend to 'see' what we have seen before" (ibid., p. 1026).

Tomkins (1962, 1963) and his student and colleague, Nathanson (1992), draw our attention to the importance of affect, a crucial ingredient in the mental representation of attachment and object relations, characterised by the kind of condensed/abstracted encoding to which the above authors refer. Thus, for example, in a discussion of the affect family of shame, Nathanson states: " ... each time shame affect is triggered, we are drawn backwards in time to experience some representation of our lifetime of similar or related shames, whether or not we recognize the incident as typical of shame" (Nathanson, 1992, p. 307). Affect theory touches upon something else: " ... the phenomenology of recall does far more than this ... Stored along with our reminiscences of shames past are our recollections of all the ways we have made ourselves feel better when hurt ... Intimately associated with the affect is our history of reaction to it" (ibid.).

As already recognised by Freud in the late nineteenth century, biological and emotional systems share many similar characteristics. I would like to draw attention to the similarity of function between biological immune processes and the emotional immune system.

Immunologists describe the biological immune system as a network of cells and tissues throughout the body that function together to defend the body from invasion and infection. Similarly, I conceptualise narcissism processing as the attraction to the familiar and a resisting of strangeness, and healthy narcissism as providing an emotional immune system (Solan, 1998a) that protects the self. Among other things, both rely on intact neural circuits and brain processing to function optimally. We can also recognise a common denominator between biological autoimmune disease and the pathological characteristics of the narcissistic immune system (see Chapter Six on defence mechanisms).

I assume that narcissism immunises the self against alien invasion into the familiar sense of the self by initially resisting unfamiliar stimuli (including the otherness of individuals), and by subsequently recognising the familiar embedded in the strangeness and restoring it after it has been challenged or hurt by the unfamiliar (Solan, 1998a). A few years later Britton (2004) also put forward the hypothesis of a similarity between the mental system and the immunological system. He did not, however, specifically consider the similarity with regard to narcissistic features. I obtain support for my assumption in view of Britton's remarks:

> I suggest that there may be an allergy to the products of other *minds*, analogous to the body's immune system—a kind of psychic atopia

> ... The not-me or not-like-me recognition and response might fulfil a psychic function similar to that in the somatic ... We are fearful about our ability to maintain the integrity of our existing belief systems, and whenever we encounter foreign psychic material, a xenocidal impulse is stimulated. (ibid., p. 60)

Freud (1918a, 1921c) postulated two other important phenomena, namely "self-love" and "narcissism of minor differences": "It is precisely the minor differences in people who are otherwise alike that form the basis of feelings of strangeness and hostility between them" (1918a, p. 199). Three years later, he wrote:

> In the undisguised antipathies and aversions which people feel towards strangers with whom they have to do we may recognise the expression of self-love—of narcissism. This self-love works for the preservation of the individual, and behaves as though the occurrence of any divergence from his particular lines of development involved a criticism of them and a demand for their alteration. We do not know why such sensitiveness should have been directed to just these details of differentiation. (Freud, 1921c, p. 102)

Gabbard (1993) suggests that Freud's (1918a) concept of narcissism of minor differences "can be extended by recognizing the fundamental narcissistic need to preserve a sense of oneself as an autonomous individual" (p. 232). Thus, Freud's remarks may also reflect, in my view, a state of pain, injury, or sense of alienation due to narcissistic sensitivity to a deviation from the familiar, a deviation that initiates resistance against these alien stimulations (Solan, 1991, 1998a, 1998b, 1999, and Chapter Two).

## Narcissism, the self, and object relations

I believe that the emerging sense of self is immunised by narcissistic processing as self-familiarity, and that both self and narcissism are inspired by, and evolve, during the course of object relations.

Most theories deal with narcissism as bound to the self and to representations of the self or the object, while the differences among the concepts of object relations, self, and narcissism seem to have become blurred.

Based on the insights of ego psychology, Hartmann (1950) differentiated, for the first time, the ego from the self and the ideal ego from the ideal self. Hartmann defined the ego as a mental structure (an apparatus with different functions), the self as the overall personality, and narcissism as a libidinal investment; this time, however, not in the ego as Freud had done, but in the self. Since Freud, we can see a constant attitude of attributing to narcissism the libidinal investment, while the variant element is the object of the narcissistic libidinal investment. Annie Reich (1953) considered the narcissistic libidinal investments to be in self-representations and not in the actual self and claimed that "positive evaluation of the self obviously is a precondition for one's well-being" (1960, p. 215). Since then, Kohut (1971) redefined narcissism as a positive investment in the developing self.

On the foundations of self-psychology, Kohut (1966, 1971, 1977) promoted three leading issues of the self:

a. The existence of a separate "core self" as a cohesive cluster of all its components.
b. Normal psychic development depends on the cohesion of the self and is differentiated from narcissistic personality disorders.
c. The maintenance of self-esteem is the best defence against narcissistic fragility. The concept of "the sense of a core self" was further elaborated by Stern (1985), and "results from the integration of ... four basic self-experiences" (p. 71), namely, agency, coherence, affectivity and history.

Although most psychoanalysts tend to accept the mutual influence between object relations and narcissism, as well as their impact on the formation of the child's self, a perceptional divergence still exists regarding the pattern of object relations in early life. Some psychoanalysts, such as Chasseguet-Smirgel (1975), Stern (1985), Emde (1988a, 1988b), Fonagy & Target (2002), and others, myself included, consider that the newborn differentiates himself from the non-self from the beginning of his life. In opposition to these, others, such as Kernberg (1975), Mahler & McDevitt (1968), Kohut (1971, 1977), Stolorow (1975), and their followers, assert that the infant does *not* differentiate himself from the non-self early in life, and lives as if he were in a symbiotic fusion or narcissistic merger with the object. All agree, however, that the narcissistic relationships and the choice of the narcissistic object are the result of a denial or disavowal of separateness between self and object.

Mahler (1968) describes primary narcissism as "normal autism" in the first weeks of life, in that "the infant seems to be in a state of primitive hallucinatory disorientation, in which need satisfaction belongs to his own omnipotent, autistic orbit". Mahler assumes that the baby does not yet differentiate himself from the non-self, although she claims that "the infant tries to rid himself of unpleasurable tension" (p. 200). From the second month onwards, "the infant behaves and functions as though he and his mother were an omnipotent system—a dual unity within one common boundary". This "normal symbiosis" describes a "state of undifferentiation, of fusion with mother, in which the 'I' is not yet differentiated from the 'not-I'" (p. 201).

Kohut (1971) claims that normal development is based on the cohesion of the self, which is achieved through the parent being emotionally available to match the baby's needs as his self-object. An individual who is unable to perceive the object as a separate other desperately needs or craves the presence of the self-object to maintain his self-survival. Kohut and his followers postulate a developmental line of self-objects, from archaic to mature.

Fonagy & Target (1997, 2002) coined the enlightening concept of the "mentalization of situations" describing the child's capacity to reflect and think about emotional situations. They view this capacity as being dependent on the parent's ability to acknowledge that his or her child's inner world needs to be understood according to his individuality.

## Healthy versus pathological narcissism

It is generally agreed that narcissism is an important element of the human emotional system, but, in my view, the psychoanalytic literature has not sufficiently elucidated how it operates, what its purpose and significance are, and how to differentiate normal narcissism from its pathological processing or operation. Freud perceived normal narcissism as "self-love [that] works for the preservation of the individual" (1921c, p. 102). The individual "withdraws libidinal interest from his love-objects [when he suffers] ... and sends them out again when he recovers ... we should behave in just the same way" (Freud, 1914c, p. 82). Other views consider normal narcissism as: regulation of self-esteem

(Reich, 1960); acceptance of one's imperfections and the limits of one's ideals (Duruz, 1981; Reich, 1960); a matching between the perception of reality and positive self-esteem (Van der Waals, 1965); positive self and object representations, based on primarily positive experiences in early childhood (Schafer, 1968); maintenance of self-cohesion (Kohut, 1971); maintenance of "the structural cohesiveness, temporal stability and positive affective coloring of the self-representation" (Stolorow, 1975, p. 179); investment of libido in an integrative structure of the self (Kernberg, 1975, 1984); and a mental process that distinguishes the individual from others (Duruz, 1981).

"When self-esteem is threatened, significantly lowered or destroyed, then narcissistic activities are called into play in an effort to protect, restore, repair and stabilize it" (Stolorow, 1975, p. 183). These may be understood as continuous reparative measures (Kohut, 1977; Reich, 1960).

Reich stresses, "narcissism per se is a normal phenomenon. It becomes pathologic only under certain conditions: e.g., when the balance between object cathexis and self-cathexis has become disturbed, and objects are cathected insufficiently or not at all" (1960, p. 216), as well as when "an enormous overvaluation of the body or particular organs" takes place (p. 222). "Narcissistic pathology becomes especially noticeable in the methods used for self-esteem regulation" (p. 216). Stolorow (1975) adds that healthy narcissism may be differentiated from unhealthy narcissism in functional terms according to "whether or not it succeeds in maintaining a cohesive, stable and positively colored self-representation" (p. 184). Finally, McClelland (2004) considers narcissism as a dimension of normal human psychosocial development and normal functional structure. He discusses narcissism under three broad headings: economic, emotional elation and emotional anxiety.

Most of the professional literature, however, deals with the pathological side of narcissism. Freud (1905d, in a footnote to the *Three Essays*) describes narcissism as perverse libidinal development. Later, (1914c) he refers to secondary narcissism as a potential source of pathology, when libido retreats from the object to the self/ego.

Since 1960, and especially from 1980 onward, Reich, Kohut, Kernberg and others have tended to view narcissism in terms of personality disorders. Kohut (1971) assumes that the pathology does not lie in the narcissism, but rather in the damaged or missing structure capable of maintaining self-cohesiveness. He locates the aetiology of personality disorders in the earliest stages of development, in the wake of disappointments, frustrations or traumas (all of which involve varying degrees of empathic failures with respect to developmental needs) that cause the personality to develop on fragile foundations. Kernberg (1975, 1984), however, claims that pathological narcissism is characterised by the investment of libido in a split structure of the self, by defences against integration, such as splits between libido and aggression, by dependency on the external environment for the regulation of self-esteem, and by disturbed object relations. Symptoms usually appear as defence mechanisms against negative self or object representations that surface under the impact of frustration (Green, 1978, 1999; Kernberg, 1975; Schafer, 1968). Green went on to describe the mourning process the child experiences following maternal depression, when the mother, while physically alive, is psychically dead to the child, a state he referred to as "the dead mother." Gerzi (2005) further elaborated the concept of traumatic holes.

Let us now return to the concept of biological immune processing. Immunologists recognise a link between the central nervous system and the immunological system. Dannenberg and Shoenfeld (1991), and others, suggest that the immune system safeguards the code of the human cell's protein as familiar and constant, recognises foreign invaders with a different protein code that endangers the integrity of body cells, and blocks them. Fisher (2011) defines the immune system as "the collection of cells, tissues and molecules that protects the body from numerous pathogenic microbes and toxins in our environment … This defense against microbes has been divided into two general types of reactions: reactions of innate immunity and reactions of adaptive immunity. Thus, innate and adaptive immunity can be thought of as two equally important aspects of the immune system … As its name suggests, the innate immune system consists of cells and proteins that are always present and ready to mobilize and fight microbes at the site of infection." This innate (or inborn) immune system mobilises white blood cells to destroy invaders, without using antibodies.

The adaptive immune system, on the other hand, is called into action against pathogens that are able to evade or overcome innate immune defenses. It enhances along with the person's development by "remembering" the invaders so that it can fight them if they come back. When the immune system is working properly, foreign invaders provoke the body to activate immune cells against the invaders and to produce proteins called antibodies that attach to the invaders so that they can be recognized and destroyed. Innate immune reactions generally occur much sooner and are less sustained than adaptive immune reactions. (Fisher, 2011)

I suggest considering one's narcissism as an emotional immune system, based on the innate healthy narcissism characteristic of a well-functioning, regulated system. This system is subsequently enhanced as it acquires adaptive forms in conjunction with an ego adaptation mechanism, allowing for a tolerance and befriending of new familiarities, a process that involves memory. Yet, always, healthy narcissism is based on the attraction to the familiar and the resisting of the foreign, processes very similar to those of the biological immune system.

"Autoimmune diseases refer to problems with the acquired immune system's reactions. In an autoimmune reaction, antibodies and immune cells target the body's own healthy tissues by mistake, signaling the body to attack them" (ibid.). Pathological narcissism might be considered as an emotional autoimmune disorder with symptoms very similar to the biological autoimmune diseases. The concept of (biological) autoimmunity is regarded as the inability of the immune system to distinguish between self and non-self (George, Levy & Shoenfeld, 1996). "This finding may constitute an association among autoimmunity, psychiatric disorders and smell impairment" (Ortega-Hernandez, Kivity & Shoenfeld, 2009) and might indicate that "a subgroup of patients with schizophrenia may demonstrate features of an autoimmune process, a theory supported by a growing database of investigation" (Strous & Shoenfeld, 2006).

Immunologists (Amital-Teplizki & Shoenfeld, 1991; Dannenberg & Shoenfeld, 1991) recognise links between the central nervous system and the immunological system, while further studies concentrate on psychoneuroimmunology (PNI) which is the study of the links among psychological processes and the nervous and immune systems of the human body (Goodkin & Visser, 2000).

### Summary of the theoretical background to my conceptualisation

Freud laid down the theoretical foundations—elaborated in the psychoanalytic works cited above—which contributed to my psychoanalytic reflections in general, and my attempts to define the roots of healthy narcissism in particular. I would like to summarise[3] how the accumulated knowledge has contributed to my formulation of healthy narcissism (see Chapter Two) and of "jointness-separateness" between two separate individuals in normal object relations (see Chapter Four). The connections Freud postulated between narcissism and "self-preservation as a normal measure for everybody", as well as "the instinct of self-love", and "libidinal investment evoking a supreme experience of elation, of a blissful state defined as happiness"— triggered my reflections about the normal operation or processing of narcissism, so crucial for our self-preservation and well-being. The idea of the foetus's "oceanic feelings" of elation continuing in normal development (Grunberger) piqued my interest in discovering whether innate narcissism preserves not only blissful emotional states from present life, but may itself be seen as a continuation or recapitulation of memory traces from the foetus's intrauterine life, forming the basis for healthy development.

As previously noted, the psychoanalytic literature includes widespread references to various situations in which there is a mental need for a "protective shield against stimuli" (Freud) or a "psychic protective envelope" (Anzieu). I assume that the processing of narcissism serves as a protective shield for preserving the self against alien stimuli that might endanger its blissful state. This processing reveals a narcissistic sensitivity to differentiating characteristics that emanate from any non-self (Britton; Solan). Freud described the sensitivity to these alien stimuli as the "undisguised antipathies and aversions" that people feel toward strangers with whom they must interact. The above helped to consolidate my idea of inborn healthy narcissism as a preserver of a separate self-familiarity and self-continuity and as a defence against alien stimulation, essentially, against otherness. This narcissism as a self-preserving force is irritated by "minor or major differences" (Freud) from the familiar, and is triggered "to get rid of the unpleasant awareness" (Mahler) and acute mental pain (Symington).

A person who is "tormented by organic pain and discomfort" (Freud), or the child who cannot tolerate his mother leaving the room (Mahler), tends to disengage or withdraw his libidinal interest from his love-objects "so long as he suffers" (Freud). Freud's illuminating comment led me to deepen my view of the healthy (survival) need to withdraw into one's "self-separated-space", primarily after the self has been injured or traumatised (Duruz; Reich; Stolorow). By withdrawing while the libidinal investment remains in the self (Freud; Kohut; Reich), self-familiarity is preserved and made immune to (and alleviated from) the invasion of the otherness of the non-self and painful sensations of strangeness (Solan). Hence, narcissism is tasked with regulating and restoring the "coherence of the self" (Reich; Stolorow). The outcome would be the retention of self-cohesiveness as a separate self from the object (Emde; Fonagy & Target; Stern), the strengthening of self-integrity (Kernberg), the "restoration of primary blissful narcissism" (Duruz), and the maintenance of the "emotional balance" (Mahler).

"The sick man withdraws his libidinal cathexes back upon his ego, and sends them out again when he recovers", says Freud (1914c, p. 82). In contrast, I would stress that it is precisely when his (the sick man's) self-familiarity is restored and immunised against the unfamiliar other, or when he recovers, that feelings of love might awaken toward himself and toward his object. This formulation elucidates the links, noted by many psychoanalysts, between narcissism, self-love, self-esteem, and object love (Freud; Kohut; Reich; Stolorow), as well as those between narcissism, idealisation, infatuation, and elation "in a blissful state of happiness" (Freud).

Furthermore, the concept of ego-skin as a sensory map of memory traces of stimuli (Anzieu; Pally), led me to consider narcissism as a familiar sensory map or network of accumulated memory traces of our emotional experiences, most of them interlinked, providing continuity and cohesiveness.

The network serves as a frame for recognising new occurrences as familiar or alien, for concentrating on the memory of previous states of "closeness with mother" (Mahler). It provides support for "good enough matching" (Pally) with the new experiences that cause us "to 'see' what we have seen before" (Pally). Via matching, one may attune reality perception to the acknowledgement of one's personal potential, one's imperfections, and the limitations of one's ideals (Duruz; Reich; Van der Waals).

While the domain of physiological biological systems is not part of my expertise as a clinical psychologist, for many years I have been fascinated by Freud's attempt to find a common denominator between biological (neurological) and mental processes. I am particularly drawn to the similarity between the functions of the emotional and the biological systems, and inspired by psychophysiological and psychobiological research, and by neuro-psychoanalytic theory, which, together, have led me to consider healthy narcissism as an emotional immune system (Solan, 1998a). I have learned that, from early on, these systems operate according to similar procedures and a "common language" (Martin, 1991). They share a common familiarity principle; namely, attraction to the familiar and rejection of strangeness. In this regard, I accept Stolorow's formulation that "narcissistic activities are called into play in an effort to protect, restore and repair self-esteem and to maintain cohesion and stability" (1975, p. 183).

I was also able to recognise a parallel between autoimmune disease and the pathological characteristics of the narcissistic immune system (see Chapter Two). By means of a similar autoimmune mechanism, in the wake of narcissistic injuries or trauma, and through a fatal mistake, pathological narcissism may be expressed as an attack on the self and produce mental pathological symptoms, such as nail biting, self-defeating behaviour, a false self, narcissistic disorders, personality disorders, and even suicide (Kohut; Reich; Solan). This implies that the inability or failure of one's narcissistic processing to resist minor or major strangeness/otherness (Freud) may eventually be expressed in emotional autoimmune symptoms (Anzieu; Britton; Shoenfeld & Rose; Solan).

In light of the aforementioned psychoanalytic approaches and my own assumptions concerning narcissism, self and object relations, I was tempted to elaborate the essential conditions for normal object relations (see Chapter Four). My assumptions were sustained by the ideas of those psychoanalysts who consider that both the newborn baby and his parent sense the other as a non-self (Chasseguet-Smirgel; Emde; Fonagy & Target; Stern). This inevitably produces a sense of otherness that the self-familiarity must deal with.

Hence, I conceive normal object relations as jointness-separateness (Solan) founded on the parent "recognising the fundamental narcissistic needs to preserve a sense of oneself as an autonomous individual" (Gabbard, 1993), as well as on the innate narcissistic resistance to any non-self and on narcissistic attraction to the familiar in this non-self (Solan). During the intimacy that characterises jointness relations between parent and baby (Solan), sensations of separateness and boundaries are temporarily blurred, yet are subsequently followed by the restoration of separateness between self and object. Self-familiarity is thus preserved in separateness, concomitant with the gradual acquisition of tolerance toward the otherness of one's objects, and the inborn healthy narcissism of baby and parent is reinforced (Solan). Alongside the development of jointness-separateness in intimacy, other areas are enhanced, such as communication, negotiation and mentalization (Fonagy & Target), positive self and object representations and positive object relations and representations (Kernberg; Reich; Schafer; Stolorow).

Some psychoanalysts, such as Mahler and her colleagues, describe parent and baby in object relations shaped by symbiosis, wherein the object of each is perceived as part of himself, and fulfils a "self-object" function (Kohut). Under these altered circumstances, rather than there being what I have previously described as a natural inborn separateness from a non-self, it appears that narcissism might preserve the self-familiarity of each of the two participants as (autoimmune) fused self-objects in symbiosis—resisting any stimuli that might challenge or otherwise endanger the merged self-object. In my view, this constitutes the roots of pathological narcissism. To reiterate, the healthy immune system indicates self-separateness from the object and protects the self from the other as a separate entity, whereas autoimmune pathology maintains a self that consists of fused self-object representations.

The outcome is that the individual "desperately needs the presence of his self-object to maintain his self-survival" (Kohut), and by implication, his self-cohesion and his self-esteem (Kernberg; Klein; Kohut; Mahler). This situation may result in "disturbed object relations" (Kernberg), and a preponderance of negative self or object representations (Kernberg; Schafer)—in other words, what we generally perceive as pathological narcissism. In the language of affect theory, the negative affects, and possibly a preponderance of shame-humiliation, disgust, and dissmell (see Tomkins, 1962, 1963) would take centre stage over pride and other positive affects. In the language of somatic experiencing (SE), the "trauma vortex" is eclipsing the innate, but weaker, "healing vortex" (Ross, 2008).

Drawing on and further elaborating upon the above works, I consider healthy narcissism as an inborn mental structure—an *emotional immune system*. Via a process of recognition of self-familiarity, the individual's narcissism sets the stage for self-preservation, self-regulation, and self-restoration, resists any non-self alien invaders, and is strengthened by, and assists in, promoting jointness-separateness in object relations.

## Notes

1.  Soft touching, caring, and caretaking, and a familiar, regular rhythm of massage that the mother provides to the baby, arouses the sensory system, activates a large number of neurons in the brain and in the course of development, influences the baby's immune ability (Orbach, 1996). The opposite is also true: the absence of stimuli leads to degeneration of active neurons in the brain, and the child tends more toward self-destruction (ibid). Observations of babies show that body massage affects not only the biological immune system, but also contributes to balanced weight increase, regular sleep patterns, sociability, calmness and tolerance, reduction in depressive symptoms, and relief from pain.
2.  Proprioception (noun): From the Latin *proprius* (own) + receptive. Proprioceptive stimuli are internally experienced as sensations connected with the position and movement of the body.
3.  From now on, I will mention the author's conceptualisation without re-indicating the date of the work.

# CHAPTER TWO

# Narcissism: an immune system for the self

S ean—a small, endearing newborn—emerges into a very different world from the space he came to know in his mother's womb. In the protected and familiar womb, the foetus is capable of recognising itself, of inserting a finger into its mouth, of moving around in the amniotic fluid, and of feeling the walls of the uterus. He feels his mother's rhythmic heartbeat, hears various noises and voices—most notably his mother's voice and her tone of speaking—and sounds of music, and adopts all these as part of his self-familiarity.

With birth, for Sean, as for every newborn, all that was hitherto familiar instantly changes, becoming strange and alien. The daylight is stronger than the familiar closed dimness of the womb, the baby's body weight and sensations are different in the absence of amniotic fluid, and anything touching him is experienced as an unfamiliar stimulus. Crying emanates from his throat and he is forced to both breathe and eat using his own resources. The newborn experiences chaos and boundlessness (Britton, 1989), and without the option of fleeing back to the uterine walls, he has no familiar place to hide. The strangeness seems to be invading him; it confuses him, and he experiences his birth and the transition from one world to another as traumatic. How will the newborn survive these changes without being able to prepare for them? How will he "know" how to orient himself in the new world into which he has burst forth?

If we consider how much preparation and effort astronauts in space require in order to achieve maximum control over their movements, their sensations, and their surroundings in the absence of gravity within and outside the spaceship, this may illuminate some of the processes the baby undergoes in the sudden transition from the narrow and familiar womb into an unfamiliar space; that of the novel, expanded world with its new rhythms, sequences and laws, populated by foreign figures with whom he now has to share his life.

## Narcissism as an emotional immune system

Freud (1920g) claimed that "*protection against* stimuli is an almost more important function for the living organism than *reception of* stimuli" (p. 27, my italics). The professional literature corroborates the underlying premise that the psychic system is sensitive to stimuli and requires a shield or a protective envelope to defend itself (see Chapter One).

As an analyst, for many years I have investigated the contribution of narcissism to the child's emotional development, and I have found an interesting similarity between the methods of operation of healthy narcissism and that of the biological immune system. I have come to assume the existence of a narcissistic immunological activity that safeguards and preserves the familiarity of the self against alien stimuli, as it absorbs semi-familiar stimuli—whether from an internal or an external source—into self-familiarity. This parallel is fascinating because it enables us to understand the normative development of narcissism alongside that of familiar pathological phenomena. I have previously suggested (Solan, 1998a) that these two immune systems—the biological and the emotional—operate according to similar functional processes from the very beginning of life; namely, the attraction to the familiar and a resistance to strangeness (see Chapter One).

Let us take a closer look at the newborn's emotional state at the time of birth and his or her familiarisation with the outside world. As an act of survival, the newborn clings to any hint of familiarity from the period he has spent in the womb. Resting on his mother's bosom, he identifies the familiar rhythm of her heartbeat, and her voice is the sound he has heard since his time in the womb. His mother's arms and the swaddling he is wrapped in are reminiscent of the boundaries of the uterine walls that contained him, and the mother's nipples arouse a similar feeling to that of his pre-birth thumb sucking.

I will demonstrate the above with Sheryl's story about her son Leo: "I was told that the foetus's sense of hearing develops between the seventeenth and the twenty-fourth week of pregnancy, so I began relating to my foetus as someone who could hear me, and who could even remember a melody he heard. I therefore regularly sang him a song that I like and I kept up a 'dialogue' with him. After my son was born the nurses in the maternity ward complained how difficult it was for them to stop Leo's crying, yet when he heard me singing this particular melody, even on my way to the nursery, he calmed down immediately. I am convinced that on hearing the song, I could see upon his face, even in the maternity ward and certainly at home, that he was so focused while listening to this familiar song that he immediately stopped crying."

The newborn baby is drawn to these familiar sensations or he may detach himself from the strangeness by escaping into familiar deep sleep and into experiences of nirvana and perfection, as if the strangeness in his environment no longer exists.

I was truly amazed to learn that, "fairy-wren (*Malurus cyaneus*) mothers sing to their unhatched eggs to teach the embryo inside a 'password'—a single unique note—which the nestlings must later incorporate into their begging calls if they want to get fed. The female birds also teach their mates the password. Teaching embryos the password for food helps parents avoid having to feed imposters" (Colomobelli-Negrel et al., 2012; Corbyn, 2012).

There is another fascinating biological immunological process at work during pregnancy. The foetus is a stranger to the mother's body, yet there are mechanisms in the mother's biological immune system that prevent the rejection of the foetus from the mother's womb during the course of the pregnancy. Only toward the end of pregnancy, as the birth process starts, is the foetus expelled as a foreign body.

This immunological process raises an interesting question: is it narcissism as an emotional immune system that causes us, as parents, to rave about our children as "the most wonderful on the face of the earth"? The smells they exude are pleasant to us while the smells of others may repel us. As parents, we love them even though they differ from what we experience as familiar within ourselves. We find it difficult to view them as separate and different, while at the same time we remain intolerant of the otherness of our fellow humans. Only toward the end of adolescence do we become willing to let our children leave home and pursue their separate paths, and even then the separation is as difficult as the birth process.

In a normal pregnancy, and except for certain abnormal situations, we hardly know what a foetus experiences in the womb. It is, however, quite amazing to discover, when these rare opportunities present themselves via ultrasound observations or through current neonatal research, the extent to which the unconscious familiarities with intrauterine sensations are repeated after birth, in the post-partum period.

Piontelli (1987, 1989), observing the intrauterine ultrasounds of twins, could decipher in one twin couple that the female foetus often approached the male foetus, "but almost inevitably he pushed her away". In another set of twins, she observed that the male foetus "through the dividing membrane … touched her [the female foetus's] face gently, and when she responded by turning her face towards him, he engaged with her for a while in a gentle, stroking, cheek-to-cheek motion" (p. 421). "At one year of age … their favorite game had become hiding each on one side of the curtain and using it a bit like a dividing membrane." Piontelli concludes: "Both temperament and behavior of the couple seem to continue in the same direction after birth" (p. 426), namely, avoidance of contact in the first twin couple and affectionate contact in the second.

Freud (1926d [1925]) anticipated such incredible observations when he wrote: "There is much more continuity between intra-uterine life and earliest infancy than the impressive caesura of the fact of birth would have us believe" (p. 138).

The newborn comes into life equipped with his or her innate hereditary, genetic makeup, and history of physiological sensations rooted in various intrauterine sensory experiences. We may cumulatively view the latter as unconscious and obviously pre-verbal memory traces that consolidate the familiar sense of his or her self. In my conceptualisation of healthy narcissism as an innate emotional immune system, we may presume that after birth, the narcissistic search for the familiar is invoked and is based upon unconscious resonance with these memory traces from intrauterine experience. These reverberations of prenatal memory traces affect the emotional significance that the newborn attributes to his infinite subjective experiences. The struggle for survival and adaptation to a new world filled with stimuli is dependent (among other things) on the efficient managing of narcissism in safeguarding the familiarity of the self.

Narcissism, in my view, is an innate component of personality, the operation and management of which precedes what we generally refer to as the "functioning of the ego". In accordance with Freud's (1923b) structural theory, and its further elaboration by Chasseguet-Smirgel (1976), it might be considered the fifth component, in addition to the four referred to in the literature (id, ego, superego and the ego ideals).

By means of narcissism, we are able to:

a. Identify the familiar within us and around us.
b. Resist and be alerted to the strangeness within us and around us.
c. Safeguard our sense of continuity, well-being, self-esteem, and self-integrity.
d. Restore the cohesiveness of our self-familiarity following the inevitable injuries emanating from the pressures evoked by otherness.
e. Cope with the otherness of our fellow beings.

Moreover, throughout healthy narcissistic processing we may enjoy pleasure or blissful moments of elation and happiness, whether alone or with others. When addressing narcissism, we may tend to adopt the language of narcissistic injuries and of narcissistic personality disorders and perversions, overlooking its positive and essential functions. I wish to point out that the narcissism that I refer to as healthy and normative is no different from that previously described in the professional literature, except I choose to emphasise its healthy and positive aspects.

I view the narcissistic immune system as comprising three components: *narcissistic sensors* imprint memory traces of experiences on to a *narcissistic data network* from where the *narcissistic immunological memory* retrieves relevant memory traces that reverberate during present experiences.

## Narcissistic sensors identify the self-familiar

Narcissistic sensors are generally synonymous with what we refer to as "gut feelings". Anything identified as unfamiliar is classified as non-self, or strange.

One can listen and re-listen an infinite number of times to the same symphony and derive enjoyment from the "fit" between what we hear and how we remember it, but in the presence of extreme and distant variations where a match is not obtained (for example, a different interpretation of the piece by a different, or even the same, conductor), an uneasy feeling of incompatibility or dissonance may ensue (Bollas, 1992). When we recognise that which we know, we relax with "homely" feelings of familiarity. Conversely, when we identify strangeness, the tension increases and might turn into vigilance; we prepare to adopt countermeasures as a reaction against the danger of the invasion of strangeness into the familiar sense of the self that I call "self-familiarity". Such an invasion usually evokes narcissistic injury, insult, disappointment, shame-humiliation, and anger.

Freud has already stressed that recognition of the familiar arouses pleasure (Freud, 1905c). "Minor differences" (Freud, 1930a, p. 114) may arouse feelings of strangeness and even anger, while "greater differences should lead to an almost insuperable repugnance" (Freud, 1921c, p. 101) and possibly racism (1921c, 1930a) and xenophobia. On the other hand, too much resemblance, such as between identical twins, may also be unsettling and evoke a sense of confusion within the self-familiarity.

Barak (at one month) pushes the nipple of the breast with his tongue and refuses to suckle. His mother tries to identify the meaning of the rejection and recalls that she has rubbed a new lotion on her nipples. Barak's sensors resist the strangeness. When his mother washes her nipples, Barak re-identifies them as familiar and suckles with enthusiasm and pleasure.

Harry (at seven months) is aware of the arrival of visitors. Through his senses, he identifies the familiar, but recoils from and resents the smells and the voices he does not recognise, thereby differentiating the familiar from the foreign. At the oral stage, Harry relies on his narcissistic sensors as if they project a beam of light that provides sensory orientation. Gradually this ability becomes more refined, and additionally relies on intelligence faculties (psychomotor, cognitive, and affective).

Sandy (at one month) receives a vaccination injection. When her mother sees Sandy smiling as she did on previous days, she relaxes. In the absence of verbal communication, the mother tends to rely on and "sharpen" her gut feelings in order to identify any deviation from her daughter's regular, familiar behaviour.

By means of the narcissistic sensors, bodily sensations, and the gut feelings based on innate affects (Tomkins, 1962, 1963), we function as a kind of body-sense. We orient ourselves sensorially with what is happening, in terms of both our facial/bodily displays (Nathanson, 1992; Tomkins, 1962, 1963) and our manifestations of innate affects. We sense the inside as well as our environment by way of interoception,[1] and we identify our relationships. Thus, we expand and enrich our self-familiarity with new, yet familiar, findings. Delay or inhibition of the process of becoming aware of our sensations and gut feelings, and of refining sensory abilities, may undermine both the feeling of familiarity of the true self (Winnicott, 1960) and the person's orientation in the surrounding environment.

## The narcissistic network

Sensory information flows to and from the narcissistic sensors during the many experiences that concern our self, our objects, and our relationships with them. This rich data is imprinted[2] and stored in the narcissistic network as memory traces[3] that interconnect based on links (such as that between the sensation of wet clothing followed by that of the dry diaper on the body). This creates a dynamic narcissistic information network with a rich reservoir of historical sensory-emotional information, a unique and personal data repository. It is my belief that an analogous and reciprocal situation exists between the narcissistic data network and the neural networks of the brain, vis-à-vis sensory receptors (for vision, hearing, etc.). The links and associations among the clusters of memory traces allow for the survival of the self, and possibly of the life instinct itself (Freud, 1915c).

In the wake of the constantly changing links among the memory traces and, on the basis of synergetic integration of the data (resulting from joint narcissism and ego functioning), the accumulated information is organised in a certain order, with continuity and a coherent pattern. This data may be variously formulated in terms of narcissism and of ego psychology (Hartmann, 1939), or object relations, self-psychology (Kohut, 1971) and affect theory (Tomkins, 1962, 1963; Tyson & Tyson, 1990). Sensory data is stored in sites and compressed into schemata (Sandler, 1987) such as codes, perceptions, signals, bodily sensations (positive, neutral and negative) and affectively-charged memories, representations, images, and symbolisations. Psychic textures (Bollas, 1992) are spun, and they include a unique sensory characterisation. Several authors have touched on this subject, including Stern (1985), Emde (1988a, 1988b), Ogden (1989), Modell (1993), and Levine (2010). Cumulative affective experience is abstracted, condensed, stored, and retrieved on a regular basis to form "scripts" (Nathanson, 1992; Tomkins, 1962, 1963), including cumulative trauma experiences (Khan, 1963; Levine, 2010). The overall perception becomes different from the sum of its separate components, and represents the core self (Stern, 1985) or the "autobiographical self" (Damasio, 1999; Solms, 2004), or, according to my conception, the subjective perception of the entirety and integrated "wholeness" of self-familiarity (Solan, 1998a).

Everything that is imprinted in the network, whether conscious or unconscious, becomes a self-asset and is identified as familiar by what I have described as immunological narcissistic processing (Solan, 1991). Thus, negative criticism about our children, our parents, or even our therapists, all of whom have become self-familiarity assets, is often intolerable, and we are quick to rush to their defence. In this way, we identify ourselves and our assets as a familiar entity or wholeness— an island in the chaos of a changing environment. We advertise our uniqueness to others so that they will be able to identify us as familiar. We learn to differentiate ourselves from others, to allow us to get to know them, and vice versa.

## The narcissistic immunologic memory

The narcissistic immunologic memory constitutes a mediating factor between current sensory experience and the memory traces from one's past experiences that are indelibly imprinted in the narcissistic network. Memory traces of similar past events, including experiences with affects, are retrieved from the narcissistic immunologic memory, and these reverberate within us as associative remembrance. I define the pattern of memory traces as *narcissistic schemata*, representing emotional content such as affects, associations, images, fantasies, memories, dreams, reflections, and thoughts. The terms "reflective self-function", "metacognition", "generic mental models of social relationships", and mentalization (Fonagy & Target, 1997, 2002) most likely refer to the same process. Nathanson (1992), in his account of affect theory, describes "the phenomenology of recall" of shame memories via a similar process (p. 307) involving scenes and scripts. Finally, somatic experiencing theory (Ross, 2008) refers to the language of the body/mind as that of the "felt sense", a term originally coined by Gendlin (1982). The felt sense is informed by the channels of sensation, imagery (e.g., vision and other senses), behaviour, affect, and meaning, and immediately connects us with both internal and external environments.

Leo (at one month) is crying. He is hungry. When his mother approaches him, memory traces reverberate within him, along with attributes connected to his hunger, such as taste, sucking, flow, and the warmth of the milk in the mouth—attributes that are specifically linked to, and associated with, his mother's warm affection. This is a transient sensory feeling, described by Freud (1911c) as a hallucination and by Winnicott (1951) as an illusion of the sensations of milk in the mouth. In my view, the illusion of satisfaction represents a recall of memory traces, akin to a conditioned reflex. Even prior to nursing, its sensori-motor evocation temporarily calms the feeling of strangeness arising from the irritating hunger. Leo moves his lips in sucking movements until he locates the nipple of the breast, fervently clutching at the familiar in order to satisfy his hunger.

Jane (at eight months) hears the sound of a pendulum clock in her grandparents' home. It is the first time she has noticed it and she is consequently alarmed. Her grandmother takes her in her arms and together they approach the clock and observe the action of the pendulum; the grandmother soothes her and whispers with each sound, "gong, gong". Since then, when Jane hears the melody of the clock, she mumbles to herself, "gong, gong". By means of the immunologic memory, she creates a link between the clock, the sound, and her grandmother's soothing. This association will subsequently allow for the activation of memory traces of past experiences (which may come to include action programs or coping strategies) when encountering a clock. Thus, at twelve months she points to a clock of any kind and says, "gong".

Jacob, in his thirties, says: "I tried hard yesterday after our psychoanalytic session to bring my sensations from the depths, to collect together all these tiles of memory, one after the other, so that my childhood event will be revealed clearly to me. Even now, I can smell my mother's smell."

The immunologic memory is an emotional tool that enables us to adapt to reality. Without it, we would register any new experience as alien, unexpected, or even traumatic. Cross-checking information between past and present creates a mixture of memory traces from the past and experiences in the present (Rosenfield, 1992). Thus, the processing of healthy narcissism via the filter of immunologic memory establishes a familiar meaning for the current experience—a sense of déjà vu—and imparts a feeling of familiarity recorded in the past-to-present occurrence. Furthermore, despite the time gaps and the physical distance, both current experiences and future expectations are crystallised on the basis of a model from the past.

Like all babies, the five-month-old Sean is sensitive to unfamiliar sensory stimuli. On a stormy winter night, he is awakened by the frequent thunderclaps, becomes agitated, and cries bitterly. He is clearly undergoing an over-stimulation of the unfamiliar, perhaps even a traumatic experience. His mother, as his protective shield (Khan, 1963), rushes to him and tries to soothe him. Unlike Sean, her immunologic memory offers familiar memory patterns that enable her to identify the sensory stimulus of lightning and thunder in the present as a familiar sign heralding the coming rain. While his mother's emotional reactions are modulated and controlled—thus preventing breaches to her role as a protective shield, which would have meant cumulative trauma flooding (Khan, 1963)—Sean's crying triggers additional affective reverberations; and with it, the realisation that lightning and thunder can be very frightening. Most likely, other childhood memory traces are revived within her as she picks him up and goes to the window, and between the flashes of lightning and sounds of thunder she adds in a calm tone to a familiar song she sings to him, "Boom-boom, the thunder goes boom-boom," and helps him regulate his feelings.

In the wake of this experience, new memory traces are imprinted upon Sean's narcissistic network. These traces are organised along a continuum and linked to a memory pattern (narcissistic schemata) with an affinity to a similar experience that he has undergone. The next time Sean experiences lightning and rolling thunder, his immunologic memory may retrieve these contradictory sensory and psychophysiological feelings and ways of coping with them: alarm from the flashes of lightning and the sound of thunder coupled with his mother's soothing in their wake, the "boom-boom" in his mother's voice, and the fact that he himself mumbled something similar to "boom-boom". Sean might well be alarmed the next time he hears the thunder, but he can calm down with the help of the resonance of the retrieved continuity of memory traces and of the emotional jointness (Solan, 1991) he experienced with his mother.

Sean (at nine months) is playing with a torch that switches on and off alternately by itself. Seeing the changing light, his immunologic memory apparently reverberates memory-pattern contexts of jointness with his mother during the lightning and thunderstorm, and he mumbles "boom-boom", even when his mother is not present. In the future, the memory patterns might reverberate within Sean as associations of what was imprinted at the time of the original event, including how it was responded to. It may help him to regulate himself more and more and he may even murmur the words "boom-boom" to his children without remembering the constitutive event for this repetitive reaction.

Like the baby that lives within us, as adults we also tend to grasp the familiar and constant before we are able to befriend strangeness and random changes. Our behaviour, emotional reactions, and ability to prepare ourselves for changes and events are dependent on the healthy processing of narcissism: sensing and perceiving, imprinting, retrieving, and resonating the relevant memory traces. Via the narcissistic immunological memory, which evolves during our lifetime, the ego's emotional regulation and the attributes of object relations are matched (or not) with reality.

When the parent prepares his baby for the anticipated event (such as the thunderstorm above), as he (the parent) foresees its occurrence, his narcissistic immunologic memory has sufficient time to retrieve memory traces that match the new emotional experience. This may occur automatically, as implicit memory (Kandel, 2006), rather than consciously (explicit memory); the individual's ego is free to mobilise adaptation mechanisms. Consequently, the change and the event as a whole are experienced as quasi-familiar and can be managed and controlled. It is important, therefore, before we meet or even undertake new challenges, to immunise the familiar by preserving its constancy and to assimilate incoming, quasi-familiar information regarding the changes that are taking place within us and in our surroundings. In parallel, we must make room for, or in other words accommodate, these events.

Conversely, an event or a change—whether happy or frightening—which occurs suddenly and without adequate preparation, does not leave sufficient time for resonances of matched memory traces and for emotional regulation. This might lead to narcissistic injury and anxiety, and increase the risk of trauma and post-traumatic stress disorder (PTSD). Therefore, events such as marriage, birth, a move to a new apartment, or suddenly coming into a large amount of money, can paradoxically create a crisis situation in our lives, despite the attendant happiness. An experience in the present that causes the resonance of memory traces from past trauma (even if its content is different in the current experience) drags one into a kind of reverberating whirlpool of a destructive pattern, the content of which has been repressed. Under these conditions, the self may be flooded by a sense of strangeness, evoking anxiety, which may range from vulnerability to depersonalisation or dissolution, as well as feelings of emptiness, "nothingness", depression, loss of the object (and/or its love), and of a reason for living. For example, the use of dogs to disperse demonstrations of protest arouses traumatic memories of banishment in Holocaust survivors, and may in some cases lead to annihilation anxiety.

What all information systems such as the cell, the brain, and even the Internet have in common is that information flows in as input, forming memory traces, and some manifestation of it flows out as resonances and associations. In this view, we may conceive of narcissism as an information system that comprises three components: data flowing in from the narcissistic sensors to the narcissistic network of memory traces, and then being filtered out and transformed via a process of reverberation of the narcissistic immunologic memory. Sometimes, the imprinting involves the non-processed incoming sensory data, which may remain unconscious (implicit). Alternatively, it may involve its transformation in some way before flowing back out; a process that brings this data into consciousness and awareness.

Thus, throughout the day, an infinite number of memory traces (most of which are unconscious) reverberate within us. They influence the way in which we perceive reality, the other, our relationships, and ourselves. Affectively-coloured resonances may lead to our being optimistic or pessimistic, to feelings of self-esteem or inferiority, or toward being able to enjoy what exists or being anxious about losing it. In this way, the hidden child within each of us influences our daily lives.

Sometimes we may be reluctant to face, or may fear, the domination of our memory traces over the present. We are then drawn to the familiar to steer or guide our thoughts to more manageable waters.

Detective Inspector Helen Mirkin describes this in the first novel of the detective series she inspired, *The Rosebush Murders,* as she struggles to discharge her duties in the midst of a murder investigation:

> And now, it appeared that some dark and chilling secret permeated the air. Out of a need to give a fair hearing to the multitude of voices emanating from the hospital and to differentiate among them, my own and that of my dead father, I asked myself whether I might be overly sensitive to wrongdoings at the hospital since his

premature death. As I strived to maintain my analytic neutrality until the investigation was over, I asked myself whether perhaps my judgment was compromised. (Shidlo, 2012, p. 187)

Alice, an immigrant in her thirties, and a mother of two boys, shares with me in her psychoanalytic session her suffering in her new country: "I can't find my place here in Tel Aviv. Walking the streets, I have no memories of my childhood, nothing to connect to, to belong to, only to my father's stories about his dream of Israel. I don't yet have a common language with the people here, and no common past. My boys, on the other hand, already feel part of a group of friends. They are happy and feel they belong to the country, while I feel detached."

We observe how people cope differently with failure, as a function of how it is coloured by different affective experiences: some people may retrieve memory traces connected to a supportive figure, and feel a need to share the experience of hurt with someone close. Others may retrieve memory traces that place the responsibility for their failure upon others, and say, "I failed because of him", or they may connect every failure to impaired self-esteem, "I failed because I am a loser". Finally, there are those who retrieve memory traces that are connected to motivation to compete, such as, "I have to succeed", and they initiate new and creative ventures despite the failure. Thus the feeling of what happens is always influenced by the feeling of what has already happened (Damasio, 1999; Pally 1997a, 1997b, 1997c; Solms, 2004; Tomkins, 1962, 1963).

The processing of narcissism as an emotional immune system is revealed in an example that Rachel brings to a psychoanalytic session. She talks excitedly about a memory her husband shared at a time she was seriously ill: "When I was hospitalised, my husband remembered that once, before we got married, I told him about a palm reader who saw that I would have a long life, but that along the way I would have a serious illness from which I would emerge strengthened. As he spoke, I remembered that group meeting, during which one of the participants asked to examine my palm and told me exactly what my husband recalled. I was excited by what she said, and by the fact that it was possible to read the future from one's palm, and I revealed it to my then boyfriend, now my husband. Many years have passed since that event; neither of us remembered it, and suddenly it popped up."

The husband's narcissistic sensors surveyed the trauma he was undergoing with his wife and her illness, while a subjective but compatible hint unconsciously triggered his associations. The associations surface like cross-checked information, connecting the past occurrence to the present event by retrieving a joint and familiar experiential memory from earlier days, and arousing the encouraging and hopeful message, "that I would have a long life." His narcissistic resonances awaken Rachel's memory traces, which might otherwise have remained forever hidden. This narcissistic immunologic memory processing assisted the immunisation and the restoring of the self-familiarity of each of them against the fear of death in the present.

Derek, a man in his thirties, came for treatment because of the distress and anxiety that flooded him every time his wife came home late. In the course of treatment, Derek revealed the following childhood trauma, as it was recounted to him: when he was about two years old, every morning his mother would leave him in his playpen, walk his brother across the street to school and return immediately. One morning, "on the way home she slipped, fell, lost consciousness and was taken to hospital. Only about two hours later, during which I remained alone in the playpen, did my aunt arrive and find me sobbing and terrified." This traumatic experience was seared into Derek's information network, his narcissistic immunologic memory, and until understood, unconsciously coloured any current experience of waiting with existential anxiety. Hence, memory traces of trauma resurface by means of narcissistic immunologic memory reverberations, even without a conscious memory of a particular event.

As suggested above, psychoanalytic therapy or dynamic psychotherapy may stimulate the immunologic memory to retrieve associations, memory traces, phantasms, dreams, affects, and transference attributes. These reverberations of past experiences are the means through which present experiences become conscious and familiar, are processed, managed, and understood in new contexts. This new awareness and insight may prevent past unconscious patterns from dominating present emotional experience.

## The processing modes of the innate narcissism

To recapitulate, narcissism may be seen as stemming from and building upon four interrelated processes: (1) identifying the familiar; (2) inoculating and immunising the familiar sense of the self while preserving its familiarity as an evident, tangible wholeness, and as a constant; (3) becoming alert to the invasion by strangeness and resisting it; and (4) restoring the cohesiveness of self-familiarity following injuries that undermine the sense of wholeness.

Innate narcissism functions to preserve the baby's fragile self, according to the familiarity principle, as it alternates between two poles: attraction to the familiar and resistance to that which remains strange (and to strangers).

These processes are assumed to occur against the background of the peripheral nervous system's visceral or autonomic nervous system (ANS).[4] Initially, narcissism functions in a similar way to neural-instinctive activity and is based on the absolute "all-or-nothing" principle. Gradually, narcissistic functioning becomes more sophisticated, and the repertoire between the activity poles becomes enriched with intermediate hues, such as calmness with the familiar and appropriate vigilance toward the strange, unexpected, or extraordinary.

Leo (at five months) is already sensorially familiar with his regular toys and has some notions about how to use them. When his Uncle Simon plays with him and shows him Christopher the bear, his eyes sparkle, he reacts with motor excitement, and extends his small hands toward the bear. Leo is obviously familiar with the toy as one of his self-assets. He easily befriends new toys with a similar texture or a similar form to Christopher the bear, and enriches his self-assets and his narcissistic information network with new sensorimotor representations. When Uncle Simon presents a completely strange toy, such as a drum, Leo's face reflects estrangement; appearing dissatisfied, he abandons the game.

Like Leo, all babies have to get to know a new toy. A profusion of new toys overstimulates the baby and makes it difficult for him to consolidate the familiar, to identify the familiar in the new toy, and to become attached to it. Generally speaking, pronounced and frequent sensory changes, such as changing locations, haircuts, or perfumes, make it difficult for the baby to recognise the familiar (as for the adult).

In accordance with the familiarity principle (which is enriched by more and more familiar elements), and via the resonance of memory traces, narcissism is evoked to immunise one's sense of self-familiarity and one's self-assets in their entirety as a whole against what could be experienced as an invasion by strangeness. Such an invasion might be experienced as undermining the cohesiveness of the self-familiarity and as an injury to one's wholeness. Moreover, it might result in the hyper-activation of the sympathetic nervous system, as manifested by an increase in heartbeat and blood pressure, shallower, faster or more constricted breathing, a tightening of the stomach and chest, and so forth. Once challenged or compromised, for example after one is unavoidably hurt and undermined in some way, innate narcissism is activated to restore the subjective sense of self-familiarity. This activation safeguards the familiarity of the self and its objects, as well as that of the existing relationship, especially following injury, frustration, disappointment, or trauma. Such a process entails a parasympathetic return to calmness (Levine, 2010; Ross, 2008), manifested by the opposite of the signs of sympathetic activation, including slower and deeper breathing, decreased heart rate and blood pressure and relaxed muscle tone, among others.

Jasmine (at eight months) sits on her grandmother's lap. She knows her grandmother well, and enjoys playing with her. However, when her grandmother removes her spectacles to polish them, it is clear from Jasmine's expression that she no longer recognises her as familiar. She puts her small hands on her grandmother's face in an attempt to touch and return the spectacles to where they belong, for the purpose of identification. Later, Jasmine plays at putting on and taking off the spectacles. When she becomes familiar with her grandmother's face, with or without spectacles, Jasmine takes a deep breath and relaxes. The familiarity and the object constancy of her grandmother have been immunised, and remain immune to minor variations. Henceforth, her grandmother can remove and replace her spectacles without the change causing Jasmine any sensation of strangeness.

The constancy of her bodily care and rituals in her relations with her parents enable Jasmine to familiarise herself with and get used to the family routine, which also includes experiencing regular changes, such as separating from and rejoining her parents. Her narcissistic urge to decipher the familiar gradually enhances her acclimatisation to constant changes (ego regulation), thereby strengthening the narcissistic processing.

Already during the first weeks of her life, Karen's facial expressions show she is relaxed in her regular cradle, but becomes restless when laid down in an unfamiliar place. She experiences the cradle as part of herself—a self-asset—just as she experiences her mother's bosom, her bath, and her familiar bedding and nappies. Her mother's regular presence during nursing or her father's regular presence at bath time are also already familiar to her. She holds on to her mother's habitual and constant emotional attendance, as well as to the fixed presence of physical objects, in order to befriend random changes more easily.

The habitual and constant sensory characteristics serve as a narcissistic safety net for dealing with changes, and together with the consolidation of the ego's adaptation mechanisms, the baby (at eight months) will shape perceptions of constancy, an important factor in the development of cognitive and emotional intelligence (ego regulation). Hence, the habituation process is a salient characteristic of the narcissistic immune system.

## Shaping and restoring self-familiarity cohesiveness

Self-familiarity and self-assets comprise affective memory traces of self-experiences with significant objects, as well as narratives, representations and images of the self and its objects, and patterns of object relations. All of these elements and resources are ingrained in the narcissistic immunological memory network, are interconnected, and culminate in the constant perception of a cohesive, true (as opposed to false) self-familiarity. This constant familiar sense of the self is crucial for the baby as an ultimate narcissistic frame for recognising self-familiarity, for deciphering any non-self, and for restoring self-familiarity following injuries, whether real or imagined.

It is interesting to note that the immunologists are concerned with the processing of the immunology system that deciphers the foreign invaders (nonself) into the body. They consider that: "The key to a healthy immune system is it's remarkable ability to distinguish between the body's own cells, recognized as 'self,' and foreign cells, or 'nonself.'" (NIH, 2008, p. 1). The invasion of the nonself into the self-familiarity results in the immune system "quickly launch(ing) an attack" (ibid.).

The enduring perception of self-familiarity indicates, in my view, an improvement in healthy narcissism processing. It may be connected to what Solms (2004) has called a "virtual body", one that enables us to absorb the most fundamental embodiment of the self. It facilitates the understanding that: "It's me, I'm this body, and right now, this is how I feel". However, the functioning of healthy narcissism is insufficient in itself for preserving a cohesive self-familiarity within the child. Improving healthy narcissism requires the parents' feedback—their auxiliary ego's reaction that would enhance the infant's evolving object relations and enrich the ego's adaptation mechanism. The parents' support and enthusiasm for their child's separateness and for his doings is crucial. This, however, does not imply echoing assertions to the tune of his being "the cleverest", the "best looking", or the "most successful", relative to others, but mainly "the one I love the most (as he is)".

This linkage between healthy narcissism and object relations highlights our narcissistic need to experience the approval of our loved ones, and to be loved as we are, each within the boundaries of his or her own self-familiarity. Parental approval supports the child's narcissistic immunisation of his true self-familiarity.

Parents are usually delighted with their offspring, who represent a valued component of their self-familiarity assets. For the same reason, parents are hurt by their child's insufficiency (or their own), and may sometimes experience and even express disappointment in their offspring's otherness (according to the subjectivity of their ideal narcissistic perception).

The baby submits to his parents' expressions of subjective delight, and their encouragement of his separateness builds and strengthens the infant's self-esteem and self-familiarity. These parental reactions are imprinted within the baby's narcissistic immunological memory as positive self and object attributes, and will remain an important resource or self-asset throughout life. Frequent reverberations of these positive memory traces in similar occurrences strengthen the baby's healthy narcissism and immunise his true self-familiarity and his valuable separateness.

Conversely, the parental denial of the baby's separateness and their expressions of disappointment and criticism injure and invade his self-esteem, and may cause him to feel damaged or unloved. These negative, parental reactions are imprinted within the baby's narcissistic immunological memory as negative self and object attributes. Frequent reverberations of these spoiling, damaging, and even destructive memory traces within him during similar occurrences, strengthen the infant's deviated or pathological narcissism and immunise his *damaged* self-familiarity, which includes destructiveness toward his self and his objects.[5]

For example, a baby born with a deformity in one of his limbs might experience himself as whole, or as an ideal self, despite the defect—of which he remains largely unaware—on the condition that his parents experience him as whole and complete, and love him as he is. Upon undergoing corrective surgery, this baby will feel a sense of strangeness for some time (a deviation from his self-familiarity). Only when he adapts to the change—supported by his parents' encouragement and expressions of love—will he become familiar with his new bodily sensations, and restore and update his self-familiarity. When a parent is adversely affected by his child's deformity, and transmits rejection and resistance to the lack of wholeness and perfection, the baby will experience himself as defective.

D. Quinodoz (2003) suggests that sometimes people feel a sense of the heterogeneity of the self, alongside its cohesiveness. Most people can usually tolerate this without excessive anxiety, in part due to the presence or internalisation of an object that is sufficiently constructive and benevolent (e.g., as manifest in their affective scripts). I accept Quinodoz's conceptualisation that when the individual is capable of distinguishing among and recognising his self's diverse components, and finding them compatible, these affects and feelings may be integrated into his self-cohesiveness via what I have called "narcissistic restoration of self-familiarity". Consider, for example, two feelings that appear to be opposed in the context of a relationship: the desire for exclusive intimacy with the object and the desire for independence. Presumably, these two opposed feelings can be integrated into self-cohesiveness when both partners are able to tolerate the otherness and separateness of the other.

Quinodoz, however, relates mainly to patients who suffer from excessive heterogeneity among "incompatible *components that cannot be linked together to create a synthesis*" (p. 1471, author's italics). An example might be a toddler/individual who cannot link his oral sense of perfection with the anal sense of aggression (see Chapter Six).

Throughout *the Enigma of Childhood*, I try to shed light on the complex fact that in every adult a child is concealed, one that influences our interpretations of experiences, touching upon many aspects of life. As I understand this, in order to attain cohesiveness, the mature person has to admit to, accept, and even cherish the child's attributes concealed within himself, including those features he does not like (just like the parent has to accept his own child as he is, including his otherness.).

In the oral stage, self-esteem is therefore equivalent to the value of the parents' love: "I am loved means that I am perfect (ideal self); if I am not loved, this means that I am defective". The baby, like anyone else, experiences criticism and intolerance toward him as a narcissistic injury to his subjective perception of self-familiarity. This indicates a necessity for harmonious functioning between the innate narcissistic immune processing, the ego's adaptation mechanisms, and object relations in order to consolidate self-familiarity, while simultaneously reinforcing tolerance toward the otherness embedded in the non-self object and in one's self-deficiencies.

The proper processing of healthy narcissism, supported by parental encouragement of the child's separateness, is advantageous for the permanent acceptance, happiness, and love of what is in ourselves and in those dear to us, as opposed to what is not; namely, shortcomings, deficiencies, and defects. Furthermore, people who are capable of accepting their own disadvantages are also capable of coping better with the weaknesses of their fellow men (and women), their otherness, and the strangeness they represent.

## Confronting the strangeness and the otherness of our fellow beings

Through his narcissistic sensors, the newborn baby senses his self-familiarity and is aware of the unfamiliar within or around him as non-self. At the same time, he is attracted to the familiar (non-self) caregiver, while continuing to resist the unfamiliar non-self that triggers a sense of strangeness. This narcissistic fascination with the familiar seems to provide the baby with the requisite degree of well-being necessary for accepting or joining this non-self. It also seems to supply his ego with the basic security to invest emotionally in this non-self as an object of libidinal desirability and as a potential supplier of existential and emotional needs (see Chapter Three). This process, which makes possible the ongoing development of object relations (Solan, 1998b, 1999), originates in the oral stage, and will be consolidated and refined throughout life (see Chapter Four).

However, whenever the object episodically does not respond to the baby according to its habitual familiar characteristics or the recurring relationship attributes of his familiar non-self, the baby senses mainly his strangeness. The baby, as any adult, might experience the otherness of his familiar object as a threat to the well-being inherent in his self-familiarity, an injury, or a rejection. Some activation of the autonomous nervous system may ensue. In these painful situations, the healthy narcissism of babies and adults is often triggered and evoked to protect what is familiar, to resist the strangeness and avoid exposing oneself to otherness. For example, someone told Alice (an adult woman) that he saw her father crying. "It's not possible, you're making a mistake," she responded firmly, "it's not my father, my father *never* cries." Another example: children have difficulty grasping that their parents were once children themselves because these attributes are not imprinted in their narcissistic network, and they hold steadfastly to the view that their parents have never been children. Otherness is thus one of the most difficult things for us to perceive and accept. What this implies is that otherness represents characteristics of the object or of his behaviour that are not identified as familiar within one's personal narcissistic network.

A family event is taking place at home. Sean (at ten months) is in his mother's arms, slightly overwhelmed by the large number of "strangers", and he clings to her so as to feel safe with what is familiar to him. Initially, all the strangers seem threatening and indistinguishable. Gradually Sean calms down. He begins to survey, scan, and locate (by means of his narcissistic sensors and his immunologic memory) familiar faces among the strangers, and only when he identifies his aunt and uncle, Maggie and Isaac, does he enthusiastically go to their arms. At one point, Sean surprises his parents by reaching out with his small hands to a paediatrician, a member of the family he does not know. It seems that his narcissistic sensors (gut feelings) registered that this guest has a special way with children, and he befriends him with ease. This person, who was initially experienced as an unfamiliar non-self, is now experienced as someone desirable and familiar.[6] As opposed to this, however, when a relative who Sean is familiar with approaches him, happy to see him, Sean refuses to relate to her. Her presence, despite being familiar, arouses distress. Possibly this relative arouses memory patterns loaded with a sense of threat. It is as if he anticipates her customary pinch on his cheeks, and is quick to protect himself by rejecting her. His mother wisely respects Sean's reservations, allows him not to respond to this "auntie", and apologises to her.

Freud (1919h), in his enlightening essay, *The Uncanny*, describes the sensation of simultaneously experiencing a sense of both familiarity and unfamiliarity in relation to the other: a semi-familiar person or inanimate object that may be experienced as threatening and thus disruptive to the feeling of self-familiarity as continuity.

Harry (at twelve months) holds on to an adult's legs on the assumption that he is holding on to his father, and suddenly realises that it's his uncle, Alvin. He feels embarrassed and runs to look for his father. When he grasps his father's legs and experiences the familiar feeling of homeliness, he returns to his uncle, holds on to him, and plays a kind of hide-and-seek game. The game represents his enjoyment of his ability to overcome the embarrassment arising from the sensation of strangeness within the familiar and to experience the transition from one emotional state to another, in which the familiar remains constant. In this way, he integrates strangeness within familiarity.

Jane (at nine months) is used to accompanying her parents to the door when they leave her in her grandmother's care. With her grandmother holding her, they both wave to the parents, and the grandmother says, "Bye-bye." One day, Jane accompanies her parents to the door, together with her grandfather. As usual, Jane waves to her parents as an expression of departure, accompanied by the familiar "bye-bye." Only after the parents have left does Jane look at her grandfather, and her face registers puzzlement. She identifies (via her narcissistic sensors) a difference between her grandfather and her grandmother on the one hand, and the familiar constancy of the departure ceremony from the parents (a reverberation of memory traces) on the other. She smiles embarrassedly at her grandfather and completes the process of departure from the parents in a joint game with him. It seems that a feeling of familiarity, mixed with strangeness, has been aroused in her. Small differences in familiar emotional situations quite often arouse a reaction of surprise and embarrassment (Freud, 1918a).

Normal narcissistic processing allows babies, as well as adults, to be curious about other people who are "almost-familiar", to befriend them, and to identify the familiar hidden within the strange (Solan, 1998a, 1998b). An encounter with a stranger sometimes arouses in us a feeling of familiarity mixed with strangeness, which stimulates a curiosity to locate the familiar in order to befriend it[7] and become able to accept change. For example, viewing a new movie triggers a need to connect the actor to a previous character he or she has played, or to feelings the actor had aroused in us in a previous performance.

Appropriate curiosity and the befriending of strangeness are very important for emotional development, for enriching the self with experiential emotional information, for adapting to change, and also for maintaining a well-regulated alertness to strangers. The *impaired* processing of narcissism leaves us in one of two extreme poles of immunising the familiarity: either clinging uncompromisingly to absolute and perfect familiarity, or rejecting any sign of strangeness or otherness.

Strangeness is not confined only to matters outside ourselves. It is also aroused within ourselves with respect to physical growth, aches and illnesses, sexual maturity, pregnancy, and ageing.

Sandy (at six weeks) has a stomach ache that causes a sense of strangeness within her. She makes an effort to produce a bowel movement, and calms down when she succeeds. Gradually (after about five months) it becomes clear that she has learned which muscles she must activate in order to rid herself of the pressure in her stomach, and how to extricate herself from the distress and return to the feeling of constant familiarity.

In the oral stage, the baby's sensorimotor capabilities develop at a rapid pace. He lies on his back, moves his legs, sits before he stands, rolls before crawling, and crawls before walking. Initially, each new sensation in his body is experienced as strange. His angle of vision is different when he lies down compared to when he sits, his limbs transmit a different proprioceptive sensation when sitting, standing, or crawling, and his perception of balance is also different for each action. The sensation of strangeness within self-familiarity propels the baby toward repetition of his new motor achievements and his new, increasingly familiar sensation of control over the motor changes.

Leo (at seven months) has difficulty moving from a standing to a sitting position, and calls for help. His parents sit him down, but he gets up like a tumbler doll and (again) starts crying. When he experiences the transition from standing to sitting as familiar and under his ego's control, his feeling of self-familiarity is recovered (familiarisation with the changing proprioceptive sensation).

Sean (at eight months) enjoys getting into a large cardboard box, as if it were a small house. As he gets bigger (at twelve months), he finds it difficult to crawl inside, and feels strangeness within the familiar feeling of crawling into his "house". In an attempt to safeguard the self-familiarity that has been challenged, he projects the strangeness on to the house, and is angry with the cardboard box every time he fails to get inside it. Finally, he ceases playing, and even destroys the box.

Self-familiarity evolves to be perceived as self-constancy (under the ego's regulation) to such an extent that often we become aware of our familiar sense of self only following disruptions in the feeling of familiarity. Strangeness and deviation from the familiar in the self-space elicit our attention. The feeling of hunger, a stomach ache, a different rate of breathing, a spectacular landscape—all these create sensations that are different from the constant and regular ones. When this happens, we experience a change in familiarity and are eager to embrace or otherwise cope with the change to revive the familiar homely routine (narcissistic restoration of self-familiarity). In this way, we acknowledge the constant and familiar sense of the self and we assimilate updated information on the changes that constantly take place within ourselves. Alternatively, some people are used to coping with exciting changes since childhood. They are familiar with excitement and therefore seek adventures as adults (narcissistic restoration of their self-familiarity), whereas for others, this confrontation with danger would be unbearable.

Sandy (at four months) wakes up crying, which for her mother is a signal of distress of the type that generally stems from a sense of strangeness. The constancy in their relationship enables the mother to differentiate between Sandy's various crying tones, and to identify whether the source of the strangeness is an unpleasant dampness in her nappy, illness, irritating hunger, or a wish for pampering. The mother tries to recognise Sandy's separate needs, which often differ from hers, in order to pacify her. She hugs her warmly and transmits confidence that the distress will pass. Sandy calms down as a result of her self-familiarity being restored at her mother's bosom and her breathing becomes more flowing and steady.

Steven (at four months) also wakes up crying and discontented. As always, his mother interprets his crying as hunger (she denies any other stress linked to the strangeness) and rushes to nurse him. She does not bother to identify the reason for the crying or consider that he may have needs other than her own, or those she attributes to him. The uncertainty, like the imperfect, threatens her. For her, nursing is a familiar experience through which she realises her motherly talents for soothing him. She accustoms Steven to eating according to her self-familiarity and not according to his needs (strangeness invasion). Her repetitive behaviour suppresses his immunologic need to learn to differentiate among his various types of distress and to regain his self-familiarity. The need for locating the source of the problem has not been created in Steven. Hence, etched in his narcissism are memory traces that food and feeding (or the activity of eating) are the decisive solutions for all distress. It can be reasonably assumed that in the future these memory traces will reverberate within him in the wake of stress aroused by strangeness of any kind, and that he will find refuge in food without being able to identify whether he indeed needs food under those particular circumstances.

Jerry (at four months) rests on his mother's bosom and they are enjoying being together. The telephone rings and the mother quickly places Jerry in his playpen and goes to answer it. Jerry experiences an unexpected change and strangeness, and he bursts into tears—an expression of narcissistic injury and distress.

The feeling of uneasiness triggered by change and by people's otherness is common knowledge. It may emerge in daily life; for example, when we drive a rented car or see someone dressed very differently from what we are used to. Preparing the child, as well as ourselves, for the anticipated changes enables us to cope better with the strangeness and befriend it. Doing so facilitates the narcissistic reverberation of memory traces that lead us to perceive the familiar within the changing flow of things, and thus preserve our self-familiarity. It is therefore important to prepare the baby to befriend scheduled or planned changes in the life of the family, by means of routine "code words", or a song, heralding certain events. Such actions provide a narcissistic net for preservation of self-familiarity prior to the changes, such as those inherent in people departing, going to sleep, undergoing a medical examination, celebrating something at kindergarten, and even the birth of a sibling.

Dan, a choreographer of a dance company, shares his feelings with me in the course of his psychoanalysis: "I'm depressed ... Recently I tried to add a few new dance variations to the regular program, but during the rehearsals I felt confusion—in me, and also among the dancers. It felt as if the previous dance steps had taken control over me and disrupted the new ones ..."

I (the analyst) remembered (a reverberation of my memory traces) the few times that Dan had expressed a fear that the family-group unity would be lost, and I interpreted: "For you, changing the familiar tempo is like losing the family team spirit that you loved so much."

Dan reacted excitedly: "I remember [reverberations of memory traces] the family trips in which my mother encouraged all of us to sing together in a uniform tempo as a family choir. I remember that these were always precious moments for me. I can physically feel now the anxiety that gripped me at times as a child when I sang off-key when we sang together ... I felt as if I had spoiled my mother's family musical event ... Maybe the new choreographic variations are a kind of off-key of the previous ones."

### Restoration of self-familiarity

From infancy to adulthood, despite the narcissistic immunological processes, we all repeatedly get insulted, frustrated, and hurt after experiencing strangeness or otherness from within or without. This situation causes narcissistic injury, disappointment, shame, and humiliation, and may be experienced as traumatic when it undermines the inner perception of self-familiarity cohesiveness. Being hurt is inevitable, because the other, even if he or she is a familiar person and dear to us, remains a separate entity who asserts his otherness.

When we are contradicted, insulted, or experience hurt, we usually tend to withdraw our interest from this individual (Freud, 1914c). In these painful states, we are often furious with this person for offending us, and sometimes even hate him, as if he were to blame for the intolerable feeling of strangeness. In other words, we naively expect the other to safeguard our wholeness, to respond according to our self-familiarities, and this other, in asserting his otherness, is blamed for offending us.

The narcissistic process of restoring self-familiarity after it is challenged is thus of fundamental importance for safeguarding one's self-esteem and sense of pride, as well as the awareness of self-integrity. This process is also essential for preserving and restoring the relationship with the object; reconciling with him despite his otherness, the insults he inflicted, and the pain he caused as a result of his otherness.

Much like the stepwise process of solving a puzzle, the restoration of self-, object-, and relations-familiarity is attained by reprocessing and cross-checking data; fine-tuning the present experiences in accordance with reverberating self-familiar data until one's self/object/relations-familiarity is adjusted and reconstructed.

Whenever self-familiarity is restored, the individual may feel free to re-evaluate his potential, acknowledge the limitations of his ideals (Duruz, 1981), and reconcile with his imperfections (Reich, 1953) and the otherness of his objects. This may allow him to accept that he can be loved as he is, and free him to reinvest in his interests and loved ones (Freud, 1914c).

Healthy processing of the (developing) narcissism creates an emotional equilibrium system, allowing one to befriend the familiar while remaining alert toward strangeness. In contrast, impaired processing of narcissism creates an imbalance between vigilance and befriending, and may lead to over-alertness toward strangeness, suspicion, and strangeness-annihilation anxiety. This is accompanied by the over-activation of the sympathetic nervous system. It may also lead to a lack of vigilance and to the over-befriending of any stranger, followed by frequent incursions of strangeness into the self-familiarity and damage to self-esteem. The narcissistic lacunae can be seen in the narcissistic pathologies of the oral stage that we are familiar with from the literature and in our work, such as a false self (Winnicott, 1960), feelings of deprivation and inferiority, injured self-esteem, deficient preservation of self-familiarity and the denying of signs of strangeness invasion, self-destructiveness, over-suspicion of otherness, constant abandonment anxiety, alcohol and drug dependency, eating disorders, perversions, and narcissistic personality disorders.

The processing of narcissism improves throughout life and will contribute to the development of various components of intelligence. For example, attachment to the parent and the befriending of otherness arises from the perception of the familiar in the stranger; the ability to adapt to change arises from the need to control strangeness and change; scientific curiosity grows from investigating that which is unknown or foreign, and joie de vivre—the source of which lies in the perception of wholeness, love, and feelings of vigour and familiar integrity—may be enhanced. In this regard, I follow Kohut's (1966) definition of wisdom: "Wisdom is achieved largely through man's ability to overcome his unmodified narcissism and it rests on his acceptance of the limitations of his physical, intellectual, and emotional powers" (p. 268).

## Summary

In my view, narcissism should be regarded as a personality component in terms of Freud's structural theory (1923b). Thus, in addition to the id, ego and superego, I would add narcissism. Narcissism is the first of the components that is activated to safeguard self-familiarity, object-familiarity, and relationship familiarity.

The view of narcissism as providing an inborn emotional immunity for the familiar sense of the self is relatively new (Solan, 1998b). It describes an innate process allowing for the preservation of self-familiarity characterised by cohesiveness and wholeness, the ability to resist the "invasion" of strangeness within self-familiarity, and finally, the ability to restore self-familiarity following the inevitable injuries that occur throughout life. Narcissism is activated by a dynamic process of attraction to the familiar and being on alert for, and resisting, the strange. During this narcissistic process, the recognition of familiarity confers a sense of well-being to the experiencing self, as evidenced by the silent action of the parasympathetic nervous system. In contrast, strangeness arouses alertness and, to the extent that it is stressful, may activate the sympathetic nervous system, in preparation for "fight or flight".

The healthy (balanced) processing of narcissism through the befriending of strangeness and otherness contributes to the enhancement of emotional intelligence. Yet simultaneously, and despite the normal course of healthy narcissistic development, we continue to react with narcissistic injury to strangeness and otherness in our external and internal environments. In these situations, as adults we may feel as injured and furious as the child hidden within us did—until the immunological process succeeds in "updating" the narcissistic data and affective information to restore our self-familiarity and our relationship with our objects despite their otherness. This updating and "resetting" may entail the current release of pent-up energy that was aroused but not fully discharged during the original (genetic/developmental) event/s, which were experienced as traumatic in a relatively minor, or major, way, and have now been re-triggered.

## Notes

1. Interoception and sensory information from the external senses, such as vision and hearing.
2. A body of research points to the importance of imprinting acquired at the beginning of life for the learning process. Observations of young monkeys revealed a direct association between their sensorial and rhythmical contact with soft and pleasurable skin in interaction with the environment, and their affective, social, sexual, perceptual, and intellectual development (Harlow, 1959). Neglected toddlers in hostels, lacking interaction with the environment and benign imprinting, showed impairments in emotional development, and incompatibility in social, perceptual, motor, and communication functioning. These traces were irreversible (Spitz, 1945).
3. Memory traces—a term "used by Freud throughout his work to denote the way in which events are inscribed in memory. Memory traces, according to Freud, are deposited in different systems; they subsist permanently, but are only reactivated once they have been cathected ... As far as evocation is concerned, a memory may be reactualised in one associative context while, in another, it will remain inaccessible to consciousness ..." (Laplanche & Pontalis 1973, pp. 247–248). The memories are coded and stored in the neural network and crystallise into an index of imprints that serve as comparison data for identifying

a new stimulus, for attaching it to a familiar historical sequence, and for retrieving its representation in the wake of renewed arousal (Pally, 1997a, b, c).

4. The ANS includes the sympathetic and parasympathetic nervous systems, and as its name suggests, operates independently and, for the most part, without our conscious control. It is responsible for regulating our body's basic autonomous functioning.

    To this dynamic understanding, somatic experiencing practitioners would add the necessity of slowly discharging trapped excesses of arousal energy in the body, one sensation at a time (Levine, 2010; Ross, 2008). For a more complete account of this process, see Ross (2008).

5. Rosenfeld (1971) elaborated the link between narcissism and object relations by conceptualising the positive and libidinal aspects of narcissism versus its negative and destructive aspects. Ross (2008) described the trauma vortex and the healing vortex, and how they interact.

6. A similar process may be observed in the animal world: stray cats accept a stranger when they identify a "cat smell" emanating from him, for example, from his own cats, who in turn brush up against him frequently to make him more familiar.

7. Levinas (1969) addresses the tendency of human culture to subordinate the different to the same, to include the unique in the totality, and to negate otherness. He characterises the other as separate from the self, which is defined by its boundaries, making it more difficult for the other to become confounded with it or to absorb it. Morality obligates us to allocate room for the other, for his otherness and his uniqueness.

# CHAPTER THREE

# The ego: an emotional self-regulation agency

## The emotional domain initiated by the instincts

This chapter will discuss psychic evolution from the viewpoint of innate biological energy, generally known as instinct. Although aware that these are controversial terms, I consider Freud's dualistic conceptualisation of the life and death instincts (1915c, 1920g, 1923b) an essential foundation for my assumptions below. I will elaborate the significance of these concepts by broadening their scope, as well as by expanding the id regulation function as a base for the ego regulation function, in conjunction with narcissistic immune processing. Without detracting from Freud's definitions of the life and death instincts, I would like to rename them a "connecting instinct" (toward life) and a "decomposing instinct" (toward death), respectively. Both instincts discharge bodily tension.

Let us start with Freud's conceptualisations. Freud (1920g) claims that "an instinct is an urge inherent in organic life to *restore an earlier* state of things which the living entity has been obliged to abandon ..." (p. 36, my italics), and that "in addition to the conservative instincts which impel towards *repetition*, there may be others which push forward towards progress and the *production of new forms*" (p. 37). Referring to the life instinct, Freud reminds us that "it is generally considered that the union of a number of cells into a vital association—the multicellular character of organisms—has become a means of prolonging their life" (p. 50). On the other hand, Freud describes the function of the death instinct: "… to assure that the organism shall *follow its own path to death*" (p. 39, my italics). Furthermore, "every modification which is thus imposed upon the course of the organism's life is accepted by the conservative organic instincts and *stored up for further repetition*" (p. 38, my italics).

The connecting instinct—my conceptualisation of the life instinct—stimulates survival mechanisms of synthesis. Links and associations are created among new data and information networks in such a way as to impel physical and emotional existence, sexual desire, reproduction, and the transfer of genetic data to future generations. Examples of this would be the links between a baby's hunger, suckling, the mother's breast, and the taste of milk for satiating his hunger, or the arousal of sexual tension by the attraction (links) to the other gender in order to achieve fertilisation. In parallel to the narcissistic immunological processing by attraction (links) to the familiar and subsequent resonance of associations or memory traces (see Chapter Two), we may conceive of the connecting instinct as processing by linking familiar elements.

The decomposing instinct—my conceptualisation of the death instinct—stimulates the body to discharge accumulated tension. We thus strive to eliminate secretions, expel excess gases, decompose food, and remove hair and dry skin cells, as well as to get rid of what is unpleasant and unnecessary. The decomposing instinct impels the re-establishment of the inner, familiar, constant biological and emotional state, for example, striving to restore a state of nirvana. In removing internal tension, the decomposing instinct may be triggered and understood as a compulsion to "follow its own path to death" (Freud, ibid.). We may conceive of decomposing instinct discharge processing (i.e., getting rid of the unpleasant and unnecessary) as parallel to the narcissistic resistance to the non-self and concomitant rejection of strangeness (see Chapter Two).

The decomposing instinct dissolves the links created under the influence of the connecting instinct by splitting, disassociating, or otherwise cutting off the linked data (for example, breast) from the stimuli (for example, hunger pangs); the stimuli can thus be ignored completely and the baby may fall into a nirvana-like sleep. Then, after, the connecting instinct re-links data, connections are restored for the renewal of life. In other words, we may view the decomposing instinct as striving toward homeostasis, whereas the connecting instinct implies the capacity for change and evolution.

## The id: instinctual regulation agency

Freud (1940a [1938]) regarded the id as "the oldest of these psychical ... agencies ... [which] contains everything that is inherited, that is present at birth, that is laid down in the constitution—above all therefore, the instincts, which originate from the somatic organization and which find a first psychical expression here [in the id] in forms unknown to us" (p. 145).

The id may be regarded as an archaic agency of self-regulation that is activated to regulate inborn instinctual tension according to the all-or-nothing principle, similar to the activation of the nervous system. This implies that when tension reaches a certain threshold, the instinctual response is total and compulsive (all), and that when it is below that threshold, no stimulus response will occur (nothing). It seems that the id's mode of instinctual regulation is triggered to discharge the tension by compulsion or even "repetition compulsion" in order to re-establish a familiar constant inner tension. Freud (1920g) claimed that "the dominating tendency of mental life, and perhaps of nervous life in general, is the effort to reduce, to keep constant or to remove internal tension due to stimuli" (pp. 55–56).

For example, when hunger increases and the tension crosses the physiological threshold (the "all"), the newborn is excited to identify a familiar source of nutrition and then suckles the milk vigorously until satiated. The mother's nipple is connected to the hunger as a means of discharging the instinctual tension (under the impact of the connecting instinct). Nevertheless, often during suckling and before being satiated, the baby may fall asleep, in complete relaxation, in his mother's arms. The initiation of sucking is thus totally neutralised by the split between hunger and suckling (under the impact of the decomposing instinct). The internal stimulus, which previously evoked tension, now drops below the threshold and the newborn is no longer attracted to the nipple (the "nothing"). The mother might try to insert her nipple into the baby's mouth in order to re-stimulate his suckling, but the baby remains indifferent during his sleep.

Natalie (at two weeks old) is crying from hunger. Her mother is not yet ready to nurse her and tells her gently: "Hold on, Natalie darling,

I'm going to the bathroom and I'll feed you in a minute." Nathalie does not understand the words, and is not yet able to wait. For her, the connections (hunger, nipple, suck, taste of milk) are a familiar source of survival (narcissistic processing), and her instinctual tension increases until it turns into genuine suffering. Her crying intensifies and becomes a shriek; her face twitches and turns red. Then, when the unbearable tension, which does not reach discharge, stimulates the decomposition instinct to disconnect the links, the nagging hunger dissipates immediately. When her mother comes to feed her, she finds Natalie fast asleep, or so tired that she cannot relax and suck. She appears drained of vitality (under the influence of the decomposition instinct). By soothing Natalie with love, and helping her to regulate the tension by singing a familiar song, her mother helps her relax. Only then does her hunger increase and her strength become restored. Natalie searches for the familiar source of milk, and starts suckling.

Leo (at two weeks old) suffers from abdominal pain caused by the accumulation of gas. Occupied with his stomach ache and his crying, he is unable to suckle despite his hunger. In these moments, his decomposition instinct overrides his connecting instinct. His mother helps him expel the excess gas by bending his knees and hips toward his abdomen and from side to side. Leo is clearly involved in these exercises, which ease his discomfort. Finally, he relaxes, his hunger increases, and he can suckle—under the dominance of the connecting instinct.

The first weeks of life are almost entirely controlled by the activity of the id's instinctual regulation described above. Babies differ from each other in the intensity of their hunger and satiation, by the periods of time between the arousal of tension and its discharge, and by the quality and duration of their sleep. Most of these differences follow a normative pattern depending on the baby's weight, the availability of feeding, and its genetic material; no baby, however, will relinquish instinctual regulation.

Each baby, like every adult, has a specific threshold that represents his own familiar level of tension, experienced as well-being. This sequence of stimulating and discharging tension is a familiar, circular pattern that balances the power of the instincts. The sequence represents the harmonious functioning of the two archaic components of the personality—the id, following the all-or-nothing principle, and narcissism, following the familiarity principle.

The regulation of the id usually takes place with an almost constant rhythm and in a regular, and thus familiar, circular sequence. However, since instincts are generally combined, it is often difficult to differentiate between them. For example, links between sources of survival are connected and attached together initially, and then decomposed or split off from these same sources. Following the discharging of tension, getting rid of the unpleasant, and relaxing under the influence of the decomposing instinct, the connecting instinct urges the biological system to restore connections and find sources of sustenance for survival.

When the connecting instinct dominates the sequence, it colours our activities positively with glimmers of life, passion, and vitality, and motivates us to find sources for survival and fertilisation. In contrast, when the decomposing instinct assumes ascendancy, it colours our activities with familiar signs of withdrawal and seclusion. When instinctual tension cannot be regulated by the id through the familiar circular sequence, a defusing of the instincts occurs. The connecting (life) instinct threatens to arouse unbearable craving, tension, stress, and anxiety, while the decomposing (death) instinct threatens, as a default option, to discharge the tension via extreme outbursts, repetition compulsion, and compulsive destructiveness.

## The ego: from instinctual regulation to the regulation of drives

The terms instinct and drive are often confused. Some psychoanalysts deal with this confusion by using the concept of instinctual drives. Strachey translated the German word *Trieb*, used by Freud, as instinct, while Freud defined *Trieb* as distinct from *Instinkt*:

> ... as a concept on the frontier between the *mental and the somatic*, as the *physical representative of the stimuli originating from within the organism and reaching the mind*, as a measure of the demand made upon the mind for work in consequence of its connection with the body. (Freud, 1915c, pp. 121–122, my italics)

Freud's definition of *Trieb*, what I understand as drive, is linked to three characteristics: source, aim, and object. The *source* of drive potency lies in the investment of instinctual energy; its *aim* may imply pleasure (according to the pleasure principle) and drive satisfaction (as opposed to the mere discharge of instinctual tension); and *object* "implies the presence of some degree of self-object differentiation" (Moore & Fine, 1990, p. 101). In my experience, differentiation between these two terms, instinct and drive, is useful for understanding psychic development and the distinction between normative and pathological evolution.

Let us examine this differentiation further. Innate instinctual energy mobilises the baby to discharge tension regardless of any object. However, on the path to fulfilling its physical needs, the connecting instinct stimulates the baby to attach his instinctual energy not only to the breast as the source of milk, but also as the source of emotional, warm, pleasurable sensuality with a provider. Freud (1915c) already attributed the formation of associative links among memories to the life instinct. Moreover, the decomposing instinct stimulates the baby to rid himself not only of physical waste, but also of emotional stress, unpleasure, and unfamiliar stimuli that may undermine his well-being. What this means is that instinctual energy (the source) invested by the ego in the provider (the object) of emotional satisfaction (the aim) may be considered as drive energy; namely, libido and aggression. Thus, drives may represent a mental outcome of somatic/instinctual energy (of connecting and decomposing instincts) and of somatic/narcissistic sensations (such as familiarity and strangeness), and account for psychological liveliness. The developmental aspect of drives was discussed by Jacobson in 1953 and 1964.

The primordial regulation of tension arising from instincts, drives, and emotions takes place at the oral stage according to three principles:

a.  The all-or-nothing principle—the id principle—directed toward survival of the self at a familiar level of tension, regardless of the object.
b.  The familiarity principle—the narcissistic principle—directed toward immunising and preserving the self in a familiar emotional state of well-being with a familiar object, and resisting both strangeness and the stranger (see my definition in Chapter Two).
c.  The pleasure principle (Freud, 1920g)—the ego principle—directed toward safeguarding the self in a familiar emotional state of pleasure, and resisting unpleasure, inside the self and in one's relations with the object.

The regulation of tension, based on the above three principles, describes a transition from solely physical survival (by discharging instinctual-biological tension regardless of the object) to psychological survival (by satisfaction of drives, affects, and emotions with the caregiver—thus, object-oriented). Freud (1950 [1887–1902], 1915d) indicated a parallel between the importance of maintaining a home-ostatic state (biological need) and maintaining a state of well-being (mental need).

The figure, toward which the evolving ego directs the baby's emotional energy so as to experience with it familiar satisfactions, well-being, and pleasure, is conceptualised as the object. The desire to repeat pleasurable experiences with the object represents the well-known concepts of libido and the libidinal object. In contrast, the need to own or reject the object is termed "aggression".

Sandy (at three months old) awakes from sleep issuing vocal sounds that her mother already recognises as signs of hunger. Her mother goes to her and both smile at each other. Sandy continues to smile, almost laughing, enjoying the intimacy with her mother so much that she is obviously willing to postpone the satiation of hunger, —but not the satisfaction of her drives (mainly libidinal), which become temporarily more important than the instinctual discharge. After a few seconds of intimacy, Sandy signals her hunger, and both mother and daughter get ready for suckling (instinctual discharge). Sandy enjoys suckling, and at the same time she is attentive to her mother's hand softly caressing her palm (emotional satisfaction and pleasure). They gaze penetratingly into each other's eyes, as if swallowing each other while suckling (object relations). Hence, each one becomes the object for the other—the mother for her baby and the baby for her mother—and thus, between them, patterns of relations occur that we conceptualise as *object relations*.

Drives are invested, through ego functioning, in an object deemed suitable for providing psychological satisfaction. This regulated investment consists of variable combinations of the two drives: libido and aggression. Integrating a certain amount of aggression into the libido stimulates the libido and the desire to seduce the libidinal object, thereby amplifying the enjoyment of love with it. Integrating a certain amount of libido into the aggression imbues the aggression with positive qualities such as initiative, motivation (Sandler, 1985), self-maintenance, and a desire to own the object. The emotional impact changes according to the predominance of one drive or the other. The regulation of the emotional energy occurs in the area between the two opposite poles of emotional outburst and calming appeasement.

The baby's affective experiences of satisfaction and frustration with his objects are stored as memory traces within the narcissistic immunological system, and often reverberate during later experiences. At these moments, the ego functioning regulates the investments of the drives in the appropriate object, using the retrieved memory traces.

Karen (at six months old) is crying. Her father goes up to her and Karen impatiently stretches out her arms (integration of libido with aggression). Karen expresses her craving for proximity (with her libidinal object) through her motor activity. She is impatient to repeat— according to reverberations of memory traces involving her father (narcissistic processing)—her familiar pleasure (the familiarity and pleasure principle), now, immediately and totally (the all-or-nothing principle). It is as if Karen were saying: "Pick me up now, and I'll be the happiest child in the world. If you disappoint me I'll be miserable." Her father recognises her urgent request and joyfully picks her up (object relations).

In the oral phase, the frustration threshold is very low due to the three absolute oral principles of regulation: all-or-nothing, familiarity, and pleasure. The baby thus manipulates or seduces his parents to satisfy his drives and emotions in the moment, without delay, immediately, and absolutely. When baby and parent are mutually satisfied (object relations), they experience a familiar, absolute, gratifying bonding in intimacy, joyfulness, and pleasure. Satisfaction is experienced at its fullest intensity as euphoria, exaltation, happiness, and love. When the object is not available to satisfy the baby's urges, strangeness or frustration may predominate throughout his experience, and he may become furious, despondent, or upset. He may cry and yell frequently, and be flooded with annihilation anxiety, as if his existence is on the verge of, or actually has, decomposed or collapsed.

It seems obvious that the object's response to the baby's needs must be in tandem with the baby's unique capacity to tolerate frustration (due to his low frustration threshold). However, I wish to emphasise that this matching has at least three essential roots: the object's capacity to consider his baby's separateness, the object's capacity to teach and prepare the baby to gradually restrain his need for satisfaction and become better able to tolerate the ensuing frustration, and the object's capacity to share with the baby these newly formed tolerance capacities (see Chapter Four for a discussion of jointness-separateness relations). Consequently, the baby's ego regulation processing is strengthened and his frustration threshold is increased.

In the absence of these roots, the object risks frustrating the baby's needs, either too frequently or not enough. Alternatively, the object might convey to the baby her unconscious wish of idealised motherhood, one who is always there to satisfy fully her baby's needs for a self-object. Such an unconscious parental wish might evoke within the baby what Smith (1977) called the "golden fantasy", that is "the wish to have all of one's needs met in a relationship hallowed by perfection" (p. 311). The golden fantasy is linked to anxiety of annihilation or separation, as the caregiver can never fully satisfy his baby's needs, due to their separateness. Thus, the baby might frequently experience anxiety of annihilation due to the inevitable failure of his object to live up to the unconscious messages of perfection, even when early object relations were based on jointness-separateness.

The combined id, ego, and narcissism regulation process improves at every stage of the child's psychic development, under the influence of object relations. The child's frustration threshold increases and his control over his emotional reactions grows. Subsequently, the child's gut feelings regarding the familiar object and his sources for satisfaction evolve, and he makes better use of his intelligence potential (whether psychomotor, cognitive, or emotional). An adult whose frustration threshold has not developed enough beyond the oral stage, whether due mainly to trauma, to his aspiration for perfection and for absolute matching, or even given the operation of the golden fantasy, is liable to react according to the absolute principle of all-or-nothing as regards familiarity and pleasure. Consequently, he may erupt in compulsive demonic rage in situations of frustration or strangeness.

Compulsive outbursts may indicate a regression from psychological ego regulation to physiological id regulation through a default mode of the compulsive discharging of instinctual tension that remains unconnected to any object. In such moments, the integration of drives may crumble under the weight of the decomposing instinct. In this case, the individual's libido loses the spark of life and the force of stimulation. The individual becomes helpless, depressed, and apathetic, while his aggression loses its motivational focus and becomes destructive. Hence, both child and adult may react with a tantrum or even a compulsive outburst of demonic rage. This reaction seems to reflect a default mode of instinctual discharge (of the accumulated aggressive tension split off from the libido).

Whenever Bill's demand is not responded to immediately, it seems as if a volcano is about to erupt. Bill (at two years old) throws his things around, bangs his head wildly against the wall, pulls his hair, or hurls himself on to the floor in a tantrum—in short, an uncontrolled compulsive reaction. At these moments, Bill's mother usually feels helpless; often she tries to keep away from him until he calms down. Sometimes, she attempts to comfort both of them by picking him up and swaying together.

Eric (at the age of twenty) describes in his therapy session an angry outburst: "I was disappointed that I didn't get what I wanted from my wife. I felt that my rage was about to spill out of me, destroying my wife and everything around me ... For as long as I've known myself, I can remember these horrible feelings ... Even now as an adult I am still helpless and can't control myself."

Each of us has his own individual threshold of emotional regulation. Within this threshold, we feel relaxed and content, and experience optimal tension. When we cross the threshold, we can still enjoy the emotional excitement and the thrill, up to a certain level. For all of us, the further away we move from this unique, personal threshold, the greater the risk that an intolerable level of tension may result in intense frustration or narcissistic injury, pain, or trauma. This stress may trigger the default tension discharge, a kind of wild destructive power (decomposing instinct).[1] Most of us, however, are able to reintegrate libido/aggression, as well as positive and negative emotions, by means of ego adaptation mechanisms, narcissistic restoration of self-familiarity, and positive object relations, and we renew ongoing relationships with others relatively quickly.

### The ego's refinement of emotional expression—from biological affect to psychological emotions and feelings

Freud claimed (1917e) that "An affect includes in the first place particular motor innervations or discharges and secondly certain feelings; the latter are of two kinds—perceptions of the motor actions that have occurred and the direct feelings of pleasure and unpleasure which ... give the affect its keynote" (Lecture XXV, p. 395). Freud considered affects as drive derivatives, but nowadays we tend to perceive them as responses to biological stimuli. Affective responses appear free of inherent meaning or an association with their triggering source, just as the instinctual discharge of tension takes place regardless of the presence of the object.

In the previous section, we could perceive the move from instinct to drives, which signifies a path from biology to psychology. In this regard, we follow once again Freud's assumption that psychological development is rooted in biology.

Kelly (2009) suggests that: "It is worth noting that an affect is a biological event, a normal part of the everyday functioning of our central nervous system (CNS). An affect is, in some respects, like a normal knee-jerk reflex. If one applies the proper stimulus to the patellar tendon—a tap with a small hammer—in just the right place with just the right amount of force, the lower leg will jerk upwards. Similarly, if the CNS receives a proper stimulus, an affect is triggered" (p. 2).

An affective response to a stimulus preserves the self and prevents it from being flooded by an onslaught of stimuli. I presume that the baby's basic affective expressions fulfil an adaptive survival function aimed at effectively capturing the caretaker's positive attention (i.e., a response). Hence, when a familiar object approaches the baby, this stimulus triggers a spark of positive affective response within the baby, whereas a stranger drawing near may trigger a negative one. Positive or negative affective response to the current stimulus may also be triggered, amplified, or magnified by the resonance of memory traces of previous emotional experiences (see Chapter Two), whose evocation might be likened to a hormonal secretion occurring simultaneously within both the baby and the parent. The affective expression may thus trigger the survival-connecting phenomenon between baby and parent, which defines their familiar common space of intimacy.

Furthermore, Kelly claims:

> Affects come in three basic flavors—positive, neutral, or negative. *Positive* affects are *inherently rewarding*, and we are motivated to do things to have them continue or get them back if they happen to be blocked. *Negative* affects are *inherently punishing*, and we are motivated to do things to get rid of them and avoid things that will arouse them. The one neutral affect is just that—neutral—it does not motivate us to do much of anything .... (Kelly, 2009, p. 7, author's italics)

Babies are often a barometer or mirror of their parents' emotional state, which they sense quite precisely. This is an act of survival for the baby, necessary for maintaining his own familiar emotional state. He is generally happy when his parents are happy, feels secure when they demonstrate confidence, expresses positive or negative feelings when they do, and is on alert when they are anxious. Often, he even absorbs their unconscious emotional messages, as transmitted by their facial expressions, body language, and intonation. Parents are concomitantly impacted by their baby's emotional expressions: his smile, for example, and affective expression touch them deeply and evoke their emotional responsiveness.[2]

By feeling, Kelly (2009) suggests— "we mean that person has become aware of the biological state that has been triggered in them, in other words, they have become aware of their affect. Affects and the resulting feelings are inborn parts of our biology ... We all 'know' what fear, shame, joy, and anger feel like because we have all experienced the same thing when any of these affects is triggered." (p. 7). Tomkins (1987) defines emotion as affects that were impacted by the environment; hence, emotion is not innate like affect. Instead, we may see significant differences in affective responses or expressions in families, or even across ethnic groups or cultures. Some families treat the more vulnerable affects, such as fear, shame, or distress with compassion; while others may respond with: "'Big boys don't cry' or 'If you don't stop crying, I'll give you something to really cry about'" (Kelly, 2009, p. 7).

Emotional experiences can consist of sensations, affects, emotions, feelings, or sentiments. They may be perceived as positive or negative, or both, and can be expressed as a short-term emotional state or mood or as a continuous and moderate emotional state. Pleasant or unpleasant sensations may reflect short-term emotional experiences linked to the senses. Pleasant or unpleasant emotions, emotionality, or excitement may be linked to a sudden realisation of a wish, or to deviations from the familiar. They may be experienced as short-term, impulsive emotional outbursts, and are frequently expressed by psychosomatic signs as well. Pleasant or unpleasant affects, feelings, or sentiments may resonate with the narcissistic memory traces of emotional experiences, and are presumably linked to mental representations of the object and object relations. The duration of this reverberation will determine whether it is experienced as a continuous or episodic emotional state.

Let us further differentiate among these various emotional experiences. As I have already mentioned, Tomkins (1962, 1963) proposed an affect theory that may be helpful to my elaboration. He describes affect as the purely biological portion of emotion, as a response to physiological conditions. He claims that the affective behaviour of infants is a programmed, inherited, muscular-glandular response to the relative intensity of stimuli. For example, an infant is overtaken by affect in response to a sudden alert; this is manifest in his or her entire body posture, which becomes visibly more "alive". We become aware of a stimulus following our physiological affective responses to it. Affect is seen as an intervening variable between stimulus and response. Tomkins's affect theory tends to organise distinct affects by categories, with each affect stimulating a distinctive "family" of responses. He identifies nine affects or affective pairs (ranges) that consist of inborn protocols. When triggered, they mobilise physiological responses that are conveyed mainly through facial expression (for example, joy can be perceived via smiling). Tomkins describes two positive affects—enjoyment/joy and interest/excitement, a neutral one—surprise/startle, and six negative ones—anger-rage, distress-anguish, fear-terror, disgust, dissmell, and shame-humiliation. Surprise-startle is considered a "resetting" affect, whereas shame-humiliation provides the important information that good feelings (e.g., interest) have been blocked (Kelly, 2009).

Tomkins, and later Nathanson (1992), emphasised that, "To the extent that an organism has an intact system for the storage and retrieval of information, it will be able to call upon this storehouse for memories of previous experiences of an affect" (p. 50).

I am convinced that such an integral storage system is essential for the immunisation and recognition of our emotional experiences of self-familiarity, both within us and in our relations with others. Nathanson even stated that "today we take for granted the existence of an *immune system* that guards the boundary of what is us and what is alien to our very cells" (ibid., p. 64, author's italics). However, neither Tomkins nor Nathanson (1992) specified which of the personality agencies mobilise this system, whereas I claim (Solan, 1998a) that it takes place within the narcissistic immune system (see Chapter Two). Moreover, Nathanson's therapeutic method of helping his patients "to become somewhat immune" to the emotions of others so that they could tolerate the emotions emanating from the otherness of their objects (see his concept of the "empathic wall") might be considered as his attempt to strengthen what I elaborated as the healthy narcissistic immune system of his patient (see my conceptualisation in Chapter Two).

Moore & Fine assert that:

> Developmentally, affects arise from fixed, genetically endowed, physiological response patterns … The initial biological response

quickly becomes linked to encoded memory traces, so that familiar perceptual patterns mobilise the appropriate affective response *in anticipation* of what the infant has come to expect by association ... Affects are usually intimately linked to object representations, self representations, and fantasies related to drive states ...In current usage, then, *affects* refer to three levels of conceptualisation: (1) *clinical manifestations* such as the reported feeling state, especially in relation to the pleasure-unpleasure continuum; (2) *neurobiological concomitants* including hormonal, secretory, vegetative, and/or somatic phenomena; and (3) *a metapsychological concept* which has been related to psychic energy, instinctual drives and their discharge, signal affects without drive discharge, the ego and its structure, structural conflict, object relations, self psychology, and a superordinate organizing system. (Moore & Fine, 1990, p. 9, my italics)

Nathanson (1992) proposes that "affect is modular, capable of infinite assembly ... with any drive, with any voluntary action, with any function of the mind, even with other affect" (p. 70).

I suggest that emotional meaning (such as feeling) is attributed to affect via the resonance of memory traces retrieved from the narcissistic immunological system where emotional experiencing is stored. Although the terms "feelings" and "emotions" are often used interchangeably, "feelings refer to the central, subjectively experienced state (which may be blocked from consciousness)" (Moore & Fine, 1990, p. 9) and they describe our awareness that an affect has been triggered. Emotions refer to the outwardly observable manifestations of feelings (ibid.) and they co-assemble with our memory of previous experiences of that affect.

Affects are mainly expressed by facial expressions and body language. Nathanson (1992) says that: "An affect lasts but a few seconds, a feeling only long enough for us to make the flash of recognition, and the emotion as long as we keep finding memories that continue to trigger that affect" (p. 51). Affect magnifies the scenes with which it is linked in memory (Tomkins, 1962, 1963).

Mood refers to "a relatively stable and long-lasting affective state, evoked and perpetuated by the continuing influence of unconscious fantasy" (Moore & Fine, 1990, p. 121)—in other words, what Tomkins has described as a persistent state of emotion intimately connected to the affective scripts that accompany and nourish it (Tomkins, 1962, 1963, 1979, 1987; Nathanson, 1992).

While suckling (id instinctual regulation) with delight (ego emotional regulation), Ella (at three months old) is attentive to her mother's voice and her rhythmic heartbeat, familiar to her since the womb (narcissistic processing). She feels her mother's caring, stares into her eyes, and enjoys the pleasant sensuality of intimacy (ego regulation of libidinal drive and emotions directed toward the object, initiating an object relation). Suddenly she stops suckling and her expression changes, as if saying, "I am in pain" (narcissistic reaction to strangeness and ego regulation of aggression). The mother is attentive to her baby's signs of separateness and tries to identify the source of her distress. She discovers that her baby's hand is in an uncomfortable position (an affective response), frees her hand, and hugs her (the mother's ego adaptation mechanism). Ella stares at her with a warm smile (ego emotional regulation) and continues her suckling (id instinctual regulation).

The parent's expression of emotions in a rich variety of tones gradually comes to constitute an essential part of the baby's familiarity with various affects, sensations, emotions, and feelings. The baby then becomes aware of the diversities in his parent's states of mind and acquires tools to express the richness of his emotions. However, when the parent expresses an equal intensity of anger in different contexts, for example, when the baby throws a toy or refuses to give him a kiss, the baby is unable to differentiate between their (otherwise) diverse degrees of intensity of emotional expression. His father's equal measure of anger might signify for him that he is always a very bad boy. A baby whose parents stifle their emotions may become apathetic and sense his experiences as bland and emotionless. The baby is likely to preserve his pleasurable familiar source (narcissistic processing), and even to practice new, almost-familiar emotional experiences when he is being held in his parent's arms. With a smile, a laugh, or by looking around and making sounds, he seduces (ego functioning) his mother into looking at him, smiling at him, listening to him, and joining together in intimacy (object relations). These experiences of libidinal pleasurable intimacy, achieved by narcissism, id, and ego regulation, are permanently embedded as memory traces in the narcissistic immunological system (Solan, 1998b) as sensory, affective, and emotional information connected to the objects and to familiarity with object relations.

Optimal mental health requires the maximisation of positive affect and the minimisation of negative affect, as Tomkins (1962, 1963) stresses. I conceive that such mental health is achieved throughout the economic emotional regulation (ego faculty) directly connected to the harmonious functioning of the healthy narcissistic immunological processing of emotional data—concomitantly sustained by object relations. This means that the baby's emotional regulation is encouraged and supported by parental healthy narcissism and the parents' own emotional regulation, as well as by the emotional regulation they provide for their baby's emotional expressions (their auxiliary ego).

Happiness and infatuation are experienced as a very powerful and addictive elation, and as an oceanic mystical experience of perfection. Positive emotional experiences, such as happiness, love, well-being, and pride, experienced mutually with the object, have curative value and great healing power. These feelings reinforce the biological and emotional immunological processing and facilitate better coping in object relations, that is to say, our internal and external relationships with our objects. Negative emotional experiences, such as constantly feeling hurt, taking offense, shame, guilt, bitterness, and a sense of deprivation, may weaken the immunological processing. Some of these emotional experiences may remain unconscious whereas others may become conscious through the resonance of memory traces.

Family history may come to represent a cycle of familiar emotional scripts and states. Children who enjoy regular positive emotional interactions with their parents and experience a variety of emotional expressions, such as happiness, love, humour, anger, and pain tolerance, might also benefit as adults from their range of emotional communication resources; for example, with their spouses and children. Children of parents who tend to express their emotions in outbursts (as opposed to modulated affects) are also likely to be excessively emotional. It is, however, important to emphasise that children and adults can also create different emotional relationships from those they first experienced with their early caregivers. This may be a result of the cumulative impact of other relations they experienced while growing up, or even in adulthood. During the analysis of transference and the resonances of associations, psychoanalysis and dynamic psychotherapy may free and evoke positive and regulated emotional expressions that were unconsciously repressed and hidden under the impact of various anxieties and trauma.

David, a patient in his forties, shared with me his suffering about not being able to express feelings of love toward his wife and children: "Sometimes I repeat in my imagination how to tell my daughter or my wife that I'm proud of them, or how I'll hug them and say good night without crying." David's mother lost her family during the Holocaust and could not believe she would ever establish a new family: "She often bursts out emotionally, and says with tears: 'I'm so lucky to have a son like you.' … I can't stand her emotionality, I'm overwhelmed … A friend came to take a package for me when I was in the army, and she cried … Yesterday Mom saw a father hugging his son and cried … I myself am afraid of an outburst of my own emotionality."

Sean (at seven months old) is blissfully curled up in his mother's arms. They radiate contentment. They are infatuated, and it is unclear who is coddling whom. Both are so absorbed in their shared experience of intimacy and happiness that nothing else around them seems to exist.

Happiness and infatuation generally assume characteristics of primeval oral-narcissistic absolutism and perfection. Children and adults therefore often share the illusion that these special emotions are exclusively theirs. For example, if a parent expresses love for one child, the other child might be flooded with feelings of betrayal, possibly causing him or her to react with jealousy and rage. Even a parent may envy the child–mother bond. In adulthood, this may take the form of a pathological reaction of betrayal, or abandonment anxiety, with even a risk of a compulsive (and possibly impulsive) outburst, such as murder or suicide. Some adults feel they cannot live without infatuation, which for them is even more important than their actual "love object", but at the same time they constantly worry about losing it.

Ruth, a patient in her thirties, says: "When my husband talks on the phone, I'm sure he forgets all about me. I can't stand his attention toward others." After several months of treatment, we are becoming familiar with her fear of closeness with me (through transference). She says: "I'm afraid that if I feel close to you, I won't tolerate the fact that you also have other patients … I'm sure you'll prefer the others." I interpret: "You fear I'll betray you, just as you feel with your husband and felt with your mother." "Exactly," she says, "I'm always jealous and afraid of being betrayed … I'm sure my parents preferred my little sister. I hate her!"

In the first months of life, the ego's regulation is relatively rudimentary. Parents provide their baby with an external, auxiliary ego that guides his survival and his emotional and adaptation needs. They are concerned with their baby's well-being, identifying the sources of his distress, validating his sensations, stimulating his intelligence potential, and regulating his emotional expressions.

Barak is crying. His mother's narcissistic sensors are attuned to deciphering the cause of his distress, and familiarising her with her baby's individual modes of emotional expression. She absorbs his reactions, processes them, and usually gives them an appropriate outlet. For example, when she identifies Barak's fatigue, she says, "Barak darling, you're tired, you need to sleep," and she sings him a soothing song. Sometimes she recognises pain and says, "Barak darling, your stomach hurts," and she looks for a way of relieving his pain. She thus validates his emotional experiences, regulates (together with him) his increasing tension, and relieves his distress.

Step by step, the availability of data of memory traces related to the parent's auxiliary ego, as well as of data of both sensory and emotional origin, allows for the consolidation of the ego's regulation. During the oral stage, the characteristic modes of regulation are linked to, and expressed in, absolute principles: pleasure is experienced only when it is achieved immediately, fully, without delay or compromise, as well as when there is an absolute or almost-absolute satisfaction of familiarity, in accordance with the reverberations of memory traces.

As the baby's frustration threshold in the oral stage is very low, the experiencing of satisfaction immediately evokes pleasure, optimism, self-grandiosity or self-assurance, while frustration immediately evokes rage, despair, or hostile dependency, and annihilation anxiety. We may observe these contradictory oral character traits as greed, demandingness, excessive generosity or penuriousness, restlessness, impatience, and curiosity.

From eight months onwards, the infant begins to express affects intentionally toward the parent, such as tenderness, happiness, and joyfulness, as well as frustration, pain, and narcissistic injury. He starts talking (at around eighteen months), but still finds it difficult to express his wishes, and he reacts angrily when his parents do not understand him. He improves his capacity to communicate by means of various emotional exchanges, such as body language and facial expression, behavioural codes, and verbal expressions of distress or joyfulness.

## The oral erotogenic zones

Pleasure is often accompanied by psychophysiological changes, such as in heartbeat, blood pressure, and hormonal secretions. These changes add an erotic flavour to the experience of pleasure. Erotogenic zones are parts or areas of the body that are particularly sensitive to stimuli, and evoke sensual excitement. Generally, these are the oral, anal, and genital zones. While being cared for, and during caretaking, baby and parent feel mutual, pleasurable sensations. Both have a desire to repeat and re-experience these pleasurable (erotic) sensations located at the mouth, lips, eyes and skin, which may produce and evoke a unique sense of their intimacy.

Generally, the baby remains largely passive in order to enjoy his mother's touch during her massaging and caretaking. He therefore depends on the parent's availability in order to regulate the degree of erotic pleasuring. With his mouth and his eyes, the baby becomes an active partner in the repetition of the pleasurable gratification and its regulation. He is able to satisfy and please himself and his caregiver by opening or closing his mouth or his eyes at will. (Even a cat may wink at his caregiver sometimes, in what seems to be a purposeful manner.)

The mouth (and especially the lips) is an essential erogenous zone for satisfaction and regulation, and a source for exploration. The baby may satisfy himself by sucking a pacifier in the parent's absence. He can usually control whatever enters his mouth. He can swallow or push out with his tongue, differentiate familiar and unfamiliar items, and identify shapes and flavours. He can hold the nipple with his lips and gums, and can suck greedily while regulating the strength of his cheek muscles to control the flow of milk into his mouth, according to his ability to swallow. His mother helps him to direct the nipple into his mouth and both are invested in his suckling and in his mouth area. Through suckling and their mutual pleasure, a sense of joining in intimacy is created between them.

Oral activities, such as kissing, sucking, licking, swallowing, eye gazing, smiling, caressing, and non-verbal dialogue, reflect the emotional erotic satisfaction of libido integrated with aggression. Sensory thrills, such as biting, chewing, closing the gums, and even vomiting, reflect the emotional erotic satisfaction of aggressiveness integrated with libido. These oral sensations gradually become symbolically loaded with emotions. For example, swallowing may be emotionally experienced as acquiring something from the outside and taking it in; vomiting, or emission, as projection from the inside outside (hence the expression, "projectile vomiting"); and eye gazing as penetration into either side. Most of these oral-erotic, sensual pleasures constitute the sensory and affective basis for the baby's emotional regulation and development during his first year of life, and remain as self-assets (the increasing capacity for erotic-sexual and emotional intimacy (Spitz, 1962)) from babyhood to adulthood.

This elaboration clarifies the origin of the name coined by Freud (1905c) for the first stage of psychic development—the oral stage. During the first six to eight months of life, emotional expression is flavoured mainly with tenderness, while later, it becomes loaded with aggressive characteristics. Freud (1933a) called this second period the "oral-sadistic" phase. At this stage, teeth emerge, and the baby often bursts out crying because of the pain, presses his gums together as a reflexive response to the pain, and bites or powerfully chews anything that comes into his mouth.

Harry (at five months old) regulates the intensity of his suckling. He grips the nipple with his lips and gums, not too weakly to lose the nipple and the milk, yet not too firmly to provoke his mother's withdrawal. He therefore tries hard to overcome and regulate his need to bite while suckling. At eight months, Harry learns to differentiate the nuances of satisfaction he produces by the way he bites different items: his pacifier, toys, and the nipple of the bottle (that stops the flow of the water).

Jasmine (at nine months old) enjoys pulling her mother's hair. Sometimes she does this boisterously, and sometimes delicately, while smiling and laughing with pleasure. She digs her fingers into her mother's mouth, as if exploring what is inside. When Jasmine senses her mother's reluctance, she pulls her fingers out and gives up her pleasurable exploration. Evidently, she is sensing that some actions are agreeable to her but are not pleasant for her mother (initiation of acknowledging separateness). She has learned to direct her movements gently, in tune with her affection toward her mother, and she is aware which gestures are experienced as painful and aggressive.

The child thus gradually improves the expression and regulation of his drives and his emotions, such as tenderness and aggressiveness, as well as his psychomotor intelligence and the expression of his feelings through his body language. He differentiates a bite from a kiss, even though both are actions activated by his mouth. In response to his parent's emotional regulation, he differentiates his kiss and his smile as tools for affection and intimacy with the other, his crying as a tool for mobilising the parent, and his bite as an expression of frustration and aggression.

At eight months, Harry is enjoying not only familiar and constant emotional states, but also play that entails varying emotional states, such as playing "peek-a-boo" with his father: When his father pulls a shirt over Harry's face, Harry's emotional state changes. His face is hidden in the shirt and suddenly he does not see his father. He becomes tense and a little anxious. Then his father says, "Where's my lovely boy?" He pulls up the shirt and says, "Peek-a-boo". Harry discovers his father, is relieved and happy. He likes to repeat this exciting game, feeling secure enough with his father to regain his familiar emotional state after a momentary thrill. He enjoys the emotional changes and waits expectantly for the next peek-a-boo. If, however, his father leaves the shirt over Harry's head a little longer, he becomes overwhelmed. Unable to tolerate his anxiety, he loses the pleasure of playing.

At twelve months, Harry is hiding in a game of "hide-and-seek" with his sisters. He hides and then appears and they embrace. The alternating emotional states of "seeing" and "not seeing," "having" and "not having," approaching and distancing, as well as any version of hide-and-seek games, are exciting for him. He experiences pleasure in the changing emotional states as long as he feels secure that he will reacquire his familiar emotional state (narcissistically restore his self-familiarity).

## The ego agency as a functional component of the personality

Freud's (1923b) topographic model differentiates among three personality components—the id, ego and superego. Chasseguet-Smirgel (1975) added a fourth component—the ego's ideals—and I have proposed considering narcissism as a fifth innate primeval component (see Solan, 1998a, and Chapter Two). These various personality components function to preserve the cohesiveness of self-familiarity via self-regulation: the narcissism safeguards the self by tension-regulation with respect to familiarity-strangeness; the id by instinctual tension regulation; the ego by tension regulation regarding drives, affects, and emotions; the superego by tension regulation regarding moral prohibitions and conscience; and the ego's ideals by ideals and cultural tension regulation.

In this section, I will refer to three basic personality components (narcissism, the id and the ego) as representing the agencies of the individual's self. The faculties of the self's agencies manage the relevant emotional system (i.e., the narcissistic immune system, the id and ego's regulation systems, and the emotional attachment system), moulded by the patterns of object relations. The complex dynamic processing of these agencies usually takes place in synchronisation while each influences the other emotional systems concomitantly, thereby increasing the likelihood of psychic survival and health. Lack of coordination may produce pathological functioning. We need to bear in mind that this distinction between the self's agencies, and their functioning within the emotional systems, is arbitrary and for didactic purposes only.

For example, the ego as an agency might regulate drives and emotions (regulation system) directed toward the familiar non-self (as deciphered and identified by the narcissistic agency). Thus, the narcissism triggers within the ego regulation system an attraction to the familiar, and the ego mobilises adaptation or defence mechanisms (within the narcissistic immune system) by either expanding the data of familiarity (befriending the strangeness or denying its otherness) or resisting the strangeness. Second, within the regulation system, the ego as an agency enriches the data by incorporation, introjection, and assimilation, or defends against it via projection. Third, within the attachment system, the ego as agency might improve communication (by adaptation mechanisms, such as body language) with the familiar object (ego and narcissism agencies) or, conversely, provoke withdrawal from the object (via defence mechanisms such as projection) or compulsively erupt in destructiveness (id decomposing instinct).

Let us focus our attention on how the ego, as the individual's self-regulation agency, manages emotional tension-regulation by means of the mechanisms generally known as defence mechanisms. I propose redefining the processing of these ego mechanisms by examining the differences between defence mechanisms and adaptation mechanisms.[3] My examination will highlight the sense of pleasure and control that generally accompanies adaptation mechanisms, as opposed to the decrease in anxiety resulting from defence mechanisms. Looking at behaviour in its entirety, and keeping in mind that it is multi-determined, one may choose to emphasise or dwell upon its defensive and/or adaptive aspects, although it is never an absolute differential, as the two frequently function in combination.

I suggest three criteria for differentiating adaptation from defence mechanisms:

a. The *objective* of the ego's emotional investment.
b. The *operating mode of the mechanism*, particularly in the three major emotional systems: the (narcissistic) immune system, the (ego) regulation system, and the attachment (object relations) system.
c. The *emotional costs and benefits* resulting from the unconscious activation of adaptation and defence mechanisms.

I regard the ego's emotional regulation as an economic investment, which is why I choose to use "cost–benefit analysis", a term borrowed from economics, as a method for evaluating the operational mode of the adaptation and defence mechanisms. I wish to emphasise that adaptation mechanisms improve in efficiency and in the benefits they provide from infancy to adulthood. This reflects increasing cognitive abilities (Greenspan, 1979) and emotional intelligence. Adaptation mechanisms emerge and evolve, each from its previous function, and may regress or reverse to its preceding functions. Through adaptation mechanisms, the individual's ego manages to connect the emerging stimulus to the object that may bring satisfaction, while improving its efficiency and benefits, relative to the previous level of adaptation functioning. A case in point is the progression achieved from incorporation via introjection, to internalisation, identification, and so forth. We may assume that adaptation mechanisms are stimulated by the energy of the connecting instinct (i.e., the life instinct, see above).

Defence mechanisms, on the other hand, do not evolve from each other. Rather, to my understanding, the individual's ego manages to combine several defence mechanisms for the defence of the self in order to avoid being flooded by a specific anxiety, for example, that of separation. When these fail, a secondary line of defence may come into play. This defence faculty is accomplished by the (defence) mechanisms that decompose the links achieved by the adaptation mechanisms. For example, they may split off or dissociate the impulse/stimuli from the object that risks frustrating its expression. Moreover, they may prevent the ego from mobilising creative connecting energy necessary for adaptation. Hence, I conceive of defence mechanisms as mobilised by the ego, under the impulse of the energy of the decomposing instinct (i.e., the death instinct, see above).

Schafer defines these differences between defensive and adaptive mechanisms by emphasising that:

> ... insofar as operations are defensive, they seek to totally obstruct discharge of rejected impulses; insofar as operations are adaptive, they facilitate discharge of accepted impulses, although they may also greatly delay, refine and limit expression of these accepted impulses so as to insure maximum gratification consistent with the individual's total life situation. (Schafer, 1954, p. 163)

During psychoanalytic treatment and the process of "working through" an issue that has emerged in therapy, we may observe that an attuned and well-timed interpretation releases the patient's anxiety and the predominance of the defence mechanisms. This may liberate energy for creative adaptation mechanisms, with increased benefit to the patient, resulting in a strengthening of self-cohesiveness and self-esteem.

I will try to demonstrate this compound process through the following sequence of an analytic session. Shelly, who is in her thirties, suffers from anxiety of abandonment. Each session stimulates her symbiotic illusion that we will be merged forever and never separate. Thus, each session, she denies that we have a limited time for our meeting. When I try to remind her that we have ten minutes until the end of our meeting, she explodes, shouting that she does not want to hear it. She screams as if she were going to die and attempts to prevent me, sometimes even physically, from opening the door. Shelly's ego clearly mobilises defence mechanisms, such as the denial of separation, which splits her impulse for merging with me from what, in the transference, she experiences as her abandoning object, and she reacts in a self-destructive manner, in order to cling to me.

During one particular session, Shelly speaks about a dramatic and traumatic separation from her boyfriend the evening before. She says: "It was ten o'clock, and Barney told me that he had to go home. I screamed and yelled and took the key out of the door and stood there so he wouldn't be able to go out. He then pushed me and I fell down and injured myself ... Still he wanted to run out and I shouted that he was rejecting and abandoning me just when I most needed him ... And he left me." [It seems that her emotional reaction to her boyfriend was very similar to her reactions to my bringing up the end of the session.] Later, Shelly associated to a traumatic event when she was in kindergarten: "Mother came to take me home and I said that today I want to go to play with Sue and her mother ... My mother exploded, even beat me on the head, and shouted: 'Don't you dare to do it to me! The door will be closed when you come back ...' She became crazy ... I was terrified, I clung to her, screaming, I tore out some of my hair and she continued to beat me. I remember it as if it was today ... It's the first time I'm talking about this ... I never recalled it." Shelly is weeping; she trembles and shakes. A few seconds later I interpret her associations in the transference: "When I remind you that our session will soon be over, which allows us to prepare for our separation and the rejoining again tomorrow, you instantly compulsively repeat this same screaming and clinging as if I, like your mother and boyfriend, am closing the door and abandoning you." She responds: "It's not 'as if'; you *are* throwing me away!" Later I say: "Probably, you became aware now that by screaming, clinging, and preventing us from sepa-rating, you tried to defend yourself from the anxiety of abandonment. You as if forgot your traumatic [familiar] wish to go with your friend and her mother, as well as your terrible pain if you or I dare to want separateness." Shelly remained silent and then said: "I'm aware that I scream in the same way everywhere! I'm in a panic. I felt yesterday my boyfriend's hate when I didn't let him go, maybe as I hated my mother when she didn't let *me* go and I clung to her." I echoed her repressed wish: "Can you hear what you have just been saying? You are getting in touch now with your authentic, familiar, deepest wish to rejoin your mother's love after getting together with your kindergarten friend and her mother. You want to join me during our session and prepare both of us for separation until our next rejoining." Shelly replies immedi-ately: "I can never imagine that there will be another rejoining. For me it is rejection forever. Can you promise me? I won't believe you any-way ... But I can say that I want to come tomorrow, that I'm craving for our sessions and that I'm always scared of their ending ... [Weeps silently] Will you wait for me tomorrow if I dare to tell you that it is four o'clock now, time to close our oneness, and that I want to meet my boyfriend who I hope is waiting for me downstairs despite what happened yesterday?"

During these unique moments, I could feel our authentic closeness; feel her trembling about relinquishing her defence and not bursting out screaming. Would she have enough creative energy to mobilise adaptation mechanisms, I wondered? After some minutes of her inner struggling, she said, to my surprise: "I bought a present for my boyfriend because of yesterday, but I don't want to give it to him now, I'm much too shaky. Can I leave it here now and take it tomorrow?"

I was greatly touched by her deriving benefit from the reappearance of her adaptation mechanisms. Probably during our session she had cathected her present for her boyfriend with our sharing of the emotional reappearance of her authentic, familiar wish to join him without threat to our closeness (adaptation mechanism of transitional phenomenon—see below in this chapter). I knew that she could also feel our closeness now, and at the same time befriend her repressed, familiar wish to go with her friend's mother—today with her boyfriend—and be sure to find me, her present for her boyfriend, or even her mother's love, tomorrow.

After some sessions, we discovered that this particular adaptation mechanism was not a new one. She used to mobilise it with her father (in secret from her mother), by giving him objects, such as presents that he had given to her, to keep for her until the next time. She would play with them again before returning them to him and their secret place. Obviously, this adaptation mechanism, when it could be released in the therapeutic context, was connected to object satisfaction, to her father's love. The mobilisation of this adaptive mechanism and its working through within the transference (as it emerged in relation to the therapist and the boyfriend) allowed for the emergence of the wish for reconciliation with us all. In other words, this adaptation evolved and became more sophisticated.

Let us compare ego regulation by adaptation mechanisms to regulation by defence mechanisms, with regard to the ego's objectives, the operating mode, and the costs and benefits entailed in the use of each mechanism.

## Adaptation mechanisms in the oral stage

In accordance with the pleasure principle, and from the oral stage onwards, the ego's adaptation objectives are:

a. To achieve pleasure and avoid unpleasure (Freud, 1900a, 1915c).
b. To adapt the inner urges to the environmental possibilities of satisfying them (as we shall see, from the anal stage onwards, this is also according to the reality principle).

c. To "cope appropriately and advantageously with the environment" (Moore & Fine, 1990, pp. 5–6).
d. To invest emotional resources economically; in the self, the objects, and the relations between them, using resources from within (instincts, drives emotions and memories) or from the outside (one's objects).
e. To coordinate between the different objectives of the emotional processing (preserving self-familiarity, tension regulation, and relations with one's objects).
f. To improve the cross-checking of information among experiences in the present reality (ego function), reverberations from the past (narcissistic function), and interaction with the parents (object relations).
g. To foster creativity and maximise the potential of intelligence assets (psychomotor, cognitive and affective).

The adaptation mechanism's operating mode, which is unconscious, is characterised by the ego integrating libidinal and aggressive drives, as well as positive and negative emotions, into cohesive psychic energy.[4] This psychic energy[5] is invested actively by the ego in an appropriate object capable of producing satisfaction and pleasure within the self, as well as a pleasurable interaction between the self and its object. This implies that the adaptation mechanism is mainly impacted by the connecting instinct and designed differently for each of the three emotional systems.

The costs and benefits to the self in the use of adaptation mechanisms rely on its economic mode of operation. This implies maximising the benefits of pleasurable adaptation, with minimum harm from frustration and narcissistic injury; maximisation of positive affect and minimisation of negative affect; and the activation and efficient management of more adaptations than defensive manoeuvres.[6] In general, the cost relates to the necessity of moderating alertness to strangeness, which might expose the self to the calculated risks of unexpected injury, disappointment, frustration, and even anxiety and trauma. Furthermore, the benefit obtained relates to the development of potential intelligence (psychomotor, affective, and cognitive), the wisdom of mentalization (Fonagy & Target, 2002), and the developmental aspects of cultural values. This benefit generates pleasurable experiences, self-gratification, self-control, and self-esteem, and also enriches communication with the objects in times of both joy and distress.

*Defence mechanisms in the oral stage*

(Sigmund Freud, 1915c; and Anna Freud, 1936)

As the name implies, the ego's objectives are to protect the self from:

a. Being flooded by anxiety.
b. Alien invasions that might overwhelm the self.
c. An undermining of the cohesiveness of self-familiarity, object-familiarity, or object relations familiarity.
d. Exposure to narcissistic injuries, frustrations, outbursts of aggression, and self-destructiveness.

Defence mechanisms are mainly impacted by the decomposing instinct, by disconnecting drives and emotions from the designed object—as opposed to the adaptation mechanisms, which invest drives and emotions in the designed object.

The operating mode is designed differently and uniquely for each of the three emotional systems. For example, in the emotional (narcissistic) immune system, a defence mechanism such as denial operates against the anxiety of strangeness; in the attachment (object relations) system, admiration and, to my understanding, symbiotic relations operate against the anxiety of object loss or of abandonment; and in the emotional ego regulation system, repression or inhibition and projection operate against the anxiety of annihilation.

When assessing costs and benefits for the self in the use of defence mechanisms, the ego's operating mode is also economic, which implies maximum protection of the self with minimum anxiety. The management of defence mechanisms demands enormous emotional resources (cost), which sometimes leaves the ego with limited emotional reserves for creativity, adaptation, self-control, self-regulation, and the maintenance of relations. The benefit derived from defence is the "primary gain" (Freud, 1914d) of moderating the level of anxiety and strengthening the ego's functioning. The "secondary gain" (ibid.) is that of producing symptoms, which detract the object's attention from the individual's original anxiety towards his symptoms.

Defence mechanisms are necessary in everyday life to release the ego from an excessive state of alertness and to free it to activate more adaptation than defence mechanisms. When anxieties increase, however, the ego is more likely to mobilise defence mechanisms rather than adaptation mechanisms, and to produce inhibitions as well as symptoms.

### Examples of adaptation mechanisms in the oral stage

Let us scrutinise, step by step, an emotional situation allowing for the ego's mobilisation of adaptation mechanisms within the three emotional systems. Eric, a three-month-old baby, is awakened from his nirvana sleep (influenced by his id's regulation of the decomposing instinct). After some minutes of well-being (the narcissistic immune system), he cries. Eric probably senses (through his narcissistic immune system) feelings of strangeness, this time akin to hunger, which in turn stimulates his tension (the id's regulation system). In order for him to be able to immediately discharge his tension, it is necessary for the powerful, connecting (life) instinct to latch on to nutrition sources. His mother approaches him and he senses (narcissistic immune system) his familiar non-self (his object), which resonates with memory traces of warmth, smell, and the taste of milk. This soothes him momentarily (narcissistic immune system). His mother picks him up affectionately and smiles at Eric, hugging and coddling him (mother's ego's adaptation mechanism within the attachment system) while Eric stares into her eyes with a tiny smile (Eric ego's adaptation mechanism within attachment systems). They are both enjoying their intimacy while each affects the other (object relations). Yet the tension of hunger increases the readiness to swallow immediately (the id's agency triggers the connecting instinct). Now, Eric's ego functions begin to regulate this emotional storm, mobilising libidinal attraction to his familiar appropriate object (an adaptation mechanism), and investing the emotional energy in joining his mother for suckling in proximity (object relations). He satiates his hunger (connecting instinct discharge) and satisfies his drives and emotions, experiencing pleasure (the ego's regulation system).

### Resistance and inhibition

In my view, resistance represents one of the archaic adaptation mechanisms that function in the healthy narcissistic system. This enables the baby to adapt to his familiar objects as he interacts with them (e.g., action sequences, requirements) while simultaneously resisting strangeness and strangers. Resistance also prevents, or inhibits associations from emerging into consciousness, most likely associations evoking feelings of threat and danger that are alien to self-familiarity.

Inhibition (Freud, 1926d [1925]) represents, to my view, one of the archaic ego's adaptation mechanisms, which functions to restrain and regulate the expression of the drives. We may say that inhibition prevents drives and emotions from being expressed (from the inside outside), while resistance serves to guard against the penetration of strangeness (from the outside inside). Both resistance and inhibition may be seen as serving as "brakes" and as strengthening the baby's boundaries. People diagnosed as suffering from ADHD, frontal pathology, character disorders, or psychosis often lack inhibitions.

Familiarisation and orientation

What characterises these mechanisms is their flexibility in composing and decomposing the incoming data (based on the connecting and decomposing instincts), thereby giving the baby a better orientation and helping him to familiarise himself with his self and his environment. This group of mechanisms includes four types of operations: association, integration (which includes assimilation and accommodation, as described by Piaget (1936), differentiation, and separation.

Association and integration emphasise similarities among separate components in order to create connections between them, combine them in a single concept, and then associate other elements with these components or integrate them differently.

Differentiation and separation stress the uniqueness and the differences between elements that are linked together. These mechanisms can thus transform data into representations (Freud, 1915e, 1940a [1938]; Hartmann, 1939; Jacobson, 1964; Kernberg, 1980; Piaget, 1936) and especially into a "representational world" (Sandler, J., 1987; Sandler, A. M., 1977) populated by emotionally-coloured memory traces of objects, relationships between the self and object, and the mode of communication ("Representations of Interactions that have been Generalized", or RIGs (Stern, 1985)). This representational world may be seen as comprising a series of scripts, (Tomkins, 1962, 1963) magnified by affect (Nathanson, 1992),[7] and impacted by object relations (Sandler & Sandler, 1998).

These mechanisms, mobilised by the ego, process innumerable sensory-emotional experiences (narcissistic immune system) and facilitate the child's learning by allowing him to gain ability in analysing, synthesising, and mentalizing the accumulated data (accommodation). Language, intelligence, mentalization, and ingenuity evolve and contribute to familiarisation with (narcissistic immune system), and orientation to, the environment (regulation system), the fostering of positive self-esteem (narcissistic immune system), and the potential of endearing oneself to others (attachment system). These attachments, grounded in the body and based on the experience of affect, form the basis of one's patterns of object relations.

## The perception of constancy

This group of mechanisms consists of four types of constancy: self-familiarity constancy, object constancy, object-relations constancy, and environmental constancy. They are processed by the ego agency, which combines with the narcissistic agency that stimulates attraction to the familiar and resistance to strangeness (Solan, 1998a), and with the biological source that aims to maintain a constant tension threshold.[8]

The perception of constancy (Hartmann, 1952; Piaget, 1977; Sandler, 1987; Solnit, 1982; Spitz, 1965a) facilitates recognition of the familiar when confronting changes, otherness and cyclicality (narcissistic immune system). The baby learns to experience the presence of his objects as constant, even when they disappear from view (attachment system). Gradually, he may become able to perceive the "half-full glass"—to immunise (narcissistic immune system) and invest in (regulation system) the constant assets he has, rather than in what he feels he is missing or has lost. His self-immunisation and his emotional security thus improve in the face of separation, frustration and strangeness—he is more immune to their influence.

Karen (at nine months) needs her parents to follow the same familiar routine every evening before she separates from them to sleep. She always wants her father to read her the same story—even though she does not understand all the words—a routine which provides her with a sense of constancy, security, and continuity, and facilitates her separation.

## Transitional phenomena and related concepts

This group of mechanisms includes four types: transitional phenomena, a transitional object, transitional communication, and transitional space. In my view, transitional phenomena are one of the highlights of adaptation mechanisms. These crucial concepts were first described by Winnicott (1953), and I wish to expand their scope.

Winnicott (1953) introduced the terms "transitional object" and "transitional phenomena" "... for the designation of the *intermediate area of experience* ..." (p. 89, my italics). I fully embrace Winnicott's important idea that:

> ... it is an intermediate area of *experiencing* [author's italics], to which inner reality and external life both contribute. It is an area which is not challenged, because no claim is made on its behalf except that it shall exist as a *resting-place* for the individual engaged in the perpetual human task of keeping inner and outer reality separate yet interrelated ... (Winnicott, 1953, p. 90, my italics)

I also agree with Winnicott's emphasising that: "This intermediate area of experience ... constitutes the greater part of the infant's experience and throughout life is retained in the intense experiencing that belongs to the arts and to religion and to imaginative living, and to creative scientific work" (p. 97).

However, to my view, the essential significance of the experiences within the "intermediate area", which evoke the various phenomena characterised as transitional phenomena, is that they encompass the multimodal resonances of senses of both the baby and his or her caregiver.

Let us examine Winnicott's example that "an infant's babbling or the way an older child goes over a repertory of songs and tunes while preparing for sleep come within the intermediate area as transitional phenomena" (Winnicott, 1953, p. 89). To my view, the baby can prepare for sleep by babbling due to the resonances of senses related to a familiar song that he heard his mother singing to him (perhaps even during his stay in the womb). The song reverberates within partners, mother and baby, (narcissistic processing) as affectively-coloured memory traces of familiar senses (sound, sight, smell, touch). In other words, it is the actual sharing of these linked senses and attendant affects/emotions that may yield a basic emotional network for the transitional phenomenon.

Recently, neuroscience researcher Rizzolatti (2004) discovered an interesting bio-physiological-psychological connection in a phenomenon he named the "mirror neuron", and I think his finding may illuminate an aspect of the transitional phenomenon. Rizzolatti claims that the same brain cells were activated whether the monkey he worked with in his lab accomplished an action or observed the same action executed by another. Stern (2004) takes this innovation further and proposes that: "It permits us to directly participate in another's actions without having to imitate them. We experience the other as if we were ... feeling the same emotion ... This 'participation' in another's mental life creates a sense of feeling/sharing with/understanding the person, in particular, the person's intentions and feelings" (pp. 78–79).

I suggest that this sharing, experienced in the joint "intermediate area", occurs when each is attuned to the other's senses. Under similar circumstances, resonances of these sensory memory traces may be triggered.

Stern claimed that in order to realise affect attunement:

> ... the parent must be able to read the infant's feeling state from the infant's overt behavior ... to perform some behavior that is not a strict imitation but nonetheless corresponds in some way to the infant's overt behavior ... and to read this corresponding parental response as having to do with the infant's own original feeling experience and not just imitating the infant's behavior. (Stern, 1985, p. 139)

Stern claims that these three conditions are necessary for the "feeling states within one person to be knowable to another and that they can both sense, without using language, that the transaction has occurred" (p. 139). This is supported by Tomkins's formulations regarding the contagion of affect and role of facial mimicry in empathy (1962, 1963).

We may consider the discovery of mirror neurons (Rizzolatti, 2004; Rizzolatti & Fabbri-Destro, 2010), Stern's terms like "affect attunement" (1985) and "participation" (2004), and my concept of the "concomitant resonance of sensory (multimodal) memory traces" as contributing to the understanding of the basis for the creation of transitional phenomena.

To my mind, such essential settings rely on an important condition— that the parents will consider their baby's *separateness*. Stern (1985) expresses this slightly differently: "The channel or modality of expression used by the mother to match the infant's behavior is different from the channel or modality used by the infant" (p. 141). Hence, participation, affect attunement, and "media" sensory communication (see below) will become a familiar emotional framework for communication between the child and caregiver.

Transitional phenomena reflect, in my view, this unique sharing; that is, a participation with each other's senses (the triggering of the mirror neuron) invested in a third shared emotional phenomenon, such as when the baby is staring at the movement of a mobile toy and the mother joins him in watching, saying in a rhythmic tone, "It moves from side to side." During these precious moments, blissful feelings arise, as if there, in "an intermediate area of *experiencing*" (Winnicott, 1953, author's italics)—or, as I renamed it, in the "third shared space" (see below)—their senses temporarily bond and evoke feelings of sharing. The joint emotional investment of both the baby and his caregiver in an event or an object triggers resonances of senses within this unique shared space, experienced as phenomena. This feeling sequence is stored and preserved in each individual's narcissistic immunologic memory, ready to resonate during similar occurrences. The resonances represent this unique sharing in the "intermediate area", bridging between imagination and reality, or between subjective and objective, as Winnicott claimed. According to my conception, this sharing also bridges between the past and present, the self and other, and over the separateness of the baby's and object's resonances of senses. It may also encompass an imagined future; an imagining of the real (Buber, 1947).

The resonance processing comes to be perceived by the partners as shared bonding, experienced in the virtual shared space. Each may resonate this shared transitional phenomenon in similar occurrences; much like the baby preparing to sleep by babbling, reminiscent of his mother's unique singing to him.

The following are some characterisations of transitional phenomena.

## Transitional phenomena in general

These emotional phenomena are experienced as *virtual bonding* that mediates between separate individuals, such as baby and parent, and they arouse a sense of satisfaction, enjoyment, and communication between partners. These phenomena are cathected with a sense of closeness to the extent that whenever the two partners are physically distant from one another, there nonetheless remains a sense of continuity and of sharing in similar occurrences—following reverberation of these unique memory traces of multimodal senses—even across generations.

Winnicott (1953) was "concerned with the first possession and with the intermediate area between the subjective and that which is objectively perceived" (p. 90). Taking the example of the baby's hunger, we can understand Winnicott's idea of the baby's first possession: the hunger stimulates sensory memory traces, such as taste, sound, smell, and touch, associated with the mother and the milk she provides. These may represent a sensory phenomenon that will relieve the hunger even before the baby is satiated. As previously noted, this sensory phenomenon is most likely connected to the physiological sensory arousal known as a "conditioned reflex", as well as to the "hallucination of satisfaction" and "hallucination of the object" (Freud, 1911c), or the "illusion of satisfaction" (Winnicott, 1953). We therefore observe the hungry baby moving his lips as if he were suckling; when he sucks his pacifier, his hunger is momentarily relieved. The baby is obviously attracted to the familiar taste (narcissistic processing) as well as by his connecting instinct of the hunger. Yet, soon thereafter, these sensory memory traces will be linked to an object that shares with him, in affective participation, these sensory phenomena, which then will be cathected as transitional phenomenon. Like Proust and his famous madeleine, we may recognise this experience when we eat food that evokes or resonates immediately with memory traces of those with whom we partook of it. The taste or the smell become the transitional bridge between us, over our separateness.

> No sooner had the warm liquid mixed with the crumbs touched my palate than a shudder ran through me and I stopped, intent upon the extraordinary thing that was happening to me. An exquisite pleasure had invaded my senses, something isolated, detached, with no suggestion of its origin ... this new sensation having had on me the effect which love has of filling me with a precious essence ... And suddenly the memory revealed itself. The taste was that of the little piece of madeleine which on Sunday mornings at Combray (because on those mornings I did not go out before mass), when I went to say good morning to her in her bedroom, my aunt Léonie used to give me, dipping it first in her own cup of tea or tisane. The

sight of the little madeleine had recalled nothing to my mind before
I tasted it. And all from my cup of tea.

Marcel Proust (1913)
*Remembrance of Things Past*
*(A la Recherche du Temps Perdu)*

A thirsty person in the desert may suck a stone and feel a range of tastes
in his mouth, associated to his object, which may temporarily relieve
his thirst distress. Unlike the baby, an adult knows that this is only an
illusion. When an adult fails to distinguish between reality and illusion, this initial adaptation mechanism is now being used as a defence
mechanism. A hallucination, such as may be seen in psychosis or other
pathological emotional states, may emerge.

Sensory transitional phenomena serving as adaptation mechanisms
temporarily assuage the arousal of tension and briefly suspend the
compulsive discharge of the instinct. This enables the baby to adapt
himself to states of minor frustration, such as when the mother is not
available quickly enough. This illusion, however, is useful only briefly,
as it will be followed by another increase in hunger (drive).

Jerry (at six months old) is tired. He wants to sleep and conveys (ego
agency) the message of tiredness to his mother via their shared transitional phenomenon (attachment system): he babbles in a rhythmic "ah,
ah, ah," accompanied by eye rubbing. His muttering tone is similar to
the lullaby his mother sings as she lulls him to sleep (narcissistic immune
system). Through this transitional phenomenon of murmuring, Jerry's
mother is able to help him fall asleep by singing this same song back to
him, separating from him until he wakes up (object relation).

## Transitional shared space

Transitional shared space represents a sophisticated transitional phenomenon, reminiscent of Winnicott's concept of the "intermediate area
of experience", in which separate individuals maintain their relationship. Each partner emerges from his self-space in order to join the other
person in the virtual shared space (see Chapter Four). The emotional
phenomenon of closeness in the shared space is a subjective, illusory,
and non-specific sensory perception.

## Transitional objects

A transitional object (Winnicott, 1953) is a concrete object in which two separate individuals, such as a parent and a baby, are emotionally invested. Transitional objects, Winnicott proposed, help the baby fall asleep, and are the first "not-me" possession, the precursors of his autonomy and of his true object-relationships. The object—whether a toy, book, or even a person—is emotionally loaded as very significant for both, akin to a "buddy", and is as dear to the parents as to the child. The parents regularly remember to put this object in close proximity to the child. Hence, it is perceived and experienced as object constancy, which facilitates self-security even when the parents are absent—that is to say, "absent-present" (Solan, 1989a, 1998a, 1998b, 1999) (see Chapter Four).

Among my daughter Sheryl's toys I felt a clear preference for her tiger, probably because it was given to her by very dear friends. I enjoyed seeing her, at the age of ten months, embracing it lovingly and murmuring "mine, mine", just as I would whisper to her when I hugged her. Sheryl refuses to sleep without her tiger, and in states of fatigue, pain, or anger, seeks it out as a buddy-partner.

## Transitional "media"—beyond verbal communication

Media sensory communication, the name I have given to this phenomenon (Solan, 1991), represents an emotional investment in sensory communication by separate individuals who jointly share a unique language. This sensory communication bonds them with a deep understanding of each other. Their communication consists of far more than words, in that the words are loaded with intonation, body language, and sensory characteristics, all of which give the communication its affective flavour and nuances, as do shared associations. This transitional phenomenon might be refined to include various unique languages—non-verbal, verbal, slang, professional communication, art, and cultural expression—all of which bridge otherness, and are understood by members of the group investing in them.

In illustrating his views regarding the difference between external speech aimed at others, and inner speech, Vygotsky (1962) provides some examples taken from Tolstoy's *Anna Karenina*. He shows that when two people share the same thoughts, the role of speech is reduced, and the speech abbreviated. When Kitty and Levin declare their love to each other, they use initial letters:

> "I have long wished to ask you something."
> "Please do."
> "This," he said, and wrote the initial letters: W y a: I c n b, d y m t o n. These letters meant: "When you answered: it can not be, did you mean then or never?" It seemed impossible that she would be able to understand the complicated sentence.
> "I understand," she said, blushing.
> "What word is that?" he asked, pointing to the n which stood for "never."
> "The word is 'never,'" she said, "but that is not true." He quickly erased what he had written, handed her the chalk, and rose. She wrote: I c n a o t.
> His face brightened suddenly: he had understood. It meant: "I could not answer otherwise then." (*Anna Karenina*, Pt. IV, Ch. 13, cited by Vygotsky, 1962, p. 140)

Most of our emotions and memories are interwoven with the unique flavour of transitional phenomena, which represent the intimacy and the continuity of emotional jointness with parents, family, or friends (attachment system). By means of these transitional phenomena we continue to feel a sense of belonging, the enjoyment (regulation system) and the presence of our dearest, even when they are physically absent, because their sensory memory traces remain sharp, clear, and tangible, despite the passing years (narcissistic immune system).

The pivotal significance of these transitional phenomena/objects, created through jointness relations (Solan, 1991; see also Chapter Four), is based on the baby's increasing capacity to separate from and subsequently rejoin his parents. Furthermore, these transitional adaptation mechanisms may be enriched over the lifespan under the influence of the child-partner's joint investment (Slutzky, 1996; Solan, 1991; see also advanced elaborations of transitional phenomena in Chapter Four).

## The pleasure/unpleasure principle (Freud, 1911c, 1915e, 1920g), linked with the narcissistic familiarity principle (see Chapter Two)

This adaptation mechanism helps the baby to pursue appropriate familiar opportunities for experiencing satisfaction and pleasure with his objects, and to avoid unpleasure in the form of strangeness, frustration, and vulnerability.

Jane (at eight months old) hears footsteps outside her self-space. By means of her narcissistic sensors, she recognises them as her father's familiar footsteps. Using her ego regulation function, she initiates psychomotor intelligence activity in order to actualise and repeat the familiar pleasure (narcissistic immune system) triggered by her father's footsteps. Memory traces of pleasure and transitional phenomena resonate within her. She crawls quickly (ego agency) and directly into his arms, without bumping into anything and without waiting passively until he comes to her. Her father responds immediately by spreading his arms invitingly and whisking her up with delight. Jane thus endears herself to her father. She evokes his tenderness toward her and succeeds in bonding with him in a shared happiness.

Enjoyment and pleasure are the by-products of the data that we attach to our experiences and the significance we ascribe to them (Bloom, 2010).[9] The affective network of associations, representations, and scripts gives meaning to our relationships and communication with others, to our distress, and mainly to our happiness.

This point is poignantly exemplified in the following excerpt from *The Little Prince*, where he describes his attachment to his rose, which he clearly misses.

> THE LITTLE PRINCE went to look at the roses again.
>
> "You're not at all like my rose. You're nothing at all yet," he told them. "No one has tamed you, and you haven't tamed anyone. You're the way my fox was. He was just a fox like a hundred thousand others. But I've made him my friend, and now he's the only fox in all the world."
>
> And the roses were humbled.
>
> "You're lovely, but you're empty," he went on. "One couldn't die for you. Of course, an ordinary passerby would think my rose looked just like you. But my rose, all on her own, is more important than all of you together, since she's the one I've watered ... Since she's the one I listened to when she complained, or when she boasted, or even sometimes when she said nothing at all. Since she's *my* rose." (Saint-Exupery, 2000, p. 63)

The familiar emotional experiences of pleasure, happiness, joining, familiarity, and love represent, in my opinion, some of the most important emotional transitional phenomena appearing very early in life, in relation to objects. These are essential emotions that strengthen the biological and the psychic immune systems, thereby enhancing their vital role in survival, while representing our need to re-experience pleasure and positive affects throughout life. Yet, adults often feel humiliated by needing to search for the love and pleasure they have longed for so much since childhood. In a parallel process, the experience of discontent represents our need to resist strangeness and to get rid of and/or avoid unpleasure (see also Chapter Seven).

## Introjection

Introjection (Freud, 1915c) operates when the baby absorbs the object's sensory characteristics from the outside, into him, similar to the oral physical activity of swallowing. It is as if the baby is swallowing parental sensual characteristics—such as voices, reaction tones, warmness, and rhythms—without digesting them. The introjections facilitate recognition of the objects via the senses (attachment system) and enable the baby to familiarise himself with the sensory uniqueness of each of his parents separately, and to preserve their characteristics exactly as he senses them (narcissistic system). This is one reason why children growing up in the same family have a different sense of their parents (see Chapter Seven and the Rashomon effect).

The absorbed characteristics often distort representations of the objects. For example, introjection of the mother's aggressive tone may undermine the "broad-spectrum" sensation of the mother's good nature.

An adult patient says in his session: "I can't believe what came out of my mouth towards my son. I remember promising myself as a young boy of ten that I would never speak to my children the way I heard my mother speaking. It simply burst out of my throat, as if my mother had suddenly screamed. I am even ashamed to tell you what I yelled at him."

In our adult lives, we can make sense of some of the introjections whenever we hear ourselves speaking in a way that is surprisingly similar to our parents' unique intonation (sometimes we may enjoy this, but generally we do not).

Sometimes, reverberations of memory traces of these introjections and introjects enable the ego to assimilate and integrate (or digest) them into a sense of object constancy and accommodate them to present experiences, in which case they cease to function as introjections and become an integral part of oneself. In later stages, adaptation mechanisms such as imitation, internalisation, and identification develop on the basis of the introjection mechanism.

## Idealisation

Idealisation (Freud, 1914c, 1915a, 1920g) operates from the inside outward, contrary to the direction of introjection. Parent and baby invest each other with narcissistic idealisation in order to preserve the wholeness and perfection of self-familiarities (oral narcissistic processing) against the appearance of strangeness. Thus, the parent experiences his baby as "the best in the whole world" and avoids facing his baby's painful otherness (see Chapter Two). The baby senses his parent's response of idealisation as if he were reflected in a mirror, and this feedback makes him feel loved as an ideal, grandiose self. The baby then projects the sense of his familiar narcissistic perfection outward, on to his parents, and on to his relation with them.

Idealisation (Solan, 1989b) may be experienced as happiness accompanied by euphoric feelings of falling in love. These feelings strengthen basic trust and "blind faith" in the object, as well as the person's sense of self-esteem and the value of his love object.

My patient Michael describes his idealised woman: "This is the woman I always dreamed of finding … she is such a wonderful person, she is perfect … she understands me without words." These are typical oral characteristics of idealisation and infatuation, manifesting the unawareness of any possibility that she might disappoint him. Two months later his beloved was late for their meeting, exactly when he needed her most. His rage overwhelmed him and was powerfully projected on to her, as if she were a demon. "My world collapsed," he says, and he immediately broke off contact with her, without even being able to listen to her excuses (her otherness).

During adolescence and adulthood we tend to idealise the object of our infatuation and we experience temporary narcissistic euphoria. Later, the idealisation might suddenly turn into de-idealisation and devaluation, giving way to disillusionment and disappointment in the beloved object.

Until about the age of six, the child idealises his parents, a useful outcome of his adaptation mechanism. During latency and adolescence the child can no longer deny the perceived incompleteness and otherness of his parents. Often, he expresses anger toward them, blaming them as if they had "spoiled" his ideal image of them, and reacting with disappointment. The adolescent may enter into disputes with his parents, or retreat into mourning for the loss of their idealisation.

Barak (aged fourteen) drags his parents into infinite quarrels on a daily basis: "Why are you working in such a dull profession, don't you have any motivation to advance? ... I don't want you to come to my school, I'm ashamed of the way you dress ... I thought I could trust you, but as I found you're cheating even Grandpa, I can't trust you anymore ... When I go to Raphael's home, I'm jealous he has such wonderful parents."

### Jointness, adjusting, and timing between separate individuals (Solan, 1991)

These are very important for comprehending object relations between separate individuals, such as baby and parent. Both baby and parent try, unconsciously, to ascertain the appropriate emotional states that lead to proximity (object relation), based on the parental capacity to accept their separateness (narcissistic agency). The baby senses (narcissistic immune system) when he is welcome, ignored, or rejected, and by trial and error he adjusts his timing of when to approach the object or distance himself from it (regulation system). He tries to act affectionately toward his objects and to befriend them via the familiar transitional phenomena of their relationship (attachment system), but often, he may be hurt by the object's lack of availability when he tries to create proximity, experiencing this as an empathic failure on the part of his object or his self-object (see Chapter Four). This adaptation mechanism serves as the basis for the development of separateness, intuition, empathy, partnership, and intimacy in object relations.

### Examples of defence mechanisms in the oral stage

The concept of defence mechanisms is not new. It was initially proposed by Freud (1894a) and elaborated by many psychoanalysts, most notably his daughter, Anna Freud (1936). In this section I would like to suggest some major mental states that lead the ego to mobilise defence mechanisms; namely, experiences of vulnerability, strangeness, frustration, hurt or deep disappointment, and shame-humiliation. Such experiences of unpleasure tend to dissolve the matching function of the self's agencies, sometimes described as "the synthetic function of the ego" (e.g., Nunberg, 1931). These experiences, which may achieve the status of "states", may undermine the cohesive sense of self-familiarity, the integration of libidinal and aggressive drives, as well as the harmonious relations with the object. Moreover, these impediments, disintegrations and dissolutions, governed by the decomposing instinct, might trigger an outburst of aggression, and expose the self to anxiety. In these situations, I claim that the ego mobilises defence mechanisms for both short- and long-term protection of the self from being flooded by anxiety.

Freud defines anxiety as:

> ... an affective state ... the reproduction of an old event which brought a threat of danger; anxiety serves the purposes of self-preservation and is a signal of a new danger; it arises from libido that has in some way become unemployable and ... it is replaced by the formation of a symptom. (Freud, 1933a, p. 84)

From the oral stage onwards, three types of anxiety are evoked in each of the three emotional systems:

a. *the anxiety of strangeness*—in the narcissistic immune system
b. *the anxiety of annihilation*—in the id and ego regulation systems
c. *the anxiety of object loss or abandonment*—in the attachment system.

A mother of a newborn (of two weeks) says in her session: "When my baby cries I feel an urgency to calm him down and coddle him with my love as quickly as I can, as he doesn't yet have the patience to wait, and I must hurry before the cries become the howl of a wounded animal that is afraid to die."

It is important to bear in mind that the baby has a very low frustration threshold in the oral stage. Hence, the baby responds affectively both immediately and with extreme over-reaction to frustration, strangeness, or threats of unpleasure. His anxiety seems to threaten his existence with decomposition, dissolution, collapse, or annihilation. The oral characteristics of low frustration thresholds may continue to reverberate as memory traces in subsequent emotional stages, as well as during adulthood. They might influence the person's emotional reactions and interpretations of his emotional and relational experiences, and consequently the intensity of his defensive operating mode.

During the different developmental stages, the above three anxieties acquire novel, more moderated forms. For example, *anxiety of strangeness* (and of the stranger) is experienced in the oral stage as a threat of a chaotic invasion of one's familiar anchor of existence, in the anal stage as anxiety of the unknown, and in the oedipal stage as anxiety of mysterious gender differences. *Anxiety of annihilation* is experienced in the oral stage as existential anxiety in its starkest form, in the anal stage as anxiety of helplessness or of losing control of one's body or self, and in the oedipal stage as anxiety of castration (Freud, 1933a). *Object-loss anxiety* is experienced in the oral stage as anxiety of abandonment, in the anal stage as anxiety of losing control over the object, and in the oedipal stage as anxiety of losing the object's love.

Defence mechanisms provide us with tools for coping effectively with anxiety, for example by disconnecting the emotional experience from its stimulus (a drive, act, or wish) or from the designated object. If, however, these mechanisms fail to achieve rapid relief from anxiety, the self becomes stalled in a state of hyper-alertness and vigilance, and the ego needs to maintain a defensive emotional state for an extended period. The ego is therefore left with insufficient emotional resources for sustaining the functioning of the adaptation mechanisms, for preserving relationships and communication with the object, for activating the person's emotional potential and his progress to the full, and for maintaining creativity or enjoying life. In extreme cases, defence mechanisms produce pathological symptoms. For example, paranoid symptoms may indicate a boundary disorder and serve to differentiate between self and non-self.

In order to clarify the momentum of the ego's mobilisation of the defence mechanisms, let us once again examine, step by step, an emotional situation similar to that described above: the mobilisation of adaptation mechanisms. Eric, a three-month-old baby, is awakened from his nirvana sleep when his decomposing instinct is activated. Following some minutes of well-being, he cries. Eric probably senses, through his narcissistic immune system, strangeness sensations in his body, this time akin to hunger. His mother approaches him holding her smartphone, not yet available for soothing him (object relations pattern). Eric's narcissistic agency deciphers her as a non-self stranger, which stimulates the narcissism and the ego functions to mobilise resistance to this strangeness. The mother, however, also triggers the narcissistic resonance of familiar memory traces of smell and the taste of milk. This stimulates Eric's id agency to initiate the connecting instinct and increases the tension of hunger. Yet, the ego's resistance to the strangeness of the mother is intensified via affect amplification and elicits strangeness anxiety (narcissism immune system). Eric screams. Now the ego immediately mobilises defence mechanisms (within the narcissistic immune system) against this anxiety; for example, by denial of this painful strangeness. As the desire for food and emotional sustenance is frustrated, the id's decomposing instinct (regulation system) produces outbursts of rage and may trigger an anxiety of annihilation (within the regulation system). The ego agency is immediately invoked to protect the self from being flooded by this anxiety, for example, by repression of the instinct and drives, so that no frustration is experienced (regulation system). At the same time, Eric may experience his mother as present while he is unable to join her, a painful experience that may lead to the anxiety of abandonment (attachment system). Again, the ego immediately mobilises another defence mechanism, such as withdrawing or detaching from her. Eric becomes exhausted; under his decomposing instinct he falls asleep, his hunger unrelieved.

Presented below are examples of the major oral defence mechanisms and their (unconscious) operating modes. In my view, the ego mobilises different defence mechanisms against the particular anxiety emanating from each of the emotional systems:

## Denial

Denial (Freud, 1926d [1925]) operates against anxiety of strangeness evolving from the narcissistic immune system. This is one of the earliest mechanisms for ignoring strangeness and the disappointment or harm caused to the sense of self-familiarity, object-familiarity, and object relations constancy. We deny everyday threats, strangeness, or deception in order to continue behaving normatively. For example, most drivers deny the risk of accidents, and conduct themselves as if nothing will happen to them. A soldier on the battlefield also has to deny the risk of injury or death, otherwise he would be unable to carry out his assignments.

*Repression*

Repression (Freud, 1894a, 1914g, 1915c, 1915d) operates against anxiety of annihilation evolving from the regulation system. Repression is activated to disconnect certain drives and emotions from the stimuli or from the object that may trigger reverberations of unbearable frustration and the anxiety of annihilation.

Anita (at one month old) is lying in her mother's arms during her mother's therapy session. "She's hungry," says her mother, "but she doesn't suckle." The mother's nipple is in Anita's mouth but she does not have sufficient strength or motivation to suck it, or possibly her mother does not have enough milk. The mother is not yet ready to forgo suckling, while the baby apparently relinquishes the emotional craving for her object-mother to feed her, and drifts into sleep until she is woken by new hunger pangs and the temptation to suckle is renewed.

Anita's repeated experience of frustration causes her ego to mobilise repression in order to disconnect completely (all-or-nothing principle) from her urge to be fed by her frustrating object. Furthermore, it removes the libidinal drive from her consciousness, as if craving for feeding were alien, thus avoiding the awareness of hunger and pain, frustration, and existential anxiety (pleasure/unpleasure principle). Anita's hunger lessens in general and she fails to put on weight. Finally, her mother pumps her maternal milk into a baby bottle and Anita sucks easily, but apparently without pleasure. Most likely, Anita is sensing her mother's anxiety that she could not suckle. Anita then begins to cling to her mother; she seems anxious about separating from her (annihilation anxiety).

Twelve years later, Anita came with her mother to consult me, as she was showing signs of anorexia; signs that seemed familiar to me from her babyhood.

Let us examine the dynamics of this symptom. In normal development, hunger represents the connecting instinct (life instinct) that connects the hunger to smell, the taste of milk, and the object. This mental state induces the ego to mobilise adaptation mechanisms that associate hunger with drives and emotions, as well as with the transitional phenomenon of intimacy in the warmth of the caregiver. Hence, the baby senses the need to be fed physically and emotionally.

Whenever the baby is repeatedly frustrated, his ego mobilises a defence mechanism—such as repression—to eliminate this particular stimulus, which in turn might provoke reverberations of unbearable frustration, trauma, and anxiety. However, the physiological sensation of hunger that is repressed continues to emerge in consciousness, and is repetitively, and unconsciously, repressed again by the ego to avoid anxiety of annihilation. This painful emotional state induces regression to a regulation by the id (rather than by the ego), in which the decomposing instinct (death instinct) disconnects the hunger instinct from smell, the taste of milk, and the object—associations that were created by the connecting instinct (see Section 2, id regulation and narcissistic processing). The result is that the baby (or adolescent) becomes detached from the need to be fed physically and emotionally, and rejects food as alien. In other words, this individual does not recognise hunger as a sign of the need for food, nor does he recognise the need (as part of his self-assets) for his caregiver to feed him emotionally and physically. Under these circumstances, the sense of being physically hungry and of possessing a thin body becomes a constant familiar emotional state; the individual's (narcissistic) self-familiarity, has been pathologically immunised.

Anita, like other adolescents who suffer from anorexia, presents symptoms of auto-starvation (biological and narcissistic autoimmune manifestations). The tendency to anorexia, which generally appears in adolescence, may be traced back to the initial familiar sensations observed at the oral stage and preserved from then on.

## Projection

Projection (Freud, 1911c) operates against the anxiety of abandonment evolving from the attachment system. Based on the narcissistic and ego resistance to strangeness, projection is activated to expel oppressing inner sensations of strangeness or of aggression outward, in order to defend the self against the anxiety of object loss or of abandonment. While, initially, this may provide some relief from the inner negative ("bad") sensations, they will return like a boomerang to threaten the baby: the object on to whom he projects his aggression becomes a threatening one.

Barak (at eleven months old) calls his father to play with him, but his father is not available at that moment. Barak is angry and probably cannot express his aggression. Like any baby who vomits unpleasant food, Barak projects, and thus unconsciously expels, his "bad" sensations of anger on to his father. He therefore experiences his father as a stranger or a bad person who is angry. Feeling as though he had better keep his distance, Barak is not aware that he is actually anxious lest his own aggression harm his beloved father.

The unconscious use of the defence mechanisms of denial, repression, and projection is common in normal psychic development. As long as they are mobilised ad-hoc in stressful situations, they contribute to mental and emotional organisation in the face of external or internal threats that might otherwise paralyse daily behaviour. Experience shows that:

- Most denials relate to existential threats and to the threat of strangeness and imperfection.
- Most repressions relate to libidinal derivatives and seldom to aggressive derivatives.
- Most projections relate to aggressive derivatives and seldom to libidinal derivatives.

In addition, aspects of these three primary defence mechanisms, based on the decomposing instinct, may be recognised in most other defence mechanisms.

## Splitting

Splitting (Freud, 1940a [1938]) operates against the anxiety of object loss in the context of the attachment system. The ego mobilises splitting on the basis of the narcissistic attraction to the familiar and the resistance to strangeness. The ego, through this defence mechanism, "splits" the particular object into a good familiar object and a bad stranger object, reminding us of Klein's (1957) concepts of "good object" and "bad object". The split is based on the object's alternating ability to satisfy or frustrate the baby. Whenever a caregiver offers familiar pleasurable satisfaction and responds immediately and totally to the baby's emerging needs, he is experienced by the baby as a good object—triggering attraction toward it. Whenever the same caregiver frustrates or arouses sensations of strangeness or unpleasure, he is experienced by the baby as a bad object—triggering resistance to it. The upshot is that the same parent-object is experienced alternately as good and ideal, or as bad, evil, and strange.

Up to the age of six to eight months, the splitting mechanism serves a normative, emotional-developmental function. From this age onward, in order to preserve the good and familiar satisfying object as a whole entity and to avoid extreme emotional oscillations, the ego manages to integrate (integration = adaptation mechanisms) the split-off good and bad object into a single, constant parental figure. The object is experienced as a good-enough, albeit frequently frustrating object (object constancy). At the same time, in order to get rid of the oppressing sensations and to regulate outbursts of aggression toward the frustrating good object, the ego projects aggression (projection = defence mechanism) on to another figure or displaces aggression on to it (displacement = defence mechanism; see below). Hence, the unfamiliar is now experienced as an evil stranger, while the object is cathected as a good object, despite the frustrations. Instead of splitting the object into good and bad, the ego now enables the child to differentiate (differentiation = adaptation mechanism) between good and bad sensations, between familiarity and strangeness (narcissistic processing), or between the satisfaction and frustration (regulation function) that he experiences with the same object.

Beyond the age of twelve months, the ego's mobilisation of the splitting mechanism indicates an excessive vulnerability to disappointment and frustration, and anxiety of abandonment. Hence, the object is sometimes experienced as perfect and idealised, and the next day as evil; it is loved one day and hated the next.

In certain exceptional cases of extreme trauma or anxiety, the ego may split its own self instead of the object—as if opposing entities are functioning unconsciously within his own self (disassociation, borderline personality or psychosis; multiple personality).

## Displacement

Displacement operates against the anxiety of abandonment evolving from the attachment system. This mechanism is mobilised to defend the self by the eruption of aggression against the love object. The baby is unconsciously anxious that his rage might harm his object and his relations with it. Hence, these oppressive sensations, especially aggressiveness, are projected and displaced from the beloved object on to a stranger, mainly in order to maintain the object as good and worthy of admiration, thereby avoiding the risk of losing the good object. Aggression is often displaced on to strangers and animals. Sometimes, libidinal or sexual attributes, or even ideas or body parts (obsessive ideas, or perversion) are displaced on to other people rather than the original cast. Displacement might trigger stranger anxiety, hate, suspicion, demonization, xenophobia and racism, and also phobic or hysteric reactions. In subsequent stages of development, however, the displacement on to imaginary monsters or cruel people often triggers nightmares.

## Admiration

Admiration operates against the anxiety of abandonment stemming from the attachment system. Admiration as a defence mechanism may remind us of the adaptation mechanism of idealisation. There are, however, important differences between the two. Idealisation enables the child to experience his object as ideal and loved, and himself as beloved by the object, whereas admiration represents a defence against the child's unbearable aggression, projected on to one of his parents, or displaced on to a stranger, in order to preserve the beloved parent. Hence, the child admires his parent, sometimes loaded by projection and experienced as despotic, while he perceives his own self as worthless, rejected, or humiliated. This implies that the child renounces his true self in order to attain security in the shadow of his revered object. Admiration thus easily turns into hatred, and emotional upheavals of this kind in adulthood may even deteriorate, in extreme pathological cases, into destroying the internally represented admired/hated object.

Steve, one of my patients, said to me: "You are a perfect woman and therapist … Whatever you tell me is always exact and I admire you … but I also feel that you find me worthless …" Several weeks later when he arrived for his session, he saw someone at the foot of the stairs leading to my clinic. Steve decided that it was another patient of mine and he could not bear the envy he felt toward this person. When he entered the therapy room, he said: "I can't believe that you're the same person I admired so much. I hate you for having other patients that you value more. I can't trust you any more." Before storming out, he added, "For me you are nothing."

From the oedipal stage onward, these defence mechanisms may also be exhibited as a phobic (usually in boys) or hysterical (usually in girls) neurosis.

## Somatization

Somatization (psychosomatic symptoms), autoimmune symptoms, and hypochondria operate in all three emotional systems. These mechanisms operate against the anxiety of strangeness, annihilation, or object loss/abandonment, and regulate aggression by attacking the body self (instead of the object) and producing real or illusionary symptoms. *The Imaginary Invalid* (Le Malade Imaginaire) by Molière comes to mind in the latter context.

These oral self-destructive symptoms include self-deprivation, self-inferiority, self-humiliation, and self-punishment (for example, putting oneself down, knocking one's head against the floor or wall). Physical symptoms include anorexia, hair pulling, nail biting, tics, chronic constipation (Solan, 1973), and psychosomatic disease. The symptoms provide emotional secondary gain, such as obtaining a sense of control over the object, eliciting the object's care and concern for one's pain, anxiety, or illness, as well as exemption from tasks that provoke anxiety.

## The false self

The false self (Tustin, 1990; Winnicott, 1960) operates against the anxiety of strangeness, abandonment, and annihilation, evolving mainly from the attachment system, but may appear in all three emotional systems. Anxiety might flood the self to such an extent that the baby (or adult) would "sell his soul" to permit alien invasion into his self-familiarity in order to please his object, or to retain self-familiarity in a state of fusion with his object. By mobilising this defence mechanism, the baby's ego denies separateness (narcissistic immune system), represses its own needs (regulation system), hides its true, separate, self-familiarity and masks it with a false self, while attempting to please the parents by fully accommodating to their needs.

The following example indicates how an extreme state of false self arises in a session. Dana, a single woman in her thirties, and an excellent student at university, suffers from a strong need to please and acquire the love of everyone around her: "I can't decide what I really want but I do know what my parents want for me ... I know how important my achievements at university are for them. So it's really for them that I'm making all the effort to learn and to get good grades ... It has reached the absurd situation that I need to consult with my mother how to respond to some situation, because I myself have no idea ... I remember that my parents always asked me to tell them everything, otherwise, my mother said, they wouldn't know how and when to help me. My mother is a worrier, vulnerable and easily hurt, and I always feel guilty towards her. She reacts with panic if she doesn't know what's going on with me. Everything needs to be done in a way that is best for my mother ... I am her shadow."

### Fetishism and perversion

Fetishism and perversion (Freud, 1905d, 1927c) operate mainly in the attachment system. The baby's anxiety of annihilation and object loss (even if the loss is only in fantasy) might be so strong that he attaches magical powers to one of his object's belongings in order to safeguard the object from impairment, injury, or illness. Fetishes and accessories such as keys, pieces of jewellery, shoes, shirts, or any object loaded with smell, serve as a substitute, providing security in place of the "lost" object. The child thus becomes completely dependent on the fetish, at the expense of self-reflection and of assuming responsibility for his life. With the development of sexual instincts in adolescence/adulthood, the fetish may become a source of sexual arousal directed toward a part-object, thereby perverting the sexual relationship.

The fetish is a kind of talisman against anxiety (an anti-phobic object), ostensibly similar to the adaptation mechanism of transitional objects. Sometimes it is difficult to differentiate between the two, even though they are actually very different. The fetish is chosen by the baby (or adult) alone, independent of the object and it represents a part-object, an anti-phobic object, and a source of deviant (or perverse) enjoyment. A transitional object, on the other hand, is chosen by both baby and parent and represents a source of pleasure for both of them in the partnership relationship. From latency onward, in rare situations of anxiety, the transitional object (adaptation mechanism) might be transformed into a fetish (defence mechanism).

### Symbiotic relations

Symbiotic relations (Mahler, 1968) operate against the anxiety of strangeness, annihilation, and abandonment evolving from the three emotional systems. Symbiosis may be regarded as an archaic defence mechanism, mobilising the three archaic defence mechanisms of denial (narcissistic immune system), projection (attachment system), and repression (regulation system). This mechanism operates by denial of separateness and by the relinquishing of the true self and of individuation, while simultaneously merging the self with the self-object, as if in symbiotic unity.

Tamar, a patient in analysis, and a mother of a newborn baby, tells me in her session: "I am so delighted with my little baby David, especially when I hold him in my arms and I feel as if we are once again one. The idea of separation between us arouses panic in me ... I can't stand it; I even hate him."

The mother admires her baby as long as they are clinging together, but if he dares to separate, she panics. She thus holds on to her baby as if they were merged like Siamese twins, without any boundaries between them. She unconsciously conveys to David that separation would disrupt their symbiotic unity and their existence, and she compels him to remain fused with her. Both Tamar and David are elated when they feel merged and retain the illusion of fusion. Little David will probably continue his life with the same need for symbiotic relations as his mother did, as a defence against the anxiety of abandonment and annihilation, and against narcissistic injuries caused by the otherness of his peers (pathological preserving of the self-fused familiarity within the narcissistic immune system).

It is important to distinguish between symbiosis as a defence mechanism against the anxiety of abandonment and annihilation in the face of separateness, and jointness as an adaptation mechanism for attachment, safeguarding self-separateness. Both emerge at the beginning of life, and even though they appear to be similar, they are vastly different experiences (see the above section, and Chapter Four).

## Summary

The baby's emotional world develops on the foundations of its biological instinctual regulation and biological stimulus-affect-response (id regulation), from which it gradually moves to psychological regulation of drives and emotions (ego regulation) throughout the relations with the object. The id's regulation is characterised by repetition compulsion and emotional eruptions as a default instinctual discharging of tensions, regardless of the object and the source of the stimulus.

The ego's regulation is characterised by satisfaction—as the default fulfilling of drives and emotional tensions/urges in relation to objects. The ego invests and cathects emotional energy in the self, objects, and relations with objects in an economic fashion.

The oral stage is characterised by three regulatory principles: *all-or-nothing* (biological-instinctual id function), *familiarity/strangeness* (narcissistic immune processing), and *pleasure/unpleasure* (ego function). These categorical principles produce unique features of the baby's character in the oral stage and the oral personality in general. Due to his low frustration tolerance, the baby's urgent insistence that his (oral) emotional needs be met immediately has the characteristic of an uncompromising demand.

Adaptation and defence mechanisms (mobilised by the ego) differ in their objectives, their mode of operation, and their costs and benefits. By means of adaptation mechanisms, the ego regulates adaptive processing, whereas defence mechanisms protect the self from being flooded by anxiety.

Uncontrolled outbursts of instinctual compulsivity in the face of strangeness, frustration, injury, or trauma can undermine peace of mind. Such an eruption indicates accidental, temporary, or constant regression from psychological regulation by the ego, to instinctual regulation by the id. It implies deregulation of the nervous system.

Intelligence potential (psychomotor, cognitive, and affective), when improved upon by adaptive ego functioning, can increase the individual's capability of extricating himself from the id's instinctual vortex, and returning to being "on track" by means of the ego's emotional regulation, thereby safeguarding self-esteem and expanding relationships with others.

Balanced emotional experiencing and maintaining a predominance of positive emotional experiences over negative ones are both highly significant for healthy emotional development. They are important for immunising the growing cohesiveness of self-familiarity, as well as for the individual's capacity to experience love, both from and for his object, and to enjoy life. Hence, one of my pivotal therapeutic working-through targets is to scrutinise, together with my patients, the roots of their suppressed and buried positive emotions, and to release memory traces of love and the enjoyment of life from their respective shackles, so that patients can resonate with and engage more fully in everyday life. Patients' healthy narcissism and ego regulation are thus strengthened, allowing positive resonances to prevail over negative emotions, as primarily seared in their narcissistic immunological systems. The patient may then be able to tolerate better the emotions emanating from the otherness of his objects, and improve his relations and communication with them.

## Notes

1.  While it is beyond the scope of this book to attempt to integrate this with the topics under discussion, we may bear in mind the connection between the soma and the psyche. Hence, we may note that traumatic levels of stress may be understood to reflect the deregulation of the limbic and "reptilian" brains by the neocortex in response to threat. When the current threat cannot be managed by the higher cortical functions of reason and communication, this triggers the amygdala to initiate an emergency response, where non-emergency functions (e.g., digestion) are shut down and stress hormones are released. The brainstem takes over, initiating fight-flight-freeze responses to threat. These survival processes are further described by Levine (2010) and Ross (2008), in particular the freeze response, which is most relevant to a contemporary understanding of trauma. When incompletely discharged, perhaps due to the fear of a loss of control, the freeze response results in blocked or "stuck" energy in the body, and may become a major cause of trauma symptoms in humans. According to the somatic experiencing (SE) understanding of trauma, it will require some degree of conscious awareness of one's bodily sensations to "unfreeze" the freeze and return to normal or, in my formulation, to restore the self-familiarity.

2.  Within the treatment setting, this affective attunement (or lack thereof) has been discussed extensively in terms of transference and countertransference (e.g., Kohut, 1971, 1977; Racker, 1968).

3.  Hartmann (1939) introduced the concept of adaptation in psychoanalysis, and I wish to draw attention to his formulation: "We call a man well-adapted if his productivity, his ability to enjoy life, and his mental equilibrium are undisturbed" (p. 23).

4.  Psychic energy—"A hypothetical, quantifiable energy, analogous to physical energy, postulated to be responsible for the activity of the psychic apparatus and thus of all mental events ... The concept of psychic energy is central to the economic point of view and is implied in the dynamic point of view" (Moore & Fine, 1990, p. 151).

5.  Social psychologist *Roy Baumeister* follows Freud's concept of psychic energy and argues for the connections between psychic energy and physiology, claiming that psychic energy is more than a metaphor. He suggests that "relatively small acts of self-control are sufficient to

deplete the available supply of glucose, thereby impairing the control of thought and behavior, at least until the body can retrieve more glucose from its stores or ingest more calories" (Baumeister, Vohs & Tice, 2007, p. 351).

6. This may apply to the expression and communication of all affects (Nathanson, 1992; Tomkins, 1962, 1963). See also Matthew et al., 2007.

7. "Love, then, is an example of a script in which the most important scenes of need and nurturance have been assembled and magnified with tremendous intensity. For each of us, love will depend on whatever scenes, whatever interpersonal interactions of nurturance, have become generalized. Love is not merely a RIG, but the result of a series of RIGs nested within each other, all magnified by the positive affects of excitement and joy that we anticipate will reward our experience of anguishing loneliness and need" (Nathanson, 1992, pp. 246–247).

8. Freud used Fechner's (1801–1887) constancy principle for his elaboration of the pleasure/unpleasure principle.

9. Bloom (2010) claims that, similar to the pleasure enjoyed by animals, the human sources of pleasure have survival objectives—such as obtaining pleasure from sugar and fat, quenching one's thirst, resting when tired, and sex. But the knowledge we accumulate throughout development becomes an integral part of the pleasure, and has an even greater impact on it than the effect of the original sources.

# CHAPTER FOUR

# Object relations: the attachment system

> Opposites come together and from what is different arises the fairest harmony.

> —*Heraclitus*

This chapter deals with the normal pattern of object relations, which I have named "jointness-separateness" (Solan, 1991), and traces how patterns of object relations are formed and how they may come to deviate from the normal path.

## *Appealing familiarity and unbearable strangeness in the formation of object relations*

Finally, the baby is born. The parents are delighted that the birth went well, their baby is healthy and all his limbs are intact. The mother too feels fine. Now they are three separate members of their unique family. Innate affect scripts first link infant and caregiver (Nathanson, 1992; Tomkins, 1962, 1963), allowing the parents to intuit what it is the newborn infant needs them to do for his survival and well-being. A mutual learning process ensues, and the parents try their utmost to become familiar with their still-unfamiliar newborn baby and his facial and bodily displays and affective expressions. At the same time, their baby intensely seeks indications of something familiar in his parents, presumably some sensation first experienced and subsequently preserved from his time in the womb (see Chapter Two).

The parents gaze at their child with love, and compare what they see now, in the present, to the hitherto imagined baby. Do they like the colour of his eyes and hair, his face, and the shape of his body? Is he good-looking? Are they disappointed his skin is wrinkled? Does he look like them?

During these typical moments of unbearable strangeness, which are often glossed over or even denied, the parents tend to scrutinise their baby for familiar hints of his belonging to them. One can thus hear them saying: "His eyes are just like yours; his cute nose is like your mother's; his skin and the colour of his hair are similar to mine." In this way, they befriend the otherness of their offspring and gradually restore each other's strained or injured self-familiarity. Their newborn baby's smooth and relaxed face, his big eyes, and even the spasms of his facial grimaces—all stir their hearts, which brim with happiness, and steadily evoke a sense of complete wholeness and perfection. They sniff and savour his distinctive and addictive odour, are proud of and adore him. They hold in their arms their most cherished self-asset, the fruit of their love, who confers on them the title of mother and father, the privileged and happy parents. The unbearable strangeness of their newborn temporarily dissipates, and each parent revels in the opportunity to restore and sustain some of his or her family legacy.

Inevitably, the parents again experience unbearable strangeness when their baby cries and they feel unable to help him. The first month of the newborn baby's life is perhaps the most difficult for him and for his parents, as they do not yet sufficiently recognise each other's separateness, as well as the evolving attachment behaviours and signals that are derivatives of affective expression (Nathanson, 1992). From time to time the parents' happiness may shift to feelings of strangeness, and they may wonder whether they have the necessary parental skills and wisdom to care for their baby. In their distress, they may turn to their own parents for support, or to a doctor, nurse or psychologist; upon experiencing pain and shame in needing the help of a stranger to better comprehend their own flesh and blood, they may resist doing so. The sense of familiarity draws them to their baby, while the sense of strangeness distances them from him.

During the first ten days of Barak's life, his parents said he was a quiet baby who "cries only when something, such as stomach pains, is bothering him." A few days later Barak was crying in his crib and his mother could not identify the cause: "He's not hungry or wet and cold, so what's bothering him?" Feeling helpless, for a fleeting moment the irrational idea crosses her mind: "Have we lost our peaceful baby"—an idea that indicates unbearable strangeness. Finally, the mother sees that Barak's tiny hand is pressed under his body. She changes his position and he immediately calms down. Her maternal self-esteem is rehabilitated and her self-familiarity is restored following her narcissistic injury of being so helpless in the face of his need and utter dependency upon her.

After a month of living together, parents and baby are more familiar with the signals and signs of their communication, and their joining, and their mutual affective attunement to each other flows more easily.

What takes place on the newborn baby's side? For him, the womb is still a familiar self-space. Thus, when he hears similar sounds or feels similar bodily sensations to those he first sensed in the womb, he usually focuses his attention upon them. These sensations reverberate in what I have referred to above as the newborn's narcissistic immunological network, which is available as memory traces. These memory traces serve as emotional perceptual containers for new, albeit somewhat familiar, sensory experiences and perceptions (see Chapter Two for an elucidation of this process). This narcissistic processing of self-recognition is consistent with the way the brain "automatically and continually processes sensory stimuli, matches patterns and generates perceptions" (Pally, 1997b, p. 1025), as well as with the psychic "organizing activity" (Sandler, 1987) that arranges sense data into schemata and perceptions. While the elucidation of the biology is beyond the scope of this book, I wish to emphasise that this processing is an active and dynamic process.

Let us examine this important occurrence of the newborn sensing the non-self. At birth, the newborn is propelled into a different and strange world, one in which he undergoes a sharp transition—from a closed constrained space without any foreign presence into a boundless space where he is surrounded by strangers. All these experiences of unfamiliar stimuli provoke a sense of non-self strangeness that overwhelms his peacefulness.

As mentioned, memory traces of the newborn's experiences, particularly from the period in the womb, reverberate in his present experience and serve as a frame for sensing familiarity or strangeness emanating both from within and from the figures around him (narcissistic processing). I suggest considering the sense of the unfamiliar as being on a continuum of emotional differences from the sense of the familiar self, ranging from minor to greater (Freud, 1918a, 1921c, 1930a).

The sense of self-familiarity thus refers to a subjective sense of the familiar self. This perception of the self "constitutes an internal frame of reference by which the outside world is assessed," and is thus the "necessary basis … for the successful distinction between the 'self' and the 'not-self'" (Sandler, 1987, p. 3).

The newborn baby is susceptible to almost-familiar sensory experiences and emotional stimuli, and no less "to just these details of differentiation" (Freud, 1921c, p. 102) from the familiar. During these vulnerable moments the baby's inborn healthy narcissism is triggered to resist or even expel these strangeness sensations sensed as non-self or "not-me" (Chasseguet-Smirgel, 1976; Emde, 1988a, 1988b; Sandler, 1987; Stern, 1985; Winnicott, 1960, 1962) or "I-It" (Buber, 1947). This primal occurrence of the (narcissistic) noticing of a non-self may be experienced as an injury to the baby's primeval narcissistic perfection (Chasseguet-Smirgel, 1976; Mahler, 1968; Winnicott, 1960). What this means is that the other, the non-self, may be experienced as a stranger threatening the sense of well-being and familiarity, evoking resistance that injures and undermines the sense of peacefulness, thus indicating that he [the infant] is not as perfect as he feels.

Let us differentiate here between three kinds of subjective self (Schafer, 1968):

a. the self-as-place (as a sensual and demarcated entity for which no pronoun is specific)
b. the self-as-agent (the "I")
c. the self-as-object (the "me").

From the moment the newborn is able to experience minor or major differences and sense the non-self, he may withdraw into his self as a familiar, sensual, and demarcated place of well-being—his self-space. When he invests his libidinal energy in himself, his self may be represented as his object, for example, "It's for me", and when he activates his ego function his self is experienced as agent, for example, "I do it". The self is the agent of his life, the creator, and the interpreter.

Along with the baby's interaction with the non-self, his inborn narcissism is constantly triggered to identify and recognise traces of familiarity both within himself and outside the subjective self. Narcissism is activated to preserve his familiar sense of a primeval "core self" (Kohut, 1966, 1971) or "sense of self" as "an invariant" (Stern, 1985) vis-à-vis any hint of strangeness stimuli that feel alien to him. The outcome of this calibration might be recognition of this non-self as familiar (minor differences), eliciting libidinal attraction, or identifying it as a non-self object and enabling object relations. This non-self might also be decoded and perceived as a stranger non-self (major differences), provoking alertness, resistance, narcissistic injury, shame, and stranger anxiety—that is to say, preventing relations with it, whether positively imbued or not.

## The emergence of object relations

Object relations are the *structures* that establish and shape the template of an individual's relations to others (Skelton, 2006). The outline of the mother's relations to her baby begins during pregnancy. The mother is attuned to her foetus's movements and the foetus is attuned to her voice, heartbeat or noises—a variety of sounds that trigger his motor activity, and whose absence reduces it (Maiello, 1995). The foetus enjoys a rich sensorial-emotional life in the defined space demarcated by the uterine lining.

One of the marvellous processes of the normal development of object relations is how the baby familiarises himself with his parent as a familiar non-self object. The baby relies on his senses (as narcissistic sensors) to recognise the familiar object. He identifies the heartbeat and tones of speech heard while in his mother's womb, smells the odours, and senses a touch or a glance. This allows him gradually to befriend the familiar "clues" concealed, as it were, in the non-self caregivers. The baby is narcissistically attentive to the sensory characteristics of each of his parents, to their affective reactions, and to the nature of the emotional bodily care and rituals that they provide. It is as if he swallows (incorporates and introjects) these parental sensory characteristics just as he swallows his milk; they are subsequently stored in his narcissistic immunological network as self-familiar assets.

These introjected parental attributes reverberate within the baby and serve him as an identity card (ID) for each of his caregivers and as the "password" for the relational rituals with them. Consequently, the baby is not confused by his different caregivers. Each experience of rapprochement[1] with his object begins with the baby's examining of the object's "sensory identity card" and relational password anew. This scanning enables him to cope with the familiar, and may trigger alertness to strangeness. Hence, whenever his mother approaches him, the baby senses her particular odour and hears her voice; unconsciously comparing them (primary processing; implicit memory) with his ingrained self-asset reverberations before engaging in bonding with her. Throughout life, the individual enriches his narcissistic data of characteristic sensory information of the familiar non-self objects around him, leaving the stranger's non-self outside the boundaries of his self-familiarity space (Solan, 1998a, 1998b). A very similar process also takes place between individuals who have just met.

Harry (at six weeks old) differentiates his mother from his father through his senses. He "knows" that he can suckle only with his mother, who has a unique odour and softness. In his father's arms, even when he is hungry, he does not seek a nipple, but rather indicates by grimaces that he is hungry.

Human babies, like most other young mammals, cannot survive without being cared for, fed, and protected by their parents. Food and protection, however, are insufficient for their survival. They also need the familiar emotional feedback of tenderness and warmth from their caregiver, which may be experienced as familiar shared signs of recognition in an alien world. On these foundations, an attachment between the newborn baby and his parents (Bowlby, 1988) is gradually enhanced, and an emotional connection is made.

Chimpanzees and other monkeys express their attachment in comparable ways to humans. In his well-known studies, Harlow (1959) found that the emotional development of monkeys reared by their biological mothers was normal, and that when they grew up they related to their offspring with a similar attachment pattern. By contrast, the babies of monkeys that were reared by a replacement mother—made with metal wires shaped like a monkey, and with a bottle of milk inserted into the area of the breast—remained secluded, their emotional and cognitive development impaired, and they lacked the sexual urge to reproduce and care for their offspring. When a young mother raised by a substitute mother gave birth, she would contemptuously reject her offspring, lacking this familiar perception of maternal emotional love.

While some may view object relations as encompassing all human relationships, it seems important to differentiate object relations from other relationships between people (for example, during occasional meetings or shared tasks). I prefer to define object relations not only from the baby's viewpoint but mainly as *mutual* dynamic relatedness.[2] Object relations are created from birth, whenever both partners (such as baby and parent, and later on, couples) invest in each other's emotional attraction, and attribute to each other a unique significance of a non-self object capable of providing emotional well-being, bonding, and drive satisfaction.[3] However, the ability of the parent (or partner) to always satisfy his baby or his spouse is largely limited, due to their separateness. Hence, frustration and injury frequently underscore separateness and make it necessary to cope with the other in object relations. Relationships that lack this mutual investment in the other as a significant non-self object do not evolve, in my view, toward object relations. Clearly, the formation of relationships between individuals is influenced by their childhood object-relations patterns.

Parents make a tremendous emotional investment in their baby. They love him, cherish him, and wish for him (their non-self object) to emerge as a happy and successful individual. They wish him to continue their family legacy, cultural characteristics, and ideals. They also hope that he will be able to assist them in their old age, and they unconsciously wish to repeat with him their own positive childhood narratives. In this respect, children probably represent the most "profitable" long-term family investment.

The baby, on his part, transmits affective signals to his parents, invested as his non-self objects; this provokes his parents' (biological) instincts and affects, motivating them to protect him, take care of him, love him, and respond to him with sensory and affective resonance (Nathanson, 1992; Tomkins, 1962, 1963). His survival instincts and affects therefore lead him to adapt himself and adjust his responses to his parents' bonding characteristics.

The mother's bonding with her offspring begins with total devotion, conceptually described by Winnicott (1952b) as a "primary maternal preoccupation", an adaptive, temporary withdrawal from other interests. This attitude on the mother's part facilitates her intimate joining with her offspring, her gradual recognition of his or her separate needs, as well as her physical and emotional recuperation after childbearing. Nowadays, many fathers also allow themselves to experience primary paternal preoccupation and, like mothers, maintain this unique contact with their offspring, and seem to discover the secret of happiness in doing so (see Chapter Three).

This primary bonding between parent and baby is accompanied by physical contact such as suckling, hugging, kissing, and affectionate expression that provides them both—as physically- and psychologically-separated individuals—with a sense of proximity and belongingness. They both gaze at each other, smile, and enjoy experiences of primordial satisfaction, with these pleasurable and erotic sensations evoking a sense of constancy and continuity. On the baby's part, existential security and basic trust (Erikson, 1950; Sandler, 1987) will emerge; these experiences will be crucial for them both on their joint journey of love throughout life.

The joint journey actually begins at the start of pregnancy, and commences proper mainly from the fourth month onward, for at this time, the hearing capacity of the human foetus is well-developed, and the foetus not only passively hears his mother's voice but is also attuned to and attentive to it, differentiating it from other sounds. Maiello (1995) postulates an interesting view that: "the maternal voice introduces an element of discontinuity in an environment that is otherwise characterized by continuity. At times the voice speaks and at times it is silent" (p. 27). Sometimes other sounds appear, often quietly, although an intense noise may emerge against a background of continuously rhythmic sounds, such as the mother's heartbeat. Hence, most of the sounds are unpredictable, uncontrollable and "not always in harmony with the child's needs and can therefore be a source of both well-being and frustration and anxiety" (ibid.) which "may give the child a proto-experience of both presence and absence" (p. 23).

Furthermore, Maiello (1995) hypothesises that "the child can have proto-experiences of separateness and differentiation in utero" (p. 25) and that he "may begin before birth to lay the ground for some of its future patterns of defence and develop the precursors of its later response to the further and more diversified frustrations to which it will be exposed after birth" (p. 28).

Following Maiello's assumptions, I would like to speculate that the child's attraction or sensibility to certain noises can be grounded in these archaic foetal experiences, imprinted on his narcissistic immunologic memory and henceforth, on similar occurrences, reverberate as unconscious memory traces. In this regard, the narcissistic immunologic memory may be considered an archaic psychic envelope of the developing foetus's senses. Stern (1992) referred to such structures as the "pre-narrative envelopes". A requirement for their formation is "for the events that lead to them to be repeated often in the infant's life" (p. 298) and thus come to "be recognized as global patterns" (p. 299).

For Spero (2009), "the psychic envelope begins as a virtual mental proto structure ['proto' because it is not yet based on fully symbolised representations] that holds the budding mind together pending further developments" (p. 193). Spero elaborates "the joke envelope" as being linked to "the psychic envelope concept in Freud's writing (1905c)." Furthermore, Spero attributes to Freud, inter alia, a remark that "a joke is rich in pleasurable acoustical qualities, drawn from the sheer *sound* of its words and the laughter that it elicits" (p. 207, author's italics). However, for a joke to evoke this familiar pleasurable excitement of laughter, both the joke-teller and his audience need to mutually "loosen up" or "disinhibit" themselves.

Hence, I suggest considering "the joke envelope" as part of the narcissistic immunologic memory, one whose network makes it possible for memory traces, dating back to the primeval sensory relations between baby and parent, to resonate. Freud (1905c) already stressed "that the rediscovery of what is familiar, 'recognition,' is pleasurable" (p. 121).

To follow Freud's and Spero's concept of the "the joke envelope", I propose considering the interval during which a person tells a joke and his listener bursts out laughing upon hearing it: this laughter resonates with memory traces of previous babbling and laughter with the mother or a close caregiver, the pair now joining together in a shared space enveloping them. Both partners join together via communication transmitted by the senses, expressing pleasurable and familiar common sounds within what Spero described as "a special kind of sound envelope" (p. 209). After birth, sight and smell will also facilitate their joining. Sometimes, these sounds may turn into unpleasant sensations or evoke embarrassment and related affects.

Jerry (at two months old) begins to produce vocal sounds. He babbles in order to catch his father's eye but his father, busy preparing a change of clothes, does not pay attention. His mother, who was standing next to them, suddenly realises that Jerry is calling out for his father's interest and consideration. These intentional sounds were new, almost unbelievable. At the same time, they resonate within her as familiar from her other children, and possibly reflect her own childhood experience of object relations. She calls her spouse's attention to their infant, and the moment he looks at his son, the baby stops babbling and all three burst out laughing and smiling, and the father hugs his baby with love and admiration for his progress.

Freud (1905c) compares the momentum of the exploding of the joke "to an *'absence,'* a sudden release of intellectual tension, *and all at once the joke is there—as a rule ready-clothed in words"* (p. 167, author's italics). This "explosion" brings to mind the resonance of the archaic, mutual, sensual giggling of both baby and caregiver, for when the child expresses funny idioms, parent and infant may burst into uncontrollable laughter. This laughter most likely resonates with giggling memory traces from the parent's childhood.

To reiterate, we may consider this "joke envelope" as an archaic transitional phenomenon (see Chapter Three) that bonds parent and infant in proximity, elation, and happiness, and concomitantly safeguards them as it were, in an envelope containing the explosions of their uncanny, often embarrassing, and unconscious affects. Spero concludes:

> Instruments of humor are applications of a wider encasement, the joke envelope, which contains the earliest interaction between explosive gasping, crying, laughing, and other auditory crises at the dawn of psychic development, uncannily remembered through mimesis, empathy, and the enveloping function of the mind. (Spero, 2009, p. 219)

Memory traces of these primary object relations patterns resonate within most of us, and initiate a lifelong longing for proximity with a familiar charismatic authority figure in whom we may once again feel blind faith and, with them, enjoy these blissful moments (Solan, 1996, 1999).

An alternative, yet similar (or at least consistent) approach, is that of Tomkins (1962, 1963). While it is beyond the scope of this chapter to examine his affect theory in depth, his view of the operation of affect as an analogue of what triggered it, "and [of] how it interacts with its receptors both to stimulate more affect and to provide the information from which we come to know that an affect has been triggered" (Nathanson, 1992, p. 69), is relevant here. So too is the notion of affect contagion (such as occurs when a baby starts crying in a nursery, and the other infants follow suit) as a precursor of empathy.

### Consolidating perceptions of constancy strengthens object relations

At the age of six to eight months, sensory data and information accumulated from the baby's repeated experiences are organised under the ego's adaptation mechanisms into a series of narcissistic schemata, and into various perceptions of constancies. *Self-constancy* refers to the baby's recurrent sensory inputs and bodily experiences (presumably processed by his proprioceptive sensors, his nervous system, and subsequently triggering his effector systems (e.g., muscles and glands) into action—an interaction rather than a reaction). *Object-constancy* is based on repeated perceived characteristics of each of the objects, enabling the individual to differentiate among his objects, update their characteristics and mainly preserve the object's presence through narcissistic sensors, perception and mental representation even when absent. *Relations constancy* is stabilised by the consistent, observed features of the unique joining with, and separation from, each parent. Optimally, throughout life, the constancies are enriched and predominate over the uncertainties.

Sean (at nine months old) is aware of exactly the kind of fun he will have with his mother when she coddles him in her arms, which he is able to differentiate from the other special fun that he loves, for example when his father throws him into the air. No one else knows how to coddle him with these special flavours. These unique relational constancies of his experiences with each of his parents and his various objects are ingrained in his narcissism and will accompany him throughout life as self-assets, and he will probably be motivated to revive them with his own children.

Natalie (at eight months old) enjoys repeating the particular bonding rituals she has with each of her parents. Up to around four months it was her mother who maintained the rituals, but now Natalie also requires her parents to maintain their "password" relational characteristics, and if one of them "forgets" his or her password, her babbling and body language reminds them of what was forgotten. For example, she needs her mother to separate from her at bedtime in a certain sequence (a story, a song, a kiss, tucking her in tight and saying "sleep well"), and in the morning, she must wake her up with a special song.

One morning, Natalie's parents had to leave home earlier than usual, while Natalie was still fast asleep. When she woke up, she recognised her babysitter, but as she was unprepared for having to forego her mother's regular coddling and her habitual morning ritual, her familiar babysitter was re-experienced as a non-self stranger. Natalie thus withdrew; secluded in her bed with her pacifier in her mouth, she rejected any attempt to approach her. Gradually, as Natalie's hunger began to irritate her and her survival needs took precedence over her nagging sense of object loss, she was willing to "swallow" the familiar bottle of milk (instinctual survival), but subsequently "vomited" the babysitter, refusing to look at her or establish a relationship with her (emotional seclusion). When the mother came back and hugged Natalie to comfort her, Natalie remained suspicious and angry for a few minutes. She needed time to verify her familiar non-self mother's ID and the password of their relationship before she could restore basic trust in her mother and resume their emotional closeness.

Her mother was narcissistically injured by Natalie's resistance and the unbearable strangeness of her daughter's reluctance, which she experienced as an impediment to her interest in her child (eliciting the shame family of emotions). However, she quickly understood her daughter's reaction and was able to respect her separateness (mother's healthy narcissism) and to feel sad about not having been able to prepare Natalie for the morning changes. As she patiently transmitted her regular signals to Natalie (such as affectionate words), both were able to recognise the other's familiarity. Excited and relieved, they felt renewed confidence in their emotional proximity.

The baby also needs the security that his parents will always recognise him. It is as if their recognition reassures him of his existence, as the following example demonstrates. Jane (at eighteen months old) visits her grandparents with her mother. They ring the bell and Grandma opens the door in a ritual game. Grandma looks at Jane and asks, "Who are you?" Jane replies, "Jane". Jane becomes a little anxious at first, very much needing the recognition. Grandma immediately stops the game and says affectionately, "Oh, it's my darling Jane?" Instantly Jane's appearance changes, the anxiety of strangeness disappears, and she resumes being the usual happy girl who Grandma recognises. Even though it makes her a little anxious, she enjoys the game, as it has become a password ritual of their meetings.

From the age of seven months, as his sense of self-constancy, object constancy, relations constancy, and motility improve, Harry is willing to crawl and explore his home space. With his parents' encouragement, he is even eager to befriend nearby spaces beyond those he is familiar with, and comes to recognise them as his self-familiarity assets. He is therefore charged with courage—not only to crawl toward his mother when he hears her voice or needs pampering, but also to crawl away to explore other spaces or to go from mother to father and back again. Motivated by his parents' enthusiasm, Harry is even willing to risk a temporary separation from them and tolerate a certain degree of insecurity and threat when he does not sense their proximity. He feels a secure attachment (DeHart, Sroufe & Cooper, 1996; Fonagy & Target,

2007) and a basic trust that he can return to his maternal base, that his parents will be there if, and when, he needs them (Solan, 1991).

Unlike Harry, Steven (at seven months old) does not feel fully self-confident, nor does he have basic trust in his parents, as they are often absent, and any temporary caregivers are frequently replaced by new ones. This lack of basic trust is most evident in times of stress, when he does *not* search for his mother's coddling and appears to lack the courage to crawl to his father. Rather, he withdraws and remains enveloped in his solitude, shifting from side to side and sucking his pacifier.

As the sense of constancy consolidates (Hartmann, 1950; Jacobson, 1964; Sandler, 1990, Sandler & Sandler 1998; Solnit, 1982), the baby begins to attach more significance to the constant presence of his objects, rather than to their random absence from his view. In the face of any new encounter with his objects, the baby, like any individual, checks and rechecks his objects according to "the 'good enough' matching" (Pally, 1997b, p. 1025) based on the reverberations of previous familiar codes. Object relations and communication with separate objects are thus enhanced.

As suggested in the above example (Steven), babies who lack stable caretaking and whose caregivers change frequently may experience difficulties in attaining secure attachment, at least temporarily. Often these babies (and later, adults) are unhappy with their lot and preoccupied with what they do not have. Their self-familiarity is shaped as being constantly deprived, their sense of continuity and belonging harmed, and they often seem wary of being abandoned, or display an affective state characterised by an excessive alertness toward strangeness.

Maintaining the constancy of caregivers, consistency in the caretaking rituals with the baby, and the constancy of family customs and routines, make it easier for the baby to immunise his self-familiarity as self-constancy and self-confidence, and to recognise the separate members of his family. These comments are also applicable to psychotherapists, who should adhere to regular procedures and maintain the constancy of the therapy setting, including the unique familiar communication they develop with each of their patients.

### Crying, smiling, hugging, and kissing signal emotional communication

Crying is one of the primary affective/emotional signals in the oral stage, indicating minor or major differences in the baby's emotional/physical state (for example, hunger, pain, distress, panic). Crying is a kind of alarm that triggers an immediate emotional response in the parent and a need to urgently decode the significance of the crying and respond accordingly. Affects are always urgent (Tomkins, 1962, 1963) as they are the primary emotional expression linked to a low frustration threshold. Eventually, the baby grasps the emotional feedback evoked by his message of crying. It is as if he obtains approval, a kind of amplification or mirroring of his sensations, legitimisation for his having alarmed the caretaker, and confirmation that his message was received and acknowledged, and will hopefully be acted upon.

Progressively, the caregiver becomes familiar with the emotional messages being conveyed in the tones of the crying and the baby's various pleas for help when feeling hunger or pain or a need for pampering and learns to respond appropriately. A parent who is able to decode the messages being conveyed by the baby's crying, and to relate to the baby's need for separateness, is less likely to become captivated by the crying.

In her psychotherapy session Stacy expresses her helplessness, and even rage, toward her four-month-old baby who cries constantly. She acknowledges that she never tries to understand *why* he is crying, especially between feedings; rather, she immediately picks him up and holds him in her arms for hours. She is exhausted, and feels desperate. He calms down in her arms but when she places him in his bed he starts crying again. Slowly, in parallel to her working through these feelings in therapy, she begins to recognise his separateness and to decode the reasons for his crying, until she reaches the point of joyfully taking him in her arms for coddling when he does not cry, finding other ways of resolving his various signs of distress. She is amazed that she was so blind to his needs.

Our narcissism retains memory traces of crying as a means of alerting the object. Therefore, even as adults we often feel we are about to burst into tears in states of distress, pain, or even excitement; this may be seen as an archaic call for a familiar figure to comfort, support, and share our emotional state. Crying appears to be a universal human signal of distress and pain.

Diana, a mother of two daughters, complains in her session that she easily bursts into tears "at any nonsense" for as long as she can remember: "Yesterday I went to visit my mother, and, as usual, I burst into tears and was ashamed—but this time I understood why. I realised that mother is always alerted to comfort me or my girls when we cry … but she shares only my distress, not my joys."

Facial expressions are crucial for refining affective attachment signals between the baby and his caregivers (and others) throughout life. The mother often feels fascinated by her baby's affect expression, responds to it, or even imitates it, which, according to Basch (1983), marks the beginning of the empathic response. From about the age of two months, the baby uses grimaces to attract his parents' attention in order to connect with them or frown and withdraw from them.

Smiling in general, and a baby's smile in particular, has a magic effect on other people, causing them to respond sympathetically (Kelly, 2012). The smile is not an inborn characteristic. Rather, it develops gradually, starting as a muscular spasm manifested as grimacing (up to two months), followed by a reflex response to a cruciform-shaped or symmetric stimulus (Spitz, 1965b), and finally, from three months, develops into a smiling response (Spitz, 1965a; Tyson & Tyson, 1990) signifying recognition of the familiar (healthy narcissism). The smile becomes a survival sign of communication, a familiar signal of positive affect.

I suggest that people are attracted to smiles, aesthetics, and subjective beauty because of their *innate* familiar attraction to a symmetrical and familiar face, which evokes a sense of constancy and wholeness. On the other hand, most people recoil from expressions of pain and anger, as well as from crying, and from the sight of people making faces because the asymmetry of facial grimaces (or tics) and their random and irregular appearance elicits a sense of strangeness. Moreover, as described by Nathanson, we may erect an "empathic wall" to protect us from the contagion of negative affects.

Parents respond with delight and elation to their baby's reflex smile, thereby stimulating its need to repeat the smile and regain the positive bonding experience it initiated. From five months onward, the smile becomes a clear, positive signal of rapprochement; the baby smiles at a familiar human face and recoils at the sight of an unfamiliar one. Finally, with the solidifying of object constancy, the baby selectively smiles at those he or she wants to, as an expression of communication, and reacts with stranger anxiety (Spitz, 1965a) and distress to an unfamiliar face. I suggest viewing stranger anxiety as a normal developmental continuation of the baby's primal narcissistic resistance to the non-self.

The baby generally reacts to the unfamiliar with anxiety as the stranger or the encountered strangeness, or both, trigger his sense of vulnerability, which is accompanied by crying and the need for flight, evidenced by head turning. At the same time, he seeks out his mother's eyes to comfort him and signal that she can protect him from the unfamiliar. A. M. Sandler (1977) elaborates this sequence as "an attempt to replace dissonance by consonance, to gain the security of the experience of the dialogue with what is known and recognised—above all, to be as close as possible to mother" (p. 197). Moreover, "the child *constantly and automatically also scans and has a dialogue with his own self to get refuelling and affirmation, through the perception of cues, that his self is his old familiar self, that it is no stranger to him*" (ibid., author's italics). Here, Sandler is attesting to what I conceptualise as the attempts of the baby's healthy narcissism to restore his self-familiarity, or rediscover the familiar, following injury (e.g., the unexpected appearance of the stranger) or trauma.

During his therapy session, Clem says: "My parents came over for a visit, and as they cheerfully approached Jonathan [seven months old] to pick him up, he burst into tears. They were hurt and gave him back to me. I felt ashamed. I wouldn't dare reject them in this way … I felt as if Jonathan wasn't my son, but rather a strange baby … Without thinking, I put him straight back into my mom's arms and he cried out in terror. I certainly did it not from affection for my mother but rather from anger toward and disappointment in my son." The boundaries between the mature Clem and baby Jonathan became momentarily blurred, and Clem felt as though he himself was rejecting his parents. He was unable to see his baby as a separate entity; one allowed to feel a sense of strangeness toward his grandpa and grandma, who were still relative strangers.

Clem the father is angry with his son Jonathan for daring to act in this way toward his dear ones, and for "embarrassing his father". In this emotional turmoil, the anxiety of Clem the son about losing his parents' love prevails over his partnership with his child as a father, and his ability to contain his baby son's stranger anxiety. Hence, he needs his infant to be nice toward the unfamiliar (stranger) grandparents. In parallel, baby Jonathan's anxiety of losing his father increases due to the message that it is "not okay" to adhere to the familiar or, indeed, to reject the strange, unexpected response he has just received from his father. The result is that Jonathan the baby finds himself in the eye of a storm; he surrenders to the imposition and falsifies his own self-expression. Instead of externalising the stranger anxiety that he is feeling, he expresses a false affection he does not feel toward the grandparents in order to please his father.

Conflicting interests press upon the parents, namely the separate needs of their baby, his vigilance toward and rejection of strangers, and their opposing need that their baby recognise his grandparents as familiar. The closer, emotionally, the strangers are to the parents, the greater the difficulty the parents will have in accepting the alienation and the strangeness their infant feels. We may feel positive affection and a sense of familiarity with one or both of our own parents and wish to preserve our self-familiarity while in interaction with them. At the same time, one of our children may sense strangeness and resistance toward the same person, given his own need to preserve his self-familiarity, and we may respond with intolerance toward his reaction. Conversely, we may sense a lack of proximity and affection with either or both of our parents while he/she finds affectionate communication with one of our children: To our astonishment, delight, or jealousy, they may exchange warm smiles with our children. We need to be aware of this dilemma, and be empathic to the opposing mixed feelings, and the otherness and separateness, of our dearest.

The significance of the smile is similar to other signals of contact that evoke a sense of closeness, such as a hug, a kiss, and expressions of tenderness and affection.

Ella (at four months old) places her mouth on her mother's cheek in a kiss position and conveys a warm, positive emotion to her. The mother "melts with pleasure". She feels a strong affection toward Ella and responds by embracing and kissing her. At around eight months old, Ella is able to control her facial muscles and give affectionate kisses to her mother, father, and brother. Gradually, but noticeably, she chooses when and to whom she wishes to give a kiss or a hug—at the same time that her emotional repertoire progressively becomes differentiated into feelings of love, happiness, frustration, anger, or pain. At fifteen months old she can almost pronounce, "I love mommy".

Smiling and verbal expressions can arouse closeness despite physical distance, whereas hugging and kissing obviously require physical proximity. Kissing and biting signify opposing drives and emotions, even though the same organ—the mouth—expresses them both. Biting is easier, as it is an automatic physiological response to gum pain, and a step toward the expression of aggression. The kiss develops chronologically later than the bite; it requires emotional intent, deliberate effort, and the activation of several facial muscles. It is therefore not surprising that aggressive expressions erupt more easily than expressions of love.

Gradually, as object relations progress, the baby is able to differentiate between his smiling and kissing, which evoke a tender emotional reaction on the part of his parents, and his biting and hitting, which evoke negative reactions. Slowly, he regulates (through ego functions of adaptation) his libidinal and aggressive affective expressions so that his bite will not be too hard, and his kiss not too limp.

The biological motivation for survival gives rise to two separate psychological channels for emotional proximity with the object: a channel for emotional expressions of *soothing*, signalling the need for intimacy or the wish for mutually pleasurable proximity between individuals, and a channel for the expression of *distress*, signalling the need for the sharing of suffering as a means for relieving the distress. Gradually, baby and caregiver jointly weave a unique pattern of attachment for each of these channels based on increasingly coordinated affective attunement. Each partner transmits a sensory thrill that profoundly influences the other to participate in the joining along both channels (Solan, 1991). Some parents, however, are capable of emotional sharing in only one of these channels (like the above example of Diana).

From the age of three months, Leo grasps his mother's hand, no longer as a reflexive response, but rather as a controlled expression of bonding. At this age, he is already able to connect sensory and motor systems, and he tries to direct his movements toward the objects and people he desires. From the age of five months, Leo and his mother signal signs of bonding to each other by means of familiar yet differentiated body language, affective expression, smiling, and gazing—all of which make it possible to confidently communicate in both channels. When one of them feels that his or her object-relation signals are not motivating the partner to respond according to his or her needs, they intensify the message or activate distress signals. When, for example, the mother does not know where Leo is crawling, she calls out loudly with a concerned intonation, "Where's my darling Leo?" Leo receives the "plight signal" and immediately returns to her. When he bangs against a table, he responds with heightened distress signals, such as crying, and he knows that his mother will come to his rescue and calm him.

In everyday life, we are not sufficiently aware of the significance of a smile, a handshake, a hug, or a kiss, and its power as a magical tool for conveying affection to others. These affective expressions initiate openness and emotional rapprochement among people, as well as a sense of well-being, which follows the alleviation of tension.

A very close friend shares with me an emotional experience that conveys the continuing significance of affective expressions of body language for adults. In the wake of an illness, her immune system has been weakened. As a result, she has to avoid temporarily any hand contact, hugging, or kissing in order to reduce the risk of contagion. She expresses her feelings via e-mail: "When we met I felt your instinctive desire to hug me, which as close friends we usually do, and I also felt my desire to embrace. The fact that I had to stop you allowed a strange, icy barrier to invade our warm, close feelings. It was painful for me. Fortunately, we still have our smiles and our gaze, which were strong enough to maintain our usual emotional dialogue. I suppose you felt it too. I feel the same with my close family. It hurts us all so much, even though we know the reason for avoiding touching, and that it is temporary. This painful experience has made me realize how much a handshake, a hug or a kiss might mean for everyone, and how much they link us, even when we feel so close to each other. Their impact goes far beyond the act of politeness."

These rapprochement processes indicate the progress of object relations between separate individuals. Each of us tries to restore and re-experience closeness while concomitantly avoiding the threat of invasion of strangeness into the self-space and shared space of proximity. Unfortunately, because of its otherness, the object repeatedly, and often inevitably, arouses in us an experience of strangeness and injury. Consequently, we constantly attempt to improve the proximity and the channels of communication with the otherness of those nearest and dearest to us. Relationship and communication in their various forms have always had the same goal; namely, to re-experience a sense of love, closeness, and security with a familiar affectionate figure.

### Jointness and separateness, familiarity, and otherness in object relations

As described above, the initiation of object relations emerges when baby and parent recognise the other as a familiar non-self and are able to reinvest in this non-self as a familiar libidinal object for satisfaction and emotional attachment. Two mutually-attracted but separate individuals bond (ego function), while concomitantly preserving their self-separateness (narcissistic immunisation) against the otherness emanating from the libidinal (non-self) object.

Whenever this mutual engagement of baby and parent, like that of any couple, results in a shared sense of intimacy they are both delighted and elated. However, if one of them experiences frustration or injury, the familiar object is perceived as an alien non-self, which arouses alertness. In these moments, one's narcissism is triggered so as to rid oneself of any unpleasant sensations (Freud, 1914c; Mahler & McDevitt, 1968). Hence, the baby/adult might withdraw from this bonding and retreat into his self-familiarity space or even attack his frustrating non-self object.[4]

During this seclusion, the baby/adult reloads his or her self-space with a familiar sense of being enveloped and secure, reminiscent of sensations in the womb. This involves the narcissistic restoration of self-familiarity, object-familiarity, and the bonding between both partners, characterised by a sense of well-being. It may re-elicit the baby's/adult's libidinal attraction to reconcile with the non-self familiar object, and renew attachment. The primary love object thus resumes being regarded as constant, as well as a worthy object and a significant other.

Therefore, the emotional experiences of both, whether baby and parent or spouses, fluctuate from a libidinal attraction to join the familiar object, to the other end of the pole where each "withdraws libidinal interest from his love-objects ... and sends them out again when he recovers" (Freud, 1914c, p. 82). Both vacillate between a sense of well-being and happiness during their intimacy (indicating minor differences) and a sense of frustration, alienation, and hurt (indicating major deviations and differences from the familiar).

The jointness-separateness pattern of object relations (Solan, 1991) relies on the capacity of the partners to join in intimacy and tolerate separateness and withdrawal. This means that for jointness-separateness relations to take place between baby and parent, it is the parent who must be capable of perceiving his offspring as a non-self object (rather than, say, a self extension), and be able to respect and tolerate separateness between them. Furthermore, jointness-relatedness seems to depend on the parent's ability to enjoy intimacy and to set the rhythm, quality, and intensity of the rapprochement-separation balancing process. Thus, parents provide their child with an "internal working model" from which the basic cognitive and emotional patterns of behaviour will be derived (Solan, 2002; Solan & Mikulincer, 2003), as well as a sense of basic trust, self-security, self-confidence, and "secure attachment" (Fonagy & Target, 2007).

During the first five months of the newborn's life, the parent is the main initiator and synchroniser of jointness-separateness, while the baby signals his longing for bonding, his attraction to other objects, or his withdrawal into sleep. From this age onward, as his motility and individuation improve, the baby—influenced by his parents' object-relational attitude—also initiates the timing of jointness and of separation. This primal sense of free movement back and forth between separateness and jointness, and from familiarity to otherness, immunises and consolidates the baby's sense of self-familiarity and security in his ongoing jointness with his parent, and the coping with alternating sequences of separation and intimacy.

At eight months old, Danny's narcissistic sensors detect his mother's appearance, and he crawls to her quickly and happily. Unfortunately, his sensors do not register that she is talking on the phone and this time does not "come out of her shell toward him", despite his attempts at courtship. Danny is frustrated. He senses that he "has" his familiar mother, while at the same time he "does not have" her. Because of his low frustration threshold (a normal reaction in the oral stage), he is narcissistically injured by her otherness, as if she does not recognise him, or is even rejecting him. He experiences an impediment to his interest and excitement, which evokes shame (Tomkins, 1962, 1963) and causes him to withdraw (Kelly, 2012). His positive libidinal initiative to crawl toward her and join in pleasure falls apart. Danny secludes himself in his self-space "shell" and withdraws by sucking on, his pacifier and sobbing. The mother is also frustrated as Danny has disturbed her conversation. Both Danny and his mother have missed the opportunity of a jointness encounter at that moment.

A few minutes later, memory traces of their jointness reverberate in each of them, restoring self- and object-familiarities. This time, Danny's narcissistic sensors correctly detect his mother's willingness to rejoin. They are both motivated to repeat and revive the familiar coddling (a "password" for their jointness). They hug each other warmly, smile, and kiss each other, which they love doing, and the mother murmurs the familiar words that Danny likes to hear, "You're mine, mine, you're always mine." Both have recovered from the unbearable strangeness that caused them to seclude themselves and they are motivated to reconcile and re-experience the blissful state of jointness.

The time needed for withdrawing or reconciling depends on the degree of each person's self-immunity, and his or her capacity to tolerate the otherness of the object and to restore the self- and object-familiarities. Jointness relations might be described as an adjustment from withdrawal from the objects to reconciliation with them—from individuation and separateness to "joining" in proximity (Solan, 1991).

This, I feel, is the essence of healthy narcissistic relations, in which the partners narcissistically regulate their separateness relationship in order to enable familiarity constancy to prevail over strangeness. Concomitantly, each partner's ego regulates the bonding/disbanding of their relationships, so that reconciliation (an adaptation mechanism) prevails over disconnectedness and an over-compulsive eruption of destructiveness.

Kohut (1972) defines object relations from early in life as narcissistic because the "I-you differentiation has not yet been established" (p. 245). In my view, object relations may be regarded as narcissistic in a different sense; namely, that which recognises the significant healthy narcissistic attempt by *both* partners to preserve the familiarity of the non-self object, overcome the unbearable hurt of the otherness emanating from it, and nurture both intimacy and separateness between self and external object.

### The jointness-separateness pattern of object relations—as experienced in shared space

It is precisely the minor differences in people who are otherwise alike that form the basis of feelings of strangeness and hostility between them (Freud, 1918a, p. 199).

In this section, I shall describe the compound formation of object relations from the perspective of the art of jointness relations woven by two individuals—baby and parent—who join in intimacy in a shared space while bridging their separateness. This jointness-separateness pattern (Solan, 1991) of object relations progresses throughout the lifespan.

Every evening (at the age of two months), Karen's father prepares a bath for her. Despite his fatigue (as he relates to his separateness), he is happy to spend these gratifying moments with her (relates to their jointness). He knows what water temperature is pleasant for her (relates to her separateness) and brings Karen to the bath. He gently removes her clothes to the accompaniment of his usual song (relates to her separateness), by which he conveys the message that they are going to enjoy a bath (jointness), and dunks her gently in the water. Karen's face radiates her enjoyment of being in the pleasant warmish water; she gazes into her father's eyes, and her muscles relax (completely) in response to the blissful moments of their joint encounter while the boundaries between them seem to be temporarily blurred. Karen's basic trust in her father, who holds her properly in the warmish water, may resonate with her having been in the familiar amniotic fluid in her mother's womb (memory traces). After a gentle washing, it is time to separate. Her father sings another song to prepare Karen for removing her from the water. Initially, she protests by crying, wishing to continue the blissfulness, but very quickly concedes and allows the caring and caretaking to continue. Her father dries her tenderly, swaddles and dresses her, and separates from her by gently placing her in her mother's arms for suckling.

Karen suckles from her mother's warm breast while gazing into her mother's eyes, and both join in a new emotional quality, quite different from the emotional texture she experienced with her father. Karen and her mother are now immersed in total serenity and a sense of happiness floods them, facilitated by the apparent blurring of the boundaries between them. When Karen finishes suckling they prepare to separate from each other. Karen sinks into a relaxed sleep; her mother places her in her bed, kisses her, and calmly returns to her other activities. Memory traces of these different emotional textures of jointness will probably be preserved in each partner's narcissism and will reverberate in similar experiences.

Jointness-separateness is a relatively new term (Solan, 1991), by means of which I describe the dynamic pattern of normal object relations that occurs following the birth of the baby. Jointness-separateness represents relations between two individuals, two separate self-spaces—the baby's self-space and the parent's self-space—temporarily taking place and coming together in a virtual third shared space. It indicates a triangulation[5] in object relations (a triad), which differs from the dyadic relation of symbiosis.

I visualise the self-familiar space as a shell, symbolising one's fortress of separateness. This formulation is similar to that of the "protective shell" (Tustin, 1981) and of the "ego-skin" (Anzieu, 1985). Via his senses and physical sensations, the baby/adult recognises the boundaries of his own shell, which are shaped by, and resonate with, reverberations of the boundaries of the womb.

From the self-space of separateness, the individual can partially emerge and be in touch with what he experiences as a non-self; that is, another individual also partially outside his shell. In these moments,

Picture 1. A snail (representing the parent or the baby) emerges from its shell and approaches the other snail. Their tentacles, which act as sensory organs, inform them whether to advance toward each other or to withdraw. They *sense* their shared space even without physical touch, and demarcate it with a secretion that flows from their exposed bodies.

the narcissistic sensors of both are activated to recognise minor or major differences or deviations from the familiar before making contact with each other. The individual, however, always preserves his separateness and his inner sense of freedom to join the object in intimacy in a shared space or to withdraw from this non-self and remain secluded in his self-familiar space.

I shall demonstrate the jointness model of object relations by means of a somewhat banal example pertaining to snails—a metaphor that illustrates the complex process of object relations.

I observe Sean, a four-year-old boy, who finds a snail hidden in its shell during an outdoor excursion. He puts it in his hand and says: "Snail, o snail, come out and be fed, first your feelers, then your head."[6] When the snail emerges, Sean is delighted that he managed to "seduce" his snail. However, when he finds another snail that does not respond, he becomes frustrated and angry, and throws it away. One might surmise that Sean would react in a similarly delighted manner if his mother were "seduced" by his courtship to join him in intimacy, or in a similarly frustrated manner if she or his father failed to join with him in their shared space.

Winnicott (1951, 1971) coined the seminal concepts "potential space" and "transitional phenomena". On the basis of these concepts I have elaborated (Solan, 1991) the significance of the virtual third shared space in which jointness-separateness between individuals is experienced. In the third shared space, a variety of transitional phenomena, such as affective expressions and sensory communications, mediate between the two individuals' separateness and otherness (see below). However, a deficiency of mediation might leave the self in a state of fusion between self and non-self, or in excessive alertness in the face of intimacy, otherness, or the absence of the object.

In my view, there is no jointness without separateness, no third shared space of relationship and communication without a self-space of individuation, no familiarity without otherness, and no presence without absence. Or, as Heraclitus put it: "They are separated from that with which they are in the most continuous contact" (Fragment 93, transl. by G. W. T. Patrick).

Throughout the process of encountering each other in shared spaces, jointness partners attempt to maintain a delicate balance between alertness to hints of strangeness in the partner, which trigger resistance, and openness to the partner's familiar hints, eliciting attraction to join with him. Hence, due to their separateness and the changing circumstances, each new encounter with the familiar object in the shared space alters the distance and emotional intensity between the partners.

Most people feel secure and familiar when ensconced in their own shell, and recognise their own self-familiarity, while in the third shared space, the emotional ambience usually changes. Therefore, ahead of every encounter, we unconsciously test the mood of the interlocutor, as well as our capacity to join with him or not, to separate and return to our own self-space. Through fine-tuning, in this unique shared space both individuals are constantly coordinating their interaction and trying to determine the appropriate distance they wish to maintain from each other. This continuous adjustment of rapprochement-distancing creates for each partner vibrations, sensations, and feelings that demarcate their virtual shared space.

We may view jointness as a concert that takes place in the shared space of the auditorium. The parent is like the conductor who regulates the sounds and adjusts the rhythm and relative volume of the different musical instruments according to the pattern of the musical notation. We hear music that blurs the separateness of the instruments and transcends it, even though each instrument safeguards its own uniqueness.

If one of the musicians were to play out of tune (e.g., timing, pitch), it would affect the harmony or relationship between the different instruments, and we would hear this deviation as an irritating and discordant experience of strangeness.

The third shared space is experienced as something virtual; a subjective, illusory, non-concrete, sensory perception, emerging from the joint creativity and the partners' mutual emotional investment in this unique encounter. The "third shared space" (Solan, 1999) may therefore be conceptualised as a transitional phenomenon mediating between the otherness of parent and baby, or of partners and spouses. Furthermore, the variety of experiences within the virtual shared spaces between different individuals adds value to intimate interactions and enriches the narcissistic immunological network with emotional assets of partnership.

In light of the resonances of these memory traces in present occurrences, child and adult are motivated to repeat, "re-find the gratifications" (Winnicott, 1952a), and revive those blissful moments they experienced in the shared jointness space.[7]

Besides, we are narcissistically wired to preserve the assets of these shared spaces—invested with qualities of intimacy experienced with the unique objects—from foreign invasion. This may be the source of the intensely emotional outbursts of jealousy and betrayal between siblings, or between competitors for the same shared space, such as spouses. During the lifespan, these reverberating resonances will enhance the developmental significance of this pattern of object relations and will influence the individual's relationships with others.

Jasmine (at eighteen months old) plays a new game with her grandmother. The following week, when she comes to visit her grandparents, she insists on playing the same game. It takes some time for her grandmother to understand her wish and when, together, they find the same game, Jasmine is delighted and insists on playing it only with Grandma, refusing to let her cousin join the game. It is clear that it is not the game per se that is important to her, but rather the unique jointness in their shared space that she and Grandma had previously created, via the game.

We may notice that bodily and sensory contact such as a hug, a kiss, a massage, or sex reduces the magnitude of the shared space, while eye gazing and body language extend it. Avoidance of eye contact seems to reduce the sense of proximity. On the other hand, communication through various means, such as the telephone, the Internet, and various private languages extends the frame of the shared spaces.

## Enjoying happiness in the shared jointness space

In the virtual third shared space, baby and parent, like any couple, touch each other physically and emotionally and are attracted by each other's smell and glances. They are engaged in a non-verbal emotional language that is known only to them and is often loaded with pleasure, love, and erotic or sexual sensations—yet, they are not fused into each other's self-space. Together, they may experience the sharing of intimacy, happiness, and communication, or the sharing of alleviating distress, pain, disappointment, and even rage. Sometimes both succeed in synchronising their rapprochement, while often one tends to approach and the other to distance; one wishes to convey love and the other to express his current interests, injury, or anger. Each attempts to overcome the sense of strangeness or hurt emanating from his object and to reconcile with his partner. To my mind, this process represents the art of couplehood.

My model of intimacy between individuals is achieved in a virtual third shared space, where both succeed in synchronising their rapprochement. On venturing from his or her self-familiar shell/space, each person exposes his or her relevant self-assets and communicates with the other, who also exposes his or her deepest relevant self-assets. The partners' sharing of this mutual emotional exposure and interest in their shared space facilitates those privileged moments of bridging their separateness, and the emergence of a blissful state of proximity (see the above examples of Danny and baby Karen).

Although it may often seem to us that there is nothing simpler than the experiencing of intimacy, in my view we need to fulfil some basic emotional conditions in order to enjoy intimacy and the art of couplehood. These include:

a. the capacity to narcissistically preserve one's self-separateness and concomitantly tolerate the otherness emanating from the partner;
b. the capacity to expose the deepest relevant self-assets and concomitantly attune and adjust one's personal expression to the ability of the partner to engage with it;
c. the related capacity (of the ego) to regulate affective expression in attunement between both partners, which makes possible the temporary relief of alertness to the otherness;

d. the capacity to express positive affects recognised as familiar and pleasant to both partners;
e. the capacity to tolerate the emotional intensity of mutual experiences of elation, love, and happiness which evoke a transient sense of blurring of boundaries;
f. the capacity to tolerate separation and to be alone following the experience of intimacy;
g. the capacity to experience positive emotions as prevailing over negative ones;
h. the capacity of both partners to reconcile and recreate proximity following injury, frustration and disappointment;
i. the capacity to be interested in the messages conveyed by the partner and to tolerate his or her deepest affective exposure, as well as enjoy this mutual sharing.

Kelly (1996, 2009, 2012) stresses that intimacy is often inhibited due to the hidden shame of emotional exposure. Moreover, he suggests we learn how to use the shame family of emotions to identify and subsequently be in a position to negotiate the impediments to intimacy.

Whenever baby and parent or significant others/spouses manage to recreate experiences of intimacy, their mutual emotional involvement in the shared space of jointness fills them with a feeling of supreme satisfaction and a sense of wholeness. They seem to be drifting in a *temporary* sensory intoxication and for some moments are unaware of each other's presence in their shared space; there is no otherness in their common space and the illusion of primeval narcissistic perfection is restored. In these moments, nothing other than their narcissistic addictive elation exists, and they float in the aura of an eternal and perfect experience that permeates them and bonds them in sheer delight. This pure, emotional occurrence of transcendence, and the powerful positive emotional experience that floods the entire space of the shared experience, is what Freud defined as the feeling of happiness (Freud, 1915e, 1920g, 1930a).

A unique and transcendent emotion of this kind might unfold between a baby and his mother while each gazes into the other's eyes during suckling, as if penetrating each other with their eyes. A similar emotional experience occurs during a burst of infatuation or during sexual intimacy in adolescence and adulthood. These transcendent feelings are engraved in the narcissistic immunological network and reverberate throughout the lifespan as subjective data of perfect and pure emotional experiences.

Infatuation, happiness, and love seduce us all. They alleviate the injury emanating from the non-self object, provide hope and initiative, and add valuable flavour to our lives, making it painful to live without them. Throughout life we are moved by urges and longings to revive this authentic, blissful happiness which represents the "narcissistic ideals" (Duruz, 1981) of our object relations.

Nevertheless, it is surprising to discover over and again how difficult it is to revive this genuine experience of happiness. The intensity of the experience of happiness is based on oral narcissistic rudiments such as absolutism, perfection, and exclusivity, which, of course, are always subjective (principles of pleasure, "all-or-nothing", and familiarity). Therefore, whenever we manage to realise our narcissistic ideal and re-experience this blissful happiness, we are delighted. However, any digression from the subjective realisation of the narcissistic ideal may arouse emotions of vulnerability, disappointment, and pain that instantly risk reducing the perfect delightfulness to "nothing".

The longing to revive these archaic, blissful emotional states never vanishes—only the degree of addiction to them changes. Therefore, happiness may be experienced through infatuation, parenthood, love, euphoria, mysticism, creativity, erotic excitement, and sexual relations, and chiefly through a couple's urge to embrace their own baby.

In her therapy session, Doris shares with me the happiness she feels with her baby: "I held my darling Ben to my chest, looked at his peaceful face and felt him completely relaxed, totally devoted to our bonding [a reference to the baby's separateness and their jointness]. I was overjoyed! In moments like these, I forget all my troubles. It's as if every event other than this supreme experience doesn't exist [a reference to their shared space]. This is exactly what I dreamed about when I was pregnant with Ben [reference to her narcissistic ideals]. Still, I was surprised to discover that when Ben stared at Ian, my other son, who played beside us, it didn't interrupt our pleasure, and when Ian called me I could also give him my full attention [a reference to her son's separateness, and to another shared space]."

## The art of couplehood: preservation of the shared space of jointness

The experience of jointness in a shared space might be likened to an exciting dance, in which each of the dancers adapts his or her pace and steps to those of the other. The synchronisation gives rise to a coordinated rhythm in a shared dancing space that may temporarily blur the sense of boundaries between the dancers. Each dancer maintains his or her familiar rhythm while attuning themselves to the rhythmic synchronisation that produces a new and unique rhythm of their shared dance, perceived by each of the dancers as a specific creation for this dance alone. Finally, the dance comes to an end. The dancers separate and each returns to his or her self-space with its own rhythm, which now includes new memory traces and a new familiar ability to attune oneself to the other's rhythm and steps.

Experiencing jointness, such as in a dance, the shared singing of a choral piece, or listening to a symphony concert performance, comes to a close relatively soon, because, due to their separateness, the well-being of the partners-in-joining cannot be sustained indefinitely. Whenever one of the partners senses that the other intends to leave the shared space, he prepares himself and the other by means of a familiar password of their ritual separation, such as "see you later" or "bye-bye", a smile, or a hug.

Sharing the ritual of separation enables each partner to prepare for the distancing, and to preserve in his self-familiarity the positive phenomenon of jointness as a self-asset, accompanied by the knowledge (i.e., basic trust) that they will rejoin. Such preservation of self-assets despite the partners being apart soothes the pain of separateness and of separation, and enhances each one's "capacity to be alone" (Winnicott, 1958). Whenever the process of separation cannot be achieved, or when individuals separate with hurt and anger, the partners may suffer from the anxiety of object loss, abandonment, painful solitude, or a wish for revenge.

After the separation, each person returns to his familiar self-space with a new emotional load of memory traces from their recent shared encounter, such as intimacy, communication, or possibly disappointment with the object. Each may be delighted and fulfilled by this encounter, or sometimes needing to "lick their wounds" after having been hurt by their partner. Then, in the self-space, each may digest the processes and load the shared experience with personal meaning and subjective significance via processes of assimilation and accommodation (Piaget, 1936), while simultaneously restoring his or her self-familiarity separateness. The person may realise that, despite his hurt and despite the separation, he still appreciates the relations he has with this significant other and that it is worth the effort to reconcile and renew communication. Failing this, he may remain stuck in his injury and possibly a need for revenge, incapable of restoring his self-familiarity and jointness familiarity. Finally, we all enjoy knowing that our sharing of jointness experiences in the past was not forgotten and that our partner's memory may also resonate with associations to our past sharing experiences.

Michel, an adult, remains secluded in a long and calm silence through most of his session, and I share the silence with him. Then, after some time he says: "I sense that you are with me but not as usual ... I have the impression that you are tired today ... or that you are thinking about something that's bothering you, or maybe I flooded you with my silence ... It's amazing to sense such fineness. I remember a song that my mother used to sing and that I loved: 'Come to me my sweetheart, we'll soothe each other and will then fly back happily.'"

I interpreted: "When you feel the stress that I'm not with you as usual, you wish that we'll soothe each other before we fly back happily." After a while Michel continued: "Last weekend, when I read a story to my son before his going to sleep, a strange thought crossed my mind: was Mummy really with me when she read the same story to me? ... When I visited my mother yesterday, we exchanged some memories about those blissful moments of reading a story to my son, just like those she and I had when she read me stories ... Out of nowhere, I suddenly asked her: 'Were you really with me when you read me the story of Bambi?' Mummy was somewhat taken aback by my question, and replied along the lines of: 'I usually loved being with you so much before you went to sleep. I do remember though a short period that I was anxious about your father's health when you were nearly four, and I read the Bambi story to you automatically, without being fully present. I was sure you hadn't noticed.' ... Although I don't remember these episodes, it seems that I did notice her presence-absence."

From the oral stage onward, the characteristics of the shared space are mainly concerned with experiences of intimacy, proximity, and happiness. In the different stages of development these characteristics will be shaped differently, for example, negotiation in the anal stage (as will be elaborated in Chapter Eight). However, the need for expressing and receiving love will always motivate personal relationships and will shape the experiences of sensuousness, intimacy, and happiness in the shared spaces.

Throughout our lives, we create a rich variety of virtual shared spaces (intimacy, communication, negotiation, play, stories, meals, etc.)

with each of our objects (mother, father, siblings, friends, spouses, etc.), based on their quality of cognitive and emotional intelligence as well as nuances of communication (i.e., body language, professional language, cultural language, etc.).

A jointness pattern of object relations, in my view, indicates healthy ongoing emotional development from birth and leads to consolidation of self-cohesiveness, creative individuation, enjoyment of solitude, partnerships, intimacy, and the ability to communicate in different ways. Jointness relations imply an emotional balance between tolerance of the object's otherness and alertness toward his strangeness, and produce a variety of transitional phenomena that create a sense of proximity despite distance, a sense of presence even in absence, and a sense of freedom to join others in the shared spaces or to separate from them.

Throughout jointness object relations in babyhood, it seems clear that the parent "soothes each other before … flying back happily," as in Michel's mother's song, and nurtures separation and joining, individuation, and jointness. The parent encourages his baby's capacity to feel blessed with happiness as well as "to be alone" (Winnicott, 1958), and even to enjoy "the sense of solitude" (J. -M. Quinodoz, 1996). He assists his baby to endear himself to his surroundings, but at the same time to enhance his alertness toward strangers and strangeness. Hence, the parent may strengthen his child's inborn healthy narcissism and his ego adaptation mechanism. He may promote the refinement and honing of his child's "motivational systems", allowing participation in human interactions and the enjoyment of relationships (Emde, 1988a, 1988b) in various shared virtual spaces, as well as enable him (the child) to feel the sense of loneliness (Klein, 1959).

The capacity to enjoy one's sense of solitude is related, in my view to the capacity to participate and enjoy relationships, as well as with the capacity to tolerate the other's need to enjoy his or her own "space." None of these experiences may be observed in isolation.

I fully agree with J. -M. Quinodoz (1996), who has emphasised that, during the lifespan, the sense of solitude (or loneliness) is crucial for the integration of psychic life.[8] According to this author, solitude, experienced in being a unique individual or in being alone, is "the hallmark of the human condition" (p. 486). While some people can tolerate this sense of solitude, for others it may evoke an anxiety of object loss or separation.

I suggest that this sense of solitude may also enhance the parents' capacity, during the baby's oral stage, to enjoy intimacy with the baby, at the same time encouraging and promoting his or her separateness. Experiences of both intimacy and separateness (while seemingly opposed) are imprinted as memory traces upon the narcissistic immune network of the baby (and the parent, for that matter). Each partner (baby and parent) maintains their own separateness while enjoying a shared intimacy. In other words, in intimacy, one is both with the object and yet alone.

J. -M. Quinodoz (1996) has proposed:

> the use of the word *buoyancy*[9] (author's italics) to denote this sense of rediscovered unity of the ego, which is characterized by the impression of being able to 'fly with one's own wings,' as patients often put it when they succeed in working through their separation anxieties … The feeling of buoyancy reflects a sense of ego integration and corresponds to the internalization of a well-developed capacity to be alone, with the consequence that each protagonist becomes able to enjoy the presence of the other while at the same time feeling comfortably unique and alone. (ibid., p. 492)

I fully concur with Quinodoz's sense that "the possibility of feeling oneself existing, alone and unique, in the presence of the other, without losing our integrity and while retaining a sense of permanence in the relationship, seems to me to be an essential condition for the comfortable, long-term living of a relational life" (ibid.). These memory traces reverberate incessantly within us during our daily life experiences, and are the foundation for enhancing the capacity to both enjoy solitude and intimacy with our objects, as well as promoting the art of couplehood.

## Transitional phenomena

The transitional phenomenon is one of Winnicott's (1951, 1953) most important concepts. I will attempt to widen the significance of the concept in jointness relations by focusing on transitional phenomena as particularly pertinent ego-adaptation mechanisms (see Chapter Three on adaptation mechanisms). Transitional phenomena may emerge when individuals invest mutually in an occurrence, object, or common interest in their shared spaces, thereby adding value to the sense of proximity between partners and bridging their separateness.

A variety of transitional phenomena emerge in the shared spaces of jointness-separateness, which, already from the oral stage, may have a magical impact on our creative skills and capacity to enjoy doing things together. Transitional phenomena provide a sense of constancy that sooth and ease our pains of separation, and help create tolerance toward the otherness we confront in our relations.

Throughout life, an infinite number of transitional phenomena are created. They follow a hierarchical sequence, from preliminary forms, such as illusions, progressing to more complex forms, such as rituals, and evolving into higher forms, such as virtual shared spaces, body language, transitional objects, non-verbal sensory communication, intimate language, narratives, ethics, and professional and cultural values. During the process of maturation, these phenomena may become more central than the actual partners with whom they were created (see below).

I suggest that transitional phenomena should be viewed as the foundation upon which psychic potential flourishes, psychomotor, cognitive, and emotional intelligence develops, and communication and creativity skills are enhanced.

In this respect, the exposure of babies—via jointness with their parents—to music and songs, stories and tales, play, and imagination, elicits creativeness, which may crystallise as talents by the time they grow up or reach adulthood.

Transitional phenomena are often transmitted unconsciously and non-verbally, as described in the following examples.

Sean (around the age of two) was taken by his parents to the park to feed the animals. His mother watches him feeding the ducks and suddenly becomes very excited. The reverberation of associations remind her of the pleasure she had as a child when feeding swans on Lake Geneva with her parents (a transitional phenomenon). Sean senses his mother's excitement and also becomes elated. They both experience an added value to the feeding of ducks, now a familiar and unique bond between them. A transitional phenomenon can thus be transmitted as emotional heritage from generation to generation. Unlike these two, Sean's father, though present, does not share their excitement. For him, it is pleasant to feed the birds, but not much more. However, even though he feels like an outsider to the intimate bonding between his wife and his son, he is moved by their jointness (Solan, 1991). Sean's mother, too, has similar feelings when she witnesses the unique bonding between father and son when they play a game of cars with that special flavour of involvement that she does not share. Her husband often tells her how excited he is by associations with a car game from his childhood, and that it means so much to him to give Sean some of the cars from his collection.

Sean (at age ten) says to his parents: "We will bring our children, your grandchildren, to you every Wednesday, just as we go to Granny and Grandpa and have fun together with the family." As he says this, he feels his parents' and grandparents' pleasure at the idea of passing down the family legacy of jointness (a transitional phenomenon) from generation to generation.

As a young couple, my husband and I spent a few years studying in Switzerland. We loved to sit around the fireplace, revelling in the warmth on cold winter days, so different from the Israeli climate we were both used to. This space became for us a shared space in which we felt an intimate proximity, a blissful state of enjoying the special smell and sounds of the burning logs, and the heat radiating from the fireplace. At various times, we shared these delightful experiences from the past with our children. A few years ago, one of our children shared with us her pleasure in sitting around the fireplace in winter. She said that their joining around the fireplace had an added value that she had absorbed from the way we had shared our experiences with her, and that she felt the emotional "flavour" of our presence when joined by her family around their fireplace. As I write these lines, I still feel the same emotional flavour of this transitional phenomenon that I sensed so long ago.

Another example of a transitional phenomenon concerns my late father who loved to cook borscht, which our children and we loved. After my father's death I cooked the borscht, but my children refused to compromise on the taste of "Grandpa's borscht", even though it was prepared according to the original recipe. Apparently my borscht lacked the emotional "flavour" of Grandpa's closeness, which they preferred to keep in mind as "the special borscht that we all miss" (as they said that they miss in reality, but have narcissistically preserved as self-assets). From then on, the word "borscht" has come to represent our code: a transitional phenomenon that evokes a sense of closeness in us all.

Ella (at four years old) is in the car with her mother. They often hear foreign-language songs on the radio, which she does not understand. That day, however, Ella suddenly asked: "What song is this?" Her mother is perplexed as she realises that in fact the song has family significance, and that she had not noticed that she had probably reacted emotionally. She said to Ella: "It's a song that Grandma and Grandpa are very, very fond of."

During psychoanalysis, via the associations and themes weaving through the patient's narratives and his transference feelings toward the analyst, we may recognise together with our patient the absent figures (missing in consciousness) with which his transitional phenomena were created, for example, a love of music. Furthermore, the patient may come to recognise that his injuries or traumatic emotional data have buried the treasured narrative, experienced as a transitional phenomenon with a parent. Until they surface, these concealed memory traces of valuable experiences with an object may remain unconscious, compressed under various stresses, anxieties and traumas.

Ernest, an adult patient, constantly experiences feelings of being hurt or abandoned by his father, accompanied by rage toward him and perpetual suspicion toward people in general. His associations and transference have led us to acknowledge hidden layers of valuable transitional phenomena linked to his father, such as reading books, collecting/studying insects, and watching sports on the television. When Ernest was three, his brother was born. Presumably, the newborn was experienced as an impediment to the bonding (positive feelings) with his father. Jealousy and feelings of abandonment flooded him and resulted in his repressing the positive feeling of jointness with his father. He remembers refusing to play with his father, and his feelings of hate. The emergence of this precious concealed closeness to his father triggered a deep longing for him, accompanied by guilt for having caused the rift between them. He developed an urge to read books with his little daughter, just as his father had done with him; something he had completely forgotten.

The various phenomena—as will be described below—are interconnected, share a continuity of associations, and are shaped as personal narratives that influence the significance that people attribute to their life experiences in the present.

## Transitional objects

A transitional object (Winnicott, 1951) is a concrete object, which, I claim, may become cathected as a result of the joint emotional investment in this particular object by the baby and his caregiver within their shared space. This unique object, such as a blanket, doll, or teddy bear, is loaded emotionally, as long as it is as dear for the parents as it is for their child. Together, they enhance their feelings of partnership by ennobling the object through personification and giving it the special attention accorded to a new family member.

The transitional object becomes the third concrete figure that virtually bridges the separateness of the other two (baby and parent), so much so that the baby senses the constant presence and protection of his parent via their shared transitional object, which in turn enables him to initiate a separation from his parents (Solan, 1991). I agree with Sandler's (1987) view that "the constant presence of the familiar things makes it easier for the child to maintain its minimum level of safety feeling" (p. 8).

Since Sandy's birth, her parents feel how important it is always to put her teddy bear, Bubu, into bed with her when she goes to sleep. At eight months, Sandy actively searches for her teddy bear (perceptual object constancy) and her parents hand it to her as an object of comfort and security: "Our darling Bubu is here with you, good night sweetheart, sleep well." Sandy embraces Bubu affectionately and relates to it with the same warmth that her parents relate to her. One night, as Sandy (at twelve months old) lies down to sleep, her parents cannot find Bubu, and everyone is stressed. Sandy cries and her parents feel exhausted and nervous. Her mother has the idea of offering Sandy an almost-identical teddy bear (one that her mother has kept for her), but Sandy easily differentiates the teddy bear by its smell and touch. The new one is simply not Bubu, and her crying continues. She wants the one that is so familiar and significant for her. Her mother is surprised she detects the differences, and respects Sandy's gut feeling, searching for the "real" Bubu until she finds him. Everyone is relieved. Sandy hugs Bubu, the parents hug them both, and Sandy calmly falls asleep.

Nadine, the mother of Danielle (who is eighteen months old), shares with me in her therapy session her stress in relation to her daughter's sleeping. Whenever she puts her down to sleep and leaves her room, Danielle starts crying. She adds: "Until last month, we regularly played a game before Danielle went to sleep. We would lay Danielle's fluffy doll-dog down to sleep and then after I gave my baby a kiss, I would cover her, whisper good night and leave the room ... Recently I lost my involvement in the game. I'm too tired to play, and I do it technically, automatically ... surely my attitude to the game couldn't cause Danielle's reaction." Nadine's insight into foregoing the ceremony enabled her to reinvest authentically in the doll-dog, giving it even more attention than before, and they were both able, once again, to separate easily from each other, with each preserving their absent-present object.

*Media sensory communication in the shared space (another transitional phenomenon)*

How do individuals who are so different succeed in understanding each other, in conveying messages and absorbing their profound meaning, and in creating authentic communication? This is not self-evident. A patient once told me: "I am constantly amazed when I feel through your interpretation that you really understand me. I got attention and love in my childhood, but I often had the feeling that nobody really understood me, except my grandfather."

I use the word "media" (Solan, 1991) for the transitional phenomenon describing sensory communication between individuals. The Oxford English Dictionary defines media as: (1) "A means by which something is communicated or expressed," and (2) "The intervening substance through which impressions are conveyed to the senses."

It is through media sensory communication that individuals convey their messages so that their partner will become attentive, identify their communication, and, by and large, understand it. Media sensory communication often becomes the secret language between people, so much so that they may understand each other and guess each other's wishes without words. Partners who mutually invest in their transitional media may broaden the scope of their own sensory communication with different jointness couples (classmates, spouses, colleagues), to the family and the peer-group ultimately reaching unlimited combinations of media partners. Finally, it seems that in dialogue generally we are more affected unconsciously by sensory messages than by the contents of verbal language, even when mastery of verbal language is attained.[10]

Intimate communication includes the physical dialogue of body language and verbal or non-verbal private communication, and makes it possible to extend the physical distance between the communicating partners, and to some extent may compensate for it (Solan, 1986). The dialogue between partners is augmented by senses, signs, symbols and representations, known only to them, and may include art, religion, jargon (colloquial language), and even scientific terms. Regular communication between individuals thus crystallises into a somewhat "secret" language, agreed upon by, and unique to, such partners. Its range expands (and may subsequently contract) during the life cycle.

Unspoken media communication is frequently unconsciously sensed by partners and used as "intelligence" information about each other's moods, any minor or major deviations from the usual sensory dialogue, and occurrences in their jointness relationship—just as Michel (in the above example) tried to attune himself to my emotional partnership with him. This information is detected by delicate sensory signs; such as facial expressions, breathing, intonation and pitch, cadence and rhythm of speech, and body language. Media are also used to convey secret emotional messages of intimacy, love, and enjoyment, or alertness, frustration, and anger. One may recognise whether the other person's messages are authentic, and whether the other person has deciphered one's messages correctly.

Obviously, there are links between what I have labelled "media sensory communication" and concepts such as emotion sharing (Emde, 1988a, 1988b), mutual regulation and mutuality (Erikson, 1950; Sandler, 1988; Stern, 1985), empathy (Basch, 1983; Kohut, 1966; Winnicott, 1960), mentalization (Fonagy & Target, 2002, 2007) and intimate communication.

The theme song of the movie *Rain Man* (1988, directed by Barry Levinson) reflects the impact of media sensory communication on the relationship between individuals. Charlie (portrayed by Tom Cruise) tells his girlfriend that the *Rain Man* song has a tranquilising effect on him, without his knowing why. Sometime later, Charlie reveals he has an elder, autistic brother named Raymond, who has been institutionalised for many years. However, when Charlie manages to reunite with his autistic brother, he is amazed to discover that when he was a little boy, he used to pronounce his brother's name as "rain man." Furthermore, Raymond suddenly sings this particular song, which he used to sing to Charlie when he was a little boy, to soothe him. Obviously, Charlie condensed the title of the song with his brother's name and thus the *Rain Man* song was narcissistically preserved within his self-assets as their shared media of soothing sensory communication. It continued to be a current tranquilising medium even though its origin was forgotten, and his older brother, the partner of this media sensory communication, was absent (Solan, 1989a, 1991).

In dialogue, the individual is tuned to the shared language communication. Each one attempts to be understood by the other and to coordinate the speaking according to the mutual openness and willingness to communicate. In contrast, in monologue, the individual has the illusion that he will always be understood and accepted, due to his denial of the other's separateness.

In the oral stage, the baby (due to his low tolerance threshold) needs to feel that his parent understands him immediately and completely, and he may become distressed and agitated when he is not understood. Hence, from the oral stage onward, and throughout life, we long for someone to understand us without words, and we are fearful of not being properly understood; on the other hand, we are sometimes afraid that others might understand messages we do not wish to reveal.

In psychoanalysis or psychotherapy, the use of media sensory communication as a transitional phenomenon provides the clearest proof of the usefulness of this conceptualisation. Media communication flows between the therapist and his or her patient in their jointness relations in the shared space of the therapy room. They both require several sessions until a familiar therapeutic medium which both understand is woven between them. The analyst develops a unique media sensory communication with each of his patients, based on the sensory messages that each conveys to him. The patient too hones his senses in order to become familiar with his analyst's pattern of clarifying and interpreting, and to find the appropriate ways of conveying his associations to his analyst.

The analyst tries to absorb and decipher the sequence of his patient's unconscious phantasies, narratives and associations, as well as his own associations, and to decode the transference and the countertransference (the analyst's unique reactions to his patient and his material), which are naturally occurring processes upon which the therapy evolves. On this basis, he may interpret his patient's unconscious by repeatedly referring to associations connected to his patient's main narrative that colours the events in his life. The analyst has to attune his interpretations to his patient's ability to absorb them, and to use his patient's words and integrate them into the familiar, unique media sensory communication that is developing between them. Generally, when the timing is right, these media interpretations are congruent with the patient's emotional state and feelings, touch him emotionally, and trigger reverberations of new transference associations that may lead him to deeper layers of experience.

Incorrect interpretation, however, is unavoidable. The analyst is a separate, different personality with his own jostling subjective associations, feelings, anxieties, and foreign influences (countertransference). All of these might be unrelated to his patient, but are triggered by him, and they may disrupt their media communication.

Michel, my patient, tells me in one of his sessions: "I think of our special way of dialoguing here in my session. If somebody would suddenly hear us, he definitely wouldn't understand anything. Since I began my analysis, we've created so many private signs. You are always able to transform my words into our special dialogue. I like this very much. It makes me feel close to you. Maybe with your other patients you have something else that I can't even guess … Wow, I've just remembered that as a child I was always curious to understand what my parents were saying to each other in their secret language."

Different languages and types of media communication (verbal and non-verbal) enable us to absorb and convey information that elaborates the mysteriousness of life (Laor, 1990). The constant flow of data can bridge the otherness of people, and even nations, and lead to a sense of partnership despite physical or ideological distance. From infancy to adulthood, human dialogue is essential in order for communication to take place in our alienated world (ibid.), and optimally it will culminate in an exchange enriched by ethics and social and cultural values.

## Symbiosis as a disturbance in object relations

Symbiosis, the term coined by Mahler (1968; Mahler, Pine & Bergman, 1975), has become embedded in the psychological literature as representing the normative development of object relations in infancy. However, I wish to draw attention to its pathological aspects, which are present from birth. To my understanding, while Mahler emphasised the merger aspects between the baby and his mother, she did not relate to the component of each one's separateness. A careful reading of Mahler's theory, however, reveals that she does differentiate or accept a separateness of mother and baby in symbiosis by asserting that the infant's need for the mother is absolute, whereas the mother's need for the infant is relative.

In later observations and studies, evidence indicates that the baby differentiates itself from manifestations of non-self (Emde, 1988a, 1988b; Sandler, 1987; Solan, 1991; Stern, 1985). Pine (2004), Mahler's collaborator, also recently claimed that, at the time, Mahler did not pay attention to the full constellation of the baby's behaviour in this respect.

Pine reformulated the theory of symbiosis, in which he continued to postulate that the baby indeed merges with his mother without differentiation, but that he also experiences differentiation of himself from his mother.

Symbiotic attachment, as I see it, represents an emotional illusion of fusion of two individuals (mother and baby) in what Mahler described as "an omnipotent system—a dual unity within one common boundary" (Mahler, 1968, p. 201). Symbiosis often stems from the mother's need to contain herself and her baby in an exclusive, common space as a defence against her own separation or abandonment anxiety. Because she feels threatened by her baby's separateness, she denies it, and depends on him to supply a feeling of completeness and security.

The baby senses his mother's anxiety and clings to her physical presence in an excessively strong attachment in order to feel secure (Winnicott, 1951). Symbiotic relations seemingly supply the baby with his emotional needs, his mother's protection, feedback for his existence, and denial of their separateness, but at the same time he unconsciously sacrifices his true self and his individuation, both of which may give rise to anxiety.

Symbiotic partners, particularly baby and mother, can be fully satisfied as long as there is no hint of separateness. They seem to resemble Siamese twins: distancing by one of them is experienced as injury, abandonment, or traumatic disruption. Symbiotic partners may remain almost addicted to this excessive closeness, and be driven throughout life by a powerful need to cling to anyone who can satisfy their familiar narcissistic need for immediate and constant merger.

Symbiotic experiences leave predominant memory traces of fusion "un-separateness" between self and object, as if there is not any non-self in their relations. According to Kohut (1971, 1977), such relations may be described as narcissistic object relations in which the other is loaded as an archaic self-object.

I wonder how and when a baby, who experiences the other as undifferentiated from himself (Kernberg, 1975, 1980; Stolorow, 1975), or who is engaged in fusion with the object as a self-object (Kohut, 1971, 1977) or in symbiosis as if they were a unity (Mahler & McDevitt, 1968), can ever be willing to forego (Freud, 1914c) this self-luxury. How will the child overcome his anxiety of abandonment, which resonates and makes its appearance as archaic memory traces whenever he confronts any hint of separateness and otherness?

Symbiotic partners, in my view, will seek their self-object even at the expense of their individuation, true self, and self-esteem. Both are often flooded with anxiety that neither will be able to survive without the other, so that the craving for merging seems stronger than the need to preserve self-familiarity separateness.

The following examples might elucidate some of the consequences of symbiotic object relations. Miriam is very sensitive to all my gestures during the analytic session, and any time she hears me breathe deeply, blow my nose, or move in my chair, she feels abandoned and even bursts into rage. When I offer an interpretation that does not precisely match her feelings, she rejects me as a stranger. In one of our analytic sessions she says: "When I lie down on your couch, and you are behind me, I always feel how much I need your presence with me … I feel totally alone if I don't see you … Closeness with you for only few moments isn't enough. I so much long for complete nearness with you … where there is no distance between us, where we can feel as one … How can I overcome what separates us?"

Herb (a four-month-old baby) lies in his mother's arms during our therapy session. He gazes at his mother with a tiny smile, and she replies with a warm smile and hugs him. We start talking, and Herb suddenly turns his head toward me, probably to discover where the sound is coming from. He looks at me and smiles. Immediately, his mother turns his head back toward her, and says: "When Herb looks and smiles at you, like now, or with his father, I feel like I'm going crazy … because I'm left out … I feel that I'm losing him."

I then understood that the little indentation I noticed in Herb's chin was a result of the pressure of his mother's finger to turn his head toward her whenever she felt a threat of abandonment, which presumably resonated with her childhood.

It is both impressive and distressing to see this step-by-step transfer of symbiotic needs from the mother to her baby. The mother unconsciously conveys to her baby that his individual need to look at me threatens to disrupt their symbiotic unity. Herb probably senses and absorbs his mother's distress and anxiety. He foregoes the temptation to look at me and tenaciously grasps his mother in his desire to release both of their anxieties. In so doing, he falsifies his self's needs.

Because the object is *not* perceived as a non-self—an external object to the self-separateness—but rather as a self-object, I maintain that the urge for merging does not occur in a third shared space but rather "within one common boundary" (Mahler, 1968). Hence, symbiosis represents dyadic object relations in which individuals do not have to carry out attunement and timing with other non-selves. In their illusion, the merging is permanent, unrestrained by time or place. Memory traces of these symbiotic experiences from early babyhood reverberate throughout life as an axiom that only symbiotic fusion is proof of security, survival, and ultimate love. They reverberate as the "Golden Fantasy", described by Smith (1977).

It is obvious, however, that the symbiotic experience cannot always be realised, even at the start of life, possibly because the parties are, in reality, separate, and one of them is not always able to respond to the other's excessive need for fusion. During these moments of frustration, anxiety of abandonment is evoked. "It is as if the mother's felt withdrawal fixed the anxiety in the child's mind" (Smith, 1977, p. 313). Such anxiety of separation can be reactivated later in life when facing any sign of separateness, such as "when the spouse is away out of some necessity, when the analyst is absent, or when the appearance of some new responsibility underscores the need for the patient to act independently" (ibid.).

Symbiotic relations may be characterised as follows:

a. Extreme dependency on the self-object's immediate and total presence.
b. Extreme narcissistic injury (including the shame family of affects) whenever the self-object is frustrating.
c. Vulnerability in the face of any hint of separateness, separation, and otherness, followed by anxiety of object loss, abandonment, and annihilation.
d. A perpetual need to please the object, including falsification of the true self and the foregoing of individuation.

The experience of symbiosis resonates as unconscious but harmful memory traces, which expose the symbiotic individual to infinite and unavoidable narcissistic injuries, frustrations, and anxieties.

A symbiotic pattern of object relations may be considered as the outcome of pathological narcissistic processing that immunises self-familiarity—*as a fused self-object*—against "alien" data emanating from the true-self's need for separateness. In the wake of injuries, the fused self-object is narcissistically restored as un-separateness, while defence mechanisms are mobilised to deny the non-self and its separateness, which would otherwise trigger anxieties of abandonment and annihilation. A symbiotic pattern represents pathological object relations and indicates a fusion with the self-object within a common boundary. As previously mentioned, this prevents the enrichment of transitional phenomena in a third shared space, foregoes individuation, and exposes a false self. Communication is often conducted as a monologue, accompanied by the illusion that the partners fully understand each other, while, in fact, intolerance toward the otherness of the partner is increased and the anxiety regarding strangers is intensified.

Both symbiosis and jointness-separateness relations commence at the beginning of life, and even though they appear to be similar experiences, they are quite different. In order to ensure their existence, partners of symbiosis can only be fully satisfied in the constant presence of the self-object. Jointness partners, on the other hand, may join in happiness despite their otherness and their frequent separations, which generate the normal development of separation-individuation, communication, and relationship (see below). Symbiosis, in my view, represents a pathological, emotional crystallisation, from birth, which leads to self-fragility, difficulty with self-regulation and vulnerability. An immature personality is formed, accompanied by a false self, limited individuation, and anxiety of separation-abandonment and annihilation—all of which may emerge in personality disturbances (including narcissistic disturbances), and disturbances in relationships with others.

### Separation-individuation and jointness-separateness

Mahler and McDevitt (1968) first described the concept of separation-individuation, using it to represent the baby's emergence as an individual from the symbiotic dyad with his mother, and the awareness that his mother is differentiated from his self (at five months old). In my view, this complex process of separation-individuation begins at birth, with the newborn baby's emergence from the womb and the primal momentum of resistance to any non-self in his new environment, concomitant with his attraction to a non-self that is recognised as familiar and cathected as a libidinal object (see Chapters Two and Four). Furthermore, I claim that the baby's inborn initial sense of separateness is improved and sharpened by his parents' recognition of his separateness, by encouraging his individual expressions of his needs, by supporting his bonding with others, as well as by validating and assisting his resistance to an unfamiliar non-self.

The baby is born with the capacity to breathe, eat, digest food, safeguard his self-familiarity, and join his familiar non-self object in intimacy. Furthermore, he is born with the ability to discharge or expel what he does not need or what is unpleasant inside him, to separate for sleep, and to resist the non-self stranger. The baby very much needs his parents' love and support as they encourage him to develop these innate functions. He needs his parents' assistance in enhancing the capacity for jointness despite their separateness, and in enriching his separateness via his individuation. In this view I concur with Smith's developmental views of separation and individuation:

> Individuation is reflected in the development of a host of ego functions having to do with reality testing and its dependence on perception and autonomy, while separation is connected with boundary functions and most importantly with the capacity to break free from mother even if only for short periods of time before returning to her reassuring presence. (Smith, 1977, p. 312)

In the first three months of life, there is a near-perfect matching between the baby's and the parents' needs, along with signs of their separateness. The parents try to avoid distancing themselves from their baby or leaving him with a replacement caregiver, while the baby depends entirely on his parents' familiarity and avoids strangeness. In these initial months, the parents may acknowledge their offspring's separateness, while the baby, on the other hand, still experiences separateness via resisting to a non-self.

During the first few months of Barak's life, his parents are available to fulfil his needs at all times, while concomitantly fully respecting his separateness, even though they are required to wake up several times each night to feed and comfort him. At three to four months, Barak may already sleep for about five hours at a stretch, allowing his parents a relatively restful night of sleep. Gradually, his parents become more aware of their own needs, and those of other family members, and thus the process of separation-individuation of both the parents from Barak, and of Barak from his parents, gathers momentum.

This situation alters the initial harmonious matching between the parents and their offspring, and conflicts of interests begin to arise. For example, having become accustomed to uninterrupted sleep, the parents feel they need this, so, if Barak wakes up at night for some reason, they are not as emotionally accessible for the desired cosiness as before. More time is therefore required for the parents to decipher Barak's unusual night-time distress and put him to sleep again. In contrast to the parents, Barak still needs them to alleviate his distress by means of the matching that he has been familiar with from birth. Because their re-comforting is delayed, Barak senses strangeness and finds it difficult to relax, separate, and fall asleep. Finally, the parents resume their habitual rituals; they hug him lovingly with his elephant in his arms, and soothe him until he is able to separate from them and withdraw peacefully into sleep, with a sense of familiarity regarding his objects.

Through these experiences, Barak gradually discovers his parents' separateness in addition to their non-self characteristics. He realises that he needs to actively attract their attention, express his separate needs clearly, be assertive—even by crying—and, finally, not allow them to leave without a ritual reconciliation having occurred. Although Barak's assertiveness often irritates his parents, from Barak's perspective, however, these affirmations of separateness indicate the normative development of separation-individuation.

In the initial period following birth, Bennie falls asleep while suckling and his mother does not know if he is satiated; she needs a sign from him that he is satisfied. A month or so later, she can easily decipher Bennie's signs and can rely on his signalling to express his desires as well as his emotional states: pleasure, hunger, fatigue, withdrawal or pain, and even his wish to gaze around before continuing his suckling. When blissful moments of intimacy emerge, she is delighted, and feels no need to make an effort to decipher his signals. The mother obtains satisfaction in being able to understand her baby, despite the fact that he is only three months old. She senses that she is developing a real partnership with Bennie as a separate individual. In adopting this attitude she encourages his separation-individuation and jointness.

Bob is six months old. His mother looks at him and is pleased to see that he can play alone with his toys. She joins him emotionally by paying attention when Bob notices that something is moving, that something else is making pleasant music, or when he tries to catch the monkey's tail, just as he grasps his mother's finger. In short, he seems happy. So she picks up her book and reads relaxedly, sitting close to him. Their occasional reciprocal smiling bridges the physical distance of their separateness and their individuation, and gives them a feeling of emotional partnership. Gradually, the mother begins to briefly leave the room while Bob continues to play, but she never forgets to tell him that she is leaving for a moment and will soon be back, even though he does not yet understand the words—only their tone meanings. She is proud of his growing capacity to separate from her.

At eight months, while Bob still enjoys playing alone with his toys as his mother watches him, he notices when she talks on the phone. Even though she continues looking at Bob, remains seated in the same armchair and even smiles at him, he senses from her intonation that she is not speaking to him and is not his usual partner. Bob becomes stressed. He expresses his individuation by throwing a toy and starting to cry, until his mother is forced to stop chatting. It seems easier for him to tolerate his mother telling him she will be back than to sense her near him but not with him.

Picture 2. One snail transmits signals of rapprochement while the other demonstrates aloofness.

Interestingly, a long conversation that our partner conducts on the telephone in the bounds of our shared space (an impediment to intimacy) arouses in us, at any age, feelings of disruption of jointness and betrayal.

## Suckling and weaning

Nelly, at six months old, cuts her first teeth. She bites everything that comes into her mouth, including her mother's nipples. The bites hurt, and her mother reacts by recoiling at every bite. Nelly senses her mother's reaction and restrains her bite reflex in order to allow the flow of milk. Gradually, her mother accustoms Nelly to new foods and reduces the number of nursing sessions. Nelly adapts relatively quickly to the new regimen: she can now bite and chew the new food with pleasure without hurting her mother or needing to restrain her aggressiveness. She gradually relinquishes suckling, while preserving her pleasure of intimacy with her mother.

The mother maintains only the last nursing before sleep time, until, at ten months, she completes the weaning. She is surprised to discover that the complete weaning is as difficult for her as it is for Nelly. Both are loath to give up these special moments of closeness. The mother feels narcissistically injured by having to admit that Nelly no longer needs her good milk. However, the insight that the weaning is important for Nelly's individuation prevails over her reluctance to separate. The mother is also released from her absolute obligation to nurse; Nelly's father can now also feed her. Both Nelly and her mother are able to adjust the primeval model of intimacy to new forms of proximity, and discover new transitional phenomena for mediating separateness and enjoying jointness.

When her mother is happy, Nelly is as well. She is drawn to jointness with her mother and has the courage to demonstrate her separation-individuation. However, when her mother is anxious or distressed, Nelly becomes sad, secludes herself and does not dare to express her separation-individuation needs.

In the normal course of events, the baby, on the basis of his experiences, consolidates his self-familiarity separateness and strengthens his ability to regulate the rapprochement distance from his parents. From around five months old, the separation-individuation process manifests itself actively through body language, motor activity and rapidity of reaction, gaze, facial display, and the expression of affects.

Steven (at eight months old) senses that whenever he moves away from his mother she immediately becomes anxious. Therefore, in order for him to feel secure he keeps her constantly within his gaze. Generally, he crawls close to her, follows her wherever she goes, and does not dare to crawl away from her toward other stimuli, even though they attract him. His mother, unconsciously, leaves limited room for Steven's separation-individuation. He thus becomes increasingly dependent upon her, needs to be picked up, and relinquishes his separation-individuation experimentations.

With Jasmine (who is six months old) in her arms, the grandmother accompanies Jasmine's mother to the door, says, "Bye, bye," and encourages Jasmine to separate actively from her mother by waving goodbye and by pushing the front door to shut it behind her departing mother. The mother, too, says, "Bye, bye, see you soon." It is as if Jasmine is initiating the process of separation-individuation by sending her mother on her way, rather than it being the mother who is leaving Jasmine behind. Gradually, it seems that Jasmine even enjoys the regular separation ceremony (a transitional phenomenon) that enables her (adaptation mechanisms) to preserve a positive image of her mother and lays the groundwork for the consolidation of basic trust, inner security, and evolving confidence that her parents will be there for her.

It is always easier to actively separate from someone than to be unwillingly left behind. This process is clearly observable in psychotherapy, when the patient going on vacation feels far better than when the analyst takes a holiday.

Getting the baby ready for sleep may be considered a prototype of the process of separation-individuation. It is a beneficial process for both the baby and the adult to separate lovingly, and for the baby to be able to withdraw calmly into his self-space and into a state of relaxed sleep. For the baby, preparing for sleep means separating from his parents and the activities of the day, and even from his capacity to see and control his surroundings. As adults, we know that when we are stressed our sleep tends to be troubled. It is thus crucial for all of us, whether baby or adult, to separate positively before any parting, and especially before withdrawing into sleep; it is significant for all of us to separate in conciliation with our dearest ones despite possibly having experienced conflicts of interest earlier.

Parents, no less than babies, need the regular rituals of separation accompanied by transitional phenomena, which help each party to positively preserve the other. The baby needs his teddy bear (transitional object), just as his parents need their intercom (to supervise the baby's room), mobile phones, SMSs, e-mails, Internet, and social networks—all of which help us to keep in touch with our objects during their absence and thus avoid the anxiety of separation.

## Summary

Object relations, defined as jointness-separateness (Solan, 1991), are created at birth and represent a triangulation (a triad) in normal object relations, whereas symbiosis involves a dyad, and represents a form of object relations I have come to consider as pathological. Jointness-separateness takes place between two different and separated self-familiarity "spaces": that of the baby, and that of the parent or of any partners who temporarily join each other in a variety of third shared spaces. Concomitantly, each preserves the freedom to "withdraw libidinal interest from his love-objects … and sends them out again when he recovers" (Freud, 1914c, p. 82). Within the shared space, partners may express their individuation, their positive and negative feelings, and enjoy the sharing of pleasure or the alleviating of distress. They may endure distancing, injury, and even rage, which will usually culminate in reconciliation. Partners may experience intimacy, love, communication, and infatuation, all of which temporarily blur the boundaries between individuals and facilitate the emergence of those privileged moments of a blissful state of happiness.

From the oral stage onward, jointness-separateness object relations may therefore be seen as representing a psycho-evolutionary system based on the harmonious functioning of instinctual bonding alongside inborn narcissistic immune processing and the ego's (economic) adaptive functioning. These processes elicit attraction toward an increasingly significant, familiar non-self object that may satisfy drives, emotions, and bonding needs. However, the object's ability to always or continually satisfy the baby or any other partner is usually limited because of their separateness. Frustration and injury are thus inevitable, underscoring the necessity to regulate relations between the self and its external objects. Moreover, most people experience separateness and otherness, as well as the actual separating from their beloved ones, as almost unbearable, as they usually trigger the concealed anxiety of object loss. The capacity of baby and parent, as of any couple, to maintain positive harmonious relations and even happiness, and to respectively improve their own individuation along the poles of jointness-separateness (without being overwhelmed by otherness) constitutes the art of couplehood in virtual shared spaces.

## Notes

1. I suggest a somewhat different conception of rapprochement from that of Mahler (1972b): Mahler considers rapprochement in the middle of the second year of the toddler's life, as evidence of his "hatching out" of the symbiotic relations via the separation-individuation process and object constancy. Mahler emphasises that when "the toddler's aware-ness of separateness grows, he now seems to have an increased need and wish for his mother to share with him his every new acquisition of skill and experience. These are the reasons for which I called this sub-phase of separation-individuation, the period of rapprochement" (p. 493). My conceptualisation of rapprochement is very similar, except that it starts from *birth*, following the evolving sensory recognition of the non-self, and consists of a mutual rapprochement (baby–parent) to proximity with the familiar non-self and a withdrawing from the stran-ger non-self. It represents a process of scanning the non-self's "sensory identity card" and relational password anew, thus bridging the sense of separateness; this is not a sub-phase, but rather, a lifelong process. My view is supported by modern infant studies (e.g., Stern, 1985). See also Nathanson (1992), in this regard. According to Nathanson: "Only by ignoring the facial display of affect and the interplay of facial communi-cation can one defend a theory that says infants are fused with mother until they can walk away from her ..." (p. 222).
2. This relatedness is also manifest in the affectively coloured internal (mental) representations of self and other in interaction, such as those that emerge, for example, in one's early memories and dreams, and may appear (or be implied) in representations of/relations with significant others, such as one's therapist. Mental representations are thought to evolve on a continuum from the rudimentary to the mature, and vari-ous attempts have been made to map out their developmental levels, so as to compare them over time (for example, at different points during the psychotherapeutic process) or among groups of people/nosological categories.

3. In self psychology this significant non-self object is conceptualised as fulfilling a self-object function that progresses along a developmental line.

4. See Kelly's (2012) discussion of "the compass of shame".

5. I am using this term differently from its usage in systems theory and family therapy, where a third object is triangulated into a dyadic inter-action or relationship (see Glossary).

6. The snail song seems universal, with each culture having its own, unique lyrics.

7. These resonances may be re-experienced at the level of the body when attention is focused on them, and become part of what Ross (2008) has described as "grounding a resource."

8. Both the author and I refer to the subjective sense of solitude that can co-exist with being part of a caring environment.

9. See J. -M. Quinodoz's (1993) book, *The Taming of Solitude. Separation Anxiety in Psychoanalysis*, for an elaboration of the concept of buoyancy.

10. See Oliver Sacks's (1985) account of "The President's Speech," in his wonderful book, *"The Man Who Mistook His Wife for a Hat"*. In this clini-cal tale, he describes how aphasics respond affectively to the sensory communication that accompanies spoken language, in contrast to the reactions of a patient with tonal agnosia and to those of "normal" people. (He does not, however, specifically refer to media as described here, yet it might enrich the subject.)

# PART TWO

## THE ANAL STAGE—A TIME OF NEGOTIATION

### FROM TWELVE MONTHS TO THREE YEARS

## The child's emotional state in the transition
## from the oral to the anal stage

The first part of *The Enigma of Childhood* dealt with the many challenges of the first year of life, as seen through the prism of the oral stage, setting the stage for future developments. The second part of the book deals with the complex process of how improvements occur in the baby's narcissistic functioning, in his adaptation and defence mechanisms, and in certain features of his object relations, as he (or she) grows older.

The second, anal, stage in emotional development starts at approximately twelve months and continues until the onset of the Oedipal stage around the age of three. The comfortable fit or familiarity matching between parents and toddler (see Chapters Two and Four), which was achieved during the six first months of life in the oral stage, is undermined, mainly because the toddler is awake longer, his demands increase, and his parents are no longer available to immediately satisfy his needs as before. Another very significant change takes place around the age of twelve months: the baby's psychomotor intelligence and mobility have improved and soon he will start walking. He now tends to touch everything and carry out various activities on his own. In the wake of these crucial changes, the parents have the very tiresome task of being constantly on the alert in order to protect their child from injuring himself or damaging the family's belongings. They have to limit his activities, indicate what is permitted or forbidden, and be creative in their educational parenting.

In confronting these changes, the toddler is often offended by his parents' restrictions, and he experiences new frustrations which tend to modify the nature of their relations. The toddler becomes more assertive in his separation-individuation demands and may even react aggressively; at the same time, he often becomes sensitive and vulnerable, and craves to revive the familiar intimacy with the parents and make sure of their love for him. In addition, he gradually and increasingly becomes aware of his parents' separateness and realises that in order to remain close to them he must obey their demands. During the oral stage, it seemed to the toddler that the parents understood him even without words, while now, in the anal stage, he senses that he has to strive to make himself intelligible in order for them to understand what he wants. This new fact of life encourages him to improve his verbal communication with others as well.

In this emotional stage the infant experiences weaning and other significant separations, such as from suckling, from his bottle, his diapers, and even his pacifier. Finally, his development reaches a stage where he is ready to separate from home and go off to kindergarten, a new and foreign place where he finds himself without his familiar parents, and with new caregivers and friends as well.

These changes are far from simple, both for the infant and his parents. The toddler's emotional skills—acquired in the oral stage—affect the way he handles new situations and balances his inner requirements with the new demands from his external surroundings.

In general, it is difficult to unravel the unique functioning of each of the emotional systems (narcissism, ego, and object relations), as well as the specific impact of the parental role, life circumstances, or genetic factors. My attempt to separate them is, of course, arbitrary, and is done only for methodological didactic purposes, in order to facilitate a better understanding of normal and pathological development.

# CHAPTER FIVE

# The progress of narcissism in the anal stage

This chapter deals with the processing of the narcissistic immune system during the anal stage, which draws on previous oral memory traces. It is generally assumed that each developmental stage recapitulates those that preceded it, as these memory traces, imprinted on the narcissistic immunologic network, both shape, and are integrated with, ongoing development.

The toddler's improved psychomotor skills, based on greater experience, enrich his narcissistic immunologic network with new "almost-familiar" memory traces involving body motility, mastery of bodily activities, purposeful action, and a sense of power. These memory traces are assembled with, and enhance the oral memory traces of bodily sensations linked to pleasurable vibrations. Constant reverberations from the narcissistic immunologic network of these integrated memory traces in present occurrences facilitate the toddler's coping as he befriends and masters his new experiences, intensifying his pleasure.

## The formation of body self-image

During the oral stage, the baby's sense of his familiar self is usually based on his bodily senses and sensations, which are linked to joyful activities and experiences of pleasure with his parents. Furthermore, the baby's attention is mainly focused on his constant, familiar, pleasurable body senses, rather than upon resisting the occasional appearance of strangeness. We may assume that his sense of the familiar self is formed, consolidated, and refined throughout the lifespan via the endless combinations and permutations of three layers: the narcissistic immunologic network; the reverberations of memory traces, (often reflecting narcissistic ideals) and the juxtaposition and combinations of new and older memory traces, presumably stored in the body/mind in an abstracted and compressed fashion.

In the anal stage, following reverberations from his healthy narcissistic immunologic network of his bodily sensations and activities in his daily experiences, we may observe how the toddler's self-confidence is consolidated These resonances arouse within the toddler the sense of familiarity, and an attraction to instigate and repeat these bodily actions and movements at will (familiarity principle) as he masters and copes with, and even improves upon, his achievements.[1] The toddler is thus inspired to revive his almost new impressions of power and mastery, which tend to boost his confidence in his self-capacities and come to represent his narcissistic ideals.

Narcissistic ideals represent the narcissistic familiarity principle for the preservation of the self-familiarity, which is enriched along the developmental stages: the oral narcissistic ideal represents perfection and the grandiose-self-familiarity, while the anal narcissistic ideal represents powerfulness and omnipotent self-familiarity.[2] Concomitantly, the toddler resists unfamiliar or unpleasurable activities, and at times resonances of negative memory traces may surface and the toddler may feel threatened by failure. Will the toddler remain stuck in the mire of these inner threats, or will he be able to restore his positive (self-familiarity) capacities via his healthy narcissism, pursue his bodily activities and try overcoming the obstacles again?

Jasmine (at two years and ten months) enjoys her physical ability to control her bodily motility while she performs dances in rhythm with the music. When her father joins the dance, she matches her movements to his steps, looking at him from below, and recognising the differences between their bodies. After a few successful attempts, Jasmine falls down, bruises herself, and starts crying. "Can't do, can't do," she screams. She seems to experience this falling as an injury to her body image, and as failure. Her father comforts her and exhorts her to try again. A few minutes later, Jasmine invites her father to dance again and says: "Pappy, I can dance even if I fall down." It seems clear that her body self-familiarity has been restored by her healthy narcissism as a wholeness of coordinated, even though separate limbs. Her self-confidence is also restored by her ego's adaptation mechanism of adjusting and coordinating her movements, and by her father's encouragement (object relations).[3]

The toddler's narcissism is thus constantly mobilised to immunise his enriched self-familiarity and assets against alien intrusions from within or from without, intrusions that may challenge, threaten or even harm his body self-image. Furthermore, as will be elaborated below, the narcissistic immune and restorative processing systems are clearly supported by the body's memory traces and resonances from past occurrences of the parent/s having "enveloped" the infant and encouraged him to overcome his distress. Part of this "overcoming" involves discharging excess nervous energy at the level of the body and its felt sense (Ross, 2008). This is achieved by the child being contained by the parent, who optimally helps him to integrate his experiences by talking to him, explaining what is happening in a few words, and linking the child's self-assets with what he is experiencing. In this sense, we may perceive the narcissistic immune system as one of the psychic envelopes "that holds the budding mind together pending further developments" (Spero, 2009, p. 193). In *Beyond the Pleasure Principle* (Freud, 1920g, pp. 24, 28–29), as Spero reminds us, "Freud describe(s) the way in which the system Pcpt-Cs[4] envelops the other psychic systems, providing a 'primitive superficial layer' and 'special envelope or membrane' that are resistant to noxious stimuli, protecting the developing ego" (p. 201). Following Freud, I consider healthy narcissism as one of the psychic envelopes that serves as an "envelope or membrane" protecting the developing self by integrating the familiar or almost-familiar while being "resistant to noxious stimuli" and to a sense of strangeness.

### Narcissism as an envelope or immunologic membrane

Narcissism, as an envelope or as an immunologic membrane, processes three layers as previously mentioned above:

a. The *narcissistic immunologic network*, consisting of sensorimotor memory traces of past experiences and their attendant sensations, and previous action patterns involving our senses, autonomous nervous system, and body. This includes our personal familiarity with (and history of) "flight or fight" situations, and with (initially adaptive) "freeze" response to trauma, whether physical and/or emotional.[5]

b. *Affective resonances* (often unconsciously, and with bodily referents) of memory traces in response to present occurrences, and an emerging sense of familiarity in coping with new experiences. This often leads to the formation of narcissistic ideals as well as the formation of the familiarity principle.

c. The *juxtaposition* of new, "almost-familiar" memory traces of actual experiences and sensations with the previous ones, and their integration within the narcissistic immunologic network.

Anzieu's (1985) conceptualisation of the ego-skin (*"le moi-peau"*) stresses the contribution of the narcissistic envelope to the secure boundaries of the self, whereas I propose that the narcissistic immune envelope contributes particularly to the consolidation of the sense of the familiar self (i.e., self-familiarity).

As previously noted in Chapter Four, Spero (2009) adds some interesting points to the concept of the psychic envelope (as elaborated by Freud) in his paper: "The joke envelope: A neglected precursor of the psychic envelope". Spero views the joke envelope "as [a] container, serving its most crucial role during early development while remaining a latent element of 'the work of humor' that is central to the pleasure of each and every joke throughout life" (p. 195). He emphasises that psychic envelope attributes, such as "shielding, immunizing, containing, and encapsulating functions, operate throughout the many phases of human development, on ever-increasing levels of symbolization" (ibid., p. 199). "A psychic envelope", Spero claims, "is perpetually involved in two main double or looping functions. On the one hand, it provides a contact barrier and form-giving template that functions within the mind of the individual; on the other hand, it maintains the complex rhythms of binding and differentiating between the self and the selves and other elements it finds in the environment" (p. 198).

I share Spero's view that "jokes and joking symbolically repeat the early rupture and rapture of breathing and self-other differentiation and the internalization of maternal containing and envelopment" (p. 194). Spero's notations accentuate, among other things, the importance of self-other differentiation for the self-protection afforded us by the psychic envelope.

I wish to emphasise that the parents' perception of separateness (already from their baby's birth) serves the toddler as a containing and enveloping foundation for his burgeoning capacity to differentiate between self and others. Furthermore, the parents' respect for and acceptance of the toddler's separateness, is crucial for the improvement of their toddler's innate healthy narcissism processing, and the preservation and consolidation of his self-familiarity throughout development during the anal stage and onwards.

During the oral stage, as elaborated in Chapters Two and Three, the frustration threshold is very low, and the functioning (and survival value) of healthy narcissism, the ego, and the relations with objects are affected by three absolute, primeval principles: the (id) all-or-nothing principle, the (narcissism) familiarity principle (based particularly on sensory memory traces), and the (ego) pleasure principle. These fundamentals produce the oral narcissistic ideals of perfection, upon whose foundations, the formation of oral self-familiarity will be consolidated as an ideal and grandiose self-familiarity.

From the anal stage onward, the toddler's frustration threshold increases—a result of his mastery of psychomotor actions and restraining experiences—accompanied by parental containing and encouraging of separateness. In the wake of this emotional development, the narcissism and ego principles are enhanced and become less absolute. The (enhanced) narcissism thus evolves from a familiarity principle linked to perfection and preserving the grandiose self-familiarity, to a powerfulness-familiarity principle linked to boundaries that preserve the omnipotent self-familiarity. In addition, the enhanced ego was hitherto characterised by the pleasure principle's regulation, which sustained the ego's investment in absolute, albeit short-lived pleasure, the immediate gratification of love and happiness with the libidinal object. Now, the ego regulation becomes linked to the reality principle, which sustains the ego's investment in mastery of, and adaptation to family and societal rules involving the libidinal objects.

The toddler becomes able to invest long-term emotional energy in experiences of controlling his physical-bodily motility, bodily sensations, proprioception, and self-representations, including those of body image. Memory traces of these fundamental experiences provide the essential attributes for the toddler's anal narcissistic ideals of power and mastery. In light of these narcissistic ideals, his memory traces of the bodily mastery experiences are integrated and moulded into a sense of a cohesive body self-image, immunised and restored by the narcissistic processing as positive self-familiarity integrity.

Furthermore, the parents are proud of their child's psychomotor achievements and of his productions. They encourage his creativity and autonomy and are elated by his capacity for mastery and control of his body. Hence, the toddler experiences his bodily actions and achievements as profoundly satisfying, and feels intense delight in jointness with his parents. He enjoys bonding with them and the sense of belonging evokes a sense of being part of a powerful family. Reverberations of these combined memory traces of bodily achievements, together with ongoing parental encouragement in present occurrences, constitute a psychic envelope of the toddler's sense of his familiar self and inner resources. Thus, following the inevitable disillusionment of the child's oral ideal and grandiose self-familiarity, he expands his narcissistic ideals through his healthy narcissism to include powerfulness, mastery, and status, which reward him, and to some extent compensate, for the lost oral perfection.

The anal self-familiarity of body self-image complements oral and anal positive bodily representations, which, in interaction, may also include object and relationship representations. In other words, we (optimally) represent, internalise, and consolidate our sense of the familiar self as being engaged in emotionally charged interactions ("scripts") with others. Resonances of these memory traces in present occurrences inspire the toddler, as well as the adult, to attain bodily control and physical fulfilment (such as when climbing stairs) and attest to his individuation and autonomy, his personal potency, and his place in his family. Hence, we may notice that the toddler often insists: "No, no," or "I want," or "I'll do it by myself," etc., as he attempts to realise his new narcissistic ideals. The toddler becomes capable of "marketing" his psychomotor, cognitive, and emotional intelligence to others through his appearance and his body language.

"Grandpa, look how big I am," says Jasmine (at two-and-a-half years). "For sure," he responds, "you're already a big girl and I'm proud of you." "I'm bigger than you," her brother exclaims, "and I will always be bigger, because I was born before you." Jasmine reacts angrily: "I know, but I'm big," and she bursts into tears, indicating that her self-familiarity representation of being big has been injured. When she manages to come to terms with her self-deficiency in relation to her brother, she becomes able to integrate the data into a continuum.

Thus, she restores her self-familiarity cohesiveness and is again happy to market herself to her grandfather: "Grandpa, my sister is smaller than me, my brother is bigger than me; you are also bigger than me, but I am big now and I'll grow more and be just like you."

The consolidation of body self-familiarity enables the toddler to compare himself with others. Concomitant with his parents' encouragement of his bodily activities and his improved mastery, the toddler may demonstrate pleasure in, and with, his body, love his body image, and feel self-confident and proud. At the same time, as the toddler's body self-image is cathected with the narcissistic ideals of mastery and powerfulness, he becomes vulnerable to criticism, lack of support, and mocking, as well as to a sense of losing control. When triggered, the shame family of affects (Kelly, 2012; Tomkins, 1962, 1963) may attenuate his natural interest and curiosity, as well as his enjoyment and joy of life.

Barak (at two-and-a-half years) discovers new pleasurable experiences of body mastery and body sensuality when he goes down a slide in different positions, or when he crawls through narrow and wide passages. He can sense that his trousers have become too small for him, and he enjoys wearing scary disguises. He seems to like his body and usually wants to take care of it: to brush his teeth, take showers, and avoid dangerous activities. He presumably senses that his parents are proud of him. Barak tries to befriend his growing body by enjoying his wish to resemble his father. Yet he is also often narcissistically injured, for example, by his older brother, who laughs at his attempts at mastery, or even when he has diarrhoea. These injuries sometimes trigger the anxiety of losing control over his body. However, he manages to maintain a sense of integrity with regards to his body image, despite its changes and despite his big brother's insults.

In his analytic session, twenty-five-year-old Ted speaks of his inferiority feelings regarding his body. He is often jealous of men who have a vigorous appearance: "I have a tiny body and I never liked it … I've just remembered a very painful scene in our old home, so I was probably about three years old. I was standing in front of the mirror in my parents' bedroom with my hands on my hips, just like my father used to stand. I felt powerful and secure. I was sure that my pants also had pockets, just like my father's, but when I tried to put my hands inside them I discovered there were no pockets! I can still feel the sharp pain of losing my strength, and my dismay. I screamed,

'Where are my pockets?' I feared my father would taunt me ... My mother found me a suitable belt. I put it on and with my hands on the belt I could feel the power returning to my expanding chest. It was not exactly the same as pockets, but still ... Actually, I really like belts. Only now I understand why."

Like any adult, the toddler obtains new information about his body image (Freud, 1923b), and about his ability or inability to control his body, through his mastery of psychomotor activities and his achievements.

Ella (at two-and-a-half years) says: "Mummy you should know that I can already get dressed by myself." In other words: "I've updated my self-representation and you need to update yours as well."

Furthermore, the toddler becomes aware of, and sensitive or alert to any deviation from his constant body self-image—such as a bodily wound, interoceptive or proprioceptive deficit, pain, illness, or failure—which produces a sense of strangeness within him. He may therefore summon his parents to help him and even pinpoint the source of his distress, and will be motivated to cooperate with the proposed medical treatment.

Jasmine (at almost three years) says to her mother, "Mummy, it hurts in my mouth." It is clear to her that the pain takes place in her own body, as opposed to her mother's. She summons her mother's help to obtain release from her suffering. Her mother looks at Jasmine's open mouth and says: "I will put ointment on your finger and you will put it by yourself exactly on the sore that hurts you, and it will stop hurting." The mother is surprised that Jasmine so readily accepted treating the sore by herself. She is obviously ready to cooperate in the treatment and clearly sees her parents (or a doctor) as a factor that alleviates her pain. Their acknowledgement that something is amiss, their ministrations, and even "pampering", help to restore not only her familiar body self-image despite the injury, but also to recognise that she does not have complete control over her body.

Jane (at almost three years) wears a hat during a trip with her parents. Back home, she goes to the mirror and calls to her mother in astonishment: "Look Mummy, it feels strange. I feel like the hat is still on my head, but I can't see it." The gap between feeling the "attachment" of the hat to the head while at the same time acknowledging that it is missing temporarily undermines her sense of body self-familiarity. As the following example demonstrates, the toddler feels the same attachment toward his diapers.

Ella (at two-and-a-half years) has diarrhoea. On the way to the doctor, Ella asks her mother why she is taking her diaper to the doctor and she proclaims: "It's mine, not to give it to the doctor." When they get to the doctor the mother suggests that Ella put the used diaper in the proper place. Under her own control, Ella is ready to separate from her assets.

Most of us seem to have difficulty adapting to physical changes at any age. Becoming familiar with our new body-appearance takes time; for example, upon losing or gaining weight, modifying one's hair colour or haircut, the appearance of secondary sexual characteristics and voice change in adolescence, and body changes during pregnancy and after delivery. It is particularly difficult to adapt to and accept permanent disabilities due to illness, ageing, or accidents such as paralysis or amputation. But even seemingly mundane or transient injuries, such as fracturing a bone in the leg, may have major consequences; as Oliver Sacks (1987) has eloquently elucidated in his fascinating account of his own uncanny experiences of living through and recovering from a proprioceptive scotoma (blind-spot) secondary to the denervation (and de-afferentiation) that ensued from his injury. Every change of body-self-image familiarity requires the mobilisation of narcissistic immuno-logic processes to restore body image (Solan, 1998b).

Bea, a patient, describes in our psychotherapy session her sensations associated with the start of pregnancy: "My breasts become full. It's pleasant, but it's like they're strange to me. They're not the breasts I know. The nausea drives me crazy and I feel I'm not in control of my body. I know there's a foetus inside me, and I'm really happy getting ready for it, but I still don't feel it, only the side effects. These are alien and confusing feelings." After the birth, her body will change again; the sensation of fullness in her womb will be replaced by emptiness, and she will have to restore her self-familiarity anew, around her new body size.

Morris, a young man, reveals his feelings about his body in an analytic session: "I don't like my body … I react with disgust, just like my mother did, to any sore or wound … My mother told me that she enjoyed feeding, washing and dressing me as a baby. When I reached age two she felt disgusted by my excretions … I know that she was obsessive about cleanliness … My body was as repugnant to her as it is to me."

Steven (at two-and-a-half years) falls, injures himself, and complains that his leg hurts. His mother, for whom any expression of pain instantly evokes panic, is unable to comfort him or help him handle his pain. She reacts by denying it, "It's nothing," she says. In order to please his mother, he allows her alien, anxious reaction and her denial that something has happened to invade his self-familiarity. Hence, he too denies the pain and begins to befriend his limping. When his kindergarten teacher asks him the following day why he is limping and whether something hurts, he replies, "It's nothing." Steven's impaired narcissism detects no further deviations from his body image, such as pain, and his body self-image is restored abnormally as someone who limps.

Parental attitudes toward the toddler's body are crucial for the formation of his body self-familiarity. Encouragement rewards a child's body self-esteem, as described above, while criticism, revulsion, and physical punishment harm his body self-image and may traumatise him. This painful experience may arouse within the toddler a narcissistic sense of being debased or violated, of being unable to protect his body self-space and his privacy. In this case, narcissism is triggered to restore his self-familiarity—so that it associates this now familiar sense of humiliation with a negative body self-image, and a sense of being hated and abused. This process reflects what I have referred to elsewhere (Chapter Three) as *narcissistic autoimmune processing* or pathological narcissism: Steven adopts his limping as part of his self-familiarity, does not resist it, and no longer complains; whereas referring back to the clinical vignette of Morris, we can see that he does not like his body, just like his mother who was repulsed by his excretions.

In this context, the term "autoimmune processing" indicates that the narcissistic restoration of self-familiarity is dictated by the presence of an alien invader, as if this invader were mistakenly deciphered by narcissism as part of one's self-familiarity—as belonging to one's body self-image. Hence, instead of a narcissistic resistance to this alien invasion that triggers strangeness to the true self-familiarity a damaged self-familiarity is restored, under the impact of the outside critic's power. The current sense of the familiar self is thus shaped as negative, repulsive, or humiliated, and the body image may be experienced as dirty (Orbach, 1996, 2007) or dishonourable, with a consequent loss of alertness to bodily dangers (strangeness) from both inside and outside.

One way this may manifest itself is by the person being accident-prone. Another example of pathological narcissism may be that of an abused toddler who learns to experience being beaten as part of his familiar body self. He thus restores his damaged self-familiarity via his (pathological) narcissistic autoimmune response. In parallel, his ego mobilises defence mechanisms, such as identification with the aggressor, and he may later become a parent who beats.

Jason, a father of two boys, is flooded in the analytic session by painful childhood memories: "My father used to hit me with a belt from the time I can remember ... I felt offended, humiliated, and violated ... My body became stiff, like a fossil, a collection of limbs that don't belong to me ... I abandoned my body to my father's beatings but I managed to protect my mind ... With each lash I taunted him inside myself: 'You, the powerful man won't manage to hurt me' ... I decided to consult you when I realised one day that I was capable of hitting my boys, which would mean that my father succeeded in hurting me."

In preserving his true self-familiarity, the infant may come to anticipate his parents' reactions to his bodily activities, whether with affection and encouragement that reward his self-esteem, or with criticism, disappointment, and anxiety that decrease it. Children (from the age of two-and-a-half) often tend to take on these representations of self-esteem as part of their self-familiarity.

Al's father wished for a fearless son; he subjectively experiences any of his little boy's physical difficulties as cowardice. He feels terribly deceived and is unable to acknowledge and encourage his son's capabilities. When Al goes to the park with his father, even though he has the motor ability to climb the ladder and then slide down, he often hears his father's mocking: "Don't you know how to climb? You're such a coward." Al admires his father despite the disdain, and he is too young to understand that his father's insulting behaviour reflects his own emotional problems and his inability to consider Al's separateness. Al tends to think that his father knows better and he (his healthy narcissism) surrenders to his father's criticism. Thus, he does not dare react in response to his father's taunting, so as to preserve his self-familiarity capacity. In this emotional state, Al's healthy narcissism fails to preserve his body self-image abilities, and gradually his father's constant mocking invades Al's self-familiarity, now consolidated as that of a cowardly boy, and Al abstains from mastering physical activities. Rather than developing a sense of mastery and pride, and given his pathological narcissism autoimmune processing, Al's self-familiarity is "restored" (and preserved) over and over as damaged self-familiarity.

Jenny shares with me in her session how upset she was with the way she reacted to her daughter: "On our way home from kindergarten, Annabel told me: 'Today we had a lot of fun. We went crazy and then I fell down and cried.' Although Annabel's message was essentially 'we had a lot of fun' and only afterwards, 'I fell down and cried,' to me it sounded quite the opposite, just as my mother would say: 'Oh, my darling baby what happened to you? Where is it hurting? Show me.' So, when I reacted in a similar way, guess what Annabel replied: 'Mummy, you don't understand. We had fun today!' … I was proud of her and ashamed of myself." Jenny had reacted to destructive memory traces that invaded her (pathological narcissism) and were introjected (ego regulation) within her self-familiarity, for they now reverberated from her narcissistic immunologic network as a script or narrative. Consequently, she was not attentive to her daughter's pleasure and her fun experiences.

In turn, Annabel might have felt a gap or dissonance between her true self-familiarity and representation as a happy girl who wished to share with her mother the fun she had had, and her mother's anxiety, which almost penetrated her. However, it appears (through Jenny's sharing with me her being upset) that Annabel's positive self-familiarity integrity was quickly restored by her healthy narcissism. Probably, with the backing of her mother, who became aware of the destructive impact she had had on her daughter, Annabel resisted her mother's invasion of anxiety. Given Annabel's ego adaptation mechanism, as manifested by her reaction to her mother, it seems that she has internalised her mother's or father's consideration of her separateness and the backing they generally provide her, which constantly consolidates Annabel's healthy narcissism. Hence, Annabel, for her part (her healthy narcissistic immune processing), is not willing to give up her true self, her genuine wish to share pleasure with her mother, and she proclaims spontaneously: "Mummy, you don't understand …"

Maya (in her forties) tells me, with some agitation, in her therapy session: "Yesterday, my daughter Nina (ten years old) complained to me that I'm never really there when she needs me. Is this how she sees me [object representation]? … I wanted to spew her words out of me, to hear her say that she didn't mean it … I love her so much and am always there for her ... How can she see me this way? I'm not like that at all, and this doesn't match our relationship ..." Maya, who is desperately trying to restore her daughter's representations of her, resists her daughter's alien invaders, which she experiences as not being part of her true sense of self-familiarity, and as potentially undermining her self-representation.

Parents are often offended by the representations that their children preserve of them. They wish to restore a presumably better, more benign image, but of course are powerless to change the subjective memory traces that their children carry. But moving forward, their behaviour in the present may form the basis for a new relationship that will possibly offset the weight of the past.

## Three essential periods in the advancement of narcissism in the anal stage

Freud (1905d) coined the terminology used to describe the pre-genital (oral and anal) and genital stages, viewing each psychosexual stage of development as representing the predominant body zone on which the infant focuses his pleasurable/erotic activity.

In the oral stage the baby relates to his mouth and skin as the major body self-familiarity "erotogenic" zone of sensitivity and pleasure. In the anal stage, the toddler relates to the anus as the essential body self-familiarity erotogenic zone. The anal stage can be divided into three phases that describe the progression of narcissism and of the ego.

The first phase, from approximately twelve to eighteen months, is centred on the toddler's physiological maturity and the initiation of toilet training by the parents (see Chapter Six). The toddler discovers pleasurable erotic sensations in the anus as he empties his bowels (of excretions and flatulence). He senses the release of pressure in the abdomen and also the agreeable warmth and dampness in his nappy (the ego's pleasure principle of immediate satisfaction). In this phase, the toddler experiences the diaper that he constantly wears as part of his body self-familiarity and as belonging to his self-space, and he experiences his faeces, excreted into the diaper, as his body's pleasurable products (narcissistic familiarity principle). This is why the toddler regards the parental demand to change his diaper or do his business in the toilet as a narcissistic injury, an invasion, and a "kidnapping" of his anal pleasures.

Following the pleasure of emptying his body, which he controls, the toddler may also experience various anxieties that become juxtaposed with older, oral anxieties. For example, he may experience the anal emptiness as absolute and irreversible, in accordance with the oral all-or-nothing principle, which would elicit the anxiety of the body self-image remaining empty, akin to the oral anxiety of annihilation.

In the second phase, from eighteen months to about two-and-a-half years, the urine and faeces represent for the toddler his self-productions, which his narcissism is triggered to preserve and to resist giving up. If the toddler's separateness is respected, he will enjoy owning his productions and separating from his diaper as he sees fit (and under his control), which may coincide with parental demands. If the toddler is forced to go to the toilet, he may experience a loss of his product—a quasi-physical injury accompanied by the anxiety of loss of control over his body.

In the third phase, from two-and-a-half years onward, the toddler recognises distinct internal and external body self-images. He enjoys the sensation of retaining his productions (excreta) inside and evacuating them outside—an event that he begins to experience as a reward for his mastery of his body. He enjoys his body image and mainly his psychic representation of his belly as being full of assets. He discovers the threshold of his ability to restrain the release of pressure on the belly, that beyond which continence may hurt, and can now enjoy the welcome release.

During this period, the toddler masters new rituals of separation from parts of his body self-image, such as when he flushes the toilet and says, "Bye-bye" to his products. When he experiences such separations, memory traces of a "bye-bye" separation from his parents during the oral stage presumably reverberate within him as familiar.

The toddler thus tries hard to balance his contradictory narcissistic needs: preserving his self-asset products inside so that no one can remove them without his consent, versus handing over his self-assets in order to gain parental approval for his "products" and cooperation. He wants to be regarded as a "big boy", like all the big, powerful people around him. This will raise his self-esteem and compensate him for the loss of productions implied in having to separate from his bodily excretions.

In the anal stage, the toddler begins to draw a narcissistic parallel between ownership of many assets and sensations of power. His ownership is cathected as a symbolic replacement of his body excretions, which at a later stage can account for the narcissistic significance that wealth has for mankind. Possessions, in this sense, indicate one's powerfulness, and the marketing of one's self-assets comes to be valued as expanding one's self-esteem. This symbolisation process represents the origin of possessiveness in the anal stage, of attributing narcissistic meaning to self-belongings, to self-assets, and even to secrets—a symbol of the person's hidden secretions.

Simultaneously, to the extent that the individual experiences possessions and secrets as symbols of self-assets, his narcissistic vulnerability will intensify whenever anyone discovers or reveals his secrets, or touches his possessions without his permission. The child may feel injured, as if his secrets are now out of his control, and he may scream as if his entire body image were being undermined. Later, in the latency stage from age six, he may also feel intense shame or humiliation that his secrets have been disclosed.

Barry, a young father of a little boy, suffers from "emotional constipation". In his analytic sessions he often complains of what he does not have that others do. From his intonation and his associations, I sensed that he was not talking only about jealousy, but rather of something more archaic. After a few months of analysis, he said: "On my way here I wanted to tell you that I feel better, but now on the couch I feel just the opposite … [very long silence]. If I told you that I feel better, even content, I'm sure you would ridicule me that it isn't possible, or you might say I don't need to come any longer. So I keep it secret." After another long silence, I interpret his feelings: "You fear that if you tell me you feel content, I'll snatch it away from you or lose interest in you." Barry responded: "I never reveal that I enjoy anything, not even to my wife. I always say that I have nothing good in life … I guard my pleasure, even my sexual pleasure, as a secret." Nonchalantly, I ask him: "Do you remember anything from your toilet training?" Barry is perplexed by the question and replies: "I don't remember anything, but now that you mention it, I think my mother had a veritable obsession about cleanliness. When she thinks my little boy's diaper is full, she urges Stella, my wife, to change it. Stella is in no rush, saying: 'What are you worried about? I'll change it later. He likes to have the diaper full and damp.' But my mother can't bear even to hear this. I too really can't understand how Stella knows that Jack likes it; he never told her … I imagine that if my mother reacts to Jack like this, she probably used to change my diapers very often …"

I emphasise what he is saying: "It seems, as you said, that your mother's activities were focused on cleanliness and not on pleasure." He replies: "I now remember that my mother once told me that when I was a little boy I used to hide my poo in different places at home and that she would go crazy whenever she discovered it. If Jack were to hide his poo I'm sure Stella would also go crazy … But I don't understand how all of this is connected to my restraint about revealing my enjoyment." I continued: "It's as if your story from early childhood, of hiding your secrets, continues in your present life." Before I'd even finished the sentence, Barry interrupted: "I can't believe my ears. You think that I conceal my pleasure the same way as I hid my poo from my mom? It's not possible!" Barry is perplexed and surprised at the association that he has just acknowledged.

Nancy (at two years and eight months) is already toilet trained, and is comfortable about using the facilities at home and in her kindergarten. She probably perceives these places as a familiar part of her body self-image, as she used to experience her diapers. Nevertheless, outside her home or kindergarten she refuses to use an unfamiliar toilet and will restrain herself for hours. One day she expressed her strangeness anxiety: "Maybe my poo will not find the one I left behind at home." She fears losing her bodily products in a foreign toilet. It is likely that narcissistic alertness to strangeness is combined with the ego's defence mechanisms against being flooded by the anxiety of object loss.

It seems that concealed anal childhood experiences often prevail in the lives of mature adults. Examples include avoidance of using toilets outside the home, even in familiar places, such as the analyst's consulting room; restrained emotional expression or enunciation of words; and taking pleasure in keeping secrets and maintaining professional confidentiality. To these we may add: sensing the fullness of one's belly; collecting objects or any kind of possessiveness symbolising fullness of assets; a tendency to economise or, alternatively, thriftlessness; feelings of mastery, power and omnipotence, or, on the contrary, the feeling that one has nothing; and a sense of emptiness, low body self-image, and low self-esteem.

### The "No, no" child and the narcissistic struggle between the toddler's autonomy and parental authority

The toddler stands up, walks, or runs, and senses his mastery over his body as well as his control over his parents' reactions. He experiences his self-familiarity as filled with power, self-esteem and even omnipotence, and feels that he can do everything alone.

Barak (at two-and-a-half) demonstrates to his father, in their shared space, his new mobility achievements, and his omnipotent power by saying, "Look, I'm sliding" [down the banister]. His terrified father shouts, "Barak stop! You'll fall." Barak is offended and angry, as if his entire body self-image and autonomy were under attack, and he is prepared to mobilise all his narcissistic power to protect his wounded self-familiarity. He responds, "I'm sliding." Now the father's sense of authority, representing *his* self-familiarity, is jeopardised by his little boy's otherness, and he is prepared to mobilise all his narcissistic power to protect his wounded self-familiarity. The father shouts louder: "No. If I say no, you won't do it; don't you dare." "Yes I will," Barak replies. They are both dragged into a situation of having to protect their own injured self-familiarity. They have relinquished the precious proximity of jointness and confront each other in an upsetting battle over separateness, a struggle of narcissism versus narcissism (NvN). Each confronts the otherness of his beloved object, now experienced as a rival and stranger. Both are exhausted and hurt. The confrontation continues until the more mature of the two, the father, manages to grasp the absurdity of the situation, picks up his beloved son, hugs him, and proposes an alternative game. Barak is delighted. The struggle has ended in reconciliation, love, and coping in their shared space. Each has restored his self-familiarity and object-familiarity and has regained his composure.

After some minutes of pleasure, the father decides to separate from their shared jointness space and says: "I have some work to do now my darling. What do you want to do now?" Barak replies, "I'll play with the cars." Each moves to his own self-space and each will elaborate through his memory traces, albeit unconsciously, the struggle of NvN, their reconciliation, and their separation.

Ella (at two years and ten months) is not yet weaned off diapers. One morning before she goes to kindergarten, her father says to her: "Sweetheart, you know what happened—we forgot to buy new diapers and we don't have any at home. What should we do?" Ella immediately replies, "I'll wear underwear." She is happy to go to kindergarten and her father leaves some extra clothes for her in case of a mishap. When her mother comes to fetch her, the teacher tells her that Ella went several times to the toilet. At home, Ella urinates a few times in her underwear, and the toy rabbit she is holding gets wet. It is now clear that her refusal to go to the toilet at home indicates her need to assert her autonomy in the face of parental authority. Her mother decides to avoid a quarrel. Toward the evening, her mother informs Ella that her beloved rabbit (a transitional object) is still wet with her urine and that she cannot take it to bed with her. Her mother is certain that an upheaval will ensue, as her daughter is never prepared to go to sleep without her rabbit. This time, however, Ella says quite calmly: "OK, let's clean and dry him and I'll take my Dora doll to bed now." She is, in fact, conveying to her mother her refusal to submit. This time, however, the mother feels proud of her daughter's assertiveness (ego's adaptation mechanism).

At kindergarten, Ella has no need to enter into a struggle over her narcissistic omnipotence, but at home she needs this NvN struggle for consolidation of her self-autonomy in the face of her parents' authority. A few days later, her mother says to Ella: "My darling, you can choose by yourself to wear new underwear also at home and go to the toilet, or you can wear diapers." Ella chooses to wear the underwear and manages to remain clean the whole day, both at kindergarten and at home.

The anal stage is important for the enhancement of healthy narcissism and ego processing, and the immunisation of individuation and autonomy. The toddler demarcates his autonomous self-familiarity space by saying, "I am," "I am not," "I want," and "No, no." Because of the toddler's narcissistic body self-image illusion that he can do everything by himself, his parents are obliged to set clear limits of what is permitted and what is forbidden. Criticism and eruption of rage on the part of the parent or caregiver are generally experienced as a narcissistic injury, implying that the toddler is incapable of doing what he would like to, or as an ego grievance, implying that the toddler has done something bad.

Following injury, healthy narcissism is triggered to restore the individual's self-familiarity according to the new demarcation of his body self-image, be it in regard to body-size changes, physical abilities, or handicaps. The ego's adaptation mechanisms are mobilised to establish inner boundaries of what one is allowed to do and what is forbidden, representing family rules that do not threaten the toddler's self-autonomy while simultaneously promoting his grasp of the reality principle. The child's self-esteem thus becomes cathected as powerfulness within the bounds of what he is able and permitted to do, and he may also familiarise himself with his parents' limits of tolerance of their NvN struggles and refuse to follow their orders.

At two-and-a-half years, Barak's mother suggests that he come with her to the park. She prepares his clothes and wants to dress him quickly but he immediately reacts: "No, no. I [want to] do it by myself." Again she tries to help but he insists: "No, no, I don't want." He cannot yet completely dress himself, and it takes a long time, but it seems more important for him to demonstrate his autonomy, even at the cost of his mother's anger. Finally his mother says that it is not worthwhile going out. She is offended and exhausted, and reacts with an angry outburst. They are both sucked into the familiar NvN struggle. In the course of these struggles, Barak often exposes the demon of rage in his parents, and their weakness in the face of his stubbornness. When Barak senses that his mother has come to the end of her tether, he approaches her to see if, despite her rage, she is still "there" for him. He says, "Do you love me?" The question immediately soothes his mother. She hugs him, helps him dress, and they go out reconciled—each one's self-familiarity restored, until the next battle.

When the toddler looks at his parents from below, he experiences himself as a dwarf next to Gulliver, even though in his play, fantasy, and imagination his subjective body self-image is that of being far bigger and even more powerful than his elders (an expression of his grandiose self, now loaded with a sense of omnipotence). Whenever the toddler exposes his parents' helplessness he becomes worried that his power-fulness might harm his loved objects, and that he may lose their love, protection, and approval. Thus, as a security net against his imaginary strength, his healthy narcissism restores the image (representation) of his parents as powerful, equivalent to his body self-power, if not more so. He asserts: "My father is stronger than all of us, the strongest in the whole world."

Barak (at almost three), like many children, is unable to conceive that grown-up people were once little children, or that his father was once small. The fact that he has no narcissistic information (memory traces) of his father being small elicits his anxiety of strangeness and he asserts: "Dad was never small like me. He was always big and I'll be big like him." He asks, "Mummy, will I be big like Dad? Can Dad suddenly be little like me?" The next day he suggests doing a show with his father: "I'll be you, the big father, and you'll be my little boy." As they begin the show, Barak is flooded with anxiety that the role swap might actually occur and he stops the game: "No, no, you can't be so little, you're my father!"

The toddler thus oscillates between a sense of self-omnipotence and self-impotence in the face of the Gulliverian authority, and from a sense of control over his parents to a sense of being controlled by them. Gradually, the toddler's healthy narcissism processing immunises and restores his self-familiarity: Belonging to a powerful family compensates for his sense of impotence in the face of authority. Hence, from toddlerhood to adulthood, mastery, power and autonomy constitute a source of anal narcissistic self-familiarity delight, and of ego assertiveness, which, however, may become an addiction to powerfulness, at the cost of reality testing and the suspension of judgment. As the saying goes, "success has gone to his head".

## Sibling rivalry

From the anal stage onward, the toddler becomes very possessive of his self-assets (as symbols of his "self-productions", i.e., his excretions), especially of his place in a powerful family and his parents' love. He is therefore very sensitive to the fact that his parents' love is given also to another, for example, his little sister. In this situation, he is liable to feel narcissistically injured and to be flooded by a sense of betrayal and jealousy, given "the way of life which makes love the center of everything, which looks for all satisfaction in loving and being loved" (Freud, 1930a, p. 82).

Sean (almost three years old) has a new baby sister. Their grandpa wants to take her in his arms and pamper her. Sean reacts immediately with anger and tries to capture his grandfather's attention. Sean is no longer as sure about his grandfather's exclusive love (his self-familiarity asset) as he was before his sister's birth. He is even more jealous when he sees his grandfather or his father playing with his little sister than when his mother or grandmother takes care of her. He feels injured and sad, as if his place of family self-familiarity has been taken away. Sean seems to differentiate between the caring function (mother/grandmother) and the playing function (father/grandfather), so that when he observes his mother having fun with his sister he becomes furious, as if his mother is changing the rules.

Gradually, Sean befriends his sister and even feels affection for her. She is so cute and he is proud to have a sister, especially one that he owns. He associates her with his self-family assets, and thus experiences his family as expanding into a large and vigorous tribe. Belonging to a powerful family compensates for the loss of his unique place, usurped by his sister. Increasingly, Sean invests in her not only as a rival, but as his object, and starts to relate to her as a tiny, separate sister that he has to take care of, be attentive to her likes and dislikes, and, as her strong big brother, protect her. Despite this, his jealousy still resurfaces whenever he senses or sees his parents expressing loving feelings toward her.

Every week, Jasmine (at two years and ten months) and her brothers visit their grandparents. At mealtimes, each has their usual seat at the table, And each is narcissistically attached to this familiar place, recognising it as an extension of body self-place image. One day, Jasmine's mother remains with them at the grandparents' home and, almost instinctively, goes to the familiar place where she used to sit as a child. Jasmine looks at her mother and says angrily: "That's my place!" Her mother quickly grasps what has happened, and with love relinquishes her place to her daughter, and adds gently: "When I was a little girl it was my place." Jasmine does not understand how her mother could have sat there before. She recognises her mother only according to her own memory traces, and any other information triggers strangeness. She thus continues to assert vigorously: "It's my place from always!"[6]

Another time, during a family gathering, Jasmine is sitting on her mother's lap enjoying their proximity. Out of the corner of her eye she notices her father, who is seated some distance away, beckoning her cousin to come to him. Even before the cousin can take a couple of steps, Jasmine leaps off her mother's lap and dashes to sit on her father's knee, in order to protect her place from her cousin's invasion. In the anal stage, the self-familiarity body-place image is still fragile. Consequently, Jasmine experiences her father's invitation to her cousin as a betrayal and as a threat of invasion into their shared space. Sitting on her father's knee, her self-familiarity is restored and she is now willing to participate in a shared game with her cousin and her father, each of them sitting on one of her father's knees. Directed by her healthy narcissism, Jasmine's family self-familiarity is now broadened to include her cousin.

> ... [the] way of life which makes love the center of everything clings
> to the objects belonging to that world and obtains happiness from

an emotional relationship to them … it … holds fast to the original, passionate striving for a positive fulfillment of happiness." He then clarifies, "I am, of course, speaking of the way of life which makes love the center of everything, which looks for all satisfaction in loving and being loved … But this does not dispose of the technique of living based on the value of love as a means to happiness. (Freud, 1930a, p. 82)

Claude, a father of two children, reveals in his analytic session the extent to which he relinquished his place in his nuclear family. He refused to be embraced and kissed, and felt that he was worthless and unlovable. His associations lead him to childhood memories: "I remember two pictures as clearly today as they were more than twenty years ago. In the first, I feel my mother embracing me, her love flowing over my body. I am happy. In the second, I return home from kindergarten with my father. My mother comes towards me. I jump on her gladly and she says: 'We brought home your baby brother.' I remember now that we all looked at him sleeping, a cute baby, and my mother, standing next to me, was really delighted … Even now I sense that she looked at him with the same expression of love that she always looked at me [with] … I'm beginning to recognise the link between my avoidance of hugs and kisses and the feeling that my brother robbed me of my mother's love … I'm aware now that I don't kiss or hug my children, because I'm always afraid that one of them will see me embrace the other with all my love and be jealous … I imagine myself coming home and hugging my daughter. She'll think that something has happened to me … When I visit my mother, will I be able to hug her after all these years? I'm sure I won't. It would be such a strange situation that I wouldn't dare … I long to hug and be hugged … I possibly missed out on my parents' love due to my jealousy … I wonder why I didn't fight for it … Why did I forgo my mother's love? Was it easier for me to give up than to struggle? … It seems to be one of my personality characteristics."

The patient's acknowledgement in analysis—through his associations and reactions to the analyst's interpretations—of the influence of his past experiences in the present is crucial. Admittedly, these insights do not change the memory traces, but they may help the patient be more open to what is happening in the present time, in the here-and-now. It may free him from the dominance of his childhood narratives (such as jealousy), over his other wishes, thereby allowing him to want to be hugged.

Claude, the infant, seems to have been more preoccupied with what his sibling was receiving than what he was being offered. Thus, his insights of anal jealousy evoked the sharp pain of having missed out on the love that was available for him in childhood. Yet changing the familiar habits in the present seems to evoke strangeness. Sometimes, however, the pain of the missing love is so unbearable that the patient remains stuck in his past interpretations, such as: "But my parents really loved my sister and not me." In these circumstances the patient may resist the benefits he could obtain from these very important insights. These insights often evoke further reverberations of associations of a longing for particular expressions of familiar love, which the individual was not aware he had experienced, and now may free his wish to re-experience and bestow on his children and his spouse what he received from his parents, albeit without being aware of it. I end this section by quoting Freud (1930a), who said: "The love which founded the family continues to operate in civilization … it continues to carry on its function of binding together considerable numbers of people, and it does so in a more intensive fashion than can be effected through the interest of work in common" (p. 102).

### The consolidation of healthy narcissistic immunologic processing

Healthy narcissism, which develops in the oral stage (as was elaborated in Chapter Two), may be considered as the innate self's preservation agency, already affecting the foetus in the womb, and safeguarding the baby's familiar sense of self and resisting strangeness. I suggest we view the consolidation of the baby's innate healthy narcissistic processing as the fruition of his involvement with his parents' healthy narcissism. The parental delight with the familiarity they sense emanating from their baby and their joining with him in intimacy—accompanied by their tolerance of his otherness, his separate needs and occasional withdrawal to his self-space, and mainly their encouragement of his separateness—substantiate the parental healthy narcissism.

The individual's here-and-now resonances of these primeval memory traces evoke his sense of familiarity and facilitate coping with his current, actual experience and the resistance of strangeness. Regular experiences that produce frequent resonances with the objects—in both separateness and jointness—consolidate the self-familiarity integrity.

As described above, the toddler is often offended by his parents' restrictions, which he experiences as foreign to his sense of the familiar self, and he tends to resist this invasion of strangeness. I consider the toddler's resistance as a healthy narcissistic reaction, although it may prove difficult for the parents to tolerate. The new frustrations cause the toddler painful narcissistic injury, involving a sense of not being understood or of being rejected, which undermines the cohesiveness of his omnipotent self-familiarity.

Let us examine in detail these occurrences of normal emotional development from the viewpoint of the healthy narcissistic immune system. We may thus consider whether and when the toddler experiences parental restrictions as if they were a foreign "implantation" of antagonistic instructions and scripts invading his body self-familiarity, eliciting the shame family of emotions and threatening his integrity. The toddler (through his healthy narcissism) resists this restrictive sense of strangeness and tends to reject it by frequent explosions of rage toward his caregivers, and, if need be, even tantrums. He thus forcibly drags the parent's healthy narcissism to resist his child's rage, and both erupt in a tiresome, painful struggle of the infant's narcissism versus the parent's. Finally, the toddler withdraws to his self-space, often with his pacifier in his mouth and his transitional object in hand. There, he can process unconsciously or consciously (via narcissism, ego, and object-relations processing) what happened, until his self-familiarity is eventually restored.

The individual in these occurrences has some steps to overcome in order to cope successfully with the "invasion" of parental restrictions. Like a child and parent, siblings or any individuals who dispute each other's views (each believing he is right and the other wrong, and both being susceptible to injury), couples (or team workers) have the same steps to overcome in order to deal successfully with their relationship. First, each expresses his anger toward the other's statements or actions (or lack thereof), and sometimes one (or both) may deny he or she actually heard the other's restrictions. This is followed by disillusionment and mourning of one's omnipotent self-familiarity or of aspects of one's object representations. One may experience the realisation of being a little child manifesting its autonomy upon facing grown-ups and parental authority, or the awareness of one's loneliness when facing the other. This may lead to the recognition of one's capacity to preserve and immunise one's own sense of familiar self despite the injury and the otherness of one's object. It may be necessary to differentiate or separate the restriction from one's self-familiarity and object representations (that is, separation of the object from the self, and differentiation between restrictions and self or object representations) so that the restrictions do not necessarily indicate that the child/adult has been a "bad boy" (or girl) and that his parents no longer love him.

This separation process helps the person rejoin his (or her) libidinal object, symbolise the restrictions as boundaries or rules for his behaviour, and sublimate his rage toward the libidinal object's unwelcome potency. He may thus learn to cope in harmony with his family while undergoing the transition from being an omnipotent infant to one who can master his behaviour and reactions. Finally, the individual's sense of his familiar self is narcissistically restored as positive and omnipotent, or robust (within the accepted rules), as he is better able to immunise his self-familiarity, at the same time coping more successfully with the otherness of his parent or spouse.

This processing of the separation of the self from the object, and then rejoining the object under the umbrella of family rules, allows for:

a. the toddler's narcissistic restoration of his positive omnipotent self-familiarity
b. the (ego) internalisation of his parents' restrictions (an "implantation")
c. their subsequent integration as self-familiarity boundaries
d. his symbolised and sublimated behaviour according to this (ego) internalisation of family rules.

The child is rewarded for his separation and individuation by his increased (narcissistic) self-esteem, confirmation of parental love (object relations encouragement), and experiencing his cathected family as a strong unity (as they now appear in his narcissistic ideals). He can choose to obey the boundaries of authority and feel himself part of this strong family, or dare disobey the authority, feel powerful but possibly guilty, and risk punishment. His self and object representations are integrated into his consolidated positive self-familiarity.

The healthy narcissism of a toddler who is unable to improve upon his inborn differentiation of self from object during his oral stage might, however, not be strengthened in the ways described above. This may occur mainly because of his caregivers' intolerance of his otherness and their imposing of restrictions that tend to evoke a sense of terror, or their pathological narcissistic need to perceive themselves/him as an unseparated oneness or an undifferentiated family ego mass.[7] He risks being invaded by the caregiver's restrictions without the possibility of resisting them, and as a result the toddler may falsify his self-familiarity. Because of the anxiety of abandonment he may also tend to relinquish his autonomy and do his utmost to please his parents. Thus, the restrictions may not be sufficiently internalised; rather, they are merely introjected, and constitute a reminder—a threat of rejection from the oneness. Consequently, the toddler usually feels that he is unable to satisfy his parents who seem to be generally disappointed in him. His self-familiarity is thus narcissistically restored as negative, vulnerable, and damaged.

It is worthwhile, in this regard, to look at the recently published study by Neukom, Corti, Boothe, Boehler and Goetzmann (2012) that examined "the relationships between lung transplant recipients and their unknown, deceased donors". They present interesting patient narratives that "are discussed within a theoretical model of psychical organ integration" and the "psychoanalytic contribution to organ integration and the donor relationship". In reading their essay, I was struck by the similarities between the emotional processes of internalisation of organ transplantation, and the narcissistic processes regarding emotional invasion into self-familiarity, given that both "implantations" originate from an external donor/parent. The healthy narcissistic processing can be elaborated according to the metaphoric similarity with the biological immunologic system's reaction to transplantation of organs. From this vantage point, the parents may be considered as the donor of the restrictions (transplantation organ) and the toddler's memory traces of his experiences of the restrictions may be considered as the recipients of the transplanted organ.

The authors reveal a gradual internalisation of the transplantation, which I find similar to the infant's narcissism and the ego's gradual processing of the internalisation of the parental restrictions—first perceived "as a *foreign body* i.e., as an object separate from the self" (ibid., p. 118). Afterwards, the "transplanted organ is cathected with narcissistic libido and might be perceived as a *transitional object*" (ibid., my italics).

Regarding healthy narcissistic immune processing, I would say that the parental restrictions are primarily perceived as foreign antagonistic instructions—that is to say, as an object separate from the self. Then, afterward, the implanted orders are cathected with narcissistic libido via the sharing of rules in jointness relations in the parent–child's shared space of encountering each other. There, in the shared space, the parents may consider their child's separateness and encourage him to be rewarded for his autonomy. Thus, the instructions may be perceived as transitional phenomena, symbolised as the self-familiarity boundaries and family rules, and sublimated in the toddler on coping with his parents. In this regard I share the authors' view that an adult patient with a mature and intact symbolisation ability, as well the capacity for sublimation, may come to experience both the transplanted organ and the unknown donor as foreign, or as located within a transitional space.

Adult patients with a damaged limb, due say to an accident or a fall, will also be confronted with a myriad of feelings, including a sense of strangeness regarding their own affected limb, which, because of its lack of functionality and/or associated peripheral (or even cortical) processing issues, may lead them to experience it as non-self, as did Oliver Sacks (1987) as per his own account.[8] This may occur both literally (as in the more prevalent left hemi-inattention, where the left side of the visual field and body is not perceived or is neglected until attention is drawn to it, or due to proprioceptive scotoma) and emotionally (as not being part of their body self-familiarity). The fascinating field of clinical neuropsychology and rehabilitation, and the brain-damaged individual's struggle to come to terms with his loss of function and create an updated version of his narcissistic ideals, is too vast to be fully explored here.

From birth and throughout the lifespan, one's healthy narcissistic immunologic network is endlessly enriched by versatile connections of the ingrained memory traces with new, almost-familiar, positive and negative memory traces of one's constant experiences as they occur throughout life. Resonances of memory traces, such as those of blissful moments in intimacy with one's parents in the shared spaces, as well as of separation from them and withdrawal within one's own self-space of separateness (in both the oral and the anal stages), assist the individual in enhancing his perceptions of jointness and separateness along the lifespan, tolerance of the otherness of objects, and attentiveness to the appearance of inner sensations of strangeness.

The reverberations of the memory traces described above may be considered as positive perceptions and representations of the individual's experiences—of his self, his objects, and his relations with them.

Resonances of such positive traces in present experiences stimulate the individual's creativity and achievements and strengthen his self-esteem and communication with others. Actual experiences combined with the echoing of positive memory traces, contribute to shaping self-familiarity, the objects and the patterns of representations of relations, as beneficial, whether in separateness or in jointness. On this foundation, the individual's healthy narcissism manages to immunise the sense of a true familiar self, as well as of a cohesive self-familiarity in accordance with his narcissistic ideals.

However, repeated experiences of strangeness, frustration, disappointment, rejection, abandonment, anxiety, or trauma generally trigger narcissistic injury and are ingrained within the narcissistic immunologic network as negative memory traces. Frequent resonances of negative memory traces may harm self-esteem and may lead to the narcissistic restoration of false self-familiarity of both the objects and the patterns of representations of relations as injuring, threatening, or even destructive. Obviously, the narcissistic immunologic network includes compound positive and negative memory traces. However, the balance between their respective resonances in present occurrences is decisive for the quality of the narcissistic preservative and restorative processing of self-familiarity. When positive narcissistic resonances prevail over negative ones, healthy narcissism seems to leave its mark on the immunisation and restorative processing of self-familiarity in integrity (under the impact of the connecting or life instinct). Frequent narcissistic reverberations of negative memory traces in the present suggest that the self-familiarity cohesiveness may be decomposed (under the impact of the decomposing or death instinct). (See Chapter Three.)

We may understand this emotional dynamic process of the repeated appearance of negative interpretation as a fixation or a reversion from the predominant resonances of the positive connecting memory traces to the prevalence of negative and destructive ones. It seems that under the impact of the decomposing instinct, a regression from ego regulation to the default instinctual discharge of tension may occur. The individual risks exploding in rage, blaming the entire world for his misery, or even, in extreme cases, embarking on a destructive and deadly rampage. Hence, self-familiarity remains vulnerable to injuries each time such an individual is involved in similar occurrences, for example when he senses rejection or criticism, or experiences shame.

The healthy narcissistic multimodal and dynamic process improves and progresses along consecutive emotional developmental stages, and harmony may be achieved among parallel lines of development. This includes the enrichment of the memory traces in the narcissistic immunologic network, the formation of a cohesive self-familiarity, the inspiration derived from object relations, and the enhancing of the ego's adaptation mechanisms.

The advancement of healthy narcissistic processing implies a transition from oral narcissistic ideals of self and perfection of objects in absolutism—via the disillusionment and mourning of the loss of perfection in the following stages—toward the revision and updating of narcissistic ideals.

During the oral stage (from birth to two years), the baby's sense of his familiar self is consolidated as an ideal, grandiose self-familiarity, matching his oral narcissistic ideals of perfection. The baby, via all his senses (including proprioception) is attracted toward familiarity and resists strangeness, according to an absolute sensory and sensual familiarity principle.

Throughout the second, anal stage (from one year to three years), the toddler becomes narcissistically familiar with his psychomotor capacities, experienced as his (psychomotor) body perfection. He is overjoyed, together with his parents, to be able to control his body, his surroundings, his autonomy, and his place in the family. His sense of his familiar self is consolidated as a cohesive omnipotent self-familiarity and body image, perceived as wholeness and self-sufficiency. His omnipotent body self-familiarity matches his anal narcissistic ideals of potency, mastery, and powerfulness, which partly compensate for his disillusionment in the ideal grandiose-self and in perfection. The toddler is attracted toward the increased familiarity of feeling potent and capable, and simultaneously resists strangeness, according to a mastery familiarity principle.

All these signify the improvement of the individual's healthy narcissism and ego functioning, which may be appreciated or "measured" by his self-confidence, his pleasure in, and satisfaction with, his achievements, from his sense of mastery, and even power in separateness and in jointness. In each of the stages a process of disillusionment occurs vis-à-vis one's narcissistic ideals, and vulnerability in the face of narcissistic injuries from the inevitable strangeness, disappointments, offenses, and trauma—all which may elicit explosions of anger and the mourning of lost ideals. Yet, the individual's reconciliation with his objects, his tolerance of their otherness, and his growing awareness of his own imperfections are all gradually consolidated and generate an increased assumption of responsibility for his actions and reactions.

Although beyond the scope of this book, it is parenthetically noted that from the oedipal stage onward, this harmonic combination of healthy narcissism and ego functioning may include superego influences, and from the latency stage onward, the ego ideal's motivations as well. From the oedipal stage, well through the latency stage and adolescence, and up to adulthood, the narcissistic ideals will include representations of gender identity as well as ethical, social, cultural, and sexual values.

Joe comes to his analytic session, rings the clinic bell and discovers that his analyst is not available due to a mistaken entry in her diary. The analyst apologises very sincerely and Joe goes home. Obviously, such occurrences evoke anger, disappointment, frustration, shame, and certainly narcissistic injury, all of which undermine the cohesiveness of the self and trigger the narcissistic, restorative processing of self-familiarity. How will the patient's narcissism deal with such an unsettling or even hurtful occurrence?

At the next session, Joe speaks with emotion: "I was of course upset, even hurt and angry with you when I realised that you were not waiting for me … I had prepared myself for the session, which was important to me, and I felt disappointed. I despised you for this misunderstanding but also was astonished that I could so freely sense my anger … I decided to go to the nearby café and there I found myself speaking with you, a real working through of my feelings, but alone … First, I had to calm myself from my anger. Then I recalled your reaction and I felt how much you were concerned about me and touched by my frustration. I felt that you gave room for my anger; you respected my pain and felt responsible for this 'accident'. You didn't blame me for the error … I have known you for a long time and I recognise that you've never neglected me … I was suddenly even pleased to recognise your imperfections. I felt relieved that after all you are a human being just like me, not perfect at all … I feel I can continue to trust you. I even feel closer to you [restoring the self- and object-familiarity] … I don't know if you remember but once you went on vacation and cancelled our session. During that period my hate overflowed and destroyed everything. I couldn't trust you for a long time. I felt vulnerable to any of your interpretations. I ruined you, myself, and our analysis. Now I can measure the ground I've covered with you since then; the progress I've made."

## Summary

The toddler's healthy narcissism undergoes improvement and advancement by means of a continuous process of disillusionment and mourning of the lost perfection (with the help of a meaningful relationship, or therapy), and by adopting updated narcissistic ideals in attunement with the emotional development stage and the reality principle. At the same time, the toddler's self-familiarity (experienced as a sense of wholeness and integrity) is shaped, narcissistically preserved, immunised, and restored as a cohesive body self-familiarity in accordance with each stage of emotional development.

During the anal stage, the toddler's healthy narcissism is enhanced by a process of familiarising himself with new attributes of his self-familiarity, such as body self-image, body productions, autonomy, and his place in the family. The toddler's psychomotor developmental achievements (ego adaptation mechanisms) are cathected with new narcissistic ideals such as mastery, power, and possessiveness. Along with these narcissistic attributes, the toddler may have an omnipotent sense of his familiar self, experiencing his parents as robust and his family as a powerful unity. Any disparagement of, or threat to, these self-assets evokes sensations of injury, jealousy, disappointment, or betrayal. The toddler demarcates his individuation and initiates constant struggles with his parents regarding his omnipotent autonomy versus his parents' authority, which alternate with reconciliations with them. Through play and fantasy, the toddler cathects his creations and productions with positive narcissistic attributes. He may enjoy willingly giving or bestowing some of his assets to his love-objects, or he may use them for negotiation with his parents. Throughout life, such achievements may be sorely tested, for example in times of physical injury or illness.

## Notes

1. From the latency stage onward, anal stage achievements of body mastery may become an ego ideal (Chasseguet-Smirgel, 1976), such as being a champion sportsman or scientist.

2. Self-familiarity may be preserved as follows: grandiose-self and perfection as the oral narcissistic ideals, and omnipotent-powerful-self as the anal narcissistic ideals. Mainly from the latency stage onward, narcissistic ideals may be combined with ego ideals that represent the ideal goals which the individual's ego is motivated to achieve, or as Freud defines it: "the ego's evaluation of its real achievements" (Freud, 1914c; Laplanche & Pontalis, 1973). Hence, narcissistic ideals are linked to self-familiarity, while ego ideals are linked to motivational achievements.

3. Her sense of body is, of course, greatly dependent on three things: vision, the balance organs (the vestibular system), and proprioceptive integrity.

4. Pcpt-Cs = perception-consciousness. Freud (1920g) used this term to indicate any function of the perception-consciousness system.

5. In this context, see Levine's (2010) invaluable work with post-traumatic stress disorder (PTSD), and trauma in general, as well as that of other Somatic Experiencing® practitioners.

6. This example obviously reminds us of the famous story of Goldilocks and the Three Bears, attributed to Robert Southey (1837).

7. A term coined by Murray Bowen in the context of family therapy in the 1960s.

8. In his remarkable book *A Leg to Stand On*, Sacks (1987), then a middle-aged physician, eloquently describes "the central resonances, so to speak, of a peripheral injury" he sustained while mountain climbing.

# CHAPTER SIX

# Consolidation of the ego

*Ego regulation from the oral to the anal stage*

This chapter deals with the ego's functioning as a mental agency (Freud, 1923b) for emotional regulation. Note that even though we speak of the ego as an agency of personality or self, personality components should not be regarded as bodily organs, but rather as metaphorical descriptions of psychic functions.

The consolidation of the ego during the anal stage draws on the oral parental auxiliary ego. From the topographical point of view, the ego operates as a negotiator between inner-life needs and external reality requirements. From the dynamic point of view, the ego mobilises adaptation mechanisms for adaptation of the self to reality, which throughout life enhances the psychomotor, cognitive, and emotional aspects of psychic intelligence potential. Simultaneously, the ego mobilises defence mechanisms for the protection of the self, to avoid being flooded by unbearable stress and anxiety. From the economic point of view, the ego functions toward maximising the emotional profits and minimising the emotional cost. Already in the 1960s, Bellak, Hurvich and Crawford (1969)[1] developed procedures and rating manuals to assess the ego's adaptive adequacy, as inferred from clinical interviews and psychological evaluations, including psychological testing (e.g., the Thematic Apperception Test (TAT) and the Children's Apperception Test (CAT)). Since then, there have been numerous attempts to assess ego functions and the mental representation of object relations (both quantitatively and qualitatively) via the use of projective testing.

The ego's functioning operates in harmony with innate narcissism processing[2] toward self-preservation. This involves additional principles and the use of more sophisticated mechanisms. During the oral stage, the toddler's rudimentary ego regulates drives and emotions according to the pleasure principle, while the parent serves as an "auxiliary ego" that supports the baby's initial emotional regulation (see Chapter Three). From the anal stage onward, the toddler's psychomotor and physiological capacities become evident, and he is compelled by his parents to restrain his urges for immediate gratification and adapt to and adopt the family's rules of behaviour. Internalisation of these rules gradually leads the ego to regulate drives and emotions according to a second principle as well—the reality principle.

## Diaper weaning as a pivotal stage in the consolidation of the ego

Diaper weaning represents a crucial achievement of the anal stage, the impact of which is reflected in the progress of narcissism (see Chapter Five), improvement in object relations (see Chapter Seven), and the consolidation of the ego. From the ego's perspective, we may divide these processes into three periods.

### First period—from approximately twelve to eighteen months

At around this age, the toddler, with the encouragement of his parents, begins to master his body motility and sphincters. However, he experiences his parents' demand to replace his "heavy" diaper with a "clean" one, or to urinate and defecate in the toilet, as an assault on his body self-image and his separateness. These new requirements trigger conflicts of interest between the toddler and his parents: the toddler wishes to enjoy his body self-image "production" in his diaper (familiarity and pleasure principles), while his parents request separation from his diaper or that he restrain evacuation until he gets to the toilet. These demands imply the need to forego many of his familiar and pleasant feelings (described in Chapter Five).

Derek (at fifteen months) resists any cajoling on his mother's part to change his diaper. His mother, a very pedantic woman, is helpless in the face of his resistance. She cannot comprehend the conflicts of interest between them, and asserts, "We'll all become ill because of him ... ."

## Second period—from eighteen months to about two-and-a-half

The toddler becomes aware, for the first time, that he has the power to deliver his productions by means of his body, and to restrain their evacuation or deliver them at will.

Natalie's physical maturation enables her (at two years and four months) to control her sphincters. Therefore, if she wants to (ego regulation) she can deliver her bodily products to her parents, cause them to be proud of her, and even obtain new underwear each time she succeeds in going to the toilet. She may also restrain herself and control and guard her products inside her body, or in the diaper, which irritates her parents. In both scenarios, Natalie feels that she controls her parents' mood. Although her mother sometimes forces Natalie to change her diaper against her will, she senses at other times that she should submit to her parents' authority and even enjoy the new physical sensations that accompany a clean and soft diaper. Yet, she is anxious as to where her products disappear, and worries whether she will have more products the following day.

Steven's mother (at eighteen months) would often "kidnap" his bodily products, even forcibly, by replacing his diaper at the moment she sensed he had defecated. Ultimately, he yields to her demands, is weaned early from his diaper (at eight months), and, like a "well-trained pet", goes to the toilet at her insistence, as a defence against his anxiety of abandonment. Steven does not express pleasure with his "productivity" or mastery; rather, as a displacement of his mother's kidnapping, he often manifests suspiciousness that his siblings might steal his asset-toys from him.

Barak (at two years and five months) loves flushing the toilet. His mother promises him that whenever he uses it to dispose of his body waste, he can flush the toilet. Barak restrains his wish to hold on to his productivity (narcissistic preservation of self-assets) in order to benefit by flushing the toilet, thereby experiencing his mastery after separating from his products (adaptation mechanisms).

### The third anal phase—from two-and-a-half years onward

Here, the process of diaper weaning is usually concluded—a central step in the toddler's emotional progress. He demonstrates his mastery of his body self-image by his restraint and by evacuating like all the other grown-ups who accept the family rules. He is thus rewarded with his parents' love and pride, and his self-esteem is enhanced, which helps him to choose separation from his self-products. Henceforth, it is in his own interest to assume responsibility for his body self-image. This no longer has anything to do with his parents' demands, and he may feel a sense of shame if he makes a "mistake".

Natalie (at two years and eight months) controls the rhythm of her emptying of her bowels every morning. She enjoys sensing and watching the faeces descend into the toilet, hears them drop, smells them, and separates from them by saying with certainty, "Tomorrow I'll have more." Natalie is signalling that her cyclical perception of her changing body image is constant: a feeling of fullness, emptiness, and, again, fullness. Four months later (at the beginning of the oedipal stage), her mother hears her speaking in the bathroom to her dolls: "I just gave birth to three babies and tomorrow I'll have more babies." Some weeks later she asks her mother: "Are real babies also born like my kaki?" (Natalie demonstrates normal and ongoing emotional development along the oral, anal, and oedipal stages).

As cyclical perception consolidates, each toddler develops a series of rituals by means of which he masters his separation from his bodily products. Diaper weaning may reflect one of the main internal conflicts from the anal stage onward (surfacing even in couplehood)—whether to hand over or retain, obtain immediate satisfaction or gain long-term partial satisfaction—as well as an external conflict of whether to obey one's objects or resist them, to struggle or to reconcile. Diaper weaning may also be considered as the source of ambivalence (Freud, 1905d).

### Long-term partial satisfaction

In the face of the above conflicts, new processes of regulation are created through which the toddler may obtain satisfaction: full satisfaction according to the (oral) pleasure principle or partial satisfaction according to the (anal) reality principle. Resonance of full or partial satisfaction triggers the individual's wish for fulfilment in the present time. This activates his (ego) adaptation mechanisms to invest his emotional energy (his drives and emotions) accordingly, so as to reproduce his wished-for satisfaction.

From the anal stage, following diaper weaning and the consolidation of the ego, the toddler's (ego) investment of emotional-psychic energy may henceforth be directed in a calculated and economic manner, which implies maximising the profits, such as rewards, and minimising the costs, such as frustration and injury.

In the course of normal anal emotional development, throughout the day the individual's ego manages sufficiently well to mobilise a vast number of refined adaptation mechanisms. This ego regulation enables him to gain long-term partial satisfaction, such as management, negotiation, and bargaining with the objects with respect to "giving" his "belongings" or receiving others (in accordance with their rules/reality principle). This implies restraining his ever-present urge for immediate drive satisfaction followed by bolstering his self-esteem due to his expanded capacity to delay satisfaction and his improved tolerance threshold, which was very low during the oral stage, and from now on increases.

Concomitantly, within limits, the toddler may enjoy the increasing tension level, which elicits both a sense of self-control and of parental approval. He may thus gain the long-term benefits of partial satisfaction, such as power, mastery, love, and various significant rewards, despite the cost of missing out on something or feeling hurt or frustrated. In this sense I fully agree with Baumeister, Vohs and Tice (2007) who consider self-control as "a central function of the self and an important key to success in life" (p. 351).[3] The toddler may also grasp any opportunity for full satisfaction with his objects according to the (oral) pleasure principle, enjoying the reduction of tension to the constant familiar level, which evokes immediate pleasure, well-being, blissful moments, and happiness.

Along the lifespan, a broad range of partial satisfactions may be experienced as emotionally enjoyable, long-lasting phenomena during tension arousal (now modulated by self-control), although the wish to achieve the full satisfaction never vanishes. For example, some toddlers obtain greater enjoyment from preparing games with cars or dolls, and from the feeling of controlling their imagination, than from the actual performance of the game. Yet, the wish for the delayed reward as full satisfaction nurtures their preparation, their imagination, their emotional and cognitive intelligence, as well as their fun, which become more intense. These long-lasting phenomena of satisfaction on the path to full satisfaction are defined as partial satisfactions and result in enhanced self-familiarity as well as improved self-confidence, self-control, self-esteem, and autonomy. We may notice that these enhanced long-term partial satisfactions provide the foundation for the capacity for long-term love relations, as well as for long-term invest-ments in creativity and work, which may give rise to the emergence of happiness.

Barak (at almost three) says: "Grandma, I really like your dessert. Put it on the table. I won't eat it now. I'll keep it for after the meal and then I'll eat it very, very slowly to keep the taste for a long time [Imagi-nation and mindfulness of the enduring taste]."

Because the toddler has not yet achieved a perception of time, he plans his activities according to perceptions of constancy and cyclical-ity, such as, "after kindergarten". Barak says to his father: "If I'm good will you take me to the football game after kindergarten?" or "Mummy, the teacher [in kindergarten] said it's Wednesday, so we're going to go to grandma's and have fun."

The toddler may gain partial satisfaction through emotional chan-nels when he endears himself to his objects, captures their attention, and engenders a response that encourages his achievements: "I love you Mummy; look what I've made for you."

### Ego regulation of drives and emotions

The toddler's vital, normal, anal ego-regulation is focused on the mingling of libido and aggression, as well as of love and hate together into constructive potential (see Chapter Three), its creative or positive energy significantly intensified. We may also stress that the consoli-dated ego mobilises more adaptation than defence mechanisms.

The toddler can thus preserve his love for his objects while regu-lating aggression toward them in the face of frustration. One of the essential signs of the consolidation of the ego in the anal stage is the individual's capacity to refrain from immediately erupting into aggres-sion in the face of otherness and frustration. He may thus obtain some long-term benefits (partial satisfaction), such as retaining mastery, expressing his anger verbally, and being able to negotiate and reconcile with his frustrating objects. Consequently, his positive self-familiarity, positive object representations, and positive relations with his objects are enriched—pride overrides shame (Nathanson, 1992). Such beneficial experiences consolidate the toddler's ego maintenance of a mostly balanced libido/aggression fusion, while the positive libidinal energy prevails over the destructive aggressive energy. Consequently, the toddler's motivation to assume responsibility for his body, his behaviour, and his love relationships with others increases.

Freud emphasised the regulation of sexual instincts in a similar conceptualisation to the above-mentioned regulation of aggression and its importance regarding the capacity to love:

> In one class of cases being in love is nothing more than object-cathexis on the part of the sexual instincts with a view to directly sexual satisfaction, a cathexis which expires, moreover, when this aim has been reached; this is what is called common, sensual love ... the revival of the need which had just expired ... and this must no doubt have been the first motive for directing a lasting cathexis upon the sexual object and for 'loving' it in the passionless intervals as well. To this must be added another factor derived from the very remarkable course of development which is pursued by the erotic life of man. (Freud, 1920g, 1921c, p. 111)

Freud describes how the child (at five years of age) has found the first object for his love in one of his parents. Yet, due to repression which "compels him to renounce the greater number of these infantile sexual aims ... the child still remains tied to his parents, but by instincts which must be described as being 'inhibited in their aim.' The emotions which he feels henceforward towards these objects of his love are characterized as 'affectionate'" (p. 111). Freud proclaims that: "if the sensual impulses are more or less effectively repressed or set aside, the illusion is produced that the object has come to be sensually loved," free from criticism, and highly valued. "The tendency which falsifies judgment in this respect is that of idealization" (p. 112).

Subsequently, he notes that:

> It is interesting to see that it is precisely those sexual impulses that are inhibited in their aims which achieve such lasting ties between people ... It is the fate of sensual love to become extinguished when

it is satisfied; for it to be able to last, it must from the beginning be mixed with purely affectionate components. (ibid., p. 115)

Ella (at two years and four months) is yelling at her brother Leo (age six) who refuses to play with her: "I'm not your friend, not your friend!" Leo responds in a positive tone: "But I'll be always your brother." When Leo was her age, he sometimes shouted at his mother when she frustrated him: "I'm cross; I don't love you." His mother would respond with the same positive tone: "But I'll always love you and will always be your mother." The mother's response appears to have been imprinted in her son's narcissism as memory traces, and subsequently internalised and integrated as part of his consolidated ego regulation. We can imagine the mother brimming with pleasure and pride upon hearing her son reacting in harmony with her ego regulation, and her satisfying feeling of continuity with her children.

Freud also observes that "Traits of humility, of the limitation of narcissism, and of self-injury occur in every case of being in love; in the extreme case they are merely intensified, and as a result of the withdrawal of the sensual claims they remain in solitary supremacy. This happens especially easily with love that is unhappy and cannot be satisfied" (1921c, p. 113). In the wake of these injuries and frustrations, the mingling of drives and emotions may easily be defused.

The immediate defusing of drives facing injury and frustration indicates the instinctual power of the id's decomposing destructiveness, which prevails over the ego function of rebinding this antagonistic energy. This means that it is far easier to erupt in aggression or disrupt relations—according to the absolute oral principles of familiarity/ strangeness, pleasure/unpleasure, and all-or-nothing—than to reconcile, restore and reconstruct them. When aggression is split off from the mingling with the libido, it colours the toddler's emotional energy with negative manifestations, such as painful, if short-lived, feelings of shame, aggressive outbursts, and destructiveness. While not necessarily directed at the object, this aggression or wrath may nevertheless explode on the object or the relationship, or be turned against the self.

The toddler's aggressive eruptions and negative affects following frustrating, injuring, or traumatic occurrences colour his experiences with his objects, through which his negative self, object, and relations representations are established. Its particular nuances are a function of the unique mix of negative and positive affects available at that time in that situation (see Tomkins, 1962, 1963). The ability to fuse and remingle drives and emotions (both positive and negative) for adaptation purposes indicates the progressive compatibility of the individual's ego as a personality agency. Rosenfeld (1971) further introduced the concept of "pathological fusion" distinguishing between normal and pathological fusion of energy. He claimed that pathological fusion is "where in the mixing of libidinal and destructive impulses the power of the destructive impulses is greatly strengthened, while in normal fusion the destructive energy is mitigated or neutralized" (p. 172). Perhaps the degree of one's shame sensitivity (Kelly, 2012) determines this.

According to Kelly, "all of us are vulnerable to shame, need at times to defend against it, and therefore routinely exhibit some degree of Compass of Shame defensive behaviors" (p. 95). These include what Nathanson (1992) has described as: attack other, attack self, withdrawal (hide from other), or avoidance (hide from self).

We may notice that when the toddler's ego is consolidated, shortly after the injury he will manage to remingle and rebalance the normal fusion. Hence, the constructive energy, as it intensifies, overcomes the destructive impulses in the mingling energy. Following such constant destabilisation of the emotional state, the toddler's narcissism may consolidate and/or restore his self-familiarity according to the negative representations and self-destructiveness, which point to the pathologic processing of narcissism. At the same time, we may observe the ego's mobilising of predominantly defence mechanisms and developing disturbing relations with the toddler's objects.

Ego regulation attempts to mediate among the various demands from within (physiological, narcissistic, emotional, and drive-related) and from outside (reality and family rules). The toddler's ego mediates also between love and anger, imagination and action, permitted and forbidden, and possessiveness and giving. In normal anal ego regulation development, the toddler is able to resist and alternatively obey his parents' demands, negotiate with them and manifest his individuation and autonomy. He may withstand their anger but yield to their reconciliation efforts and maintain jointness relations with them—at the same time preserving his true self-familiarity separateness and respecting his parents' authority.

Harold (at five years) generally behaves politely in accordance with his subjective reality principle. He says, "thank you," "please," "sorry," and "excuse me," while at the same time he experiences "the brat" within himself. As he explains to me in his session: "It's not me who's the bad boy; it's a bad stranger who jumps out of me." Still, he is afraid that his father may discover his "brat" and punish him.

## Anal symptoms connected to diaper weaning

Under internal or external pressure, the ego might, either briefly or for a longer period, fail to re-establish the mingling of drives and emotions following defusing, as described above. When this mixture of drives and emotions is dominated by destructive power, such as aggression and hate, and the libidinal energy is not sufficiently developed, this may evoke anxiety of loss of self-control. In this emotional state, the ego is alerted to mobilise defence mechanisms and sometimes even to create anal symptoms.

Excessive withholding, constipation, enuresis, and encopresis are among the frequent somatic symptoms originating in the anal stage. These somatic symptoms are often unconsciously and temporarily produced as passive-aggressive resistance symptoms (defence mechanisms) to parental weaning requests. Yet, these almost-normal anal symptoms may propel the toddler toward persistent pathological symptoms.

Alma (at two years and eight months) unconsciously imposes a passive-aggressive pattern of relations on her mother. She becomes constipated, feels herself "filled" with power and in full mastery over her body, while her mother becomes increasingly anxious about her. Ostensibly, Alma cannot be blamed for being aggressive toward her mother—after all, it is she who is suffering from constipation. After three days of constipation her mother consulted me. From her presentation of Alma (whom I did not meet), it seemed to me that she had good-enough immunisation of her body self-image (the operation of healthy narcissism), but insufficient regulation of her aggression (ego function). I presumed that the somatic symptom would lose its impact, and that Alma might spontaneously recover from the symptom if her parents were able to desist from the power struggle with her. Hence, I reassured the mother by supporting her concern and instructing her not to urge Alma to go to the toilet or give her any laxative medication, even though the mother expected me to recommend the latter. Rather, I suggested that she encourage Alma's individuation, and reward her autonomous behaviour and her capacity for mastery wherever possible. By the fifth day of being constipated (two days after the consultation), and in full command of her body, Alma told her mother that she was going to the toilet to try to relieve herself. She chose to inform her mother of her decision just as the mother was about to leave home to do her chores. The mother felt compelled to wait until Alma hopefully relieved herself. Once again, Alma had controlled their passive-aggressive relations. Her constipation, however, stopped, and both of them felt much better.

Steven's (at two years and ten months) emotional state is very different from Alma's. Since the oral stage, he has been suffering from anxiety of abandonment. In addition, during his anal stage he suffers from anxiety of abandoning parts of his body self-image, of losing his body productions and of remaining empty forever. Against such anxiety, Steven's ego also mobilises a symptomatic defence of constipation, but although it resembles Alma's constipation as a symptom, it differs significantly. Alma's symptom represents mainly a passive-aggressive act that she has control over, while Steven's symptom is directed mainly against his anxiety of losing control, of being robbed—a symptom he cannot control.

The physician instructed Steven's mother to treat him with laxative suppositories and enemas in order to release the constipation. In the wake of the treatment, Steven feels his body emptying without his control, and is flooded by anxiety that someone has penetrated him and removed his body parts. He sinks into seclusion, his pacifier in his mouth, refuses to play, eat, or cooperate with his parents, and his constipation symptom remains unrelieved.

Nora, a twenty-year-old student, realises, to her surprise, that even though she wants to share her pain with me, she finds herself trapped in the same communication difficulties she has with other people, which causes her to suffer. She remains silent for hours on end. She experiences any attempt on my part to alleviate her suffering as penetration, and screams: "I can't talk, don't you understand. You'll never be able to take anything from me." After several months of psychotherapy, she is able to express her anxiety: "When I suffered from constipation, my mother used to take me to a doctor who treated me with an enema. I hated it … As long as I keep myself from speaking I feel strong … No one will remove the secrets from my head." Given this childhood experience, it seems likely that Nora transferred on to me her anxiety of being penetrated (i.e., treatment as enema). I waited patiently while silently reflecting on the resemblance between physical constipation and emotional constipation, and on the resemblance between the words "secret" and "secretion".

The toddler has a sense of mastery over his secrets—something he can hold inside, which nobody can remove without his permission. In other words, he has symbolised his secretion and sublimated his excretion. The ability to have and keep secrets is an extremely important element in raising self-esteem and may even assist in establishing a solid foundation for the anal adaptation mechanism of internalisation, which is so significant for the consolidation of ego functioning (see the section on adaptation mechanisms). Having or keeping a secret of one's own is loaded with values of strength and fullness that replace constipation, whereas revealing it—beyond the bounds of the toddler's subjective reality principle—implies weakness, shame, and loss of loyalty. Unfortunately, when caregivers miss this significance of keeping secrets they risk reacting negatively to the toddler's need to keep a secret, and blame him for being a liar, which may actually lead the infant to represent himself as a liar.

## Ego economic regulation of choices and decisions

From the anal stage onward, the individual's ego and its principles of emotional regulation have a significant impact on his choices and decisions. (This impact may even be reflected in financial behaviour.) The individual's choices of where to place his emotional investments are based on his subjective, often unconscious, resonances of memory traces. His choice expresses the probability of maximum emotional benefit (immediate or long-term satisfaction), at the lowest cost in terms of injury, frustration, loss, or anxiety. This is why I have chosen to analyse adaptation and defence mechanisms according to their costs and benefits (see Chapter Three).

Since the 1990s, advances in behavioural economic science have helped us to better understand what triggers people's choices and decisions, and why and when people prefer immediate satisfaction to long-term gains. Prospect Theory advances a cognitive psychological perspective, according to which people tend to estimate the probability of profits or losses rather than evaluating the final product. This approach is also reflected in their financial decisions (Kahneman & Tversky, 1979). People often make quick decisions according to their last transactional results, accompanied by the belief that the current situation will continue forever (Kahneman, 2009a, b).

The emotional finance view (Tuckett, 2011) focuses on decision making as "an ongoing and major emotional experience because outcomes are fundamentally uncertain" (p. 187). This approach underscores the impact of emotions—of dynamic unconscious needs, ambivalence, fears, and uncertainty—on investment decisions and motivation for investor behaviour.

My approach to both emotional and fiscal behaviour draws on a narcissistic perspective and on the ego's economic function. Making decisions may be unconsciously influenced by the individual's narcissistic immune processing, which causes him to repeat a familiar decision, perhaps a minor deviation from the familiar, as if it were the safe one, and to resist subjective major differences that evoke strangeness and the unknown.

Economists and neuro-economists have begun to examine people's financial investments from a cognitive psychology perspective. They identified the areas of the brain that are involved in decision making, such as the prefrontal cortex and the limbic system, a relatively primitive brain area situated in the depths of the brain, which, amongst other functions, is concerned with feelings such as gratification, fear, and anger.

Neuro-economists (McClure, Laibson, Loewenstein & Cohen, 2004) claim that: "Choices [that] involve an opportunity for near-term reward, are associated with limbic and paralimbic cortical structures, known to be rich in dopaminergic innervation. These structures have consistently been implicated in impulsive behaviour" (p. 506).

> The limbic system ... responds preferentially to immediate rewards and is less sensitive to the value of future rewards, whereas long-run patience is mediated by the lateral prefrontal cortex and associated structures, which are able to evaluate trade-offs between abstract rewards, including rewards in the more distant future. (ibid., p. 504)

I suggest that oral characterisations, such as the demand for immediate and full satisfaction and a tendency for aggressive outbursts in the wake of injury, loss, and frustration may be reflected in the functioning of the limbic system, while anal characterisations such as retaining and searching for long-term profits (representing partial satisfaction), may be reflected in that of the prefrontal cortex. It would be interesting to test this hypothesis with the aid of neuro-imaging techniques such as positron-emission tomography (PET) and functional magnetic resonance imaging (fMRI).

These researchers again highlight the parallel processes that exist between biological and emotional systems. This resonates with Freud's (1950 [1887–1902]) dream of discovering a scientific psychology, of finding a biological and neuropsychological explanation for emotional processes and of revealing mental processes as linked to the physiological and biochemical activity that occurs in the brain. This dream was further elaborated by Kandel (2006), a physician and neuroscientist interested in psychoanalysis and neuropsychiatry. He went on to win the Nobel Prize in Physiology or Medicine, having patiently struggled to understand the biology of mind by looking at the brain "one cell at a time" in both cellular and molecular biological terms. This approach yielded valuable insights into both animal and human models of functioning in the areas of learning and memory.

We may characterise the ego's economic regulation through the perspective of decision processes: individuals who are able to (narcissistically) preserve their self-familiarity and assets, and who can enjoy owning their possessions as well as partnership with their objects (in jointness-separateness relations), might be interested and more content with their lot, rather than with what they have lost or otherwise lack. They therefore might base their ego decisions more on the probability of future long-term profits rather than of losses, and on long-term partial satisfaction and evaluation of final production. For example, a conservative "buy-and-hold" strategy of gradually building a diverse investment portfolio maintained by periodic "tweaking" might be selected (Wild, 2009).

Individuals who are unable to narcissistically preserve their self-familiarity assets, who are always discontent and bemoan what they have missed or lost—influenced by their anal narcissistic injury or trauma to their body self-image, and object-relations experiences of losing their possessions (objects)—may base their ego decisions more on the probability of losses and on short-term full satisfaction. This might result in a bias toward growth rather than value stocks, or perhaps in an active, more aggressive approach involving greater risk in order to obtain greater rewards.

Social psychologist Roy Baumeister (e.g., Baumeister, Vohs & Tice, 2007) has spent his career studying the effects of decision-making on individuals, and has created a paradigm relating decision-making to psychological energy. Stemming from Freudian theory, Baumeister describes a store of psychic energy that can be dedicated to the complex process of decision-making. Each decision that is made depletes that energy store until the individual eventually suffers from what Baumeister terms "decision fatigue". There is physical evidence that we succumb to immediate gratification when we become mentally fatigued, rather than continue to rely on our higher-functioning cognitive centres. For example, as many people who have gone on a diet to lose weight have discovered, it is easier to succumb to the wish for comfort food at night, when tired.

## Adaptation mechanisms in the anal stage

This section considers some of the important adaptation mechanisms that emerge in the anal stage and provide the foundation for the development of intelligence.

### Internalisation, the reality principle, mastery and executive functioning

Internalisation may be conceived as the ego's psychological absorption, digestion, and integration of the inputs from the outside into the inside, providing "building blocks" for the rudimentary ego and the foundation for its consolidation. The process of internalisation thus requires the complementary processes of assimilation (absorption and digestion) and accommodation (integration), concepts that were elaborated by Piaget (1936). Greenspan has described the involvement of these processes in the "external boundary" (1979), that is, the organisation of experience that relates "more (or less) to the impersonal, often inanimate world" (p. 129), and proceeds to apply them to the "internal boundary," that is, "organizations of experience which relate more (or less) with the stimulus world connected to drives, wishes, feelings, internal representations, and affectively colored human relationships" (ibid.). As Greenspan takes care to point out, these boundary concepts should not be taken literally, but rather as a shorthand simplification.

The baby's parental "auxiliary ego" is imprinted from birth in the baby's narcissistic network as memory traces, some of which are integrated in the anal stage as inputs within his ego. For example, every evening, Jasmine's parents remind her to brush her teeth and she obeys accordingly. One day, she says: "When can I decide by myself? I want to brush my teeth before you read me the story." From that day onward, no one had to remind Jasmine to brush her teeth. It had been internalised as part of her ego; she owns it and decides for herself when to do it.

In my view, internalisation as an anal adaptation mechanism is enhanced on the basis of the oral adaptation mechanisms of incorporation[4] and introjection,[5] and by reverberations of narcissistic memory traces. These mechanisms prepare the groundwork for the adaptation mechanism of identification that is mobilised in the oedipal stage. This implies that processes of internalisation recapitulate previous gains and reflect their further elaboration (e.g., differentiation) throughout development. One may visualise development as an upwardly progressing spiral, where each consecutive loop (stage) recapitulates the previous but is organised in a more differentiated and integrated fashion (Shidlo, personal communication, 15 January 2013).

Internalisation of the parental auxiliary ego and authority serves as a subjective basis for another beneficial adaptation mechanism coined by Freud (1911b) as the "reality principle", which in turn is formed from the oral "pleasure principle" (see Chapter Three). "… in so far as it [the reality principle] succeeds in establishing its dominance as a regulatory principle, the search for satisfaction does not take the most direct routes but instead makes detours and postpones the attainment of its goal according to the conditions imposed by the outside world" (Laplanche & Pontalis, 1973, p. 379).

With improvements in the toddler's physiological ability to control his sphincters, he becomes capable of retention and restraining his immediate need for satisfaction—according to the pleasure principle—and of postponing it to a more appropriate time according to the new principle—the reality principle. This implies that the urge for pleasure is preserved despite its delayed realisation.

The reality principle defines the family rules as subjective guidelines for the toddler's behaviour, namely tangible self-boundaries to his pleasure principle that represent the permissible and forbidden activities. By behaving according to this principle, the toddler is able to attain maximum long-term satisfaction (partial satisfactions) in his individuation as well as in his relations with his surrounding objects with minimum frustrations. In subsequent developmental stages, these guidelines become refined as social, cultural, ethical, and moral values.

As the toddler in the anal stage cannot yet reflect on the logic underlying the rules he has internalised, he is constantly engaged in testing the limits imposed on him by his parents' authority. He monitors the consistency and constancy of their boundaries, seeing how far he can go and whether his parents have "fallen asleep on the job" of enforcing their limits.

The family rules might thus be internalised, or "digested", thereby becoming an integral part of the ego's function of integrating boundaries of self-familiarity into the formation of the subjective reality principle. In other words, the toddler starts to acquire self-discipline in response to the family's constant stressing of clear boundaries and rules.

Like the toddler, domestic animals also behave according to a subjective reality principle that spares them from reprimands. Our Irish setter was educated not to enter the bedrooms, but, like a toddler, he tried to be smart and examine the limits of the permissible and the forbidden (indicating an internalisation of rules, not a result of taming). Whenever the family was gathered in one of our bedrooms, the dog would place himself outside the room and begin to edge his way inside, but keeping his head facing out of the room. In this way, according to his subjective reality principle, the dog stopped at the permitted border, but also revealed a sophisticated grasp of the situation—his rear in the forbidden zone inside, but his head, which represents the knowledge of rules, outside in the permitted area. It was, of course, impossible not to laugh at his "wisdom" and accept it, just as we do with toddlers in these situations. Nevertheless, similar unscrupulous behaviour by an adult is not funny at all, such as in the case of drivers facing a no-entry sign who enter the road in reverse, opposite to the direction of the permitted traffic movement.

Jane (at two and four months) almost touches an electricity socket, and then points to it and asserts, "No, no, no!" in accord with her subjective reality principle. However, when Jane gently touches her baby brother who is sleeping, she hears her mother saying, "Jane, don't touch." Jane starts crying, "I love him and you say no!" Jane does not yet understand why, if she feels so affectionate toward him, she cannot touch him as she touches her beloved parents. She has yet to update her reality principle by realising that her mother's boundaries do not relate to her affection, but rather to her act when her brother is sleeping.

When the toddler's behaviour diverges from his ego's subjective reality principle, he often feels guilty (for his forbidden acts) and even anticipates being punished. The recognition of being guilty because of prohibited acts is different from guilt feelings due to prohibited wishes, fantasy, or thoughts, which will develop in the oedipal stage, with the consolidation of the superego's ethical principle.

In his kindergarten and with the families of his friends, the toddler discovers different rules of behaviour. How, then, is he supposed to behave? These crucial dilemmas accompany all of us from the anal stage onward throughout our lives and mainly in couplehood, when each of the partners has different behavioural rules. Each of them is sure that his or her reality principle and family rules are the best and the ultimate ones, while those of his otherness partner are less compelling. The subjective reality principle reinforces the individual's alertness to any minor or major deviation of behavioural codes from those familiar to him. These differences may undermine his illusion of the objectivity, or the universal coding of his reality principle.

Dorothy (at seven years old) asks me in her therapy session: "How can my friend's behaviour always be right and mine always wrong? I hate it when she looks in my notebook without my permission, but she says 'That's how good friends behave!' ... Who decides if somebody's behaviour is right or wrong?"

As winter approaches, Natalie (at two years and seven months), who enjoys going to kindergarten, is wearing a new sweater that she pulls over her trousers. Her mother tells her that she looks lovely. That day, the teacher assembles the children and insists that they all put their sweaters inside their trousers. Natalie starts crying: "My mother told me to put it outside: I don't want to put it inside." The teacher is very strict about her rules and Natalie yields, but refuses to go to kindergarten the next day. When her mother discovers the reason, she explains to Natalie that there are family rules and kindergarten rules, and that every day after kindergarten it will be fine to pull the sweater over her trousers. Natalie's true self-familiarity is thus narcissistically restored, her reality principle is enriched, her ego is strengthened (as is her mummy's authority), and she happily rejoins her kindergarten.

The parents' reactions to the toddler's behaviour are sometimes influenced not by family rules but rather by capriciousness. These deviations from the familiar intensify the toddler's narcissistic injury and his resistance to obey, as well as his fear of punishment and sense of solitude.

Dad returns tired from work and does not have the patience to handle the noise that Barak pleasurably produces while playing with his game. The father angrily tells Barak to stop playing in the living room, even though he usually allows him to play there. Barak is anxious about his father's rage and tends to adjust his behaviour in order to please him, based on fear, given his father's irritation, rather than according to his ego's rudimentary reality principle.

In times of stress and fear of the unknown, most people, adults and children alike, wish to rediscover their lost primeval ideal objects. They wish to rediscover their oral auxiliary ego, their leader whom they can follow blindly and securely, as if this ideal-object serves as the reality principle and knows what is good and bad in the uncertainty of the inner and outer worlds. This is the source of longing for an authoritative charismatic leader, of trust in divine providence and in ideals, and, in extreme cases, in the addiction to a messianic cult (Solan, 1996).

When an individual enters therapy, he unconsciously transfers on to his therapist the resonances of his wish for an auxiliary ego from his childhood. He often tends to rely on his therapist's interpretations without querying whether they are appropriate for his own reality principle or whether they evoke a sense of otherness to his self-familiarity. Such dependency may also reflect transference of the wish to please the therapist and gain his or her approval. This situation requires the therapist to support his patient's ego, healthy narcissism, and separateness. In other words, through interpretations the therapist needs to free the patient to preserve his true self-familiarity against the invasion of alien interpretations.

Elian, a woman in her thirties, tends to accept my analytic interpretations as the word of God. She associates: "I always obeyed my parents. I was the good girl. They knew what was good and bad for me ... When my daughter Nina rebels against me, I feel deep pleasure. I really admire her knowing what's good and what's bad for her ... I am entirety dependent on what you, or my mother think I should be doing. The only exception is with my children! I allow myself to ignore my mother's comments, and I do what *I* feel is right or wrong. They're my children, no one else's!"

Parents, community leaders, therapists, and people in authority prescribe codes of behaviour and set the rules and norms in the family or in society. As Freud (1927c) claimed: "It is only through the influence of individuals who can set an example and whom masses recognize as their leaders that they can be induced to perform the work and undergo the renunciations on which the existence of civilization depends" (p. 8).

Throughout life, from toddlerhood onward, people update their reality principle in light of the new approving authorities they come into contact with.

We can observe crucial differences in behaviour among families and cultures, which act as a carrier transferring the family legacy from generation to generation. In this sense, both familial and societal rules may be viewed as anal transitional phenomena that bond toddler and parents, or any partners in a long-term joint venture. Whenever the toddler behaves according to his subjective reality principle and true self-familiarity he may experience self-confidence, self-esteem, and ego elation (partial satisfaction). This may be comparable to the elation of a conductor of an orchestra who successfully brings together all the musicians and instruments into one coherent piece of music, while the uniqueness of each instrument is preserved.

McCloskey and Perkins (2013) define executive functions as cueing, directing, and coordinating aspects of perception, emotion, thought, and action. The aim of the self-regulation executive functions is to facilitate self-regulation in conducting one's daily functioning. They operate in four "arenas" of involvement: (a) the intrapersonal arena—with regard to the self; (b) the interpersonal arena—with respect to others; (c) the environmental arena—with regard to the environment; and (d) the academic symbolic-system arena—with respect to cultural and communicative symbols, including language, reading, and so forth.

Ben-Artsy Solan (2014) added that the efficient use of executive functioning means that the person manages the situation and not vice versa. In her view, these are part of the ego functions that pertain to mechanisms of adaptation and defence, which also operate in the domain of emotion. The individual perceives the situation in his environment according to his subjective reality principle and operates to obtain satisfaction according to the pleasure principle.

In self-regulation executive functions there is also a component of narcissistic functioning, discernible in listening to the environment and making its elements familiar; in the use of familiarity to deal with novel situations; and in the listening to one's self and making its elements familiar to one, until the consolidation of self-definition is achieved. The ego operates to fulfil self-realization in accordance with the narcissistic self-definition.

*Personification, animism, humanization (Freud, 1912-1913),*
*transference (Freud, 1912b, 1915a), and the boundary between*
*imagination and reality*

Having looked at internalisation, the reality principle, mastery, *and executive functioning,* we now turn our attention to some additional adaptation mechanisms that characterize the anal period. These adaptation mechanisms trigger imagination and phantasmatization, attributing a living person's feelings to an item or idea. Animism is probably one of man's oldest beliefs, namely that a soul or spirit exists in every object, even inanimate objects (Hefner & Guimaraes, 2011). The toddler thus personifies, transfers, and improves his imagination and creativity (adaptation mechanisms) or projects (defence mechanism) his feelings, familiarity, and mastery on to his toys. He plays with them as if they were alive and thus seemingly manipulates the reality that is beyond his familiarity (unknown in his narcissistic immunologic network) and adjusts it to his family characteristics, or to his subjective reality.

I will demonstrate personification with a personal story. Once, during the war (I was almost three years old) when the sirens sounded we quickly rushed downstairs to the air-raid shelter in the basement of our apartment building, when suddenly I noticed that my teddy bear was not with us. I remember clearly how worried I was that left behind he would be in great danger. I instantly left my parents and tried to go back upstairs, but my father followed me in panic, grasped me firmly, and categorically forbade me to leave the shelter. I remember saying: "You worry about me, but I worry about my teddy bear." I was really hurt by his panicky reply, "He isn't alive, but you..." hugging me with all his might. I recall my sharp emotional pain of disenchantment—that my dear teddy bear would remain a significant toy for me, but little more.

Sheryl (at nearly three) has a fur tiger she loves very much and plays with as if it were her protector. Once, a family friend joined Sheryl's game and whispered, "I'm really afraid of him." Sheryl tries to defend her tiger, "Don't be afraid, he's nice." The friend insisted (in jest), "How can I be sure he's nice?" So Sheryl exclaimed, "He's not alive, it's a doll!" Many years later she still remembers her anger toward this friend, who obliged her to reveal her secret and express explicitly what she knew as the reality, but hoped to hide with her magical thoughts.

Another time, Sheryl was about to leave on a flight with her family. The security officer had to examine her tiger and joked that people in the plane might be scared and that she would have to leave the tiger with the luggage. Sheryl became extremely anxious that she had to separate from her tiger and that it might get hurt travelling with the luggage.

For the toddler, the gap between imagination and reality is still unclear. Therefore, just as hidden magical forces might bring alive the inanimate, the toddler is anxious that other mystical forces of his "badness" might exit his imagination and cause something bad to happen to his family. Hence, the toddler, as well as many adults, inhibits his imagination and is afraid to fantasise about "bad" things. Between these boundaries of imagination and reality, the process of creation may take place, generally through positive sublimations (see below). Nevertheless, often in relating to the eruption of "badness" or similar negative characteristics emanating from others, creativity produces an outlet for the disconnecting (death) instinct, for example, through games of war or other games that focus on violence.

"Transference is a type of object relationship, and insofar as every object relationship is a re-editing of the first childhood attachments, transference is ubiquitous" (Moore & Fine, 1990, p. 196). Transference, in my view, is mobilised unconsciously by the ego—in the service of healthy narcissism via object relations—in order to familiarise a person with the otherness of his object. Transference, in this sense, might be considered a sophisticated mechanism of personification. The echoes of the individual's resonance of emotional childhood relationships are transferred unconsciously by the ego on to this other non-self, in order to enable relations with this person as an acquaintance rather than as a stranger. Anne-Marie Sandler (1977) describes this psychic movement, from the avoidance of the stranger anxiety toward the familiar, as a defensive or adaptive motivation, in order to replace the experience of dissonance (regarded as an overwhelming experience) with a sense of consonance: "to gain the security of the experience of the dialogue with what is known and recognized" (p. 197). In my terms, transference is a crucial adaptation mechanism that enables us to communicate with the other as if he is known and recognised. When transference functions as a defence mechanism, I prefer to define it as projection.

The individual's memory traces resonate in present occurrences with a similar (childhood) emotional intensity, and are usually compatible with this person's role images, "prototypes", or "imagos" (Freud, 1912b), such as a partner, authority figure, or rival. Occasionally, however, the transference does not match the relations in reality, but rather exposes the emotional difficulties in object relations given different expectations by each of the individuals with respect to their relationship.

In psychoanalysis, transference is one of the main tools the analyst uses to get closer to his patient's unconsciousness. This enables the analyst, the patient, or both to touch with words in the "here-and-now," the very origin of the patient's childhood's transference, the "there and then". This recognition may be used to alleviate the dissonance (Sandler, A. M., 1997) or the lack of fit of transference and actual relations, and to lessen the grasp of the negative transference on ongoing object relations, thereby freeing them to be evaluated in their own right.

### Symbolisation and Sublimation (Freud, 1905d)

Symbolisation signifies that "one mental representation stands for another, denoting its meaning not by exact resemblance but by vague suggestion, or by some accidental or conventional relation" (Moore & Fine, 1990, p. 191).

Through symbolisation the toddler manages to preserve (narcissism processing) the symbols of his precious anal body self assets and his "productions", while separating (an ego function) from the original excreta, as demanded by his objects (object relations). At the same time, through imagination and play—which represent sublimation (ego function)—the toddler enjoys the anal activities and his parents may even join him (object relations) when these activities coincide with their requests (Solan, 1989a). These two adaptation mechanisms are brought into play to solve internal and external conflicts arising during diaper weaning.

Some examples: the toddler enjoys playing and creating (sublimation) with various materials such as dough, plasticine, sand, mud, or clay (symbols of his excretions); he likes to postpone eating his favourite dish (sublimation of restraining or delaying evacuation) until the end of the meal; he attributes value to small objects outside his body (symbolisation), enjoys collecting them (sublimation) into a small bag (symbolisation of his tummy) and not allowing anyone to touch them without his permission (sublimation). He derives pleasure from keeping his secrets (symbols of secretions) untouched, avoids revealing them (sublimation of restraining evacuation), and shares them only when and how he desires. The toddler enjoys offering his possessions to others as long as the process remains under his control (sublimation), such as dispensing cookies or objects from his collection (symbols). One of the major symbols of anal productions is money. Some people like to waste money, others wish to keep an excessively tight hold on their money, others consider money as dirty, and for others money means powerfulness, often leading to avarice.

Danny (at almost three) is playing war (sublimation of aggression) with his tin soldiers and banging cars together (symbolisation of collision with his strong father). Now and again he shouts, together with the sounds of crashing and shooting. He enjoys imagining the whole scene and creates a lively game that unconsciously plays out his secret aggressive feelings toward his frustrating parent—feelings that he does not dare express openly. He then builds a garage with cubes and a hospital on the upper storey and brings the damaged cars and wounded tin soldiers in for "repair". This creative and gratifying game enables Danny to sublimate reconciliation with the wounded soldiers, symbolising his father. His father joins the game: "Danny, your soldiers are stronger than mine." Danny is proud to hear his father's encouraging words, but then becomes uncertain whether his father means that his tin soldiers will win or is anxious about his son's power. Danny answers: "Daddy, I trained my soldiers but you know that they're not really so strong." Danny thus defines for both of them the boundary between inside and outside, between imagination and reality. He succeeds in regulating the emotional flow from himself toward his beloved father in their shared space, and in maintaining love and aggression in an integrative combination through symbolisation and sublimation. The positive element dominates this integration—a sign of a healthy adaptation mechanism. Hence, they are able to continue the game joyfully, without a clash.

Symbolisation and sublimation are among the most advanced adaptation mechanisms, representing a refinement of feelings, thoughts and drives communicated through a creative cultural channel and through art. Sublimation enables people to accept feelings that would otherwise hurt or upset them, or evoke resistance. Refined aggression and libido expressed through play or any transitional phenomenon release both infant and parent, enabling them to benefit from their joint experience in a shared space and to protect their relations, which otherwise might hurt either one.

Sublimation can sometimes fail and turn into symptoms, such as emotional constipation, perfectionism, or living in squalor.

## Perceptions, conceptions, and representations

These adaptation mechanisms enhance the individual's cognitive and emotional skills and his language communication, and promote his adaptation to the outside world. This group of mechanisms is based on the oral mechanism of familiarisation and orientation, which integrate the operations of association, integration, differentiation, and separation of innumerable sensory-emotional experiences into schemata. It includes as well, mechanisms of constancy of object, self, and relationship and their mental representation, symbolisation, and sublimation.

One of the important conceptions established in the anal stage is the constancy of periodicity. In the oral stage, the internal rhythm, for example the rhythmic arousal of hunger, constitutes the baby's preliminary infrastructure of periodicity and time, somewhat like a biological clock. In the anal stage, the toddler's attunement to the sequence of transitions that are constantly repeated, such as the rituals of hunger and satiation, emptying and refilling, and joining and separating events, initiates the conception of periodicity. The toddler becomes familiar with the connection between evacuating his excretions and being refilled and full the following day and between separating from his parents on falling asleep in the dark at night and waking up in daylight and rejoining his parents. The whole cycle is repeated regularly with familiar rituals so that he feels secure about predicting what will come next, thereby avoiding the insecurity of the unknown.

Harry (at two-and-a-half) enjoys filling boxes and emptying them (symbolisation and sublimation of his evacuating his excretions and being refilled again), making sure to end the game when the box is full. Often, he finishes eating cottage cheese from a tub, closes the lid and says teasingly: "Mummy, I didn't eat anything. Look, it's closed." His mother participates in the game: "Now you'll eat all the cheese and your tummy will be full." She then opens the tub and he reacts, in a teasing voice of mastery: "Ha, ha, ha, you don't know, my tummy is already full."

The toddler integrates four separate components into an adaptation mechanism of emotional and cognitive time patterns: rhythm, periodicity, cyclicality, and the capacity to determine the delay of postponement of satisfaction. At this stage, however, he does not yet comprehend the significance of time patterns such as today, yesterday, or tomorrow (Piaget, 1936). A routine at home and in the kindergarten helps the toddler to predict the order and periodicity of his daily events as if he had a clock. A toddler for whom these rituals are not constant might suffer from the anxiety of emptiness and the unknown.

## Emotional expression

During the oral stage, the baby starts to become familiar with his bodily sensations, emotions, and "gut feelings" as a survival response to internal or external stimuli. From the second part of the oral stage (at around eight months), positive and negative emotions are regulated by the ego in accordance with the three absolute principles—familiarity, all-or-nothing, and pleasure—as well as by his low frustration threshold. These emotions are characterised by affective expressions of short duration, usually an impulsive outburst followed by an immediate release of tension.

In the anal stage, the toddler's feelings become more diversified and the emotional dialogue with his parents progressively better regulated, perceived, reflected, and "mentalized" (Fonagy & Target, 2002). As the frustration threshold increases, anal feelings can be characterised by long-term containment in the interval between the emergence of the need (or the stimulus) and the postponement of its gratification (or of reaction). These feelings are accompanied by an ongoing optimal sense of tension, a continuous feeling such as love and powerfulness, or anger and resentment. At the same time, the toddler never relinquishes oral affects; he is predisposed not to forego any opportunity for oral, love-related experiences. Sometimes, outbursts of rage may also erupt, and may be understood as defence against shame, following an impediment to unquelled interest-excitement or enjoyment-joy (Kelly, 2012; Nathanson, 1992; Tomkins, 1962, 1963).

The toddler conveys positive and negative affects, usually toward his objects, and these add flavour, significance, and emotional value to his relations with them. Positive affects bond individuals together and enrich the emotional relationship and the verbal and non-verbal communication with vitality. Negative feelings, because of their bitterness, shame-humiliation, aggressiveness, or indifference, deter people and hamper relationships.

The toddler wants to be understood and realises that he has to convey his feelings verbally in order to maintain relations with his objects, particularly his parents. Within the boundaries of the shared space of jointness with his parent, he senses his object's feelings toward him and his feelings toward his object. He senses their rapprochement or coming together, as well as their distancing and separating. Furthermore, he can sense the limits of his object's tolerance of his aggressive or loving behaviour, and also possibly his caregiver's unregulated excitement and manifestation of feelings.

> An affect includes in the first place particular motor innervations or discharges [afferent and efferent pathways] and secondly certain feelings; the latter are of two kinds—perceptions of the motor actions that have occurred and the direct feelings of pleasure and unpleasure which ... give the affect its keynote ... The core which holds the combination together is the repetition of some particular significant experience. (Freud, 1916–17, pp. 395–39)

*Affect* is defined as: "To move or stir the emotions of" *and affecting* means "exciting or touching the emotions; moving" (McKechnie, 1983, p. 32). The capacity to convey affects indeed provides the communicator with a tool for moving and touching the other despite their separateness and their otherness. The exchange of feelings, especially affectionate bodily and verbal communication between partners, may represent a transitional phenomenon (adaptation mechanism), a means of communicating, understanding, and bonding between people. Feelings, affects, and narratives, however, are always experienced subjectively. No two people can experience precisely the same feeling or affect. In part, this reflects the infinite variability in the combinations or mixtures of affects, much like a palette of colours (Tomkins, 1962, 1963), as well as the uniqueness of the affective script.

Harry (at five years old) tells his father with touching affect: "You know Pappy, I like the MacGyver movie more than any other film." It was clear that it is not the movie itself that touched Harry so much, but the fact that he watched it with his older cousin, whom he admires, his father, and his grandpa, as well as another cousin, in the weekly family reunion. Harry's words touched his father deeply, as he himself feels the same flavour of pleasure (resonance of memory traces). Harry's father also remembers himself as a little boy watching the film with his father, and reminisces how his son's admired cousin used to watch this movie again and again with his grandpa, when he was a little boy like his son. They are all excited, then and now, just like Harry. This gathering of the men of the family affected Harry and became an emotional transitional phenomenon (adaptation mechanism; see Chapter Three) that bonds them across three generations.

In the anal stage, the sounds and words emanating from the toddler's mouth are managed by his ego for similar adaptive or defensive purposes as his body products (urine and faeces). The toddler delivers the words that carry his feelings only when he wishes to do so, and he may express or conceal them. He may verbally communicate his positive or negative feelings so that his object will understand him, or he may talk in uncommunicative gibberish. At other times he may restrain himself from speaking and from expressing feelings in order to consolidate his separateness and demonstrate his individuation and autonomy. He may even withdraw in silence or in resistance, in order to annoy the other in a passive way—a constipation of words, as it were.

Jasmine (at two years and ten months) expresses her feelings verbally. She glances at her mother and tries to sense if she is really listening to her. She says: "Mummy, I'm sad. Claudine didn't play with me at kindergarten." She is already able to link her affect of sadness to the source that triggered it, in this case her friend's rejection. In their shared space, Jasmine tells her mother about her experiences and feelings in other shared spaces, like the one with her friends, so that her mother will be able to share her feelings. Her sadness and sense of loneliness, triggered by her friend's rejection, alternate with a feeling of partnership in the shared space with her mother that provides her with security and a sense of being loved. Jasmine is thus capable of "maintaining a minimum-level-of-safety feeling" (Sandler, 1987).

Let us examine the positive and negative feelings. Positive affects may be considered as affective expressions often evoked by libidinal drives and experienced in regard to the object; they represent a feeling of love and its various offshoots, such as tenderness, a sense of bliss, infatuation, empathy, sympathy, adoration, and a wish to bond.

Love is experienced differently in each of the developmental stages. Oral love is shaped by the primordial, blissful narcissistic state of being loved, of being infatuated, and of receiving absolute caring and attention from the object, accompanied by physical gestures like hugging and kissing. It is often accompanied by erotic sensations and by the symbolic need to "swallow" the loved object. In contrast, anal love is shaped by the narcissistic possession of the love object and by the ultimate sense of belongingness and exclusiveness. Anal love is accompanied by physical gestures like the need to touch and hug firmly and by the symbolic need to possess the love object. Anal love may reflect tenderness combined with aggressiveness and the flavour of mastery. Together with the separation-individuation process during the anal stage, the toddler also becomes aware of his parents' feelings, some of which are concealed and beyond his control.

Negative affects may be considered as affective expressions often evoked by aggressive drives and experienced as a feeling of anger or its various offshoots, such as frustration, humiliation and shame, rage, and a wish to disconnect from the other and to destroy him. Alternately, and in accordance with affect theory, the aggressive drive need not be postulated. Anger may be seen as "a natural response to real things rather than as a morally reprehensible animal residing inside of certain unfortunate people" (Kelly, 2012, p. 83).

> "[Since it] … feels less bad than fear, distress, and shame, it may be understood as a defence against such feelings: If we really want to understand what motivates angry behaviors, we must conceive of anger not as a cause, but as symptomatic of underlying feelings of vulnerability, especially of shame." (ibid., p. 83)

Anger, in my view, may be a by-product of healthy narcissism in the face of strangeness. Anger may be regarded as the ego's emotional safety valve, a healthy and indispensable reaction for maintaining optimal tension toward the unfamiliar within the self-familiarity. Unregulated anger, however, may escalate into feelings of hate, revenge, and destructiveness. During the anal period, advances in regulation of affect, and specifically of anger, may be observed in the toddler's emotional repertoire. In part, these are thought to reflect the operation of anal defences, such as reaction formation rather than splitting (an oral mechanism), made possible by cognitive advances (Greenspan, 1979; Piaget, 1936).

Oral anger is shaped by the eruption of consuming rage. From the anal stage onward, however, the toddler's ego is enlisted to regulate the outbursts, and to prevent their destructive potential from being unleashed on to the self, its assets, or its objects. The most difficult, yet favourable, ego regulation task is to create a mingling of opposite feelings—anger and love (see Chapter Three). Yet, in the anal stage, anger and love are often defused and the toddler cannot yet perceive how one can love when angry. This is apparent in the defence mechanism of reaction formation, where these two affects are juxtaposed rather than mingled, or in that of splitting, when they are disassociated from each other.

As a consequence of the above, at this stage the toddler persists in asking, "Do you love me?" while what he means is: "If you are angry at me, can you love me?" or "If you punish me, you don't love me." Repetitive questions of this kind are also linked to the toddler's emerging realisation that he cannot really know or control what his parents feel toward him if they do not express these two feelings (anger and love) simultaneously and explicitly. Actually, even between adult spouses or partners, there emerges this significant and important need to ask, "Do you love me?" or to hear the spouse's expression of love. It is certainly as important for adults as for children to bond together by expressions of love, so as to ensure that aggression does not destroy love. By means of gut feelings, their touch and tone of speech (in their shared jointness space) the toddler, and later the adult, tries to decipher the partner's body language and, especially, words that convey love or anger, and to differentiate these words from those that are devoid of affect.

Colin shared with me in a session his failure to handle his anger the previous day: "Last night I went to a restaurant with Lara, my fifteen-year-old daughter. It was a really enjoyable evening for both of us and I was feeling so happy until my mobile rang and I started talking with my business partner. The waitress came over and said angrily: 'You were told at the entrance not to use mobiles in our restaurant.' I went outside to continue the conversation. When I came back I wanted to leave the place that had become so offensive for me. My daughter, on the other hand, wanted us to stay and said: 'Dad, what's your problem? The waitress is right to be angry. Let's take responsibility; there's no reason to run off and spoil our great evening.' When the meal was over she handed my credit card to the waitress, smiled and apologised. The waitress also responded gently and thanked us for the tip. I was amazed at my daughter's dignity and integrity and ashamed of my reaction."

I interpreted: "For you, anger is threatening and destructive. It's as if it doesn't leave you any possibility to communicate, and therefore you have to run away." Colin reacted immediately: "You're right. For me when there is anger there are no relations! … I remember as a little boy that if my parents were angry with me and then went out, I couldn't sleep. I was so scared that something bad, like an accident, would happen to them. Or I was sure that God would punish me in my sleep …"

Some months later, after missing a session, Colin said: "I couldn't come yesterday and had no way of informing you. For the first time in my life I am not afraid of your anger. I can take responsibility and apologise. I'm even ready to hear your anger and to tell you frankly that I had a more important meeting than our session … As it was my free choice, I'm willing to pay for the missed session."

Because the loved object often frustrates, criticises and deceives, the toddler's feelings of anger appear, and with them a central emotional dilemma that confronts us all from the anal stage onward: how to contain both love and anger toward the same object, and how to maintain love as constant even in the face of periodic angry outbursts. This dilemma demonstrates a continued interest in the object or relationship despite the implied impediment. Other questions that arise in this context include how to regulate angry outbursts following an insult, threat, or feeling of betrayal; and how to assume responsibility for this anger demon and recognise it as part of one's *self-assets* that can be imagined, fantasised and mentalized before giving free rein to the reaction. Finally, how can we reconcile quickly enough so as to confirm the presence of love, respecting the otherness of the objects, and creativeness over aggression and destructiveness?

Fear is a primeval feeling: it often arouses anger that becomes intertwined with the healthy narcissism function in the face of strangeness. Fear alerts us against danger, strangeness, or change in emotional states. In the oral stage, the baby responds with panic when he senses danger and may freeze, while in the anal stage the toddler can already feel fear and the need for fight or flight. He can communicate his fears verbally, and at times even identify the source of the fear and possibly find ways of coping with it (adaptation mechanism), for example fearing pain but coping with the doctor's treatment. Fear often results from the toddler's projections of aggression on to strangers or inanimate objects (defence mechanism).

Jasmine (at two-and-a-half) is afraid of lizards. One day in the kindergarten yard, the teacher and the children suddenly came across a lizard that had frozen in its tracks, transfixed. The teacher explained to the children that the lizard is afraid of them, which is why it does not move. When Jasmine returned home she tells her mother: "We saw a lizard in the yard that didn't move. We're not allowed to frighten it … It's afraid of me like I'm afraid of it." Thus, through personification (an adaptation mechanism), she could cope better with her fear.

Fear that cannot be regulated by the ego might be transformed into free-floating anxiety that blocks the ability to identify the source of the distress and to deal with it. While fear and anxiety seem to be similar, they are actually very different. Both are unpleasant and manifest themselves as a reaction to a sense of danger. Fearful feelings are usually a conscious emotional response to a tangible danger relating to objects or to clearly-defined emotional states. In contrast, anxiety represents mainly inner unconscious danger, connected to reverberations of traumatic memory traces from one's personal history.

Fear of sleep is one of the most common fears in the anal stage. For the toddler, sleep represents a situation of non-control or even non-existence.

After the goodnight ritual is completed, Natalie (at two-and-a-half) calls her mother back and asks for water. Her mother brings a glass of water, covers her, and says goodnight again. A few minutes later, Natalie calls her again. This time she needs to pee and her mother takes her to the toilet. The separation ritual is then repeated. Some minutes later, Natalie calls again: "Mummy, will I see you in the morning?" By now her mother is exhausted and fed up with Natalie's repeated requests. Natalie senses that her mother's patience is wearing thin, and asks her mother for just one song. Her mother sings the lullaby they both love, which succeeds in calming them both. Then Natalie says, "Good night, Mummy, I love you." She separates from her mother on her own initiative and under her control, enveloped with feelings of reconciliation, and promptly falls asleep.

Alma (at two years and eight months) dreams that a monster is attacking her mother and she runs to her parents' bed to be comforted. She cries: "Pappy, what happened to Mummy. Did the monster do something bad to her?" Alma fears that she was not only dreaming and that the situation was, in fact, reality. She is anxious about losing control over her aggression toward her mother, which is projected on to, and given room in, her dream.

With the development of verbal language, the toddler's dreams are loaded with emotional content. The dreamer (whether a toddler or an adult) is the screenwriter, director, set designer, and also the main actor of his dream/movie. He projects his emotional scenario on to his self-space screen. The dream, like imagination and play, is the personal subjective fruit, the emotional creation through which the dreamer expresses disguised and symbolised feelings and contents that interrupted his rest or disturbed him during the day.

At night, the toddler fears his bad dreams and his impotence in the darkness. He is afraid of seeing a parent sleeping and not moving; maybe the parent will not hear if he calls out, like inanimate objects that do not move or communicate. Sometimes the toddler may even try to open his sleeping parent's eyes to verify that he or she is alive.

## Examples of defence mechanisms in the anal stage

This section considers some of the important defence mechanisms that the ego mobilises in the anal stage to safeguard the self against being flooded by anxiety. The anxiety evoked in the anal stage is mainly concerned with the loss of control over the body or over one's objects (Freud, 1926d [1925]). The anxiety may be triggered within one or more of the three emotional systems (the narcissistic immune system, the attachment-object relations system, and the ego-regulation system).

The physiological manifestations of anxiety include hyperarousal (faster heart and pulse rate, rapid breath), constriction (a tightening in the chest, muscular tension), gastrointestinal distress (e.g., "butterflies", constipation or diarrhea), as well as shaking and sweating. Its psychological manifestations may include shame, a sense of dread and impending danger, which may invoke a defensive orienting response, and feelings of uncertainty, insecurity and helplessness (Ross, 2008; Skelton, 2006, cited in Tuckett & Levinson, 2010).

### Resistance and opposition

"In psycho-analytic treatment the name 'resistance' is given to everything in the words and actions of the analysand that obstructs his gaining access to his unconscious" (Laplanche & Pontalis, 1973, p. 394).

Freud (1950 [1887–1902]) first conceptualised resistance as an obstacle to the elucidation of the symptoms and to the progression of the treatment. In *Inhibitions, Symptoms and Anxiety*, Freud (1926d [1925]) differentiates among five varieties of resistances, three of which are related to the ego function: repression, transference resistance, and that resistance which proceeds from illness and which is "based upon an assimilation of the symptoms into the ego … It represents an unwillingness to renounce any satisfaction or relief that has been obtained" (p. 160). Freud also mentioned the resistance arising from the id (the fourth variety), in the form of the power of the compulsion to repeat. The resistance stemming from the super-ego (the fifth variety) "seems to originate from the sense of guilt or the need for punishment; and it opposes every move towards success, including, therefore, the patient's own recovery through analysis" (ibid). This can account for some instances of the so-called "negative therapeutic reaction" (Freud, 1914g, 1923b, 1937c), where the patient does *not* appear to improve, and may actually deteriorate, despite what would generally be considered adequate treatment.

In my view and complementing this definition, resistance would be to the unknown that is an inevitable part of the progression to health (whereas the symptoms are familiar to the patient). Resistance prevents, or inhibits associations from emerging into consciousness, often associations which evoke feelings of threat and are alien to self-familiarity. Resistance may also be conceptualised as originating from the narcissistic immune system, which constantly resists minor or major differences or deviations from self-familiarity. Resistance might take the form of inhibition of drives and emotional expression, and of opposition, mobilised as a defence against the anxiety of losing mastery or against any attempt at coercion triggered within the object-relations system. These mechanisms are based on oral mechanisms of withdrawing.

Mother calls Jasmine (nearly three) to the table and she immediately resists: "No. I'll decide when I come to the table." After a while she asks: "Mummy, who decides the rules in our family?"

### Avoidance, ignoring, and undoing (Freud, 1926d [1925])

These defence mechanisms are mobilised against the anxiety of being harmed by strangeness (narcissistic immune system) or by aggression (ego regulation system). They are accompanied by magical thoughts, normal in the anal stage, evoking the illusion that the unpleasant, painful, aggressive incidents have not really occurred. Ignoring and undoing remove an act or thought that might evoke anxiety from consciousness, while avoidance allows one to refrain from an act or thought that might evoke anxiety. People often use expressions and gestures to ward off the "evil eye", such as "touch wood". These mechanisms are mobilised on the basis of the oral mechanism of denial and are generally a reaction to an external trigger.

Guy (at two-and-a-half) is playing with his older brother's toys, knowing full well that his brother forbids him to do so. His mother surprises him, "Guy, what are you doing?" Guy does not reply, as if he did not hear her. He tries to avoid her anger by quickly putting away the toys, as if undoing his forbidden act. This mechanism attempts to change the stressful reality, even though it is obvious to all.

Annette says: "Seeing that I can't protect my son, a soldier in the army, I avoid thinking about him, to prevent the dangers I imagine will actually happen."

## Rationalisation (Jones, 1908)

Rationalisation is mobilised as a defence mechanism against the anxiety of uncontrolled occurrences or the unknown, or against strangeness triggered within the narcissistic immune system and the ego regulation system. The toddler uses rational, logical thinking to alleviate his anxiety, and produces excuses, explanations, and justifications for his acts and thoughts in order to regain control. Adults often use rationalisation under the guise of ideology and principles.

Jasmine (at two years and ten months) experiences strangeness in envisaging that her parents were once babies because she has no such memory traces in her narcissistic network. Hence, she provides a rational explanation: "Mummy, you are still a child, because you also have parents."

## Isolation, reaction formation and obsession (Freud, 1926d [1925])

These defence mechanisms are mobilised against the anxiety of loss of control over emotions triggered within the ego regulation system. The outburst of emotions is blocked by:

a. isolating the emotion from the experience
b. reaction formation that converts the emotion into its diametrical opposite, for example, from attraction to repulsion (disgust and dissmell)
c. obsessive repetition (moderate or intensive) of an act or thought that prevents the emergence of the original forbidden impulse.

Reflecting the all-or-nothing principle (discussed earlier), these defences are based on oral denial, splitting, or repression mechanisms. Despite their oral origins, they represent further cognitive and emotional gains observed during the anal stage.

The mother of George (at two years and ten months) says: "Until about a month ago, George loved to play in the dirt, crumble food, romp in the mud, and sometimes hide his faeces around the home. His father discovered this, shouted at him, and even beat him. Since then George 'changed his tune' and has become very pedantic. He feels aversion, is repulsed by any kind of dirt, and now maintains order and cleanliness in a really excessive and obsessive manner."

Morris (at two years and ten months) tells his mother matter-of-factly and with no visible affect, "Gil's mother fetched him and hit him." It was impossible to ascertain his emotional reaction. Was he startled, fearful or empathic toward Gil?

In his analytic session, Rafael (aged thirty) describes his emotional difficulties in a monotonous monologue lacking any affect. He says: "My wife says she married me because she loves me, but I don't know what she means by love. For me it's important to establish a family just as it is to establish a business ... Feelings are impossible to measure ... they are not logical."

## Fixation (Freud, 1905d) and regression (Freud, 1900a)

Fixation and regression are interlinked. They represent defence mechanisms against anxiety connected to change, strangeness, trauma, physical illnesses, or loss of control, triggered within the three emotional systems. Regression refers to a retreat to a previous level of functioning, for example when "unresolved conflicts and anxieties from earlier developmental phases may have left the mental apparatus with 'areas of weakness (fixations)'" (Moore & Fine, 1990, p. 164).

In regression, the toddler (or adult) may behave or react momentarily or even constantly according to a primeval principle such as the oral all-or-nothing principle, even though he generally behaves according to the reality principle. He may also regress to behave according to earlier, usually traumatic, familiar situations, even if they are inappropriate to his present developmental stage. Other sources of fixation might originate in an addiction to immediate satisfaction or to a particular erotic zone, continuing to maintain dependent relationships because of anxiety; or an inability to cope with new emotions, such as jealousy. These fixation points may persist throughout life and serve as a refuge for regression in the face of anxiety; one tends to regress to one's fixation points. These fixation points may also allow one to regain a familiar emotional state in relations with one's objects.

Roy (at four years and two months) was weaned off diapers relatively late (element of fixation). With the birth of his brother, he was flooded by the anal anxiety of losing control over his aggression toward his sibling. He now regresses to the oral anxiety of abandonment, clamouring for his mother's attention immediately and absolutely, according to oral principles, precisely when she is holding his baby brother. Because his anxiety is not sufficiently relieved or contained, he unconsciously relinquishes his (anal) accomplishments, regresses and becomes encopretic—emptying his excretions into his pants. This regression enables Roy to behave affectionately toward his baby brother, while his symptom conceals his jealousy. Outside his family, however, for example in his kindergarten, he continues to behave in accordance with the (anal) reality principle.

*Identification with the aggressor (Anna Freud, 1936)*
*or attraction to aggression*

These defence mechanisms are mobilised against the anxiety of loss of control over one's rage, triggered within the three emotional systems. When the toddler is frequently exposed to his object's aggression, abuse, criticism, or humiliation, he may become anxious that his rage will hurt or even destroy his admired object. By means of these defence mechanisms, the toddler may identify with his abusive and threatening object by adopting his or her aggressive behavioural characteristics. Often, individuals are drawn to situations of violence, danger, or sadomasochistic pleasure as a repetition of memory traces of physiological and emotional excitation. Through these defence mechanisms the toddler preserves his admired object's image as part of his self-assets, based on the oral admiration mechanism and anal isolation and reaction formation mechanisms.

While the primary gain of these defence mechanisms is that of reducing anxiety, the secondary gain might be the individual's benefit of having his parent pay attention to him. At the same time, the secondary gain might be the individual's addiction to the thrill of threats, violence, and danger, and the attendant adrenalin surge. He may even repeatedly seek the challenge of living at the edge of life and death. This may explain the popularity of watching violent wrestling competitions or fights between animals, events that may attract people for whom the path toward criminality is often quite short.

Brian (aged thirty) tells me in his session: "I'm addicted to scenes of violence on the TV, even reaching orgasm … At times I behave aggressively toward my assistants. I hate behaving like this … I always struggle with myself not to hit my children. I never do, although I am tempted … Sometimes when I am being humiliated I hear myself whispering, 'You can't hurt me because I enjoy it.'" After a long silence he adds: "When I pushed my father to the edge he would beat me. This went on until I was ten years old. The older I got the more I would sneer at him and I got pleasure from seeing his craziness, although he continued to beat me … Still, I admired him, wanted to be like him or ask his advice, but couldn't enjoy his love."

## Summary

This chapter describes the toddler's ego regulation of drives and emotions during the anal stage, and the pivotal role of the diaper-weaning process. The toddler's ego is focused mainly on mixing or mingling aggression with libido, safeguarding his love for his object while regulating his aroused aggression toward the same, yet frustrating, libidinal object. The toddler asserts his individuation and often competes in a power struggle with his parents' authority. From the anal stage onward the individual finds it difficult to admit that aggression constitutes part of his self-familiarity assets and that, like his parents, he is able to feel both love and anger toward the same person.

In addition, from this stage onward, the individual, via his ego's economic regulation, can postpone immediate satisfaction and undertake emotional investments for the long-term, choosing profitable objectives at minimum emotional cost. His assertiveness, individuation, and self-discipline, as well as psychomotor, emotional, and cognitive intelligence may be enhanced, as are his language skills, creativity, play, and joint ventures involving mentalization, phantasmatization, and the expression of feelings.

Internalisation and the appearance of the subjective reality principle as well as symbolisation and sublimation, constitute the toddler's main new adaptation mechanisms in the anal stage. Via these mechanisms, the toddler may adapt to behavioural standards and upgrade his self-esteem and self-values by mastering the permitted family rules and avoiding those that are forbidden. Moreover, by mobilising his adaptation mechanisms, the toddler's ego enhances the potency of his intelligence (psychomotor, cognitive, and emotional).

These milestones contribute to the development of two other personality components, namely the superego that emerges during the oedipal stage, with its emphasis on ethical values, and the ego ideals that emerge in the latency stage, with their emphasis on social and cultural values.

Defence against anxiety, while building upon previous oral defences, is now expanded to include new mechanisms, such as reaction formation and identification with the aggressor, isolation of affect, and rationalisation and intellectualization, to name but a few. These new anal defences are made possible by the co-mingling of libidinal attachment with the disconnecting instinct or with whatever may stand in the way of emotional connection.

During the anal period, the main anxiety is that of loss of control over one's body or objects. Anxiety may be triggered within one or more of the three emotional systems, that is, the narcissistic immune system, the attachment-object relations system, and the ego-regulation system.

## Notes

1. Bellak, Hurvich and Crawford (1969) view the construct of the ego as having "formal similarities with the model of intelligence underlying the Wechsler Adult Intelligence Scale: a general factor (total I.Q. in the Wechsler test being roughly parallel to 'ego strength') and some less-general group factors (Verbal I.Q. in the Wechsler test, parallel to clusters of intercorrelated ego functions)". They selected "twelve ego functions from the psychoanalytic literature, [and] delineated their component factors. These ego functions are as follows: Reality testing; Judgment; Sense of reality; Regulation and control of impulses and affects; Adaptive regression in the service of the ego (ARISE); Defensive functioning; Stimulus barrier; Autonomous functioning; Object relations; Thought processes; Synthetic-Integrative functioning; Mastery-competence" (p. 527).

2. Innate narcissism, in my view, may be considered as a primeval personality component that chronologically precedes the ego's functioning (see Chapter Two).

3. Baumeister, Vohs and Tice (2007) consider "self-control to be the deliberate, conscious, effortful subset of self-regulation. In contrast, homeostatic processes such as maintaining a constant body temperature may be called self-regulation but not self-control … Inadequate self-control has been linked to behavioral and impulse-control problems, including overeating, alcohol and drug abuse, crime and violence, overspending, sexually impulsive behavior, unwanted pregnancy, and smoking" (p. 351).

4. "Actually incorporation contains three meanings: it means to obtain pleasure by making an object penetrate oneself; it means to destroy this object; and it means, by keeping it within oneself, to appropriate the object's qualities. It is this last aspect that makes incorporation into the matrix of introjection and identification" (Laplanche & Pontalis, 1973, p. 212).

5. To this definition I would add: incorporation (an oral-stage mechanism) may be conceived as the primal biological mode of holding in inputs from the outside world, like swallowing food and the body incorporating it, or absorbing and preserving a variety of tastes. Introjection (an oral-stage mechanism) may be conceived as the ego's psychological "swallowing" of aspects from the outer world, but without "digesting" or integrating them. One thus speaks of "foreign" or "ego-alien" introjects. Internalisation (an anal-stage mechanism) involves the digestion and integration of the "swallowed" inputs from the outside into the ego's performances. In the process, the functions of the ego change and become more sophisticated. Identification (an oedipal-stage mechanism) may be conceived as the ego's psychological processing of the representations of objects into its own self-representations in order to preserve compatibility between its objects, images, values, and even ideals, and its self-familiarity. Note that the various processes of internalisation described above are coloured by affects (see Tomkins, 1962, 1963).

# CHAPTER SEVEN

# The dynamics of object relations in the anal stage

## The progression of jointness-separateness in the anal stage

At this stage, the aspect of object relations that I previously referred to as "jointness-separateness" (see Chapter Four) takes a new direction, focusing on educational requirements (cleanliness, order, and discipline), the establishment of authority, and the toddler's autonomy achievements, particularly mastery.

The parents are not as available now to satisfy the toddler's needs as they were before, during the oral stage. The toddler may often become frustrated, offended, or hurt. He might sense himself as small and not understood which, of course, is likely to irritate him. Consequently, the toddler needs to generate new adaptation mechanisms to deal with the new situation, such as refining his separation-individuation and furthering his own autonomous self (Mahler, 1972a, 1972b).

During this stage, along with diaper weaning, the toddler's capacity for postponing satisfaction, as well as his possessiveness over his assets, emerges. He does not want anyone to appropriate his possessions without his permission and he trusts his parents to safeguard his assets while he postpones satisfaction (see Chapters Five and Six). When the toddler obeys a family rule, and in so doing delays his gratification of receiving his parents' love and attention—for example, when they are busy with his siblings and ask him to entertain himself—sibling jealousy and rivalry may emerge; it is as if the parental love will be usurped by his siblings.

Sean (at two years and ten months) is called to the table to eat lunch with his family. He says to his mother: "I got my game ready, but I'll play after lunch. You mustn't let anyone touch my cars." Clearly, he senses his parents' contentment, love, support, and partnership as they see him delaying his gratification and responding to the family rules. This restraint fills Sean with new gratification and a feeling of power and control, so much so that postponing enjoyment sometimes becomes even more pleasurable than the game itself.

For the first time in his life, the toddler's relations with his parents are shaped by his assertion of autonomy, which triggers conflicts of interest with parental authority as well as competition for power. The toddler realises that he has control over his body and over his parents. He discovers his ability to negotiate and his power to affect his parents' mood, arousing their love, pleasure, and pride in him, or alternatively, testing their limits and provoking their aggression. He can please them and elicit expressions of love when he is willing to accede to their demands. His self-esteem is rewarded when his parents say, "You're such a good boy." He may also annoy them and provoke their anger when he refuses to cooperate, and he then hears them saying, "You're a bad boy." For him, this means that he is good or bad not according to what he really is, but whether they are pleased or angered by his behaviour.

The toddler experiences his good behaviour as a condition for being accepted and trusted by his parents and abiding by their rules. Conditional trust is a new anal characteristic of trust, unlike the blind, basic trust of the oral stage. He has to behave according to their rules in order to sense their acceptance, and to feel confident that they will love him and be there for him. Obeying the family rules rewards him and inspires in him a sense of belonging to a strong family. He tries to capture his parents' attention by affectionate gestures, offering them gifts, or suggesting games. He keeps trying to improve his verbal skills in order to make himself better understood, and to discern via his narcissistic sensors, in their shared jointness space, when his parent has been seduced into partnership and when he remains distant (see Chapter Four). The toddler attempts to coordinate and synchronise their mutual approaches to jointness and to transform conflicts into partnership by negotiation and reconciliation.

The main issue in anal jointness relations can be conceptualised as the creation of a balance between the parents' respecting the toddler's separateness, individuation, and autonomy versus the toddler's respecting his parents' authority and love. Until this balance is reached, both parent and child may often engage in power struggles that provoke anger and pain, or alternatively, reconciliation and expressions of love (see Chapter Five, the struggle of parental narcissism versus the toddler's narcissism). Progress in object relations leads to the gradual capacity to negotiate verbally with a separate other in a jointness mode of communication.

This new balance from the anal stage onward passes through the parental stressing of appropriate boundaries to the toddler's omnipotent phantasms. Often, parents find it difficult to impose boundaries, to thwart or refuse their child's wishes, to be stricter than they have been until now, and to frustrate their child by imposing their authority. They become exhausted by the toddler's constant willingness to enter into power struggles and to test the limits of their restrictions, their tolerance, and their authority, and they often feel narcissistically injured. They find themselves helpless in the face of his "No, no" reactions to every request, his stubborn resistance and insubordination, and their inability to handle his wrath. This is a fatiguing phase in which parents often lose their patience, allow him everything, or erupt in rage which is not always proportional to the occurrence, but rather a manifestation of the degree of their exhaustion or burnout.

Nicole (at two years old) enjoyed intimacy with both her parents in the oral stage, while at the same time they encouraged her separateness. Consequently, in the anal stage, Nicole continues her normal jointness-separateness and furtherance of her autonomy. Her mother, however, is repeatedly hurt and drained by her stubbornness and her rebellious behaviour. The mother feels strong love for Nicole yet perceives her as a "bad girl". She does not have the strength to handle Nicole's aggression by placing limits on her behaviour. Occasionally, Nicole feels she is a bad girl who irritates her mother and is liable to be punished. She is also concerned about her mother's weakness (see below), tries to pacify her, and promises to be a good girl. The father is generally not perturbed by Nicole's stubbornness and, contrary to his wife, succeeds in creating a partnership with his daughter and eliciting obedience to his authority.

With him, she dares and even enjoys struggling for power and then reconciling together. Nicole easily differentiates her mother's fragility in the face of her assertiveness from her father's encouragement of her individuality.

At this stage, the toddler is motivated to assert his autonomy and expose his omnipotence while at the same time is anxious he might hurt someone. If, however, he experiences his parents as fragile, helpless, or vulnerable (like Nicole's mother) in the face of his challenges, he may feel guilty and sometimes even seek punishment, or be over-gentle to others. Alternatively, if his parents are inconsistent in setting the limits of their authority, or constantly criticise and belittle him, he may come to feel that his individuation is not accepted. In this case, he may tend to forego any expression of tenacity, relinquish his individuation, turn his aggression toward himself, and view himself as a bad boy—all of which will intensify his insecurity and lower his self-esteem. However, when his parents consistently demarcate clear boundaries to his behaviour in accordance with the family rules, the toddler may internalise these guidelines as his subjective reality principle. Hence, he may feel confident in his self-control and emotional regulation, recognizing in their shared spaces, when he deviates from the family rules and when he respects instructions. This will help him define his self-familiarity representations, his self-esteem, and his object representations.

We see that anal jointness relations usually take place in triadic[1] relations, that is, parent and toddler, each emerging from his self-space and *joining together in a third shared space*. From the anal stage onward, there appear a variety of triadic relations, such as the toddler facing both parents as a couple, constituting his leaders and authority figures. Triadic relations may encompass all members of the family who join in the family space at a particular time to share common interests, such as family rituals, games, and meals. These common interests are invested in as transitional phenomena that bridge their separateness and otherness, and facilitate the family's representation as a strong, cohesive unit.

Each partner can master his separateness and his representations in his self-space (experienced as self-constancy), whereas the third shared space of jointness is renewed at each encounter. Hence, the parties, such as parent and toddler, join the shared space each with his own self-control and degree of tolerance toward the other, and they are thus exposed to unpredictable emotional occurrences, depending on each other's mood and emotional index. Will it be a power struggle or a joyful game played together? Both parties may achieve a matching of interests and feel elated by their love and partnership in jointness, or come to feel frustrated and offended. Whatever the case, after any disruption, they will both attempt to safeguard the subtle balance of jointness and to reconcile their differences.

Alain, an adult patient in his forties, shares with me the rigid behavioural rules of his childhood: "Already in kindergarten I decided that I would always obey my father's demands in order to avoid his humiliating beatings and win his love … Since then, it seems, I carry out any assignment I'm given perfectly, and always on time. Still, I'm usually scared that I'll make a mistake, that I'll be late for a meeting, or that I haven't properly prepared the material for the presentation … All my life I dreamed of finding someone kind-hearted who would love me and accept me as I am … Instead, I found myself married to a woman who requires me to obey her strict rules."

Some sessions later, Alain emotionally relates his conversation with his parents: "To my amazement, my father doesn't remember ever hitting me, nor can my mom recall such events. I really feel confused. Is it possible that my father never beat me in the way that is ingrained in my memory? Or maybe I sensed that he had wanted to beat me, and I experienced it as real? Or perhaps I even managed to prevent him from doing so, because I was so docile?" Processing the new insights regarding his charged relations with his father helped Alain gradually regulate his fear of the reactions of authority figures to errors he might make.

Alain's insights can help elucidate how the infant absorbs unconscious messages from his parents. I am convinced that Alain sensed well enough his father's unconscious tendency, but interpreted it wrongly, as if it were real. Such imprints in the narcissistic network are liable to affect the child's behaviour and restrict his love relations, even with those close to him, throughout his life.

Carmen's (at two years and eight months) mother tells me in her session how exhausting the struggles are for her with her stubborn daughter each morning: "Instead of leaving home happily, we leave feeling angry and jaded. I'm so sad to separate like this from my darling daughter at the kindergarten … But it drives me crazy when she resists wearing the clothes I suggest, and when she takes her time coming for breakfast. I'm afraid of being late for work because of her … I, the mature person, am helpless against this little one … I feel I'm a bad mother … She manages to bring out the evil in me, while I love her so much and am trying to be a good mother."

Through our elaboration of the source of her hurt, which appeared to be mainly a repetition of her own childhood, the mother felt a lot calmer and her creative thinking could re-emerge. In her next session she shared her achievements: "When we were doing the 'good night' separation ritual, I suggested to Carmen: 'Tomorrow morning, when we hear the beeps on the radio, we'll feed and dress Yan and Ban [Carmen's dolls] and then we'll feed and dress ourselves for kindergarten, okay? … From the next morning onward it's been like magic! Our agreement on the procedures, rules of behaviour and schedules are clear and regular. Carmen calls me when she hears the news signal and we both enjoy feeding and dressing Yan, Ban, and ourselves … I'm delighted! We are happy on the way to the kindergarten. Carmen tells me what she'll be doing with her friends, and I tell her who I'm going to meet, and when I'll come to take her home. We hug and kiss each other, say goodbye and she runs happily into the kindergarten."

A mother and her child, two separate individuals with a conflict of interest each morning, managed to create a transitional phenomenon of shared interests and partnership that binds them during their morning jointness. They also established a ritual of separation from home and from each other, and look forward to being part of other shared spaces until they rejoin in their shared family space at home.

## The significance of giving

Following diaper weaning (see Chapters Five and Six), the toddler may relate to his bodily productions as a positive aspect of his self-esteem, and as a "secret weapon" for bargaining with his parents. Because his excrement is unavailable for most of the day, unconsciously, the toddler may often be worried about remaining empty of product, of not having anything to deliver to his parents, as a means of controlling them. Hence, he produces (through his ego) symbolisation and sublimation of his act of delivering excretions.

From the anal stage to adulthood, various forms of gifts may represent symbolisation of the original body productions, as well as sublimation of giving self-productions. Gifts represent an expression of love that might meet the object's expectations. The toddler expects his giving to be rewarded, and for his parents to praise his gifts, his creativeness, and his achievements. No less, he expects them to safeguard his creations so that they will accumulate and not disappear like his faeces down the toilet. He still measures the value of his gift by his parents' response. Most people enjoy the anal, symbolised, or sublimated form of giving gifts as an expression of love, especially to their dearest ones, and expect to be rewarded for their generosity.

Ethan, in his forties, submitted his request for nomination as managing director of a car company, but on being accepted, relinquished the job and fell into depression. Later he came to consult me and said: "I'm always afraid that someone will discover that I'm a failure, have nothing intelligent to say, that I'm childish and dependent on authority." In one of his sessions, he revealed: "I always wanted my father to be proud of me. Because I was a creative child I built a car out of Lego. I was about four years old, maybe even less. I went to my father's garage and was happy to find some paper to wrap the car in as a gift for him. I also noticed that there was a puddle of water on the floor. I gave my father the present and told him about the water in the garage. He shouted at me: 'You worthless creature. You poured the water. You had no reason to go into my garage. You're a bad boy!' He then shoved away the car. I didn't pour the water, but I was worth nothing in his eyes, or mine. This is the story of my life. It's always like this. I can't be independent because I'm not worth anything."

I asked Ethan: "Do you recognise the link between your story and the fact that you were nominated as director of a car company and then relinquished the job?" Ethan seemed surprised, and responded: "No, it didn't occur to me … I remember now what I forgot to tell you, that when my father went into the garage, he discovered, of course, that the water pipe had burst. I felt that this was my revenge, even though I felt guilty about enjoying his panic." I interpreted: "It seems that you presented your nomination for managing director to this car company so as to unconsciously recreate your car present for your father. But you seem to have felt so guilty for your imaginary revenge that you refused to accept the nomination." Ethan replied: "Which means that I have stupidly ruined my life. No, that's not true. It's my father who ruined my life. I feel more anger toward him now than I have ever felt before … Would it have been so difficult for him to accept my piece of work as a gift?"

## The emotional index as a frame for emotional scanning

Gradually, in their shared jointness space, both toddler and parent improve what I have termed a subjective "emotional index", based on an ID and password from the oral stage (see Chapter Four). In jointness relations, each partner scans and gauges the reactions of the other through his own emotional index. I consider this emotional index as an adaptation mechanism for child and parent in order to detect the feelings of the other. This index is based on gut feelings and intuition, the constant characterisation of the object's responses (his ID), and the perception of the constancy of the relations (their relational password). The emotional index enables each partner to make choices and decisions, such as whether to approach the other or distance himself, and whom to choose as a partner.

The constant updating and enrichment of these scanning skills from the oral stage to adulthood, through the refinement of the jointness-separateness relationship, facilitates the flow of gut feelings and intuition between people. The decoding, deciphering, and identifying of digressions in their own emotional or physical state, or that of their objects, enables them to prepare for any changes that may arise. The toddler can thus identify with whom it is preferable, control his anal stubbornness, obey the strict rules, be especially lovable, or, rather, behave manipulatively in order to achieve his aims.

Barak (at two years and four months) distances himself from his mother. He runs away from her, knowing she will chase after him. At the same time, he intuitively feels that her alertness has been aroused, so that at an appropriate moment he turns around and runs back into her arms, to their shared space of jointness, where she excitedly declares, "My, my, my lovely boy."

## The transition from monologue to dialogue

The marvellous process of language acquisition has been a constant source of fascination for psychologists, linguists,[2] philosophers, and neuroscientists. Recent innovative computational testimonies (Solan, Horn, Ruppin & Edelman, 2005)[3] indicate the ability of computer software to identify the rules of syntax from a text, and to learn a language by means of statistical deduction and inference. Breakthroughs of this kind challenge the psycholinguistic claim that learning is based on innate patterns of language. If a computer is able to achieve such ability, we can expect the human brain to reach even further. Is it possible that this algorithm operates like synapses, whose neural connections establish constant patterns, such as those of language? Is this process similar to synaesthesia[4] between words and sensory stimuli?

Kandel (2006) claims that synapses are thought to be involved in learning (and by implication, in the memory of what was learned): learning has been found to lead "to a change in the strength of the synaptic connections—and therefore in the effectiveness of communication—between specific cells in the neural circuit that mediates behavior" (p. 200). "Strength—the long-term effectiveness of synaptic connections—is regulated by experience," (p. 202) and "learning may be a matter of combining various elementary forms of synaptic plasticity into new and more complex forms, much as we use an alphabet to form words" (p. 205).

I draw attention to the development of sensory emotional language that relies on the above studies. My claim is that verbal language represents a combination of common words that are the carriers of subjective affective meanings organised into sensual, affectionate, negative, and positive sensory communication.

Already, in the womb, the foetus hears his mother talking and singing, and he recognises the familiar melodies and the sound of the words after his birth, long before he is able to decipher their meaning. Throughout the oral stage and onward, these speech sounds resonate within the baby as familiar intonations, shades of sound, and repeated voice patterns (see Chapter Two) that evoke his smile and nurture visual communication between him and his caregiver. Emotional messages between them are transmitted mainly by means of motor, non-verbal, and sensory communication, often by mutual gazing, smiling, hugging, and kissing (see Chapter Four). The baby also absorbs the parent's verbal expressions through familiar melodies of language and intonation. The acquired milestones of the emotional language are thus ingrained, and enable parent and baby to communicate emotionally and understand each other in their shared space of jointness.

At the beginning of the anal stage, the toddler wants to make full use of his new language acquisition and to express himself verbally. He still often speaks in gibberish, the unique language that his parents understand, and feels how amazed they are that he is speaking. Yet, his talking does not always match their availability to listen attentively, which may shape his expression mainly as a monologue.

From the second part of the anal stage (from age two-and-a-half), as his perception of separateness grows and the practicing of separation-individuation improves, the toddler becomes aware that non-verbal and gibberish expressions are insufficient for him to be understood by his parents and others. This recognition represents a crucial achievement in the toddler's emotional development, as he now realises that he has to make an effort to find the appropriate words and pronounce them correctly with suitable intonation and proper syntax in order to make his speech clear to the listener.

From the anal stage onward, the toddler invests so much in words, language, and communication that they become his narcissistic assets. His urge for mastery of language with the other is intensified, just as it was regarding his body self-image and his relations with his parents. Furthermore, he tries to master his emotional expression by conveying his needs, feelings, and desires—his sensory communication—as if "piggybacking" on the adjusted intonation of the words, so that his messages become affectionately loaded. Consequently, it becomes very important for him, as it is for people in general, to be understood correctly by others and how others accept his stories and whether they remember what he tells them. When parents do not have the patience to listen to the toddler, he feels narcissistically injured. He may then take steps to capture their attention or adapt his speaking to their willingness to share his sensory communication. This motivates him to relinquish his unique oral gibberish in favour of understandable communication, which may well be the start of genuine dialogue.

Parents who always understand their toddler's gibberish leave him little room for the separateness that would motivate him to improve his language, or even to insist on knowing whether they understood him correctly. On the other hand, when the toddler frequently fails to capture his parents' attention, or when they do not have the patience to communicate with him and understand him, he might forego his efforts to engage in dialogue, thereby inhibiting or delaying the progress of his speech and language skills.

By listening to and assimilating his parents' and his older siblings' forms of speaking—their intonation, body language, and facial expressions—the toddler adopts their affective language and becomes polite or ill-mannered, quiet or brash. He establishes a unique sensory communication with each of his objects. He realises that the intonation of the same word combinations may change their meaning, conveying a different affective message. Henceforth, the toddler is capable of receiving, conveying, and engaging in dialogue by means of verbal language that includes affectionate sensory communication.

Verbal communication is a central element in symbolisation, mentalization, phantasms, playing, and dreaming. Generally, a listener in dialogue is more impressed and moved by the sensory and affective communication than by the literal meaning of the enunciated words. Hence, the shared language with others may represent a transitional phenomenon that bonds people together and bridges their separateness and otherness.

Paul dictated to his secretary an affectionate letter to his colleague. Listening to his secretary reading the letter back to him before sending it, he became upset and said to her: "You're reading dry words, although the letter I dictated was very affectionate, in order to entice my colleague to join my project."

Steven (at age three) makes no effort to speak in a way that his kindergarten teacher or others will understand. He talks gibberish with his pacifier in his mouth, which only his parents understand. He is furious at not being understood, and expects everyone, excluding himself, to make an effort. Steven ignores the need to try to attune himself to others and to explain himself in a communicative style that they will understand.

Jack, a single man in his twenties, reacted nervously to my interpretation: "You don't understand me exactly in the way I expect ..." I reflected to Jack his statement: "Exactly as you expect." He responded with an association that surprised him: "My mother always understood me, well, almost always ... No, I don't know why I said that. I'm often mad at her because she doesn't understand me exactly ... I have a vague recollection that she used to understand me without words. She could look at me and say, 'You seem tired or sad.' For me, this is a clear sign of love ..." I interpreted: "It's as if you're mad at me as well, because I didn't meet your expectations, and you're examining me just like you scrutinise your mother's love." After hesitating a while, Jack continued: "Yes, you're right. I can see now that when I told you that it's important for me that my girlfriends understand me, my hidden wish was to confirm their love. Obviously they all failed, just as you did." Jack's dialogue, especially with women, was often blocked by his unconscious need to test their love by having them understand him precisely, beyond words.

We often wish to convey emotional contents that we have mentalized and phantasised in our inner speech with ourselves, but various sources inhibit us and prevent this communication from taking place with others.

Andrew, in his thirties, started to describe to me in his analytic session an unpleasant experience that he had that day. I was attentive to what he was saying, but I sensed that he was not actually talking to me, nor was he relating anything unpleasant. When Andrew completed his monologue, I interpreted: "You want to share your unpleasant experience with me, but it seems that you're not communicating it to me, as if it doesn't really matter to you whether I get your messages and share them." Andrew hesitated a while and then said: "I think I'm afraid to discover that perhaps you aren't listening to me … I'm usually sure that no one is listening to me, that my thoughts don't arouse any interest." After a long silence, Andrew continued: "My dad, who I love and appreciate so much, never listened to me … He was physically present when I spoke to him, but I felt that he wasn't there. He was probably preoccupied with other things … It was so painful … Like I felt this morning and tried to share with you … In fact, your attention is very important to me, but I don't do anything to get it and I'm afraid to check whether you understand me and are listening to me."

Julie, a teenager, arrives regularly and punctually to our therapy sessions, but refrains from speaking and remains silent for at least twenty minutes. When I fail to repeat or include her exact words from the present or a previous session in my interpretation, she explodes: "Anyway, you don't remember what I said, so there's no point in talking … I sometimes feel as if you are empting me of my words, of my strength." In the following months of therapeutic work, Julie gradually began to share her associations with me while I, for the most part, avoided interpretations that might provoke her "constipation". The changes she was undergoing motivated her to find out more about her childhood. After questioning her mother, she shared the information she obtained: "My mother told me she remembers that I already spoke fluently at two years and five months when my brother was born. She was amazed that when I saw my baby brother sucking her breast, I screamed anxiously, 'He's emptying your strength.' My mother told me that at the time I was also constipated, and my parents tried to forcibly insert an enema, as the family doctor recommended, but I resisted, screamed, and wouldn't let them." Julie stopped her animated discourse. A long silence ensued. I decided still not to say anything, so as not to provoke her painful feeling of penetration. Toward the end of the session, Julie formulated her own insightful interpretation: "Do you think that my fear of being emptied of my words is like my fear that sucking would empty my mother's strength, or like my fear of being penetrated by the enema?"

D. Quinodoz (2003) has elaborated the theme of "words that touch" by emphasising that we are often touched by communication addressed to us, independent of the words or content being conveyed. The same formulation may touch our reasoning, our feelings, and sensations, or evoke images and memory traces. Quinodoz considers "that a *language that touches* operates more by suggestion than by demonstration. It is a form of language that is not restricted to the verbal transmission of *thoughts* but incorporates *feelings* and the *sensations* that accompany these feelings" (p. 1474, author's italics). I accept Quinodoz's concept that the analyst has to create a shared language with his analysand: "a language that touches and can remain as a point of reference between the analyst and his analysand for recalling a moment of insight" (ibid.). Such shared language is based on the patient's main area of interests, or of his main "eloquent" images, related, for example, to domains such as music, football, or information technology, "while retaining certain images that have resonated in the course of the analysis" (ibid., p. 1478).

Quinodoz's concept of "words that touch" corresponds to what I define as media sensory communication (see Chapter Six) which takes place between separate individuals in the shared space. These individuals preserve common as well as personal memory traces that reverberate in similar occasions. Consequently, the verbal language represents a combination of common words that are the carriers of subjective affective meanings organised into sensual, affectionate, negative, and positive sensory communications (see above). It is obvious that dialogue can only take place between people who are aware that their words must touch their interlocutors.

The anal stage marks the beginning of a willingness to engage in dialogue in the shared space with interlocutors who facilitate a flow of sensory communication through verbal language. This flow becomes for the partners a dossier of "secret intelligence", by means of which they may intuitively collect data on the state of mind of the other participant/s and the extent of their listening and comprehension. Love is often evoked toward those who understand us and remember our messages, but we also wish to safeguard our secrets and prevent them from being forcibly removed. Some people are able to communicate the richness of their feelings, while the dry verbal language of others lacks sensory communication, which makes it very difficult for them to convey their feelings to their partners, and for their partners to understand what they are trying to convey.

Generally, a special kind of sensory communication develops between partners who experience constancy in their jointness (such as couples, siblings, friends, work colleagues, and, especially, parents and children). This exclusive communication draws on their proximity and enables partners to transmit encrypted messages to each other and to enrich their intuitions, so much so that an outsider cannot partake in this and might even feel like a stranger—excluded, ignored, or otherwise rejected. The toddler often senses these unbearable feelings of being an outsider to his parents' bonding language, as if he is left outside of the circle and does not belong (Adler, 2003).

These feelings of being an outsider to an impenetrable parental team were very familiar to me (from the age of three). My parents used to speak a foreign language between themselves that my brother and I did not understand. I remember well my curiosity about the secrets flowing between my parents and my wish to share their jointness. Slowly, through the tone of their speaking and the emotional impact (sensory communication) of the words I heard repeatedly, I began to decode and understand their foreign language, without being able to pronounce any of the words. My younger brother used to say that he had me as his private translator and mediator, so that he did not need to make any effort to understand their private language.

### Separation from familiar shared space and the befriending of new shared spaces

Natalie (at two years and three months) is going to nursery school for the first time. Her mother decides to remain with her for a few days to allow her to befriend the new teacher and the children, but without interfering in Natalie's activities. As long as her mother is close by, Natalie quickly establishes a secure passage in the new shared spaces with her newly discovered friends, toys, and teacher. When Natalie says to her mother: "Mummy, I have new friends and I like Tony my teacher," her mother understands that her mission has been accomplished. The next day, they both establish a ritual of separation, very similar to their separation ritual every night before going to sleep. Clearly, it is not only Natalie who is separating from her mother; her mother too needs to separate from her daughter and feels she has to overcome her anxiety about leaving Natalie, and relinquishing or losing control over her. Natalie says, "Bye, bye Mummy," and takes another girl's hand. "Bye, bye my darling, have a nice day. I'll come to fetch you after the teacher's story."

Two weeks later Natalie can already happily separate and go to play, and when her mother comes to fetch her, Natalie tells her in a somewhat triumphant tone: "Mummy, I played with the teacher, with Rose and Amos and it was fun." Again, just like every night, they are both able to perceive the cyclical constancy of separation from their shared spaces and subsequent rejoining, while being able to enjoy other shared spaces in the interim.

It seems to me essential to establish the familiar before going out to meet new, unfamiliar challenges, and to feel secure and alert before separating from the familiar shared space and befriending new people in new shared spaces.

In the oral stage, separation evokes mainly the anxiety of abandonment, object loss, or annihilation, while in the anal stage, separation evokes mainly the anxiety of losing control over the parent (or other person), and not knowing in what emotional state they will eventually return to the shared jointness relations—for example, will they be loving or angry.

Guy (at two-and-a-half) is getting ready to go to kindergarten. He is a happy and outgoing child. At the kindergarten gate, he clearly finds it difficult to separate from his mother, even though he separates from his father relatively easily. His mother shares with me in her therapy session: "I am anxious that something will happen to Guy in the kindergarten ... I feel as if I am abandoning my child to a concentration camp ... I feel a pain that is resonant of being separated from my mother by the Nazis ... I know full well that we are no longer in the Holocaust but still, the same feelings obsessively keep repeating themselves."

Guy's "gut feelings" presumably identify his mother's facial display or mimicry (Tomkins, 1962, 1963) as anxiety, without being able to decipher their significance, and he thus tenaciously clings to his mother and screams. Guy's father, on the other hand, sees his son as enjoying joining with the teacher and getting along with the children, and he separates from Guy with warm words: "Have a lot of fun with your friends."

Guy's gut feelings most likely identify his father's secure attitude and he separates easily from him.

Paradoxically, individuals who are capable of separating without undue difficulties are better able to share closeness. However, those who experience excessive emotionality or anxiety in separating cause irritation both to themselves and to the other party, resulting in a resistance to disengage and separate, and they are constantly anticipating the coming separation, even while being in proximity.

As we were looking around a store, our daughter (aged three) came across a toy monkey and instantly "adopted" it. Before leaving the store, we prepared her that in a few minutes she would have to separate from the monkey and return it to the shelf. We expected her familiar, "No, no, I want to keep him," and an ensuing annoying struggle. To our surprise, she put the monkey back on the shelf, separated from him affectionately, saying she would remember him, and willingly joined us. As she took each of our hands in hers, without any protest, we were deeply touched by her affectionate separation from the monkey, which overcame her wish to keep it. We embraced her tenderly, and warm feelings of closeness encompassed the three of us. A few weeks later at her birthday party, we shared her emotional reaction when she recognised the same monkey as a gift from us. She hugged it lovingly, as if she had realised her promise to remember it despite the separation. This monkey has become a significant and important figure in our family, a transitional object for all of us, and even nowadays for our grandchildren.

## The consolidation of individuation

"I know who I am. I'm Barak … I'm not Colin … I'm not Mummy … I'm not Daddy … I'm Barak!" The toddler enhances his individuation and his identity, externalises them, and presents himself so that others will recognise him and wish to be in jointness with him. He attempts to discern and assess the level of closeness, partnership, and communication that he may be able to create with each of his partners, and then updates it.

Jasmine (at two years and ten months) and her family prepare for a bicycle outing to the nearby park. Jasmine says: "I want to ride alone, not on the bicycle with Daddy. I'm already big like Sean." Her parents agree but insist on negotiating and on emphasising, "Only in the park."

At the park, Jasmine tries to demonstrate her ability and further her individuation: "I'm big like Sean, and the whole family rides together."

In this example, Jasmine tries to promote her separateness as a grown-up, autonomous girl by saying, "I want to ride alone!" However, she consolidates her individuation within the limits defined by her parents' authority ("only in the park"), as well as safeguarding the jointness with her family by declaring, "The whole family rides together."

From the anal stage onward, the individual tends to initiate creative ideas for promoting his individuation within the framework of the limits set by his authority figures. Now and again, the toddler rebels against the boundaries set by his parents in order to test their steadfastness, practice his autonomy, and, mainly, to check their tolerance and love for him even though he is asserting his individuation. Along with internalisation of the family rules and the formation of the subjective reality principle (see Chapter Six), the toddler represents himself as being part of the "we". He identifies himself as an individual, smaller than his big brothers and parents, but one who belongs to a valued cohesive unit in which he feels secure and content. At the same time, he wants quality time for love and intimate contact in jointness with the parents, without the presence of his siblings, in order to be reassured about his parents' love for him as an individual.

Marty, a patient in his thirties, shares with me his childhood individuation memories: "When I was about three years old, my father gave me a diary and said: 'We'll play every Wednesday after supper, just you and me. Each day you put a sticker in the diary so you'll know when Wednesday is coming and that we can play any game you want.' I was so proud of my diary. I waited for the Wednesdays and felt big like my father with his diary in which he arranges his meetings. The Wednesdays in my diary, when my father was there only for me, became full of my favourite stickers. I was so happy that he approved of my games and gave me tips for improving them. I love him so much … On one of our Wednesday meetings, he told me about his regular walks with his father, my grandpa, who gave him lots of advice about things that were happening with his friends. He remembered these walks, just as I remember my diary and my Wednesday meetings with my father."

It is far from simple for the toddler to promote his individuation and feel certain that his objects will validate and approve his gut feelings, be accepting of what he says, encourage him, not criticise him or clip his wings, and, particularly, continue to love him.

Natalie (at two years and ten months) plays with her doll. She forbids the doll to disobey her demands. Repeatedly, after a brief outburst of anger, she embraces her doll and says: "I love you my sweetheart, you are always my beloved one," just as her parents say to her.

Acts of imagination and imitation, and even the practicing of object relations in games by manipulating reality (Flavell, 1963; Piaget, 1936; Piaget, 1977), contribute to the development of cognitive and emotional intelligence and mentalization (Aron, 1993). This process facilitates recovery from injuries, coping with vulnerabilities, regulating contrasting or mixed feelings, and strengthening friendly and harmonious rapprochement (see Mahler, 1972b).

Edith (aged twenty-five) shares with me in her therapy session: "I'm so vulnerable to others' criticism of me ... This morning I was wearing this black dress that I like. When my boss saw me she said, 'Black doesn't suit you.' It was enough to spoil my day. I'm always afraid that others won't like the way I express myself, and that they will discover my imperfections ... I remember longing for my parents' approval, but they always criticised me."

In the anal stage, the toddler begins to differentiate between what is permissible in his imagination and in games, yet forbidden in reality and in his relations with others. He worries, however, about losing control over his phantasms, which may overflow into reality. He therefore constantly checks his parents' love and their reaction to games in which he reveals his individuation and his creativity.

In his forties, Dan still hides his individuation. He tells me in his therapy session: "I often feel bewildered and withdraw into my imagination ... After all, in my head no one can mock what I say or criticise me. There are no boundaries of permissible and forbidden, good or bad, and I can expose my authentic self to myself ... I remember when I was still in kindergarten, my father would mock me about everything, and criticise anything I did, or any thought I expressed. Ultimately, it just seemed so much easier to enjoy my hidden thoughts and my creativity. I always imagined that sometime in the future I would meet someone who would appreciate my qualities."

Like any individual, the toddler markets his uniqueness by means of his facial expressions, body language, and verbal communication with others. He practices promoting himself by playing and imagining in his self-space, prior to exposing himself in the shared space of jointness. In his self-space, the toddler may shake himself free from the emotional burden of having to bridge the otherness of objects who may frustrate his wishes; he can relax from the effort of having to gain the attention of others, and of having to attune himself to them. There, he can withdraw into a refuge from external assaults on his individuation and devote himself to restoring his true self-familiarity as wholeness. Through his reflective functioning (Fonagy & Target, 1997) and his affective attunement (Stern, 1984, 1985), he may integrate, organise, and internalise the experiences that have affected him, such as love, anger, distress, or jealousy. Above all, in his private space, he can create a phantasmic world filled with creative imaginings, achievements, games, and the secure promotion of individuation. Thereafter, encouraged by his newly won confidence in his self-familiarity constancy (as wholeness), he will be better able to manage his fluctuating, inconstant jointness relations.

On a cold wintery day, Karin (at two years and seven months) refuses to wear the slippers her grandmother offers her and insists on wearing socks. Against this backdrop, a struggle ensues. Grandma, however, assesses the situation and decides this time to let her play as she wishes. Karin happily glides around as if she were skating, while mastering her body movement to avoid falling, making sure that Grandma is aware of her achievements. After a spell of "freedom", on her own initiative, she brings the slippers and shows her grandma how she puts them on alone. She then says, "Grandma, I love you, let's play together." Karin is thus confirming that her grandma is not angry at her refusal to obey, loves her, and is willing to partner with her.

Such events consolidate the toddler's individuation, strengthen his self-esteem, enrich his partnership with the otherness of the objects, and confirm his sense of belongingness within the family unit—a unified, powerful, tribal family structure (Solan, 1991). In a parallel process, these events bring the toddler into contact with family boundaries and expectations, and the experience of alien reactions of criticism, anger, and disagreements. He becomes familiar with his parents' intolerance and, in these situations, may come to feel bad and lonely. Therefore, along with the formation of individuation and a perception of separateness, a latent process of disillusionment and mourning emerges (Freud, 1916–1917). The toddler may feel often the absence of his (oral) absolute perfection and his grandiosity in being able continually to amaze his objects. The notion of separateness, consequently, often includes another hidden derivative—within the infant as well as within the adult—namely, painful solitude.

These anal-stage pains, losses, and injuries trigger a compound process whereby healthy narcissism immunises and restores the toddler's self-familiarity. Now, however, the restoration takes place within the new limits of his body self-image, the new family rules, his reality perceptions, and the separateness of his objects. It is an updated restoration of self-familiarity. Whenever this recovery of self-familiarity individuation occurs, the toddler declares, "I am!" and, "we are!" This implies that the infant adds new narcissistic representations to his self-familiarity, such as autonomy over and beyond dependence, wholeness rather than perfection, an omnipotent self beyond a grandiose self, and of being loved as an autonomous "I am." He then imagines himself as being as grown-up as others, and able to do by himself everything that others do. Cognitively, he is quite capable of differentiating the "little ones" from the "bigger ones", children from authority figures, permitted from forbidden, and what he is capable of doing from that which he cannot do.

In light of the above, psychodynamic relations between toddler and parents now trigger new inner conflicts, which are reinforced during the narcissistic power struggles that are so prevalent in the anal stage (see Chapter Five). The toddler unconsciously fears that because of his omnipotence, his fuzzy unclear boundaries between phantasms and reality, and his magic power (see Chapter Six), he may become even more powerful than his parents and capable of damaging them or losing them. He therefore glorifies his parents with narcissistic representations of omnipotence and senses their authority, like bodyguards hovering above, protecting him from the world as well as from his own powerfulness, thereby giving solid backing to his individuation.

The toddler's belongingness to his parents' potent leadership fills him with confidence, pride, and assurance against all the strangers surrounding them (derivatives of the oral stranger anxiety). The "we are" becomes his fortress in the face of his solitude, and any hint that the family unity is being undermined evokes in him anxiety of losing control. The sense of solitude thus seems to be compensated for by the sense of belonging to the family unit and other groups.

Sean (at two years old) is going on a trip with his extended family, including his parents, grandparents, aunt and uncle, and cousin—all in all, eight family members. Even though Sean does not yet know how to count, he clearly recognises if someone is missing. It is amazing to observe him behaving like a little shepherd, making sure his flock stays together, and becoming really worried if someone momentarily strays from the tribe.

The toddler complies with his family's behaviour codes and their leadership demands, all of which require him to refrain from doing things, restrain himself, master his aggression and omnipotence, as well as recognise warning signs and be alert to danger and to strangers. All of these are integrated into a montage of his self-familiarity and family narratives that reverberate within him throughout his life as the subjective reality principle. These resonances determine his behavioural choices in individuation, in family relations, and in society, which together constitute the foundations of humanity and culture (Freud, 1927c, 1930a, 1933b [1932]). Despite these advances, from the anal stage onward, the individual continues to seek authority figures to guide him and protect him against strangeness and strangers (Solan, 1991, 1996, 1998a, 1999).

## Parents' reactions to their toddler's assertion of individuation

For parents, the period of furthering autonomy is one of the most difficult phases in child rearing. Parents are anxious that, in a moment of distraction, the infant might stumble or hurt himself or damage one of their valued household possessions. Parents need to maintain constant vigilance and they experience an ongoing dilemma regarding the extent to which they can rely on their child to be sufficiently alert to danger and care for himself, or whether they should limit his autonomy and protect him. From the anal stage onward, parents experience the narcissistic injury of not being always able to protect their child from all threats.

Although parents wish to foster their offspring's individuality and provide them with all the necessary skills to cope with their own lives, they find it difficult to separate from their growing children and to relinquish or lose control over them (an anxiety originating in the anal stage). They also often resent the toddler's attachment to caregivers other than themselves. In a parallel process, and for their own sake, parents wish to separate from their children, free themselves from worry about them, and invest more in their own interests, which often triggers guilt feelings and reinforces the above concerns.

We may observe that these parental difficulties continue even when the children leave home. According to Ellis (2011): "Helicopter parenting occurs when parents constantly interfere and interact in their children's lives. They are always there—hovering like a helicopter—micromanaging and over-analysing every little detail of the kids' lives." This "over-parenting" may deprive young adults of their independence and of the "self-worth that is created from making one's own choices" (Rettner, 2010). In fact, a recent preliminary study conducted by Montgomery in the US (of approximately 300 first-year college students) found that "students with helicopter parents tended to be less open to new ideas and actions, as well as more vulnerable, anxious and self-consciousness, among other factors, compared with their counterparts with more distant parents" (Rettner, 2010). Some of the students studied were described as "dependent … impulsive … ultimately not ready to leave the nest" (see Rettner, 2010).

Gradually, from the anal stage onward, parents attempt to regulate highly complex, narcissistic, dynamic, and emotional storms that often occur in their relationships with their offspring. Inspired by love for their child as an individual, they encourage his individuation, initiative, motivation, curiosity, and learning. They coach him in resolving dilemmas and making decisions, as well as in assuming responsibility for his needs, his body, his choices, his actions, and his life.

## *Separateness, privacy, and sharing*

From birth, along with an urge to bond with his object, the baby seeks separateness, and he mainly demonstrates this primal need by his nirvana sleeping, where he can disregard the unknown world that surrounds him. From the anal stage onward, the toddler explicitly expresses his need for individuation and privacy by exclaiming, "I want [to do it] by myself." This statement represents his wish to distance himself from his parents' support, but still to retain their love and approval.

Secrets, possessions, and privacy become the toddler's source of mastery over his body self-space, especially in the course of the diaper-weaning process of the anal stage (see Chapters Five and Six). Parents are told by their toddler not to meddle in his affairs without his express permission, including his drawers, pockets, and various collections. Parents who are able to respect their toddler's secrets, possessions, and privacy contribute to their child's evolving confidence in them, so that at a suitable time he will approach them voluntarily to share his private concerns.

This archaic urge for separateness and seclusion, and from the anal stage onward the wish to keep secrets, arises from our inborn healthy narcissism processing that immunises true self-familiarity assets (see Chapter Two). Parents also want their children to respect their privacy. Nevertheless, it seems more complicated for adults than for children to accept that their dear children or spouse holds on to their secrets, or that they need their own private space.

Jenny, a woman in her thirties, wishes to be loved but at the same time can't bear to be hugged. In the analysis, her associations led her to remember her rage against her mother, who always entered her room without having knocked first, went through her things without permission, and obliged her to wear dresses she didn't like. Jenny felt she couldn't have any privacy, and apparently experienced being hugged as an invasion, was afraid to lose her freedom and privacy.

## The nature of anal individuation

The main personality characteristics that emerge from normal development in the anal stage are autonomy (internalisation of family boundaries and rules), mastery, assertiveness, stubbornness, possessiveness, restraint, curiosity, mentalization, and motivation for creativeness, playing, and imagining. We may also observe the extent to which individuals insist on safeguarding their self-assets, their possessions, and their place in the family and the group, often accompanied by obsessive behaviour around order, cleanliness, and discipline. Tendencies may appear toward constipation (physical and emotional), hoarding, and domineeringness, as well as toward perfectionism, greed, or lavishness, influenced by the anxiety of losing control. Excessive jealousy and feelings of deprivation and inferiority tinged with shame may flood the self. Some of the characteristics may border on the pathological, such as capitulation to one's superiors, selective mutism, acute suspiciousness, excessive meticulousness, and obsessive-compulsive behaviour (Freud, 1908b, 1915c, 1930a).

David (in his forties) is the father of four boys and has a senior position in a business organisation. He describes himself as an obsessive and pedantic person who searches for perfectionism (anal personality characteristics), while, from his presentation, there seems to be little evidence of oral manifestations, such as warmth and intimacy. David is ambitious, very successful in his profession, and is known for his decency and his ability to exercise restraint and control. When he decided to stop smoking, for example, he did this from one day to the next without any difficulty. He enjoys his economic expertise and the resulting financial benefits. However, his meticulous, compulsive behaviour and strict demands for discipline from himself, his sons, and his subordinates border on the extreme. Whenever he is offended or angry with someone, he restrains himself but maintains a deafening and frightening silence toward the "offender". When watching films with emotional content, his involvement brings him to the threshold of tears, but he generally conceals this affective response and reacts cynically.

Through psychoanalysis, David was able to recognise his loneliness and his longing for closeness and sensual intimacy, and how he avoided partaking in manifestations of love (oral attributes)—even toward his wife and children—because he was anxious of losing control. In the course of treatment, he was able to connect his anxiety of being flooded by emotionality with his mother's frequent emotional outbursts when he was a little boy. Despite David's generally positive outlook and his impressive emotional strength and integrity, his anxiety of losing control and his avoidance of seeking intimacy and love weigh heavily on him.

## In the wake of the memory—the Rashomon effect[5]

The Rashomon effect refers to how the subjectivity of perception may affect recollection to such an extent that multiple observers of an event may provide substantially different, yet equally plausible, accounts of it.

When family members exchange common childhood memories, they often encounter divergence among their narratives and their representations of objects. In this situation, each individual may try to protect his own unique story and convince the others that his is the correct version. Each person may claim exclusivity and objectivity of his subjective "Rashomon version", which matches the reverberation of his memory traces. What this illustrates is that each person struggles to safeguard his true self-familiarity and narratives. Divergences between narratives narcissistically injure each individual's self-familiarity. It is as if the strangeness in the other's narrative threatens to invade the self and undermine its true self-familiarity. This narcissistic injury represents a painful awakening from the illusion that there is a "right" narrative or that one possesses exclusivity over the truth and the nature of reality. Hence, we may experience resistance to correct our original, but inappropriate, narrative.

The infant generally communicates his gut feelings or his subjective stories to his parents. Whenever these narratives differ from those the parents are familiar with, they often tend to correct him and negate his feelings and representations. The toddler's attention may divert from his own, true, familiar intuition, and disrupt the processing of his healthy narcissism. For example, a toddler says to his mother, "I've got a pain in my leg," and the mother responds, "There's nothing wrong with your leg." Or the infant claims: "I don't like the taste of tomato juice," and the parent responds, "It tastes OK, you have to drink it." The child may feel uncertain whether what he is sensing is correct, as if there can be only one right representation, feeling, or narrative.

From the anal stage onward, following such discrepancies between the toddler's gut feelings and his parent's reaction, the toddler may mobilise similar adaptation mechanisms to those he uses in the weaning process. This implies that he conceals his gut feelings—his true-self narratives—as precious secrets that no one will be able to touch and spoil, and he (his narcissism) thus manages to preserve his true self-familiarity and self-integrity. During these critical moments, the infant might also be willing to subordinate his senses to those of his parents, who "know everything". A toddler who has retained certain oral characteristics, such as a false self, might, in these emotional situations, relinquish his gut feelings and falsify his true self-familiarity feelings. He might even distort his narratives in order to please his parents and, in doing so, also distort his healthy narcissism processing.

It is therefore important to encourage children to express their gut feelings and narratives even when divergences of narratives exist. Gradually, with their parents' encouragement, they may be able to experience that differences can exist concurrently with their preserving true self-familiarity. The toddler may thus cope with the incongruity between his experiences and those of his loved ones and acquire respect for otherness in their shared space. Toddlers, no less than adults, who feel support and legitimacy for their own gut feelings, develop self-confidence in their intuition and their individuation and feel more secure and more interested in familiarising themselves with otherness. Thus, the infant may assert: "Daddy says I'm wrong, but what I say is nice."

Stern (1992)[6] defines his concept of the "pre-narrative envelope" as an infantile subjective experience, representing a pre-verbal unit and based on repeating rhythmic prototype patterns "from which narrative will emerge, transposed" (p. 294). In this regard, the pre-narrative envelope may correspond also to the foundation of the subjective Rashomon version. In fact, it seems that Stern's idea might coincide with my view of the narcissistic childhood memory traces that resonate repeatedly within the individual, together with his present occurrences. Under the influence of these reverberations of the archaic memory traces, the individual events are subjectively experienced as familiar or foreign and accorded meaning. The resonances of these units of memory traces are gradually organised into self-familiarity and associated into narratives or a Rashomon version as self-assets (as will be further be elaborated in Chapter Eight). Hence, the pre-narratives and the Rashomon version include subjective and unique goals of desires and motives that serve as the "backbone of the unit" (ibid., p. 293) (as will become apparent in the following examples).

Sid, in his thirties, tells me excitedly in his psychoanalytic session: "I met my two brothers yesterday at the cemetery, for our father's memorial day. At the grave, we exchanged memories of our childhood with Daddy. To my surprise, we discovered that it was as if each of us had a different father. It was unbelievable! Brad, the eldest, remembers him as being almost perfect, always doing the right thing ... Nathan grinned and said: 'What are you talking about? Dad was aggressive, critical, and always angry when we didn't obey him or act according to his expectations.' Whereas I, the youngest, remember his authoritative personality alongside his tolerance toward me, and his love and support ... There and then, in the cemetery, we began to argue about who knew our dad best. It was as if we each wanted to better defend Father's image ... I felt stressed. I wished I could have been there alone in the cemetery with my 'real' daddy ... that none of them would damage my memories ... Maybe I even felt guilty about having so many good memories of my dad, which they don't."

"Guilty?" I asked. Sid responded immediately: "Yes, guilty ... Nathan quarrelled a lot with Daddy about his studying, which he neglected, and I, a little boy, maybe three years old, remember that I decided to be better than him, so that Daddy would love me and be proud of me ... I was also afraid of his anger toward Nathan ... It was like stealing Daddy's love from him. That's what my guilt and my stress yesterday were about, I think ... Maybe Nathan's protecting himself against my father's anger blocked his capacity to enjoy his love for him ..."

It is indeed incredible. Three brothers from the same family subjectively experience their father so differently; their childhood memory traces repeatedly resonate in them and each is convinced that his object image is the real one. Each one has obviously different goals of desires/motives, which nourish his Rashomon effect.

Claudine, (in her forties) a mother of two children, shares with me over many sessions her hatred for her mother: "She never took care of me ... never supported me and sometimes even hit me hard. As long as I can remember, I hated her and wanted her to die ... However, whenever my mother was late returning home, I was scared and couldn't sleep." Several months later, Claudine came to the session very irritated: "My son Fred, who is now fifteen, shouted at me this morning. I don't even remember why. He hates me! ... I suddenly feel as if it's hitting me from inside ... Perhaps there were also positive sides of love and concern with my mother, but because of my hatred they weren't worth anything ... How come I've never tried, as a grown-up woman, to understand her behaviour? ... To get to know her personality better ... Now in my head some obscure, positive episodes emerge, like going together to the beach, which I loved so much ..." After a very long silence, Claudine said: "It's amazing. Although I recognise these positive episodes and have some questions about who my real mother was, I still can't get rid of the feeling that I hate her ... The thought that perhaps I missed out on my mother's love is unbearable ... Was I living in my own imaginary world and not noticing what was really going on ... I wish I could now embrace her with all my love, and beg her forgiveness ..."

Nostalgia seems to be another aspect of resonance of narrative or Rashomon effect that represents narcissistic reverberation of some familiar emotional occurrences in the past. The emotion linked to the nostalgia may emerge through resonances of memory traces of aroma, sound, or a particular familiar affect that floods the self. Recent studies (Routledge, Arndt, Wildschut, Sedikides, Hart, Juhl, Vingerhoets & Schlotz, 2011; Routledge, Wildschut, Sedikides, Juhl & Arndt, 2012) found that "nostalgia reflection" that emerges temporarily arouses in people a sense of belongingness and affiliation and provides meaning in life and continuity between their past and their present.[7,8] As such, for many people, nostalgia may be a powerful tool for improving their state of mind and self-esteem. I presume, in this sense, that nostalgia represents the healthy narcissism processing of resonances of memory traces—of familiar narratives—that confer familiar positive meaning to present experiences.

From childhood, people preserve their narratives and their Rashomon effects, positive and negative, which represent the milestones of their self-familiarities. My conception of healthy narcissism's tendency to preserve, immunise, and restore true self-familiarity against sensations of strangeness stresses the source of the narcissistic injury, while simultaneously recognising that some details in our memories may eventually prove incorrect, or that somebody else may remember them differently.

## The art of couplehood

I am constantly amazed by the delicate relations balance people have to sustain (or to orchestrate) in couplehood in order to maintain its cohesion. Couplehood represents impressive and complex object relations between two separate, very different individuals. When we discuss couplehood, we usually refer to two adults participating in an intimate relationship. I, however, have expanded the concept to include parent and child, as I find that childhood subjective experiences and narratives reverberate endlessly in each adult. In this section, I will concentrate on couplehood only in the context of oral and anal object relations.[9]

In my view, via the couplehood that emerges between parent and child, man and woman, or any pair of adults throughout life, each partner attempts to revive the familiar patterns of object relations ingrained in him or her. Repeated resonances of these patterns, which include narratives and the goals of desires/motives, become the individual's "narcissistic ideals" (Duruz, 1981). Reverberations of these concealed narcissistic ideals stimulate in individuals an unceasing search for bonding in couplehood with a partner who will match the memory traces of the original familiar parent or the relations with him. Such a search emphasises the profound significance of "object choice", a term introduced by Freud (1905d, 1914c).[10] Couplehood thus often tends to restore the jointness-separateness pattern, occasionally the wish to revive the symbiotic pattern of object relations, and generally to renew patterns somewhere between these two. Sometimes, spouses (or one of them) are affected mainly by their oral characteristics of object relations and at other times by their anal characteristics.

Kelly (2012) asserts that spouses are mainly affected by the ways they handle shame: "From early childhood on, we all develop defences against shame in order to disguise or reduce its unpleasant nature. These defences are, in part, why shame remains a hidden challenge to most relationships" (p. 63).

> [Those who have] a "big ego" are people who have so much shame they cannot tolerate anyone seeing weaknesses in them … Their rigidity creates a wall around them that is essentially impenetrable by others to the point that they have frequent and terrible marriages. Narcissistic people become so skilled at hiding their shame that neither they nor those around them can see it. (ibid., p. 64)

Relating to the oral stage, shame may appear, for example, when one of the spouses, or both, reveals how much he or she is needy, dependent, or clingy upon the other. Regarding the anal stage, shame may appear, for example, when one of the spouses, or both, reveals his need for mastery or control, his characteristic obsessive-compulsive symptomatology, or his need to collect things (including what most people would consider garbage). Thus, as Kelly (2012) asserts, when people begin living together, "the novelty begins to wear off but surely, our guard goes back up again to protect us against hurt" (p. 94).

All of us, children and adults, strive to realise the concealed narcissistic ideals of love (or love derivatives) with a spouse. We particularly cherish a smile, eye contact, a hug, or a kiss that resonates in us as the most familiar manifestations of love and proximity. These displays of oral love seem to be indispensable for fortifying the bonding between two separate individuals (even, and mostly, adults), in an attempt to preserve, immunise, and restore in their couplehood each one's narcissistic ideals of love that draw on his or her unique historical narrative.

I need to emphasise the immensely challenging task that couplehood faces in bridging the narcissistic power struggles between partners, particularly from the anal stage onward. Spouses can become trapped in endless disputes and narcissistic power struggles, just like the toddler and parent in the anal stage where each strives to impose his own narcissistic ideals on the other (see Chapter Five, for the struggle of narcissism versus narcissism). Although both spouses experience the urge to bond in love relations, they find it difficult to compromise on the nature of the relationship, given the revival of competing sets of original patterns of object relations in the present.

At times, the couple succeeds in jointly reproducing acceptable compromises (i.e., with minor differences) of the concealed narcissistic ideals, and they are elated. At other times, one of them might try to persuade the other to accept his familiar pattern, convinced that his ideals should be realised, and becomes upset whenever the other resists him. Each wishes to prove that he is right and the other wrong, seemingly oblivious to the fact that the reality principle is always subjective. Furthermore, when the behaviour of one of the partners reflects major differences from his spouse's ideals, or when he does not respect his partner's familial roots, strangeness infiltrates the self-familiarity, shame and aggression may threaten to override the need for negotiation, and one or both partners may risk neglecting their shared couplehood interest, which was to safeguard their jointness-cohesion.

In such situations reconciliation is often experienced as weakness, while aggression and aloofness are experienced as powerfulness. Hence, although each partner craves tenderness, one or both might feel ashamed of the archaic need for love and reconciliation and prefer to linger in detachment, asserting his individuation at the expense of reviving and maintaining their jointness. Unfortunately, it may seem easier to destroy the relationship than to renew jointness. When one of the partners overcomes these narcissistic injuries, he may attempt negotiation, compromise, and reconciliation, enticing the other to renew their shared wish of love relations and thus, restore jointness.

From the above, it seems clear that in order to maintain the art of couplehood we have to maximise love expressions and tolerance towards our spouse's otherness, his or her beliefs and attitudes. Positive affects have to overcome those inevitable negative ones that risk hindering the relationship or evoking communication crises (Kelly, 2012). It behooves each partner to contribute to their mutual belongingness, restoring it when necessary, so as to safeguard the cohesion of their jointness. This process illuminates the delicacy of couplehood relations.

On the way home from kindergarten, Gary usually shares with his mother the pleasant and unpleasant feelings he experienced in his separate self-space, and in the shared space of his kindergarten. He brings his experiences to the renewed jointness with his mother in their shared space: "It was fun in the kindergarten; we built a tower of blocks and then knocked it down, and built it again ... Erwin is a bad boy, not my friend."

This sharing bridges their separateness and allows them to feel the continuity and constancy of their jointness relations even when separated. The same is true of adult couples: the more they share what happens to them in external shared spaces, the more their jointness is enriched and their couplehood strengthened.

The way in which parent and toddler, during the anal stage, resolve their power struggles, restrain aggressive outbursts, and improve negotiation and reconciliation skills despite their separateness and otherness, may shape the child/adult couplehood relations. These childhood patterns may unconsciously trigger, in adulthood, characteristic oral or anal reactions and decision choices according to pleasure or reality principles, along with adaptation or defence mechanisms. Shared sensory and emotional communication between partners is thus crucial for being able to respond, support, and get along with each other's otherness.

We can observe a step-by-step example of the complex anal jointness processing: while preparing herself for kindergarten, Nathalie (at two years and ten months) succeeds in putting on her pretty dress by herself, without any help or even asking what she should wear. Nevertheless, she wishes to share her achievements with her parents and to feel the flavour of their jointness and approval.

In the first phase, Nathalie differentiates herself as a separate autonomous individual and decides to choose her dress by herself. In the second phase, she invites her parents to join her in their shared space and see how well she has managed to dress herself. In the third phase, she is aware, because of their authority (or separateness), that they might react angrily, as they did not give their consent to her choice of dress. In the fourth phase, her mother joins her happily, even though before responding to Nathalie's achievement and upon seeing the dress she had some reservations and said to herself, "Oh no, why this beautiful dress?" However, she kept her reaction to herself, in her own self-space.

In the fifth phase, in their shared space, the mother hears Nathalie saying: "Look Mummy, I dressed myself; I won't dirty my pretty dress." In saying this, it is clear that Nathalie took into consideration her mother's otherness as she tries to negotiate what is permitted. The sixth phase of their encounter culminates in jointness partnership in their shared space. The mother overcomes her inner criticism, reacts to Nathalie with pride, and marvels at her autonomy and her undertaking not to dirty her dress, while Nathalie expresses love for her mother who recognises her individuation. This time they both manage to achieve a wonderful sense of partnership in their shared jointness space.

The description of Nathalie and her mother illustrates that if either had responded differently, for example, with her mother saying, "You can't wear this dress," and by Nathalie insisting, "I'm going to wear it," the jointness ambience would have been blocked. The aftermath would be a detachment or withdrawal from jointness, each to her self-space, angry, disappointed, and offended, until able to reconcile anew in a shared space of jointness.

Carol (in her thirties) shares with me in her therapeutic session the deterioration of her marriage: "When Simon asks me to do something, I feel compelled to always say 'yes' even though I don't want to do it. I'm unable to respond to him with a 'no' or to negotiate his request, or mine with him. He always controls me and I am always submissive … It was the same with my father, even though I am now a grown woman … I can't tolerate a relationship like this any longer."

Father returns home from work. Barak (at age three) intuitively knows that his desire to pounce on his father the minute he enters will invariably be met with a refusal because his father is tired and hungry. Barak is tolerant of his father's otherness, knowing that, despite the refusal, his father loves him. In their jointness, he learns to postpone the fulfilment of his wish and says: "Dad, after you eat and rest I want to play with you." Barak thus expresses his love and his concern for his father's separateness, and his anticipation of an attuned meeting in their shared space. His father is touched by Barak's consideration, hugs him warmly and responds, "Of course we'll play together afterwards." Barak waits patiently. When his father finishes his meal, Barak summons him with his magic smile, and they both enjoy playing together. Step by step, Barak is improving the "art of couplehood" with his parents.

I agree with those behavioural economists who assert that economic principles are also relevant for a happy marriage. For example, Anderson

& Szuchman (2011) suggest that economics studies how people and societies allocate their resources (e.g., money, libido, energy) so as to "keep you smiling" and the marriage (a business venture comprising two partners), "thriving." According to these authors, it requires "artistry" to create and maintain a highly unique, individual and emotionally intimate partnership that recognizes the partners' respective strengths and weaknesses, and allows each of them to withhold parts of themselves from the other, in order to avoid unintentional harm. In my words, they accept that it is the *healthy* part of one's narcissism that preserves separateness and yet enables intimacy in jointness.

Every time I witness the jointness process, I am impressed anew by how delicate the normal psychic process is that enables a couple to achieve these infinitely marvellous moments. I consider couplehood a relationships artwork, in that partners have to create jointly forms of management to mediate tolerantly their respective separateness. They have to preserve delicate partnership attunement and tirelessly negotiate their otherness, as well as maintain calculated expectations, requests, and responsiveness. Moreover, they have to reconcile in the wake of injuries and conflicts of interest and soothe each other's injuries by lovingly touching one another (physically and emotionally). Such an art enables partners to provide for the continuity of their shared couplehood cohesion and love relationships, improve the skill to love the other person as is, despite his or her otherness, and attain happiness and contentment through both their jointness relationship and their separateness.

## Summary

In this chapter, I have elaborated my approach to the development of significant jointness-separateness object relations in the anal stage— a stage that focuses on educational requirements (cleanliness, order, and discipline), diaper weaning, and advances in communication. Evolution along these crucial and privileged moments of rapprochement (especially in the oral and anal stages) takes place in the various shared spaces of jointness relations in which the partners attempt to bridge their separateness and otherness, and experience closeness. From the anal stage onward, these relations are characterised by a narcissistic power struggle between the parent's assertion of authority and the toddler's assertion of autonomy, as well as by negotiation between the partners (while each confronts the otherness of their partner), and reconciliation via expressions of love and shared interests. Parents and toddler may initiate separation from the shared familial spaces and enter into new shared spaces of jointness relations outside the family.

Consolidation of the toddler's individuation and the perception of separateness accompanied by the acquisition of verbal language—as the carrier of sensory and affective communication—advances the transition from speaking in monologue to communication through dialogue in the shared spaces. Jointness relations from the anal stage onward culminate in the art of couplehood between parent and child, spouses, a pair of colleagues in a team, etc. The art of relationship may be viewed as a long-term joint venture, with a common or shared motivation to respect the family rules and bridge one's separateness and otherness. The art of couplehood thus points to the complexity of relations between separate, very different individuals, yet ones who are so similar in their need for love and mastery.

## Notes

1. For triadic object relations in the oral stage, see Chapter Four.
2. Piaget (1936) claims that patterns of language are acquired as part of the baby's cognitive system, and that we have to differentiate between acquisition of language until age four and any subsequent language acquisition. See Vygotsky (1962) for a different account of the development of thought and language. Chomsky (1985) claims that the human language-acquisition ability is based on a universal innate infrastructure of grammar (*syntactic structures*), an internal structure of languages.
3. Z. Solan and his colleagues (2005) developed an algorithm that achieves computerised learning of compound syntax, and creates new, meaningful sentences without any prior knowledge, and only on the basis of exposure to the text (ADIOS—Automatic Distillation Of Structure).
4. "Synaesthesia—(noun) a condition in which a secondary subjective sensation (often colour) is experienced at the same time as the sensory response normally evoked by the stimulus. For example, the word 'cat' might evoke the colour purple." (Martin, 2007, p. 696)

    Synaesthesia is the coming together (coupling) of two or more senses. It is a neuropsychological phenomenon, whereby the stimulation of one pathway (e.g., sensory or cognitive) is coupled with, and evokes involuntary experiences in a second pathway. In working with people who have undergone stressful and traumatic experiences, it is necessary to "uncouple" this coming together, and work with one sensation at a time (see Ross, 2008).

5. Named after Akira Kurosawa's film *Rashomon* (1950), in which a crime witnessed by four individuals is described in four mutually contradictory ways.

6. Stern (1992) calls the "pre-narrative envelope" an alternative view of the "unconscious phantasy". He reminds that "the point of reference for the concept of an 'unconscious phantasy' is contained in Freud's (1916–17) earlier views of a 'primal phantasy' and in the Kleinian view of an 'unconscious phantasy' (Isaacs, 1948)," and that "these conceptions, 'unconscious phantasies' are inherited scenarios containing an object, aim and goal" (p. 291). Stern adds that "students of narrative structure have found motives and goal-orientation to be crucial *narrative aspects*" (p. 293, author's italics).

7. *Moses and Monotheism* (Freud, 1937c), as elaborated by Rolnik (2012), may also represent such a Rashomon effect.

8. Rutter and Rutter (1993) also elaborated the influence of past experiences on the present.

9. Obviously, in subsequent developmental stages, individuals confront other very important couplehood issues, such as libidinal and sexual attraction.

10. Object choice—This term is often reserved for love-objects. This may be someone like oneself or possessing attributes one would like to have (a narcissistic object-choice), or someone who can gratify one's needs for nurturance and protection (an anaclitic choice) (Skelton, 2006, cited in Tuckett & Levinson, 2010). This concept was further elaborated by Blatt (1974), who attempted to differentiate between an anaclitic and an introjective depression, linking type of depression to self and object representation. An introjective choice uses introjection and identification with the aggressor in an attempt to retain the object internally, while safeguarding its potential love. That the object is needed to provide approval, acceptance, and love, implies a more advanced developmental level (e.g., superego) than that of someone who relates to the object more in terms of need gratification/frustration. Note that Blatt's attempt to link anaclitic and introjective types of depression to developmental level of object relations (Blatt, 1974), and his original findings, failed to be replicated and extended with a large sample (Shidlo, 1985). "The term 'object-choice' is used to designate either the choice of a particular person (e.g., 'his object-choice is directed on to his father'), or else the choice of a certain type of object (e.g., 'homosexual object-choice')" (Laplanche & Pontalis, 1973, p. 277).

# CHAPTER EIGHT

# Healthy and pathological narcissistic processes

## The formation of self-familiarity

From the moment of birth and the departure from the protected space of the womb, the newborn is a separate mental entity from his mother, loaded with an inherited genetic makeup and physiological sensations rooted in his manifold intrauterine sensory experiences. This mental entity is thought to represent an initial accumulation of sensory information, imprinted, as it were, as experiential memory traces on the narcissistic immunological memory network. This primordial mental base is enriched and fortified from babyhood onward by infinite subjective experiences that leave enduring memory traces, continuously organised into familiar "senses of the self" (Stern, 1985), which I define as "self-familiarity". In other words, we can experience and recognise ourselves as familiar, and sense and recognise our familiar self in different daily occurrences. Alternatively, in certain situations, we can sense ourselves as unfamiliar or strange, as well as vulnerable, injured, or traumatised.

As we will see, my conceptualisation of self-familiarity connects with and expands on Stern's views: "Sense of the self is not a cognitive construct. It is an experiential integration. This sense of a core self will be the foundation for all the more elaborate senses of the self to be added later" (Stern, 1985, p. 71).

Moore and Fine's (1990) definitions of the self and of "self-schemata" may be closer to what I mean by self-familiarity, although I consider self-familiarity as "experiential integration" (Stern, 1985) and not as a cognitive structure:

> The total person of an individual in reality, including one's body and psychic organization; one's "own person" as contrasted with "other persons" or objects outside one's self … [Self-schemata are] enduring cognitive structures that actively organize mental processes and code how one consciously and unconsciously perceives oneself; they range from realistic to distorted self views which the individual has had at different times … represent aspects of the bodily or mental self, including the drives and affects perceived in reaction to the person's own self and to the outer world. Various self schemata are hierarchically arranged into supraordinate forms and then into an overall self organization during maturation. (Moore & Fine, 1990, p. 174)

Self-familiarity also includes self-assets (for example, personal narratives)—all memory traces of these self-experiential acquisitions are condensed and shaped as representations. We thus have representations of one's self, one's objects, manifold relationships, realisations, and achievements, in conjunction with the countless narratives that we develop throughout life. The shaping of self-familiarity and the combinations of all these memory traces into self-assets, as well as their accumulation, undergoes advanced ego processing such as abstraction (Kandel, 2006), assimilation, accommodation, separation, and reintegration (Piaget, 1977). This shaping is influenced and enhanced mainly by positive aspects of object relations, such as promotion of intimacy, separation and individuation. Self-familiarity and self-assets are influenced as well by negative aspects of object relations such as enduring self-object and symbiotic relations, denial of separateness, intolerance, shaming, and criticism.

Under optimal conditions, the infant's entire emotional organisation may be integrated into a cohesive unity of self-familiarity, in which positive memory traces prevail over negative. This cohesiveness may solidify, as it were, into a *true sense of the familiar self*, one perceived in the oral stage as perfection. The self-familiarity and self-assets are updated in the anal stage, along with the continuously accumulating and integrated memory traces of the toddler's subjective experiences, for example, those of imperfections or deficiencies, as well as those of parental encouragement. Now, the true sense of the familiar self can be shaped and perceived as omnipotent wholeness, bringing with it a sense of self-familiarity encompassing separateness, autonomy, joint-ness and belongingness. Perception of wholeness, in this regard, is not concerned with an ideal, universal, perfect whole, but rather with the subjective integrity of self-familiarity, which includes deficiencies. The subjective perception of wholeness is crucial for the individual as an ultimate narcissistic immune frame—for recognising himself, decipher-ing strangeness within his self-familiarity or emanating from the out-side, and identifying the non-self or the otherness within his objects (see the section on the narcissistic immunisation and restoration of true self-familiarity as wholeness, below).

Under the impact of constant resonances of negative memory traces, the entire emotional organisation may be constituted in false cohesive-ness or in fragile shaping or incoherence, arousing a sense of fusion with the object and resulting in self-object familiarity. Such an emo-tional organisation may solidify into the predominance of a false and vulnerable self-familiarity, alternately perceived as ideal or damaged.

It is thus important to recall that during the subjective experi-ences of childhood, the infant's self-familiarity encompasses several agglomerations of organised memory traces, providing him or her with various senses of his or her familiar self and self-assets. During daily occurrences, resonances of these variously organised memory traces of childhood subjective experiences emerge. These resonances range from positive and consolidating memory traces to negative and vulnerable ones—from rewarding to injuring ones. The reverberat-ing memory traces colour the sense of the familiar self in the present; consequently, the individual recognises himself through a predominant self-familiarity, while other, less-pervasive senses of the familiar self appear occasionally.

Injuries from within and from outside often destabilise the predomi-nant sense of the familiar self (whether self-familiarity or self-object-familiarity; true self or false self). This destabilisation of cohesiveness may lead to the appearance of the less predominant or subordinate forms of self-familiarity, whether positive or negative, in different moments of subjective experience. For example, various incisive moments, such as those following a timely creative therapeutic interpretation, the emergence of a love relationship, or even a traumatic illness, may evoke and engage the less substantial, positively-toned self-familiarity that was compressed, smothered or concealed under the impact of recurring injuries.

Whenever the self-familiarity cohesiveness is undermined (as previously elaborated in Chapters Two and Five), narcissistic immunisation and restoration processing is triggered.

## The narcissistic immunisation of self-familiarity

Generally, when discussing narcissism, we talk about "disorders" without paying sufficient attention to what I regard as *healthy* narcissism. Thus, both in practice and in the psychoanalytic literature, we may find a vast array of minor to major narcissistic disturbances between the poles of healthy and pathological narcissism. In this section, I shall discuss the narcissistic processing that occurs between these two poles, and emphasise the disparity between them, with the aim of revealing the hidden roots of what ultimately causes this diverse narcissistic immune processing.

To my understanding, from birth onward, the innate survival objectives of narcissism remain the same, namely, to immunise and restore self-familiarity and familiar self-assets according to their original or primary consolidation, and to resist alien invaders (see Chapters Two and Five). Hence, healthy, distorted, and pathological narcissism are all outcomes of the same innate narcissism processing.

I share Stolorow's (1975) distinction between healthy or unhealthy narcissism, that is, "whether or not it succeeds in maintaining a cohesive, stable and positively colored self-representation" (p. 184). One may ask why and under what conditions narcissism either succeeds or fails to maintain cohesiveness of the positively[1] coloured memory traces (representations) of self-familiarity. For example, to what extent does the self-esteem system need to be flexible so as to accept less-than-perfect positively-coloured images of the self? What does this flexibility consist of, and how is it achieved? How is the restoration of cohesiveness achieved following injuries that undermine its integrity, and how much time is needed? How is self-familiarity regained?

Stern (1992) elaborates the "pre-narrative envelope" (see Chapter Seven) as founded on the "infant's pattern-recognition abilities" (p. 299), and on his aptitude for recognising recurring experiences as global patterns. I conceptualise these recognition abilities as the innate emotional immune processing of healthy narcissism according to its attraction to the familiar and its resistance to strangeness. The individual's familiarity represents his narcissistic and ego organisation[2] of memory traces, fashioned by the repetitive and constant subjective experiences gathered and associated since the foetus's first sensory experiences in the womb. The affective frame, which is often related to objects, is subsequently condensed (and associatively linked) with sensory sensations and stored as memory traces.

The frequent reverberations of positive (rather than negative) memory traces in present occurrences evoke recognition memory of the familiar, and affect the meaning of subjective experiences. Or, as Stern suggests, the infant recognises the invariant characteristics that remain constant across all the changes, and his "unconscious phantasy" (1985, p. 301) encompasses desire, perception, action, and affect, as well as discharge.

The individual's constant recognition of his positive self-familiarity consolidates the narcissistic preservation and immunisation of the predominant, most familiar, and cohesive sense of his familiar self. In light of this subjective frame of wholeness, his self-familiarity may be narcissistically immunised, adjusted, and restored by (adaptive) flexibility, continuity, and integrity when destabilised.

During the individual's lifespan, the gradual improvement and refinement of his narcissistic processing facilitates the adjusted immunisation of his true self-familiarity and, when challenged, accelerates the restoration of self-familiarity according to the familiar subjective frame of wholeness. In this sense, the restoration of self-familiarity might be considered as similar to a jigsaw puzzle. Following injuries from both inside and outside, the successful healthy narcissistic restoration of cohesive self-familiarity relies upon the availability of one's positively-coloured memory traces. Such memory traces (as described above) may represent, inter alia, subjective experiences of being accepted by one's objects as a separate individual, in addition to "belonging" to them, that is, recognised as familiar and as part of them.

Barak (at age five) was hurt by his father's criticism of his behaviour and went crying to his room. He loves his father greatly, but in moments such as these he feels hate for him. He crushed a picture he had drawn for his father and threw it into the garbage can. He then managed to calm down, took out the painting, straightened it, and sat down to draw on another piece of paper—a family of parents and three children. He took the drawing to his father who hugged him warmly, ignoring the emotional storm Barak had gone through, and the restoration of self-familiarity that he had achieved. That night, before going to sleep, Barak told his father that he had crushed the drawing because he was angry, but that he had straightened it. He also told his father that he thought a policeman might come and be angry with him for his behaviour, but that he remembered his father once told him that he is such a good boy that a policeman will always come to help him and not to blame him. His father was very touched by what Barak said, hugged him, and said goodnight, leaving both of them filled with love and an awareness of having controlled their aggression.

The entire emotional organisation may also, under the impact of constant resonances of negative memory traces, be constituted in fragile cohesiveness or in incoherence, arousing a sense of fusion with the object, and resulting in self-object familiarity. Such an emotional organisation might solidify into a false and vulnerable self-familiarity, alternately perceived as ideal or damaged.

An interesting observation emerges: when the individual's present occurrences trigger narcissistic resonances coloured by positive memory traces, his narcissism may restore his self-familiarity according to flexible, improved, almost-familiar immune processing (flexible familiarity principle). On the other hand, when the individual's present occurrences trigger narcissistic resonances coloured by negative memory traces, his narcissism is restored via a rigid, destructive, wholly familiar immune processing (rigid familiarity principle). For example, one is either fully accepted by one's objects for fusion, or threatened with abandonment when exhibiting signs of separation. In other words, along such an individual's lifespan, his or her narcissistic processing depends so much on the self-object's conditional availability that its improvement and refinement is distorted. Under these conditions, a fragile and negatively-coloured (representation of) self-familiarity is narcissistically preserved, immunised, and restored, leading to pathological narcissism. This will become clearer below.

### The formation of narcissistic schemata

Besides their characteristics in creating self-familiarity, memory traces are organised into what I call *narcissistic schemata*. The constant resonance of these schemata with the individual's daily experiences provides him with a familiar frame for his narcissistic recognition or repudiation of the particular occurrences, and for dealing with actual circumstances as familiar or strange.

The conceptualisation of narcissistic schemata may be understood as relating to the terms "schema", used by Piaget (1936), "schemata", used by Sandler (1987), "pre-narrative envelope", elaborated by Stern (1992), "script theory", coined by Tomkins (1987), and "self-schemata", defined by Moore and Fine (1990). Script theory stresses the importance of the processing of data experiences within each primary affect category (see Tomkins, 1962, 1963) and postulates the retaining and storing in memory of whatever was experienced in previous occurrences when that specific affect or affect range was experienced. This formulation in fact represents all the terms mentioned above, while each is related to certain attributes of the self, such as: affects (Tomkins, ibid.), cognitive intelligence (Piaget, 1936), ego functioning and feeling of safety and well-being (Sandler, 1960), schemas of motivational, affective and object-related experience (Stern, 1992) etc.

I define narcissistic schemata as continuing associations of memory trace configurations that constantly reverberate as codes for narcissistic immunisation and restoration of self-familiarity. Narcissistic schemata resonate throughout the individual's experiences, consciously or unconsciously, in various emotional configurations or combinations (or "assemblies", to use Tomkins's term), such as perceptions, representations, associations, fantasies, narratives, and feelings. Hence, these schemata serve as subjective structures or keystones, by means of which the individual may review, interpret, and attribute significance and meaning to his daily experiences on the basis of past experiences. Moreover, it is likely that narcissistic immunisation and restoration of self-familiarity will take place in attunement with resonances of narcissistic schemata. Presumably, these narcissistic schemata or templates will also colour future expectations and object relations.

The most frequently reverberating narcissistic schemata become the individual's *default resonance*, his subjective keystones for handling actual occurrences and for updating self-familiarity. Individuals thus cope better with almost-familiar experiences than with unknown occurrences and may feel secure in predicting what will come next, thereby avoiding the insecurity of the unknown. (Thus, if the sun shone yesterday, surely it will shine today and tomorrow, regardless of whether this follows logically.)

Three main narcissistic schemata can be conceptualised as follows.

a. Narcissistic *beneficial* schemata (NBS), containing mainly clusters of favourable, constructive, and positively-coloured memory traces relating to experiences of the true self, of separateness, and of coping with non-self otherness in terms of jointness-separateness relationships.
b. Narcissistic *harming* schemata (NHS), containing mainly clusters of hurtful, negatively-coloured memory traces relating to infrequent experiences of being harmed, criticised, deceived, frustrated, treated with disdain, or otherwise insulted by one's objects.
c. Narcissistic *destroying* schemata (NDS), containing mainly clusters of destructively-coloured memory traces that invade self-familiarity by means of unceasing painful experiences of rejection, humiliation-shame, and trauma. Most of these NDS memory traces are the outcome of the child's cumulative trauma (Khan, 1963) and of his being repeatedly criticised, mocked, treated aggressively, neglected, physically abused, and/or abandoned. The NDS might include data of symbiotic object relations evoking a sense of merging with the self-object, and with separation experienced as traumatic and as triggering anxiety of annihilation.

To clarify the above, let us examine some examples of NHS resonances followed by NBS default reverberations.

Alvin (at about three years old) challenges his father to a game. His father refuses and orders him to stop playing in the lounge because he is making too much noise. Alvin is deeply offended, takes his game, and withdraws, crying, to his room, murmuring on the way: "You never play with me, I don't love you." [Alvin's current experience resonates with former frustrations and hurt involving his father, provoking his aggression, which we may refer to as NHS.] Some minutes later, still in his room, he chooses another game and calms down. Unconsciously, he picks out a game that he likes to play with his father [his NBS resonate with memories of his father playing with him and loving him]. Therefore, a few minutes, later Alvin goes back to the lounge and kindly invites his father to play together: "Pappy, please play this game with me." [The NBS apparently resonate a positive representation of his father.] It appears that Alvin has overcome his pain, and it is important for him to reconcile with his father. The father reacts positively [the father's NBS resonance] and the relationship is restored. One may surmise that Alvin's true self-familiarity is restored by his healthy narcissism, as he manages to preserve his self-integrity despite the injury, and his father's positive representation despite the frustration and anger. It seems as well that Alvin's ego has mobilised adaptation mechanisms that enable him to choose a suitable game and to negotiate with his father in accordance with his desire that they play together, as befitting their familiar jointness-separateness relations. Alvin's self-esteem is enhanced by his father's approval and expression of love.

An example of "default" NHS resonances: Angie (at two years and ten months) is in a similar situation to that of Alvin. She cannot tolerate her father's refusal and reacts impulsively by throwing her game on the floor. "I hate you, you're a bad father," she says, and storms off to her room. She is highly prone to being hurt and carries on crying in her room for a long time, unable to calm herself and repeatedly proclaiming, "Nobody loves me." [Under the influence of her NHS, which resonate constantly, she feels insulted and is overwhelmed by her injuries. At the same time, Angie's ego mobilises a defence mechanism: she projects her aggression on to her "bad" father and feels rejected by him, while in fact it is *she* who is being aggressive and who rejects the father.] Only when she goes to sleep does Angie cooperate with her father's goodnight ritual and accept his attempt at reconciliation [her NBS probably resonate the ritual of expressions of love before going to sleep, which enables her to reconcile with father and to restore her positive representation of him, until the next injury].

Over the course of many analytic sessions, Arnold (in his fifties) shares with me his anxiety about his professional achievements: "After success comes a blow." He remains silent, and then associates: "My mother used to say: 'Don't be so pleased with yourself; beware of the evil eye.'" Arnold then sinks into another long silence and finally adds: "Marilyn, my daughter [in her twenties], is succeeding in dance school ... I'm proud of her ... But I'm still afraid to express my pride ... Yesterday she phoned me and told me that next week she has an important performance and that she needs my support ... Then she added: "You've never genuinely encouraged me to show my capabilities. You've always said, 'Be careful.' I know that you love me but I need also to feel that you have confidence in me. Your support is important to me." I was nearly in tears, sensing a precious closeness with her … I so much wanted to really encourage her and was so stupidly reluctant to do so."

A few minutes later, I interpreted: "Your daughter could sense your love but she probably also sensed the concealed evil eye, your mother's saying, 'Beware of the evil eye.'" [An introject] Arnold responded: "Evil eye. Do I really believe in the evil eye? … No! It has nothing to do with me. It's my mother's superstition … I'm really proud of Marilyn and I want to support her with all my love."

"Don't be so pleased with yourself; beware of the evil eye," emerged as Arnold's NDS resonance alongside experiences of success, causing him repeated professional failure and a reluctance to encourage his daughter's success. In other emotional states, such as expressions of love for his daughter, his NBS resonate constantly. Marilyn, however, resists her father's NDS resonances; her own NBS default resonance prevails over her father's NDS. She is able to safeguard her self-familiarity in integrity against the invasion of her father's NDS, whereas her father failed to resist his own mother's NDS invasion into his self-familiarity. Marilyn attains success even though she never relinquishes her need for his support and is able to express this (NBS resonance). Gradually, and especially as a result of his daughter's comments, Arnold is able to recognise his NDS invader, in the form of the "evil eye", as alien to him—his mother's introjected superstition that, he realises, "has nothing to do with me." When he was able to begin resisting the invader, his motivation to safeguard his self-familiarity and his professional achievements increased, even though the "evil eye" continued to reverberate within him from time to time without, however, invading his true self and undermining his self-integrity.

Self-familiarity is enriched throughout the lifespan with both constructive and destructive data, and becomes an enormous depository of processed and processing data. This network is analogous to a huge family tree whose roots are linked to branches connected to various other subsets of self-familiarity information. This implies that all the narcissistic schemata (NBS, NHS, and NDS) resonate in each of us as an inseparable part of our daily life, and one or two may become our default resonances, through which narcissism immunises self-familiarity. We may assume that healthy narcissism is a processing that takes place mainly by triggering predominantly NBS reverberations in daily experiences. Conversely, pathological narcissism may be seen as processing characterised by the triggering of predominantly NDS reverberations in daily experiences. Usually, these schemata resonate within us without our being aware of them, rather, we are mindful only of their consequences, that is, when our true self-familiarity is affected.[3]

## The tasks of narcissistic processing

The individual's innate immune narcissism is constantly decoding minor or major differences between the self and non-self and their compatibility or incompatibility, and differentiating the self-familiarity from any alien threat. The individual's narcissism is thus programmed to process constantly (according to multiple tasks), differentially supported (or not), by ego functioning and the influences of object relations. The major tasks of narcissistic processing are as follows.

a. Immunise the sense of the familiar self as true self-familiarity.
b. Preserve self-familiarity in separateness from the non-self.
c. Maintain attraction to the familiar, and mainly to the familiar non-self object.
d. Maintain alertness to strangeness emanating from the other.
e. Maintain tolerance toward the otherness of the object through a progressive befriending of the object's separateness.
f. Safeguard the cohesiveness and separateness of self-familiarity as wholeness in situations in which boundaries are sensed as temporarily blurred, such as in intimacy and blissful happiness with the non-self object.
g. Activate resistance to the invasion of alien elements that threaten to undermine self-familiarity cohesiveness.
h. Persevere with the matching of self-familiarity (including self-assets) with the resonances of the narcissistic schemata and the incoming memory traces.
i. Withdraw from the shared space with the object/s to the self-space following injuries, or for processing the incoming data or restoring true self-familiarity before rejoining the object/s in a shared space.
j. Restore true self-familiarity following the inevitable injuries caused by otherness, unfamiliarity, and unexpected or harmful occurrences. Restoration of the true self also takes place whenever the individual discerns an invasion into his self-familiarity (for example, by an introject, as in the above example of Arnold and the evil eye).

In certain situations, however, unexpected occurrences, both positive and negative, may not trigger resonance of comparable narcissistic schemata, or perhaps not do so quickly enough, thereby putting the individual at risk for experiencing uneasiness, destabilisation, stupor, or even trauma. This implies that trauma reflects a sudden invasion of strangeness within the sense of the familiar self, and that one's narcissism is unable to preserve the self-familiarity from this sharp invasion. Paradoxically, unexpected positive occurrences may sometimes be experienced as stupefaction or be traumatic for the same reasons mentioned above or due to resonance of narcissistic schemata representing the unexpected emergence of threat, injury, calamity, or trauma (NDS). In these moments, the individual's positive or even happy experience might be transformed into anxiety, conscious or unconscious, for a few seconds or even longer. Sometimes he or she may become dazed or confused.

The following is an example of a woman in psychoanalysis whose narcissistic processing usually predominates as healthy narcissism, while her NDS resonate at occasional, if crucial moments [I address the emotional dynamics in brackets].

In one of her sessions, Mina (in her thirties) tells me: "Yesterday I had a romantic meeting in the park with Mick. We were both very happy [NBS resonance appropriate to the current experience]. Suddenly I had a panicky feeling I couldn't explain, as if some calamity was about to occur that would destroy our happiness forever ... Mick was offended." [NDS prevail over the NBS in inappropriate resonance with the current experience of happiness.] After a long silence, Mina associated her feelings to a trauma she had experienced when she was five years old: "We had a very enjoyable family outing and suddenly, in the middle of a field of flowers, my father had to lie down because of terrible pain. My mother called an ambulance and he was taken to hospital. I was afraid that my father was going to die because of me, because I was so happy ... my mother always criticised my joyful behaviour. She wanted me to be happy, but to remain calm. She would say: 'Don't be too happy, because it might end in misfortune' ... She was right; the misfortune happened."

Generally, Mina enjoys jointness relationships sustained by her healthy narcissism processing and ego adaptation mechanisms. However, in moments of exceptional happiness with her boyfriend, the unconscious destroying (NDS) reverberations of the traumatic narrative, which links her joyfulness and her father's collapse with her mother's warning, override the default NBS resonances. In the above situation, her emotional stress level rises and destroys her joyfulness. Mina's insights in the session released her healthy narcissism processing to restore true, cohesive self-familiarity. She decided to share her traumatic memory with Mick, to apologise for her behaviour, and to reconcile with him (adaptation mechanism). A few months later, she noticed that while these traumatic cues continued to make their appearance and were burdensome, they generally did not spoil her happiness.

## Narcissistic immunisation and restoration of true self-familiarity as wholeness

We can discern the individual's sense of true self-familiarity mainly through his body language, his emotional expressions, and particularly his reactions to being hurt. This sense of being hurt (NHS resonances) by our partners in the shared space undermines the well-being of our self-familiarity and evokes the shame family of emotions. We may thus feel hurt, lonely, rejected, isolated, or distant. In order not to experience these difficult feelings, we are often flooded by rage. In moments like these, when the emotional connection to our partner is broken, we tend to withdraw into our self-space, where healthy narcissism may process a restoration of true self-familiarity through NBS resonances and ego adaptation mechanisms. Thus, outbursts of rage (prevailing of NHS and NDS over NBS resonances) and mourning of the loss of well-being take place in one's self-space. Gradually, by imagining, negotiating, and reconciling (adaptation mechanisms) with the one who offended (jointness-separateness relations), a reconstruction of the positively-toned aptitudes of the self and the objects appear (prevailing of NBS over the NHS resonance). Now, the individual's healthy narcissism can restore the sense of the familiar self, according to the NBS default resonance of the predominant self-familiarity characteristics as wholeness. The individual might even restore his true self-familiarity after being invaded temporarily by otherness, for example, when made to feel guilty (NDS) by the other's accusations.

These recovery and reconciliation experiences contribute to enhancing the individual's self-esteem and cathecting his self-familiarity with the added value of narcissistic wholeness despite his deficiencies (healthy narcissism), as well as with added value to his ego of self-competence despite his failures (ego's adaptation mechanism), and added value in the relationship of love, communication, and proximity, despite the hurtful injuries and the otherness emanating from his partner (jointness object relations).

It will be recalled that during the oral stage, the perception of whole-ness is absolute (based on the all-or-nothing principle and the absolute familiarity principle). The baby experiences himself, his parents, and his relationship with them as a perfect wholeness, one that contributes to the formation of his ideal-self and ideal-object. Yet, obviously, he is very vulnerable to any deviation from these ideals and any injury to this perfection. From about eighteen months (the start of the anal stage) and throughout life—by means of the harmonious functioning between healthy narcissism and the ego's adaptation mechanisms, influenced by jointness-separateness relationships with his objects—the perception of self-familiarity is constantly updated as wholeness despite its imper-fections. In fact, healthy narcissistic processing attests to continuous narcissistic emotional organisation of associations and dissociations among inner memory traces, just as between representations of self and objects. Being hurt triggers dissociation, explosions of rage, mourning of the lost perfection, and association and reintegration around various imperfections, disabilities, and new circumstances. This ability implies flexibility and elasticity as opposed to rigidity and brittleness.

A child or adult who strives for perfection does not, in the main, experience wholeness of the familiar self. He is usually dissatisfied with his achievements, perceiving himself as lacking and insecure. This type of individual tends desperately to seek (oral) perfection by means of obsessive (anal) perfectionist wishes and activities.

The individual's sense of true self-familiarity as wholeness and as coping with his deficiencies seems, to me, essential for his self-esteem, especially regarding his capabilities and his self-confidence, gained throughout experiences of managing and restraining. Moreover, this sense of wholeness and grounding seems crucial for the progression of his individuation and for his creative communication and relations with others, as well as for his capacity to love the other and be happy. (Note that what one person perceives as wholeness may be regarded by another as impairment—the difference between seeing the half-full versus the half-empty glass.)

I wish to draw attention to the capacity to love the other and to be loved, as well as the capacity to be happy with one's lot, as the outcomes of healthy narcissism. We usually discover that it is not as simple as it seems to love the other—a fact that is strongly connected to childhood patterns of object relations.

We often realise that object relations perform a rather complex task. At least two different individuals, such as baby and parent (or spouses) are constantly enticed to experience love relationships. Each one is attracted to join the familiar non-self other and, with him as his object, to revive his own archaic or childhood experiences of intimacy as wholeness (according to his subjective experiences and his narcissistic schemata resonances). At the same time, each one is constantly attracted by familiarities, resists strangeness and otherness (narcissistic processing), and is motivated to regulate his instincts, drives, and emotions (ego function).

One of my substantial convictions is that the adult's capacity to love the other seems to pass through his parents' ability to enjoy intimacy *with him*, to consider his separateness and to respect his otherness (childhood experiences ingrained in the narcissistic schemata). This capacity must be followed by the respect adults accord to the otherness of their parents. This implies our accepting our child/parents as they are, as human—with their merits and virtues, as well as their mental health issues, emotional handicaps, or inadequacies—and particularly, our being able to appreciate the love they were able to give us throughout our childhood.

No one is perfect, and most parents are good enough. Parents can respond to their child, cherish, and love him (or her) only through or according to their personality skills and deficiencies. Up to the latency stage, the child's emotional need is to be an accepted partner of his parents, and to give and receive affection from them. At the same time, he needs to appreciate each of his parents as a valuable familiar wholeness that provides a sense of security. The problems arise in adolescence: most adolescents are disappointed to discover that their parents are imperfect and fall short of their imagined wholeness and perfection— a normal emotional development—and they fail to restore and update the parents' familiarity as wholeness. They tend to blame the parents for their own deficiencies (they unconsciously blame the parents for "spoiling" the parent-familiarity they have consolidated from childhood), and the parents are then liable to feel guilty. Maturity differs from adolescence in this regard, and characterises a situation in which one is able to appreciate one's parents despite their mistakes, and to acknowledge that no one can avoid making mistakes or causing injury (whether to parents, children, or spouses) due to one's otherness and various imperfections.

Winnicott expounds this ambiguity so admirably that, although previously quoted, it is worth repeating:

> And in any case you [the parent] will make mistakes and these mistakes will be seen and felt to be disastrous, and your children will try to make you feel responsible for setbacks even when you are not in fact responsible ... You will feel rewarded if one day your daughter asks you to do some baby-sitting for her, indicating thereby that she thinks you may be able to do this satisfactorily; or if your son wants to be like you in some way, or falls in love with a girl you would have liked yourself, had you been younger. Rewards come *indirectly*. And of course you know you will not be thanked. (Winnicott, 1971, p. 143)

## Patterns of object relations and their impact on healthy or pathological narcissism

The Dulcinea theme in the *Man of La Mancha*[4] illustrates Aldonza's wish to be recognised and loved according to her familiar sense of self. She wishes to be loved as Aldonza (representing her deficient self-familiarity and her complicated object relations) and she resists being loved as the unfamiliar lady Dulcinea. In this example, we see the persistence of Don Quixote's NBS resonances and the constancy of Aldonza's NDS resonances (the italics are mine to emphasise these issues):

DON QUIXOTE:    ...I have *dreamed thee too long,* /.../*But known thee with all of my heart.* /.../Though we have been always apart. My lady ... *Now I've found thee,* /.../Dulcinea ... Dulcinea!

ALDONZA:    *I am not your lady!* .../I am not any kind of a lady!/I was spawned in a ditch by *a mother who left me there/ Naked and cold and too hungry to cry/* ... /Then, of course, there's my father/*I'm told that young ladies/Can point to their fathers with maidenly pride*/Mine was some regiment/Here for an hour ... /So of course, I became, as befitted my delicate birth/The most casual

DON QUIXOTE:   And still thou art my lady.

ALDONZA:   And still *he torments me!*/A LADY! How should I be a lady?/For a lady has modest and maidenly airs/And a virtue I somehow suspect that I lack/.../*Won't you look at me,* look at me, /Look at the kitchen slut, reeking of sweat/.../A strumpet men use and forget ... *Take the clouds from your eyes and see me as I really am!*/You have shown me the sky, /But what good is the sky/To a creature who'll never do better than crawl? /*Of all the cruel bastards who've badgered and battered me/You are the cruelest of all! /Can't you see what your gentle insanities do to me?* /Rob me of anger and give me despair! /*Blows and* With your "Sweet Dulcineas" no more! /*I am no one! I'm nothing! /I'm only Aldonza the whore!*

[Aldonza's narcissism moves her to implore Don Quixote to recognise her self-familiarity, her being a whore and not a lady. She experiences his tenderness as a cruel invader and rejects it as alien.]

Different object relations patterns may influence the infant's self-familiarity and the narcissistic immune system by means of the parents' unconscious wishes for him. For example, parents may hope for their child to express his individuation or for him to be perfect and ideal; they may wish for him to compensate them for their difficulties or use him as their extension, establishing and representing them as perfect parents; or they may strive for family cohesion or, alternatively, neglect the idea of solidarity.

In the relationships of adults, the child concealed in each one influences the mode of the interaction between them. We may observe that compatibility between partners' positive resonances of narcissistic schemata (NBS) might generate proximity and intimacy as well as negotiation, reconciliation, and communication between partners, causing immense satisfaction and happiness. These beneficial relationships emerge as the outcome of advances in healthy narcissism, of the ego's predominant adaptation mechanisms, and of a prevalent jointness-separateness pattern of object relations. Hence, the individual encounters the otherness of his loved object, which includes his dissimilar narratives. While each senses these divergences as minor differences, he may maintain sufficient openness to integrate his spouse's almost-familiar experiences into the continuity of their relations-familiarity as wholeness. He might then enjoy the added attributes that enrich their relations.

Patrick, a married man, tells me in his therapy session: "For many years I resisted participating in the family supper gatherings of my wife's family organised on Saturday evenings. I didn't understand what they saw in these gatherings, which for me was all suffering. In my family, such gatherings happened only on special occasions. At home my brother and I would eat first and only then would my mother and father sit down to their meal. I was quite sure that my wife's family was freaky. Now that my children have grown up I've begun to love these weekly family gatherings, and I do my utmost to be there. I feel what I missed out on as a kid, and I also help my wife prepare the table for the four of us."

Incompatibility between partners' resonances of NBS, NHS, and NDS relations might, however, trigger temporary or constant strangeness, resistance, injury, alertness, distress, and anxiety, or even traumatic experiences. Incompatibility might arouse acute conflicts of interest between the individuals involved and activate defusing of the antagonistic drives and emotions—aggression detached from libido and mainly hate from love. Each partner may sense and react to the other's emotional expressions under the impact of his inherent, recurring childhood object relations pattern. Harmful relationships tend to emerge as the outcome of the triggering of distorted or even pathological narcissism, or traumatic reverberations, of the ego's predominant defence mechanisms, and of symbiotic patterns of object relations. When one of the partners senses these discrepancies as major differences or deviations from his childhood pattern of object relations (as with Aldonza and Don Quixote), he may experience strangeness, which often triggers anxiety, rage, and pain in various shapes and forms. The individual then tends to disconnect from the relationship and withdraw into his self-space, or he might erupt in rage, destroy the relations, or even attack himself or his partner.

Relationships may be conceptualised on a scale ranging from a jointness-separateness pattern of object relations to a symbiotic or traumatic pattern, with various configurations in between. As elucidated in Chapter Four, from birth to six months, both patterns characterise a similar bonding process. However, each pattern is based on an essentially different premise of the parental approach toward the baby. These premises range from recognition to denial of the baby's separateness and will continue to resonate for both (via memory traces) throughout life.

It should, however, be emphasised that nearly all babies who experience symbiotic relations with one of their parents may establish jointness object relations with their other objects. Yet, it is interesting to observe, particularly during the psychoanalysis of adults, that the search for a symbiotic pattern seems to predominate in daily experience over the jointness pattern. This is probably due to an "addiction" to the illusion of merging, and the impact, in symbiotic patterns, of the anxiety of abandonment. The individual's search for a jointness pattern might remain concealed or reappear with objects in whom a jointness pattern prevails.

Let us elaborate the differences between the two object relations patterns, namely, jointness-separateness and symbiotic relations, from the perspectives of narcissistic processing and ego functioning. From birth onward, jointness-separateness (see Chapter Four) takes place in a third shared space, which implies the temporary emergence of each individual from his self-familiarity space and a joining with the other in a shared virtual space. Joining in a shared place starts during the intimacy of the oral stage and may improve throughout life. Spontaneous variations of this joining may emerge with other family members, friends, spouses, or even among more than two partners. Each can separate from the other by familiar signs and withdraw to his self-space or join other shared spaces. Whenever partners communicate their availability, they may rejoin. Such passages or transitions between joining and separation can take place between individuals on condition that separateness between them is familiar, recognised, and respected (thanks to memory traces and healthy narcissism, as well as predominant NBS resonances).

The individual's experiences in the third shared space provide the substance for the enrichment of the quasi-familiar beneficial memory traces (NBS) in each of the partners, and contribute to strengthening his or her true self-familiarity and self-assets. Each participant may enhance communication with his partner as otherness and expand the nuanced understanding of this other. Each may consolidate his own verbal expression so as to be better understood by the other (adaptation mechanisms), while simultaneously increasing tolerance of the otherness (healthy narcissism). Such an emotional dynamic between partners enhances their mutual relationship. Thus, jointness-separateness relations represent healthy object relations that strengthen the individual's healthy narcissism in harmonious functioning with his ego's adaptation mechanisms.

Even in the shared space, however, an individual is not exempt from injury, and can often be frustrated, offended, or hurt by unexpected reactions emanating from the otherness. Injuries of this kind tend to evoke and amplify the resonance of his NHS. In the face of such injuries the person may withdraw, distressed, to his self-space, where he will try to heal his wounds, mourn his losses, and finally restore his self and his object's familiarity by preserving his losses within his familiarity (as memories), and thereafter communicate and reconcile with his objects (healthy narcissism and adaptation mechanisms).

I will elaborate the above issues through excerpts of the emotional dynamic between analysand and analyst over several psychoanalytic sessions.[5]

George tells me in our shared space of the session: "I've come here today after having had another clash with my boss who criticised me and wanted me to consult my colleague who knows the material better than me. I was deeply offended, as usual, mainly by the way he exploded at me [shared space]. I restrained myself from answering him; instead, I went to my desk [self-space] with a feeling of rage, and tried to understand what provoked his criticism, because I really appreciate his way of seeing things but I hate his shouting [preserving positive object representations, his self-assets, while separating the negative issue from the whole]." After a silence George continued: "I'm proud of myself this time [healthy narcissism], as I could understand what my boss was getting at [NBS resonances], and a little later we were able to negotiate and have a constructive conversation" [reconciliation by the ego's adaptation mechanisms in the shared space]. After a while George associates [NHS resonance]: "I loved playing certain games with my father [adaptation mechanisms in their shared space] but I was afraid of his shouting and his criticism ... I hated him, and I remember clearly that when I went in rage to my room [withdrew to his self-space] I stupidly decided to stop playing any games with him in order to punish him [defence mechanisms]." Toward the end of the session, he said: "I'm aware of your contribution to my new capability to discuss things with him [his boss/father transference] despite my shortcomings [noticing our jointness and separateness]."

As George associated, I could sense in our shared space his shortcomings and his hate and fear of his father's/boss's otherness,

which erupts in shouting in their shared space(s), but also his love/
appreciation of his father/boss [NBS resonances] transferred on me this
time. In my self-space, I reflected on George's emphasis of his restraint,
his anal adaptation mechanism that often emerged in the analysis. I was
touched by his associations of the healing of his injuries, which indicate
the healthy narcissistic restoration of his true self-familiarity through
which he regained mastery and the ability to reconcile with his father/
boss, unlike in the past, when he used to struggle with his boss and was
almost fired. That was the reason why he sought analysis. I pointed out
how his self-esteem had been enhanced in his dialogue with his "offending" boss, as well as his appreciation of our work, which revealed the
NBS of his jointness-separateness pattern of object relations.

In another session, however, George enters my clinic with the
vulnerability we have come to know, and tells me: "Yesterday evening
we went with friends to a restaurant. I suddenly saw my wife staring
into my friend's eyes [their shared space] and I couldn't bear it. I tried
not to show my rage [his self-space] … Yet since yesterday, maybe stupidly, I can't think of anything else but of divorcing her. I'm probably
morbidly jealous!" George continues cursing her without any associations or the working through that he usually does. Suddenly he says:
"I'm sure you can't wait for your next patient as I'm incommunicable
today."

I could sense in our shared space George's transference onto me as
well as his vulnerability to this stressful occurrence, and the panic that
invaded his true self-familiarity in this situation. I reflected in my self-
space that in such situations, whether momentarily or in the long-term,
his self-cohesiveness seems to be undermined; he feels unloved while
his NHS or even NDS resonate unconsciously within him [regression
to the ego's oral defence mechanisms]. These reverberations cause
his destructive urges to flood his discourse with curses, revenge, and
plans of divorce, and to remain detached from any object, whether
his wife or me. His ego's defence mechanism of projection is unconsciously mobilised, and George projects his aggression and hate on to
his wife, and to me. I view George's emotional state as characterised
by a decomposing of his aggressive drive from its integration with his
libido. It may indicate a temporary regression from the ego's regulation
of drives and emotions to the id's instinctual discharge of the destructive impulse (NDS), or, alternatively, an eruption of his decomposing
instinct, regardless of the object (see discussion of the death instinct in

Chapter Three). I therefore searched for a transference interpretation that hopefully would help him retreat into his self-space and there heal his injuries and reintegrate and regulate his drives. Such a retreat might help him to restore his true self-familiarity, as he so often did when able to acknowledge his NDS resonance, and once again reconstruct relations with his wife as he did with his boss/father.

After a while, I interpreted: "It seems that a particularly painful event in your past spurts out when you imagine my waiting for the next patient, or when your boss proposes that you consult your colleague, or you see your wife staring at someone else." George replied: "First, I'm sure every man would feel betrayed in such circumstances …" George lapses into silence, withdraws into his self-space, and I maintain an empathic silence. Afterwards, he comes back to our shared space and associates as usual. He says: "My mother used to say that when my little brother was born and I was fifteen months old, my parents would stare at my brother and I would come between them, spread my arms, and not let them approach his cradle … From about the age of three, I remember many times that I couldn't bear her staring at my little brother. I used to shout: 'You hate me, you love only him' and I refused to play with my mother …" Following another silence I interpret: "It hurts you so much that you feel morbidly jealous, and here too you imagine that I, like your wife, your boss, or your mother, am not really interested in you, and can't wait for the next patient."

In my self-space, I reflect that the young George, at fifteen months, probably experienced the unexpected staring as a kind of betrayal, abandonment or trauma (memory traces). His painful association (NHS and NDS resonances) illuminated his hate and the detachment from his father/boss (described in the previous extract) as a defence mechanism for avoiding pain.

I interpret: "You were probably a bit shocked by your mother unexpectedly staring at your brother, while you were so familiar with her staring at you. So you are always on guard, morbidly jealous, preparing yourself for her staring at someone else." After a long silence, George added: "I suddenly remember a most painful stare my mother gave a man I didn't recognise. I was maybe three years old. I don't know anything about what was between them. I never saw him again, but I remember the hatred I felt toward my mother. I never spoke to her or anyone else about this event … I wish I could ask her now, but as you know she has Alzheimer's. When I visit her, she stares at me but I feel that she doesn't recognise me ... It's very painful ..." George seems to weep silently.

I sense George's deep pain when his mother stares at him but does not recognise him, pain that is juxtaposed with that of other situations, as if a stranger (e.g., his baby brother, the strange man, his colleague) had intruded his shared space with his mother/wife/father/boss. These unconscious NDS reverberations of his "morbidly jealous" feelings probably destroy other beneficial memories of her looking at him with love.

George continues: "I imagine you think there are links to my pain when she stared at my brother or even when she— wait a minute, when she, just like my wife, stared at this man ... I'm really perplexed by this analogy ... This is what I like in our sessions, when I can associate freely, discover links by myself to what I have long ago forgotten, and feel that you understand me ... I'm curious how my meeting with my wife will be this evening."

George calmed down, and I could sense his urge to live and to love. I thought about his archaic cycle of decomposing instinct and now connecting instinct (id regulation) (see Chapter Three). He now seemed re-attracted to his familiar mother/wife object, and could reconcile with his father/boss. This implies that his ego's adaptation mechanisms could refrain from destroying the relations and his true self-familiarity was once again restored through his healthy narcissism processing; he is also attracted to his familiar love object, his mother/wife, and able to recognise his mother's love within himself. Furthermore, he is aware of the source of his rage toward them (his wife/mother and, in the transference, also me (NHS resonances)). Through his ego's adaptation mechanism, his drives and emotions toward his object/wife/boss/analyst are reintegrated and reinvested in jointness-separateness relations with her. The next staring episode will probably renew the pain, but hopefully George will preserve his love feelings better in the shared space.

As mentioned previously (see Chapters Four and Seven), I suggest considering jointness-separateness between a parent and his or her offspring as the normal object relations pattern from birth. Jointness-separateness provides the foundation for the development of the individual's capacities for relationships with others in intimacy and communication, as well as for his individuation in separateness. Furthermore, it may provide the foundation for enhancing the child's innate healthy narcissism and his ego's adaptation mechanism. In this context, I would like to stress five major aspects of jointness-separateness relations from the parental viewpoint that affect the child:

a. Parental pleasure obtained through intimacy with their baby, eliciting the sense that the boundaries between them in the shared space are temporarily blurred.
b. Parental respectfulness of the child's separateness, including his withdrawal to his self-space or his joining others in (other) shared spaces.
c. Parental encouragement for reconciliation following narcissistic injuries experienced by the child and/or the parent (via modelling).
d. Parental backing for and tolerance of the otherness of their child and loving him as he is.
e. Parental assistance and support for their child's individuation.

In couplehood, just as between parent and child, partners may jointly experience a variety of transitions from approaching to distancing, and from separating to rejoining. In these transitions, they may experience the positive and negative emotional states of intimacy, love, and communication, including anger, hurt, negotiation, and reconciliation (NBS and NHS resonances).

On the basis of these experiences, the sense of the familiar self may be shaped as a true self-familiarity that is separate from the familiar non-self object. As the narcissistic immune system usually immunises self-familiarity as it is being shaped, the individual's narcissism is triggered to immunise and restore true self-familiarity as differentiated from other familiarities. Throughout life, the differentiation between self-familiarity and other familiarities becomes more sophisticated and depends on the processing of innate healthy immune narcissism. Healthy narcissism continuously improves during the lifespan—preserving true self-familiarity during moments of intimacy, communication, and separateness, as well as upon experiencing both positive and negative affects.

Let us now scrutinise the symbiotic relations. Symbiotic relations occur within a single merged space where parent and baby, like any symbiotic couple, have an illusion of fusion, "an omnipotent system—a dual unity within one common boundary" (Mahler, 1968, p. 201). Repeated experiences of the sensation of merging into "oneness" elicit elation and an addiction to this "ideal" unity of un-separateness. On the other hand, separation, separateness, and otherness elicit within the symbiotic couple an acute vulnerability that provokes excessive anxiety of rejection, abandonment, or annihilation. Such a merging state of mind obliges one (or both) of the symbiotic individuals to falsify his true-self needs and to reinforce dependency on the self-object while trying hard to avoid being expelled from the merged space. For both, the sense of un-separateness achieved by mutual clinging and dependency represents the ultimate emotional state of love. Separation—even as withdrawal to one's own self-space or to satisfy other individual needs—is experienced as abandonment. Experiences of un-separateness and the denial of separateness emanating from the self-objects, given their excessive anxiety, leave predominantly harmful and destructive memory traces within the individual (NHS and NDS resonances).

On the basis of these experiences, the sense of the familiar self is shaped as a fused self-object familiarity, as a vulnerable false self. The narcissistic immune system usually immunises self-familiarity as it is predominantly shaped, according to the familiar subjective frame of wholeness. Hence, the symbiotic individual's narcissism is programmed to immunise and restore the self-familiarity shaped as fused self-object wholeness, as a symbiotic sense of self-familiarity. This means that innate narcissism *deviates* from its original immune processing function—of resisting the non-self and preserving true self-familiarity in separateness—and is transformed into a pathological processing that preserves a false, vulnerable, and fused self-object familiarity.

This pathological processing does not resist the alien invasion emanating from the parental self-object's anxiety of abandonment into the child's self-familiarity. Whenever the concealed self-need for separation emerges, the infant/child immediately represses or denies it, due to the resonance of alien invasive memory traces of the parental anxiety of abandonment. Hence, the infant/child tries to gratify his self-object's needs as if they were his own, at the expense of relinquishing his individuation in his efforts to please.

When anxieties of abandonment or annihilation flood the self, the individual's ego increases the mobilisation of defence mechanisms, such as denial of separateness and repression of the true-self need for individuation and separation. The outcome is dependency and clinging to the self-object, projection of aggression on to those who are not involved in the fusion, such as the second parent or caregiver, and often a split within his own self-object familiarity.

The continuous illusion of fusion (NHS or NDS) does not trigger or promote the individual's need to negotiate or communicate with the otherness of his object. The result is that individuation is obstructed, and intimacy is experienced as a permanent blurring of boundaries accompanied by a threat of abandonment (NDS). Neither party experiences a need for attunement to others, nor an appreciation of the importance of timing in communication and relationship. Moreover, neither has to expand his or her verbal expression in order to better understand the other's otherness, nor is progression achieved in their respective communications with others. In short, the otherness is felt to be threatening and separation is intolerable (NHS).

Finally, constant resonance of these narcissistic schemata (NHS, NDS) in the individual's daily experiences provides the substance for pathological attributes in his or her object relations and in his or her narcissistic immune processing: vulnerability, fragility, low self-esteem, anxieties and narcissistic personality disorder, as well as autoimmune symptoms.

The following two detailed vignettes demonstrate the symbiotic emotional dynamic of analysand and analyst in the transference, over the course of several psychoanalytic sessions.[6]

Monty, a thirty-five-year-old celibate man, shares his misery: "I'm worth nothing and I don't need anyone ... I'm always afraid of being forgotten ... Actually you're like a machine to me [no shared space] ... If I allow myself to feel something toward you, I'm liable to lose my own self in yours [fused self-object], and I'll never know again who I really am [renouncing his true self] ... When the session ends at the usual time, your next patient will arrive ... and I'll be left alone with my terrible pain. I can't bear it! ... I hate you now ... You triggered my need to be loved and to meld into you ..." Several sessions later Monty associated: "I was told that I used to cling to my mother and that I was torn from her arms when she became ill and had to be taken to hospital. I was about two years old. I don't remember anything, but I know that she never came back ... This is my pain of being left alone and forgotten."

In my self-space, I reflect on Monty's trauma of being forcibly detached from his symbiotic mother. These unconscious traumatic memory traces continue to resonate within him via his post-trauma destructive NDS and cause him unconsciously to attack and even destroy his fused self-object familiarity. This suggests that pathological narcissism preserves, immunises, and restores a detached, forgotten, and unworthy self-object familiarity that yearns for love but is also afraid of it. As the anxiety increases, Monty's ego mobilises a defence mechanism of repression to counter his urge and need to be loved.

James, in his forties, is very successful in his creative profession, but suffers from continuous breakdowns in his family life: "I know that I have the look of a vulgar young man [false self]. I sometimes even like to maintain this appearance ... I'm generally an optimistic person ... I may in secret appreciate what I have in my life [true self-familiarity] ... But at times I suddenly feel stressed. A deep painful feeling floods me that I don't know who I really am [fused self-object] ... I may then erupt aggressively for no reason [NDS] ... Sometimes I need to feel that there is an exact matching between me and my wife [fused self-object], otherwise I erupt in rage and destroy our relationship. [id's compulsive instinctual discharge] She cries but I don't care."

I reflect on the past several months, during which the analysis has been stuck. I sense that James firmly resists my otherness and does not allow me to join him in a shared space of working-through. He transfers his need for a self-object on to me, and wants me to understand him precisely, without his having to verbalise. He gets angry and reacts rudely when I do not understand him, and even shouts at me. I sense that our communication is dominated by his false self. Sometimes, for a few minutes I sense his concealed positive emotional communication, expressed mainly in the authentic smile he gives me when he leaves the room. I feel I have to wait patiently for the opportunity to convey my reflections to him through a constructive interpretation.

One day, James gives me this authentic smile at the start of the session, as opposed to the end, and I feel deeply touched. I sense that it may be possible to invite him to a shared space and to offer him an interpretation that would evoke associations from his true-self: "During many sessions I have felt that you have 'the look of a vulgar young man,' the one you told me about, but today I feel through your smile both your need to hide things and to share your hidden authentic emotions." I was very moved by James's response, "Actually, I feel embarrassed and ashamed to tell you that deep inside me I have an authentic, gentle, and creative soul, [NBS] very different from the way I appear ..."

Some sessions later, we were able to expose the roots of the vulgar self-familiarity and James could begin to release the enigma of his childhood. I present here a vignette from this disclosure that burst forth as if it had waited a long time to express itself: "My father's mockery and criticism of my gentle attitude, 'like that of a girl,' he would say, humiliated me [NDS] and I forced myself to please him [self-object; false self; 'and reveal a vulgar side that I don't like'; invasion into his self-familiarity] ... It was my father who raised me from birth, who waited up for me at night, who whispered to me quietly but constantly that he is the only one who cares for me and can protect me [unconscious messages that mother is worthless] ... His wish was that I would be exactly like him, a tough boy [self-object] ... Sometimes I had the impression that he was programming me. I remember when he accompanied me to kindergarten, and then later to school, he would always say 'do this and do that, be careful of this and that, etc.' When I participated in a competition or a race at school, my father would always be there and I had to win for him, otherwise he would get distressed, as if it were his race. He once told me that when I was running he felt as if he were inside me and that we were running together and winning ... I know he invested a lot in me, hours of sport and homework together, but I never could tell him that I wanted to be with my mother, or that I wanted to sleep over at a friend's home. He used to say, 'You have me and you don't need anybody else' ... He certainly was a wonderful father. I admired him and learned a lot from him. He still is a wonderful father, but on one condition: that I remain dependent on him ... If ever I wasn't dependent, he would become mad at me and shout as if I had done something bad to him [NDS] ... In fact, I had anxieties when I was a kid. I couldn't go to sleep before he came home even if my mother was there. On these occasions I would go to my mother's bed, but when he came home he'd be mad at me ... Quite a few times growing up, I wondered how my mother let him push her aside ... She has a kind and gentle nature ... Oh my God, I hate the idea that's just crossed my mind but amazingly, I sense that you are waiting for such thoughts for advancing our work ... Could it be that my authentic, gentle, and creative soul, which my father hates so much, comes from my mother? ... Did I hide my love for her? ... I never respected my mother, just as I don't respect you ... which is why I'm wondering how I could sense just now what you are feeling. I also don't respect my wife ... I shout at her, even in front of our child ... She says that it's as if she doesn't exist for me as a person ... I think you also tried to interpret my intolerance to her being different, but I never understood what you were talking about."

James impressed me with his fluent discourse during this session and his exhaustion. I felt it was important not to interrupt him, but rather to continue considering his associations in our shared space. This session was so different from previous ones. I wondered what had unlocked his associations and allowed him to expose his true self. Could it have been my awareness of his authenticity? I was also intrigued by what seemed a rare occurrence of symbiotic relations between a father and his baby, as opposed to a mother. Until this session, I thought that James was very intelligent, but with rudimentary emotional intelligence and difficulties in associating, and that he was unaware of his wife's suffering and incapable of connecting to my verbalising his emotions. Now I could see that he had concealed these capacities, probably due to his father's criticism and need for symbiotic relations to be one with his son, both of which had invaded James's self-familiarity from birth. The result was that James preserved his false self through a pathological processing of his narcissism, while unconsciously hiding his true self. He needed to please his idealised father, his archaic self-object who always understood him, did everything for him, programmed him, and protected him. The otherness was as unbearable for James as it was for his father.

His father's destructive mockery and shouting invaded James's self-object familiarity as malignant, destructive memory traces, so much so that these NDS constantly resonate in his daily couplehood experiences and destroy his family relations. His mother was as "irrelevant" for him as she had been for his father, and as his wife and I had become, via the transference. Nevertheless, he probably did experience a hidden sense of proximity with his mother, a relationship more akin to jointness-separateness relations, which he concealed from his father's mockery. He continued to maintain his relations with his mother as his "authentic gentle and creative soul" (that resonated as NBS), which I could sense when his smiled at me. Obviously, his symbiotic relations with his father dominate his rudimentary jointness relations.

Within the framework of my approach, from birth, symbiotic relations between a parent and his offspring are considered to constitute a pathological object relations pattern. Symbiotic relations can propel the basic narcissistic network toward the pathological processing of narcissism, one that immunises and preserves a fused self-object familiarity, a false self-familiarity and vulnerability to separation, and causes the ego to mobilise mainly defence mechanisms.

I would like to stress six major aspects of symbiotic relations that invariably encompass the following parental conceptions (I refer here to the mother, although the conceptions could apply equally to the father, or to both parents).

- The parent obtains pleasure in intimacy with her baby while the boundaries between them in the merged space are constantly sensed as blurred.
- The parent denies her child's separateness, obstructing his or her need for separation and his or her tendency to connect with others, due to her anxiety of abandonment.
- The parent supports intolerance to otherness.
- The parent obstructs her child's individuation.
- The parent encourages her child's fusion with her.
- Abandonment and annihilation anxieties often flood the parent's self and invade the child's self, flooding him with anxiety.

The above six points imply that the child/individual's illusion of being fused or merged within a "oneness space" with his self-object is at risk of being shattered,[7] thereby exposing him to the anxiety of abandonment, to falseness and the relinquishing of his true self, vulnerability, self-disorders,[8] and self-destructiveness. These emotional states are often harmful to his individuation, his self-esteem, and his relationships with his self-object. The individual's coping with frustration and injuries might become deficient, producing frequent autoimmune emotional phenomena (see below).

The following example of Ethan (in his thirties), who shares with me his feelings about his recent vacation, may illustrate the differences between a person displaying self-familiarity in integrity and cohesiveness throughout the healthy processing of narcissism, and another person (his friend, Marty) whose self reflects vulnerability and fragility, and is restored through pathological narcissistic processing.

Ethan tells me excitedly: "I had just finished arranging my photo album from my trip to India with Marty. It was such fun, as if I was reliving the trip and re-experiencing the smells, the colours, the people, the landscapes, and also my friendship with Marty … I remembered these experiences as if they were happening now, so that I could easily arrange the photos in chronological order and add some comments that describe the sequence of events." [Ethan maintains continuity of memory traces and preserves self-familiarity cohesiveness throughout his healthy narcissistic processing.]

"I also met Brad who had just returned from travelling alone in India, and we shared our experiences. Brad described the intoxicating fragrances in the spice market and I felt I could smell them as if

I were there with him [NBS]. I'm really into spices and smells, and I was sorry that we decided not to visit the place Brad spoke about. Never mind, I'll go there next time ... Brad offered me a photo that he took in one of these spice plantations, but it really didn't occur to me to put it in my album as I hadn't been there. It's not the same as the pictures I took myself or even the ones Marty took when we were together." [He safeguards his self-familiarity as differentiated from his friend.]

"Yesterday evening I went to visit Marty, really pleased with my album and wanting to share it with him. Our exchanging of memories was disappointing. Every time I recalled an experience that Marty couldn't remember, like the particular sound of the crows, or some amazing Indian people we met, he reacted angrily as if I had invented the events, or they had happened with someone else ... I was shocked; he has blocked all ways of sharing memories. He was excited when he remembered exactly the event I described, but quite crazy when he couldn't remember the precise occurrence ... Such rigidity! ... Such stiffness! ... I can't understand his vulnerability. It's as if he has to be sure that we both remember exactly the same things. Only now do I understand some of the clashes we had during the trip." [Note the vulnerability and fragility of Marty's self when he is unable to share events other than precisely those he personally experienced, remembers, or photographed. In order to preserve his self-familiarity, he probably needs to rely on a distorted or pathological processing of narcissism.]

Ethan's immunised self-familiarity and cohesiveness enable him to feel secure in his true self-familiarity and to differentiate his narratives from Marty's, or even Brad's. Ethan is willing to hear from his friends about the otherness of their experiences, but without allowing them to invade his self and confuse his own experiences. Thus, Brad's descriptions arouse Ethan's memories of related smells, his wish to experience these foreign but almost-familiar places, and to visit those he missed (indicating his healthy narcissism).

The time needed for restoring self-cohesiveness following injuries depends on the predominance in everyday life of narcissistic processing, and on the relative contributions of its healthy, distorted, or pathologic aspects. It also depends on ego functioning by means of both adaptation mechanisms (such as symbolisation and integration) and defence mechanisms (such as projection and detachment or other dissociative mechanisms).

Pathology in object relations may produce insecure and destructive relationships, dependency and clinging or aloofness, anxiety of abandonment and annihilation, paranoiac feelings and ideation (which may serve to further differentiate self-other boundaries), and psychopathic relations or states, as well as hate and loss of love.

## Autoimmune emotional phenomena

There is little solace in the fact that no one is perfect—neither we, nor our children, our parents, or our spouse. We all experience narcissistic injuries when we confront deficiency, whether in our objects, our relationships, our bodies, or our selves. Flaws consisting of normal deviations from the familiar, such as failure, illness, organ transplantation, ageing, inconsolable bereavement—even pregnancy or sexual development—are often experienced as alien to our self-familiarity. These deviations may adversely affect the integrity of the self and undermine its cohesiveness. Whenever an individual experiences these life events as especially alien to his self-familiarity, his self, or his object, he sometimes risks unconsciously activating self-destructive processes. He might deny the change or the handicap or disavow their meaning, instead of befriending them as belonging to him. Consequently, he might initiate attacks on himself, such as lowering his self-esteem in response to ageing, seeking magical and elective reparative surgical intervention or sinking into depression following a failure.

> The [biological] immune system is a complex network of specialized cells and organs that have evolved to defend the body against attacks by "foreign" invaders … It is able to remember previous experiences and react accordingly … At the heart of the immune system is the ability to distinguish between "self" and "nonself." The body's immune defences do not normally attack tissues that carry a self marker. But when immune defenders encounter cells or organisms carrying molecules that say "foreign," the immune troops move quickly to eliminate the intruder … In abnormal situations, the immune system can wrongly identify self as nonself and execute a misdirected immune attack. The result can be so-called autoimmune disease such as rheumatoid arthritis or systemic lupus erythematosus, allergy etc. (Schindler, 1991, p. 1)

Let us observe a highly intelligent, generally happy person I worked with in psychotherapy. Albert, an adult, succeeds in most of his professional, academic, and familial activities. His healthy narcissism generally processes new incoming information in harmony with his ego's mobilisation of a rich variety of adaptation mechanisms and his jointness-separateness object relations. Nevertheless, he often risks damaging his academic career due to his tendency to avoid important presentations or exams, which he unconsciously and wrongly perceives as threats to his self-esteem. Since childhood, despite being aware of his positive cognitive capabilities, he has resisted studying, sensing barriers and instrumental difficulties owing to his attention-deficit hyperactivity disorder (ADHD), as if this were an intruder that damaged his positive self-familiarity abilities. Reverberation residues from these childhood experiences of injury cause him to postpone studying until the last minute, as an unconscious defence against failure anxiety. He thus has an alibi for his eventual poor performance: "I didn't have enough time to prepare, so I couldn't have achieved more." Despite this, he generally achieves good-enough exam results.

I believe that Albert's ADHD barriers are unconsciously wrongly identified by his narcissistic immune system as alien invaders or threats to his self-familiarity. These handicaps are thus not recognised as part of his self-familiarity difficulties which he might include within his self-familiarity as wholeness. As a result, in the face of all kinds of challenges and exams, such malignant data (NDS) resonate within him, and his narcissism is triggered to attack his "intruder" self-asset, his ADHD, by experiencing failure as an intrinsic part of his familiar self, and his familiar self as a failure. Thus, instead of studying and preparing himself for this task, which would enable him to overcome his hurdles or handicaps, avoidance (defence mechanism) of learning is triggered, as well as avoidance of situations that challenge his self-esteem. Even his good-enough exam results do not help his healthy narcissism to restore his self-familiarity as a wholeness that includes these particular deficiencies, and he is reluctant to expose his self-esteem to any assessment.

Despite his difficulties, Albert's success in other areas of his life is a result of resonance of other data (NBS) that, for example, reinforce his leadership and social skilfulness by smoothly bypassing his ADHD deficiencies—a process that enables him to enhance and even enjoy his cognitive capacities.

In the wake of stress, the biological immune system may, through a fatal mistake, attack and destroy healthy body tissues and produce autoimmune illnesses such as juvenile diabetes and rheumatoid arthritis (Goodkin & Visser, 2000; Stojanovich & Marisavljevich, 2007; Strous & Shoenfeld, 2006). I assume that "autoimmune emotional phenomena" are produced in a similar way as autoimmune physiological disease.

As we have seen, the infant's accumulated memory traces of enduring injurious experiences—such as being excessively criticised, abused, rejected, or traumatised, as well as being fused with another (self-object)—are organised into narcissistic destroying schemata (NDS). These negative experiences, supported by resonance of the NDS in the infant's daily life, may invade his self-familiarity and distort his true sense of his familiar self. Thus, instead of narcissistic immune processing that identifies these "invaders" as alien and resists them, the infant's narcissism, like the biological immune system described above, *wrongly identifies this non-self as if it were the self.* Moreover, it seems that the healthy narcissistic resistance to the invasion of these NDS destructive "intruders" is paralysed. Instead, the infant's pathological narcissistic processing attacks, destroys, and turns against itself and its body, executing a misdirected immune attack against his true self in an attempt to destroy it—as if his true self were a non-self, an intruder. In these circumstances, pathological narcissism is triggered to restore a self-familiarity that matches these invaders' NDS. The infant's self-familiarity that is thus invaded, attacked, and damaged may produce symptoms best understood as *autoimmune emotional symptoms* reminiscent of the autoimmune physiological diseases (Britton, 2004; Goodkin & Visser, 2000; Solan, 1998a). The individual thus senses his familiar self as unloved, damaged, humiliated, and insecure, and experiences low self-esteem or comes to feel like a failure, self-rejected and self-exploited. He might suffer from a negative, dirty, and dishonourable body self-image, desist from pursuing his individuation, literally beat his head against the wall, and exhibit obsessive symptoms, as well as nail biting, anorexia, perversions, trichotillomania (hair plucking), cutting, and suicidal tendencies.

Furthermore, this individual might be constantly alert to change, owing to an excessive anxiety of abandonment and annihilation. Defence mechanisms against these anxieties may be expressed by permanent withdrawal (Reich, 1960), projected on to the other as hate, or directed toward the self as self-destructiveness (Anzieu, 1985, 1987), coloured by the death instinct (Klein, 1957; Segal, 1983).

We may also observe that:

> Self-preservation and self-destruction are rooted in bodily experiences and developmental processes of bodily care. The body, as a source of satisfaction and pleasure, enhances the tendency for life preservation, the attraction to life, and serves as a shield against self-destruction. Bodily sensations, such as responsiveness to physical pain and sensitivity to internal bodily processes, produce warning signs aimed at alerting systems against bodily harm due to internal and external dangers. (Orbach, 2007, p. 154)

In terms of my theory, this conceptualisation may point to a strengthening of healthy narcissism and the structuring of NBS and NHS resonances.

"Negative bodily experiences, distorted bodily experiences, and negative attitudes and feelings may enhance a self-destructive tendency. Thus, body-hate, rejection of the body, physical dissociation, physical anhedonia, insensitivity to bodily cues, and other distorted bodily experiences may facilitate self-destruction" (Orbach, 2007, p. 154). In terms of my theory, this conceptualisation may point to the structuring of destructive NDS resonances, and may increase the triggering of distorted and pathological narcissistic processing, and the autoimmune emotional symptoms. Let us elaborate one of the toddler's excessive anxieties in the anal stage, the anxiety of uncontrolled aggression (dissociated from libido) that might erupt against his frustrating loved object. He might feel terrified and guilty about his fantasies that his parent might be hurt by him, particularly if he lacks clear parental boundaries. No less, due to projection, he may be scared of his parent's eruptions of rage and might even be terrified of being killed by this rage. In order to preserve his beloved parent, the toddler's pathological narcissism might wrongly identify his aggression as alien to his self-familiarity (instead of befriending, regulating, and containing it), and thus turn his aggression (originally experienced toward the parent) toward himself, as evidenced by self-destructive symptoms, such as compulsively hitting his head against the wall. Frequently, when the infant's self-familiarity is attacked by self-destructiveness, he will search for compensatory excessive parental attention and affection. He risks unconsciously producing physical or autoimmune emotional symptoms that the object generally responds to with concern—such as chronic constipation, selective mutism, stomach pains, headaches, trichotillomania, anorexia, obsessive-compulsive ideas and acts, psychosomatic disease, and attempted suicide (Solan, 1991).

Rita (six years old), a highly intelligent girl, was referred to me in the wake of breathing difficulties and stomach pains diagnosed by paediatricians as psychosomatic symptoms. Rita is very obedient and often asks the people around her for forgiveness if she feels their resistance to what she says or how she behaves. In our play with dolls over the course of many sessions, her anxiety about being "a strong girl" emerges. During this particular session she whispers to her doll: "Someone might get hurt … Something bad will happen to your parents … maybe an accident … Because I … you are strong … You can't breathe?" Rita looks both anxious and exhausted, and I try to interpret her feelings: "You are so afraid that if your doll is strong, just like you are strong, someone will get hurt." Rita bursts into tears and turns to me, murmuring: "We had a little chick in our backyard and by mistake I fell on it, and it didn't move. Mummy said it was dead. It was terrible. It was all my fault." After a while I interpreted: "You're afraid something bad will happen to your parents, just like what happened to your little chick, because you are strong … When you can't breathe, you are sure they will take care of you." Rita gives me a wide-eyed look and responds, "Are you sure that if Mummy knows I'm strong it will be OK?" When her mother comes to fetch her, she relates to Rita's sickness, as she usually does, in an overprotective manner. Rita's reaction is surprising: "No, no, Mummy, I'm not sick. I can put on my coat by myself. I'm a strong girl, I love you." I felt really moved to see them hugging each other. It occurred to me that she was testing her mother in my presence—to be on the safe side, so to speak.

At the time, I ignored what she meant by "strong" but I tried to use her words. Only some months later were we able to comprehend that for her, "strong" means healthy and angry, and that Rita's breathing difficulties served to keep her parents' attention focused on her illness, rather than on her being a healthy, loving girl capable of what she considered "bad" acts, namely, the expression of her angry feelings.

The following excerpts taken from several psychoanalytic sessions demonstrate the pathological processing of a young woman's narcissism and her autoimmune emotional reactions.

Adela, (in her twenties) an only child, had been diagnosed with borderline personality disorder (BPD). She talks about her constant distress, profound loneliness, obsessive ideas, and frequent aggressive outbursts. She complains of serious difficulties in creating and maintaining an intimate relationship, although she "can't bear being alone anymore." During her psychoanalysis, Adela often expressed in various forms her predominant unconscious malignant narrative (which I emphasise in italics). For example, she described dramatically an event that happened the previous day: "I was waiting in line at the supermarket when suddenly *a rude elderly man pushed in front of me in violation of my rights.* I started shouting, ready to go at him and push him away ... *my evil exploded, as if I were cursed or bewitched* ..." She continued: "*I'm afraid of my violence* because *my father is extremely violent* toward my mother ... toward her obsessions (her mother suffers from obsessive-compulsive disorder (OCD)) ... *I'm sometimes afraid he'll kill her* ... I don't want to be like him! ... Mummy makes demands on the family not to sit on her chair or bed, as *she is afraid we might contaminate her* with bacteria or a virus." In the next session, she says: "Mummy told me she was overjoyed when I was a baby, and *she held me in her arms the whole time.* She felt as if *her pregnancy with me was continuing* ... Now, I'm not sure *if she held me so close only because of her love for me, or whether also because of her obsession* about infection ... *I'm always envious, especially of pregnant women* ... I also envy you; *you've got everything and I've got nothing* ... I'm often afraid that *someone will violate my rights,* maybe even you ... I don't trust you ... *I feel humiliated for needing your affection* ... You might leave me." After a long silence she continues, "I think that my *father was gentle towards me,* particularly when I was a kid ... I'd almost forgotten this." Following another silence she says, "*Just when I feel close to somebody I start sweating profusely,* and I think the person with me might see it or smell it ... Did you notice it?" she asks. "*The sweat appears just when I feel you understand me ... and I feel rejected and I hate you.*"

I interpret her traumatic narrative: "You are longing for your mother's love holding you as a baby in her arms." I pause for some seconds and then continue: "You are also longing for your father's love and for my affection but your sweat pushes itself in front of you and your evil explodes as if you are bewitched or cursed, all these in violation of your right to be loved." This interpretation was followed by one of the very rare times that Adela could mentalize her self-destructiveness. She responded: "It's stupid ... I always think that it's you or someone else who rejects me, or might violate my rights ... Nobody can love me because of my smell and my outbursts … It's true, *I so crave love, but when I feel it's coming I perspire and it spoils everything for me.*"

This time our shared space was expanded and I could sense her humiliation in needing my love, and her anxiety of losing the "almost forgotten," affectionate father who does not correspond with his violent representation. Presumably, this anxiety triggers her ego to mobilise a defence mechanism of identification with the aggressor. She thus defends her father by becoming enmeshed in violence, just as he is, as if she were bewitched.

In one of the next sessions, Adela acknowledges her rage toward her mother's obsessive-compulsive demands, *which "violate her rights" to live*, just as her father erupts in violence toward her mother: "This morning my father wasn't at home and my mother shouted at me not to sit on her chair … I hated her so much. I almost exploded at her just like he does … *I would like to contaminate her with a violent virus just as she warned me of doing … But I do everything I can to protect her* from my father's violence [ego's defence mechanism of reaction formation] … I wish I could die and escape all this brutality."

I reflect on her suicidal tendency which arises when she encounters her violence toward her beloved mother's OCD, and on her stress and fear that she might unleash her rage on her mother or on "a rude elderly man (who) pushes in front of me," [an association that recurred in many forms] and attack them instead of herself. I wonder about her father's violence that invades Adela's self-familiarity, and her failure to immunise her true self-familiarity's "right" to be loved without destroying her love-objects or being annihilated. She is longing to be loved (NBS resonances of her father's affection) but, in fact, does not feel loved by anyone and is not particularly loving of herself or others. At the same time, she is deceived and repulsed by the frightening violence (NDS resonances of her father's violence). The unconscious conflict between her longing and her repulsion is resolved through her psychosomatic symptom of excessive perspiration (an archaic defence mechanism), which leads her to avoid intimacy. As she puts it: "I'm evil, bewitched, cursed. Nobody can love me." I realise that her father's positive representation and memory traces of his love (NBS) are deeply concealed beneath her default NDS resonances. Will I be able to help her to reinstate these NBS in order to balance her NDS?

Adela's borderline personality disorder can be understood as reflecting her need to deal with the threat of impending separation or rejection,[9] and the loss of external love-objects—her deceiving father and her repelling, obsessive, symbiotic mother. Because her need for affection cannot express itself, her traumatic experience ("I'm afraid that he'll kill her") surfaces in the absence of a "good enough" containing object. Her object relations are impaired (she cannot maintain relationships), and her ego mobilises mainly defence mechanisms (identification with the aggressor, reaction formation, sweating, and the wish to die), at the expense of adaptation. Through a pathological processing of her narcissism, she preserves her self-familiarity as being bewitched or cursed by violence, as rejected, unloved, and smelling bad, and her object representations (her self-assets) are negative. She is very vulnerable, easily erupts in aggression (see Chapter Three, regarding instinctual eruption) and is anxious about her rights being violated. Her distorted self-view, outbursts of violence, perspiration, self-destructiveness, pathological object relations, and narcissistic disorder, which previously had led to a diagnosis of BPD, can alternatively, to my understanding, be considered as autoimmune emotional symptoms.

Suicidal tendencies often appear in symbiotic relations diagnosed as BPD, as described above. Orbach (2007) and his colleagues claim that "the connection between suicide and symbiotic relations rests on the simultaneous fears of either total fusion or total abandonment" (p. 157). Alternatively, according to my conceptualisation, this tendency toward suicide might be considered as an autoimmune emotional phenomenon, where the individual is trapped in his unconscious fantasy-illusion of his self-object as an alien invader who has either fused with or is welded to him, or has totally abandoned him. In both cases, the individual loses his self-familiarity, experiences the sense of an alien self, and is ready to self-destruct or commit suicide together with his self-object.[10]

The following example demonstrates the pathological narcissism of an excessively symbiotic person who has immunised self-familiarity as fusion with an archaic self-object, and who attacks separateness as an invasion by an alien being, causing her to attempt suicide (autoimmune emotional processing).

Nancy, a young woman, came to consult me following a failed suicide attempt when she discovered that her lesbian partner had left her: "My life is ruined ... I can't exist without Danielle ... We had such a close relationship, like a single unit ... My mother was like a tight coat on me ... she moved in unison with my gestures ... Only when I feel our oneness do I realise that I exist ... I feel something similar with Danielle ... I want her to be in every crevice of mine ... otherwise I have no existence."

The conception of "chimerism"[11] provides another interesting perspective on my view of autoimmune emotional phenomena:

> In its pathological bio-psychological phantasmic manifestation, chimerism describes a confused organism which may turn against itself, as parts of it are experienced as alien and are attacked by the immune system ... the creation of a psycho-genetically deformed and confused organism which cannot ... detect what is familiar and what is alien within it ... is allergic to itself and attacks itself. (Durban, 2011, p. 921)

Durban is emphasising "the pathological, self-destroying properties of being welded, in unconscious phantasy, with alien psycho-genetic materials which are felt to be branded into the body and interfere with the evolution of the psyche" (p. 910).

Normally, the biological immune system would resist any alien genetic material. Nevertheless, within the uterus the foetus might sense uneasiness, generated from alien non-self elements, such as membranes that touch him inconsistently but that he is probably unable to reject (as Durban, 2011, describes in a clinical case). I wonder whether the physiological symptoms of many autistic children and other people who avoid being touched and are sensitive to palpation (autoimmune emotional phenomena), could be an outcome of such alien, intrauterine sensations.

D. Quinodoz's (1990) elaboration of the vertigo symptom and object relationships seems to me to be relevant to emotional autoimmune phenomena. Quinodoz claims that vertigo (an autoimmune disorder) may be "an expression of separation anxiety manifested in bodily sensations connected with space and time" (p. 53). The author follows Freud (1926d [1925]) in attributing the genesis of anxiety to separation and object loss. Based on an interesting example, Quinodoz suggests that the patient relates to his objects not as existing people, but rather as extensions of his ego.

> At times when the patient becomes aware that he is living in an "objectless" world, he discovers it as *the void* and may have

a sensation of vertigo ... in a world which does not present any boundary to it. The patient anxiously seeks the boundaries of an object against which to impinge in order to perceive his own boundaries and feel that he exists. (Quinodoz, 1990, p. 56)

The patient expresses his threatened phantasm: "'I feel the cable car opening underneath me like a belly dropping me' and he redis-covered the anxiety at the idea of being dropped by the mother's belly, or by the mother; he was repeating this in the analysis with the anxiety that I would drop him out of the analysis if he did not cling tight" (ibid., p. 56). He had also an irresistible wish to jump into the "void"—for instance, to leap out of the window. He then continues his associations through another phantasm: "Remaining inside this belly also assumed a terrifying character, as if it were a whirlpool that would never let him go ... the whirlpool then turned into the mouth of a ferocious dog that was ready to gobble him up." In other sessions this patient expressed his need "to be 'one' with his analyst so as to compel her aggressively not to separate from him" (p. 57). During another session he had the sensation of losing his own breath. Or, he gave his analyst the impression that he was talk-ing to her, but was actually talking to himself, as if she were fused with him. For Melanie Klein, Quinodoz reminds us: "Claustrophobia goes back to the fear of being shut up inside the mother's dangerous body" (ibid., p. 57).

Vertigo appeared to Quinodoz in the analysis of this patient as an expression of separation anxiety. The author could observe "the vicissitudes of the object relationship by way of the development of this symptom in the treatment ... from fusion-related vertigo via vertigo about being dropped, vertigo associated with aspiration, ver-tigo connected with the alternation of prison and escape and vertigo related to the attraction of the void" (p. 62). I agree with Quinodoz's view that "agoraphobia and claustrophobia are forms assumed by vertigo when the patient becomes aware of the danger involved in fusion" (p. 57).

I propose also to consider this patient's vertigo phantasms as reso-nances of his unconscious and primitive memory traces from the time spent in his mother's uterus, which is reminiscent of the chimerism (Durban, 2011) described above. It seems that the patient was about to lose his own breath in being closed as "one" in the mother's uterus, or losing his breath when dropped into the unbounded world. In this sense, vertigo is the familiar experience that resonates as narcissistic autoimmune phenomena in daily experience.

In addition to the autoimmune emotional phenomena, other pathological forms of narcissistic processing might emerge from an individual's distorted self-familiarity or from his personality disorders, such as the formation of a false, vulnerable, and fragile self-familiarity; self-deprivation and self-destruction; an immature narcissistic personality; obsessive, impulsive, and compulsive personality; a paranoid personality; and borderline personality disorder.

## Summary

In the course of the oral and anal stages elaborated in this book, we see that the innate functions of both narcissism and the ego may be improved or distorted under the impact of various occurrences in the child's life. These occurrences include both self-experiences and object-relations experiences, on a scale from beneficial to traumatic. The resonances of these childhood memory traces are organised into narcissistic schemata that provide a subjective interpretation of the individual's present state and experiences—in essence, a filter affecting all experience. The conceptualisation of innate immune narcissism and subsequent reverberations of the narcissistic schemata may clarify why familiarity (whether beneficial or destructive) is so tempting and strangeness so unbearable: It elucidates how relationships are easily severed under the impact of these resonances—whether between children and parents, between siblings, or between couples.

I have attempted to delineate the complex process of object relations in order to facilitate a clearer differentiation of object relations patterns on a continuum between pathological and healthy, and between the symbiotic object relations pattern and what I define as the jointness-separateness object relations pattern. A specific elaboration deals with pathological narcissism and what I consider to be autoimmune emotional phenomena.

## Notes

1. Positively indicates that the positive attributes prevail over the negative ones.

2. Narcissistic and ego functioning of association, resonance, assimilation, and integration of memory traces into a cohesive unit.

3. It is parenthetically noted that, based on an ethological approach, a contemporary theory of trauma and its treatment via "somatic experiencing" (see Levine, 2010) links specific bodily occurrences with the freedom from post-traumatic stress disorder (PTSD).

4. *Man of La Mancha*, a musical written by Dale Wasserman, with lyrics by Joe Darion and music by Mitch Leigh. Inspired by Miguel de Cervantes's *Don Quixote*, it was adapted by Wasserman from his 1959 non-musical teleplay, *I, Don Quixote*. The original Broadway production was staged in 1965.

5. The excerpts are focused mainly on the narcissistic, ego, and object-relations perspectives; all other dynamic considerations are omitted in order to illuminate the main issues. Moreover, as throughout this book, no identifying data are provided, in order to ensure anonymity and maintain confidentiality.

6. As before, the vignettes given here are strictly confined to the narcissistic perspectives; all other dynamic considerations are omitted so as to focus on these main issues as well as for reasons of discretion.

7. See Ulman & Brothers (1988) for an alternative view. These authors view the concept of trauma and PTSD as resulting in a shattering of archaic narcissistic "centrally organizing fantasies" that involve self and selfobject, for example, fantasies of grandiosity or idealization.

8. "Self-disorders: Also called selfobject disorders, these occur when the self has failed to achieve cohesion, vigor, or harmony, or when these qualities are lost after they had become established tentatively. The major diagnostic categories ... always imply impairment of the self's structural integrity and strength secondary to the experience of faulty selfobject responsiveness" (Moore & Fine, 1990, p. 178).

9. The essential feature of borderline personality disorder (BPD) is "a pervasive pattern of instability in interpersonal relationships, self-image and emotions" that are often expressed impulsively. Moreover, the individual's "perception of impending separation or rejection, or the loss of external structure, can lead to profound changes in self-image, affect, cognition, and behavior. They experience intense *abandonment fears* and *inappropriate anger*, even when faced with a realistic time-limited separation or when there are unavoidable changes in plans (e.g., sudden despair in reaction to a clinician's announcing the end of the hour; panic or fury when someone important to them is just a few minutes late or must cancel an appointment). They may believe that this 'abandonment' implies they are 'bad.' These abandonment fears are related to an intolerance of being alone and a need to have other people

with   them"   (see   http://psychcentral.com/disorders/borderline-personality-disorder-symptoms/ [retrieved 12 December 2014]).

10. The same disaster processing may happen in cases of parents murdering their own children.

11. Durban (2011) notes: "In genetic medicine, a *chimera* is an organism that has two or more different populations of genetically distinct cells that originated in different zygotes ... Each population of cells keeps its own character and the resulting organism is a mixture of mis-matched parts ... welded parts residing in the body and later in a fusion of body-mind ... the chimerical child has fragments of self which are alien and malignant to themselves [and] they are an alien presence to themselves" (p. 921, author's italics). Durban indicates that de M'Uzan (2006) was the first to propose the term "psychological chimera" to describe the inevitable immune "anti-gene" reaction of the patient to the analyst's interpretations.

# CHAPTER NINE

# Summary

*T*he *Enigma of Childhood* presents my theoretical innovations and the clinical approach derived from them. The book contributes to clarifying early psychic experiences and how they affect the baby's evolution along a normal or pathological developmental path. It also focuses on how childhood experiences are reflected in adulthood, couplehood, and parenthood. My theories grew out of my understanding of the generally accepted psychoanalytic and psychological literature as well as my clinical work over the years, both of which have informed each other and been mutually reinforcing.

*The Enigma of Childhood* elaborates the infant's normal emotional development from birth through the oral and anal stages, emphasising, as can be expected, the nature of the infant's relationship with his parents. I examine in detail the emotional processing that a newborn engages in after emerging into a world that is completely different from the space he was accustomed to in the mother's womb.

The book traces the mysteries of the newborn's capacity to survive these dramatic changes as he clings to any sensation of familiarity from the womb. These survival skills help him to orient and familiarise himself with his new bodily experiences and with the new world into which he has emerged, one that includes his caregivers.

I elaborate our tendency as babies, and eventually as adults, to grasp the familiar and the constant, and to update information on the changes taking place in ourselves and our surroundings, prior to undertaking new challenges. I also direct attention to our skill as adults, by virtue of the child within us, to preserve the self and manage relations with others—often at the same time that our dearest partners reveal their otherness, and in thus doing, unwittingly challenge our familiar sense of self.

I provide many examples to illustrate the infant's emotional path of development, familiarisation, and adaptation—in a word, change—alongside his resistance to the alien, the defence against anxiety and the hurdles he needs to negotiate and eventually overcome in object relations.

This "working through" in the oral and anal stages focuses on four basic concepts: narcissism, the id and ego, object relations, and separation/individuation.

## Regarding narcissism

Here I differentiate between innate healthy narcissism and evolving pathological narcissism. Innate healthy narcissism, a new concept I have developed, is first processed in the womb, and subsequently refined throughout life in order to preserve true self-familiarity. I consider healthy narcissistic processing to function as an emotional immune system by means of which self-familiarity is immunised, restored, and safeguarded as an organic subjective wholeness. At the same time, this narcissistic immune system maintains alertness toward any strangeness that might threaten self-familiarity as wholeness, including resisting and/or rejecting any alien intrusion or invasion into the sense of the familiar self. The alien non-self may consist of any deviation from self-familiarity, anyone outside the family circle, a stranger, an unknown element, or an irregular event. Narcissistic alertness may be characterised variously as resistance to that which is perceived as alien or unknown or even as undergoing change, and may lead to repulsion, rejection, anxiety, and panic, and even to a hatred of strangers and to racism. In contrast, the alertness may take the form of curiosity, which, in turn, may lead to the befriending of otherness and strangeness, to mastering the unknown, and even to enjoying exploration, adventure, or danger. Healthy narcissism focuses on differentiating self-familiarity from the non-self, the familiar non-self from the stranger, and on developing and increasing tolerance to the otherness emanating from another person.

In moments of intimacy and blissful happiness (such as those found in jointness object relations), boundaries of separateness might be temporarily sensed to be blurred; nonetheless, narcissistic alertness is constantly maintained to identify sensations and perceptions of the alien non-self. The link between healthy narcissism and object relations highlights our narcissistic need to feel the approval of our loved ones. To be loved as we are, to be known and appreciated for our uniqueness and separateness, enhances our self-esteem and allows us to remain, each within the boundaries of his or her own self-familiarity.

From the oral stage onward, our narcissism processes incoming data mainly according to familiar sensations and "gut feelings", and from the anal stage onward also according to body image self-familiarity. We are narcissistically attracted to the feeling of the familiar, while remaining vulnerable to strangeness and otherness. The narcissistic immune system can thus be compared with the biological immunological system that identifies the familiar cell protein and rejects the foreign body.

I consider innate healthy narcissism to be one of the crucial archaic components of our personality, the fifth (if developmentally first) personality component along with the id, ego, superego, and ego ideals. Healthy narcissism undergoes constant improvement and refinement (supported by ego functions and jointness object relations), a dynamic multi-stage process based on gradually relinquishing the illusion of perfection, concomitantly mourning the lost perfection and ideals, and continually adopting an updated familiar sense of self-wholeness. Subsequently, a familiar sense of self-integrity is consolidated, appropriate for each stage of emotional development.

## Regarding id and ego functioning

I differentiate between discharging instinctual tension unrelated to objects (biological and id regulation), and discharging drives and emotional tension by satisfaction connected to objects (ego regulation). During the oral stage, the parents support the baby's ego by functioning as his or her auxiliary ego. In the anal stage, the toddler internalises the parental regulation and the boundaries established by them and/or by reality, which consolidate the functioning of his ego. I take a fresh look at the ego's regulation, and how adaptation mechanisms are mobilised differently from defence mechanisms. These differences, in my view, are based on three criteria: emotional objectives, modes of operation, and emotional costs and benefits.

Adaptation mechanisms represent infinitely sophisticated means that continually improve in efficiency from infancy to adulthood, and whose aim it is to regulate the individual's drives and emotions in a beneficial manner. As the individual develops, adaptation mechanisms make possible self-achievements, long-term investments in various kinds of tasks, including shared projects, and communication with others. Hence, relationships regarding such shared projects, and attuned to the individual's objects and surroundings, may be attained, evoking and arousing a sense of pleasure, satisfaction, self-esteem, and self-control. Defence mechanisms represent inner constellations for preventing the individual from being flooded by anxiety, tempering the intensity of the anxiety, or producing symptoms and autoimmune emotional phenomena as a substitute for experiencing anxiety.

## Regarding object relations

I differentiate between two patterns of object-relations, namely, jointness-separateness and symbiosis. To my understanding, the normal pattern of object relations should be viewed as jointness-separateness starting from birth and subsequently refined via communication with others throughout the lifespan. An important role is attributed to separateness, which, as I see it, originates in the oral stage—from birth—as an outcome of the baby's healthy narcissism, differentiating the sense of self-separateness from any non-self. It is further shaped by (and through) the parents' attitude to their child's separateness and individuation and their jointness relations with him.

I have defined jointness-separateness relations as normative triadic object relations, drawing on healthy narcissism and facilitated by the ego's mobilisation of adaptation mechanisms. Jointness takes place whenever each of the partners in the relationship (e.g., baby and parent, spouses or colleagues) emerges from his or her self-space to join together in a virtual third shared space. Each is sensorially attuned to their partner's availability to share intimacy and communication, on the one hand, as well as to their partner's signs of strangeness and otherness, and hints of upcoming separation, on the other. In large measure, through the encounters in the shared space, the fine-tuning of the relationship moves from approaching and sharing to distancing and separating, a flowing back and forth which may culminate in the art of couplehood. Jointness in the oral stage is characterised mainly by intimacy between parent and offspring, and in the anal stage by negotiation, partnership, and reconciliation.

In my view, symbiosis should be considered a primitive dyadic mode of object relations, an outcome of impaired narcissism that fails to differentiate self-separateness from the non-self object, and preserves self-familiarity in a state of fusion. In symbiosis, defence mechanisms against the anxiety of abandonment are excessively mobilised. A symbiotic object-relations pattern takes place in a merged self-object space characterised by denial of separateness and the assumption of a false self, as well as by an absence of progress (e.g., a developmental delay) in individuation, and in relations with the otherness of others. In this respect, therefore, the symbiotic pattern might be considered pathological.

## Regarding separation-individuation

My approach is predicated on the perception of separateness present from the beginning of life (the oral stage), intertwined and perceptible with the evolving of the baby's narcissistic sense of non-self. The alertness toward the alien non-self accompanies us throughout our lives. Individuation and the perception of otherness may be considered as derivatives of the perception of separateness. The infant's individuation is improved through his healthy narcissism preserving his true and cohesive self-familiarity in separateness and the ego's adaptation mechanisms. Individuation and autonomy are enhanced through parental encouragement, partnership, and intimacy, and, no less, through their mode of separation from their child and their enabling him to separate from them. In this sense, the parents become the child's "coaches"— in the management of his life toward autonomy and individuation, as well as of his relationships and communication with others.

Perceptions of separateness and otherness are among the most complex aspects of awareness for each individual, for they may threaten his sense of self-familiarity and bonding, and increase his feeling of loneliness and isolation. I emphasise throughout the book how much easier it is to disrupt relations due to intolerance of the partner's otherness than to maintain relationships despite the inevitable injuries experienced, given the otherness of the object. Yet, parents and infants, like any partners, including spouses, may mutually strengthen their belonging-ness and their common interests of jointness partnership, and enhance negotiation and reconciliation by bridging conflicts of interest in the face of otherness arising from the object. This fine-tuning is a means for enhancing the art of couplehood.

The book describes how, during the oral stage, the baby defines his self-space of individuation mainly by narcissistic sensations and by his ego's pleasure principle. He demarcates his shared space with his differ-ent objects largely through his senses, his "gut-feelings" while intimacy takes place in their shared space in jointness-separateness relations. From the anal stage onward the toddler also defines his self-space of separateness by a narcissistic demarcation of his body self-image and by assertion of his individuation and autonomy, largely by means of his ego's reality principle. In his shared spaces with his different objects, his individuation is expressed mainly by negotiating the family rules, engaging in power struggles, communicating, and adjusting in joint-ness relations. Moreover, the toddler consents to his parents' authority demands and their (by now) familiar leadership.

The book also deals with various aspects of pathological narcissism and pathological object relations. Pathological narcissism may produce what I have defined as *emotional autoimmune phenomena*, which encom-pass various forms of self-destructiveness and what we generally refer to as narcissistic disturbances, OCD, narcissistic personality disorder, or a borderline narcissistic personality. Pathological object relations may include various forms of fusion of self and self-object (including those seen in schizophrenia), destructive object relations, and what we gener-ally refer to as disturbances in relationships, excessive vulnerability to otherness, mounting anxiety of abandonment, behavioural and affec-tive disorders, as well as psychopathic relations.

*The Enigma of Childhood* highlights the unconscious emotional checks and balances that are first formed during the oral and anal stages and then accompany us throughout life—whenever individuals (for exam-ple, baby and parents or couples/spouses) are involved in a relation-ship that encompasses the following elements:

a. A narcissistic immune balance on a continuum between attraction to the familiar and the maintaining of an appropriate alertness to otherness.

b. An ego-regulation balance on a scale between emotional outbursts and emotional restraint, equilibrium and pleasure.
c. An object-relations balance on a finely-tuned scale between proximity and distancing, approaching and separating.

My essential idea is that a "child" reflecting our childhood experiences is concealed within each of us, whether child or adult. These experiences resonate with the myriad layers of memory traces and narratives from early life onward, somewhat like a Russian babushka doll. The "concealed child" reverberates in present time and thus influences our present behaviour and contributes to the significance we attribute to intimacy, love, work, and the otherness of our partners. Furthermore, our childhood narratives influence the interpersonal contacts and communications we create that, unchecked, play a large role in determining the extent to which we experience happiness or suffering in our daily life.

The memory traces of experiences accumulated throughout our lifespan are continuously juxtaposed and assembled on the layers of childhood as quasi-familiar memory traces with minor changes, which confer almost-new meanings to our past and present experiences. It is on the foundation of this constant psychic movement of associations, forward, backward, and then onward, this vibrant juxtaposition of memory traces, that the consolidation of self-familiarity as wholeness takes place. The flow of associations evokes the energy of aggression combined with the power to love and the motivation to work, which together produce self-esteem and the feeling of happiness. Like the ebb and flow of waves pounding on the surf, this complex dynamic of joining and separating associations of self-familiarity constitutes *The Enigma of Childhood*, which assumes multiple meanings and dynamic interpretations throughout the various psychic stages.

# EPILOGUE

The major leitmotif running through *The Enigma of Childhood* is the crucial role of the innate narcissistic immune system in safeguarding true self-familiarity as a cohesive entity and wholeness in the face of the unfamiliar. The strangeness, the unfamiliar, and the unknown that are hidden within and around us, and contained as well in the otherness of our partners, persistently threaten to undermine our integrity and well-being. Hence, from birth to adulthood, we seek an "external force" (parents, leaders, a partner, therapy, faith, or science) or an "internal force" (self-esteem, self-confidence, mastery, and love) to protect our beloved objects and our love relations as well as to guard us from the threats of the unknown and enable us to control the alien. We search for landmarks, tools and guidance in the unknown by being curious, exploring, conducting scientific research, and mainly by maintaining the familiar sense of self, of love and well-being.

*The Enigma of Childhood* reveals how subjective narratives of the concealed child embedded within each of us affect our daily experiences. Resonances of childhood, both positive and negative, colour our interpretations of various occurrences. Reverberations of memory traces of joint interests with others inspire us to communicate with them and to meet them in shared joint spaces, thus creating intimacy. As the boundaries between us tend to become temporarily blurred, we become enveloped in a feeling of partnership and happiness, side by side with the constant search for separation-individuation.

Through the process of individuation, we constantly distance ourselves physically and psychically from our dearest objects. Yet, simultaneously, we develop sophisticated means for keeping our objects within us, and create the technological means for keeping us abreast of each other and bringing us closer, such as mobile phones, Facebook and other social networks. We try to maintain a good-enough balance between jointness and separateness, between connecting with others in shared spaces while refining our ability to withdraw into our own self-space. Awareness of separateness seems to enhance the ability to differentiate ourselves from others, to be curious about their otherness, to befriend them, and be emotionally intimate together despite a built-in self-preservative alertness to strangeness.

The concealed child within us seems to affect our adult lives, for better or for worse. Thus, all too often, in the wake of injuries, disappointments, or frustrations, and the attendant shame family of emotions, we may be sucked, unconsciously, into struggles with others, accompanied by rage, hatred, and vindictiveness. In these moments, our tolerance of otherness and the skill of bridging the conflicts of interest decrease, as occurs between the toddler and his parents during the anal stage. The conflicts of interest may then predominate over the joint interests and the mutual sharing of respect, love, and partnership that hitherto we managed to consolidate with so much emotional effort (whether in the family, with our fellows, and even among nations). This situation may occur with our children, our parents and siblings, and especially our spouses, when love relationships that have been built step by step over many years turn sour. Cultivating the art of living seems truly essential, so that despite untold frustrations and failures, we manage to maintain steady motivation for long-term investments in family and in work, for strengthening couple-hood, and preserving continuous love over and above the destructive hatred that our object hopefully manages to survive. Happiness, when gained, is surely a result of this ancient art of love and work.

Any disturbance in these delicate "checks and balances" of jointness and alertness may produce deficient vigilance and inappropriately excessive befriending. By being excessively attracted to familiarity or loaded with extreme transference so as to make the other familiar, as it were, we may inadvertently allow ourselves to be inappropriately befriended or even sexually seduced, that is, let alien factors invade the true self-space of separateness. (In some specific situations this might be part of the dynamics of incest or child abuse.) Furthermore, disregarding alertness to the strangeness within the familiarity might cause us to be lax about taking proper care of ourselves.

The technological era in which we live increasingly confronts us with a series of existential emotional and educational dilemmas: how can we bring new technological devices such as smartphones, televisions, and computers into our protected homes and still retain appropriate tools for discerning whether these media are providing useful information or playing the role of Trojan horses? How can we improve our "gut feelings" as we encourage our children to investigate essential aspects of the unknown while simultaneously taking a calculated risk of exposing them to threats and inappropriate material?

Many of us, children and adults, "surf the web", an activity that broadens our access to important data and to various potential partners and enterprises. However, this activity may also expose us to invaders, especially if we lack the tools to determine whether the data is genuine and whether the "chat" partner is a friend or a predator. Moreover, as internet access is usually located in a secure and familiar environment such as the home, alertness toward the unseen strangeness is decreased. This constellation is liable to heighten the illusion of engaging in "familiar" chatting, and thus lower vigilance to strangers and to alien threats that can expose one to seduction, abuse, fraud, and, sometimes even physical danger. It is important to be mindful that alien factors may invade the true self-space of separateness, invoking the need for defence.

On the other hand, excessive alertness and suspicion toward any hint of strangeness, otherness, change, or novelty can lead to anxiety and a defending of boundaries tinged with paranoia, or even a racist reaction.

Many children nowadays becomes addicted to "sharing" and exposing themselves via their smartphones—rather than investing in communication with the otherness of their friends. Thus, they may sit side by side, each with his "pacifier-smartphone", without inhabiting a shared space of dialogue with the others.

Finally, I would like to address what for me is an essential issue: how can psychotherapy or psychoanalysis help us obtain a better system of checks and balances, as we acknowledge the impact of the child concealed in every adult?

In my view, even the most proficient psychotherapist or psychoanalyst cannot modify the patient's subjective narratives, because his experiences are permanently imprinted, tattooed memory traces on his narcissistic network. The therapist cannot become the desired parent that replaces the real one, and, in this respect, it is not possible to produce a "corrective emotional experience".

However, consistent attentiveness and mindfulness, by both therapist and patient in the course of therapy, to the processing of the patient's unique, repetitive, similar associations concerning his narratives (in their shared space of what we generally refer to as "working through") are crucial. Highlighting the associations allows the patient to grasp the unconscious connection between them and the actual occurrences. Drawing attention to the source of the associations and interpreting them in the light of the transference in the here-and-now, as manifested in the relationship with the therapist and with others, is likely to bring about change in the salience of the memory traces. Moreover, this process may release significant, archaic, positive memory traces that were compressed or repressed in the unconscious under other destructive narratives. Their resurfacing may redress the balance of constructive and destructive memory traces.

Psychotherapy in general, and psychoanalysis in particular, to the extent that they are based on the patient's and analyst's associations in conjunction with the therapist's interpretations and technique, provide an exceptional opportunity for the curious psychologically-minded patient. The patient may join his or her therapist in a journey into the recesses of the mind, and an encounter with his/her concealed child. This process may produce new insights into the patient's childhood experiences, which in turn may help him recognise the significance of his or her narratives and scripts, and their impact on current life experiences.

This process can trigger the patient's motivation to reveal to himself, and perhaps to his significant others, his authentic "gut feelings" and his true self-familiarity, which he abandoned under the impact of alien invasions inherent in injuries, traumas, and deficient object relations. He may be able to acknowledge the hidden roots of his present sensations, reactions, and behaviour in light of these childhood narcissistic blows and scars that have marred him and that he still carries. It might provide him with new insights into his tendency to emphasise the evil and the calamities (his mobilisation of ego defence mechanisms), and to minimise his self-belongingness, love and happiness.

He might even discover the need to familiarise himself with his parents' genuine personality, for better or for worse, and to acknowledge his parents' positive characteristics, hitherto suppressed and smothered beneath the injuries, disappointments, hate or jealousy. He may then even realise that it is futile to hope for the re-creation of relations that he missed due to these injuries, and come to terms with the fact that one can yearn only for what one has experienced and is already imprinted in one's memory traces. This "working through" will hopefully bring to light the patient's precious, inner network of relations and his hitherto concealed capacity for individuation and communication, the unfolding of his individuation skills within love relationships, and the realisation of work-related potential, all of which had remained, in large measure, fallow and unexploited.

We may then gradually re-establish the delicate balance between befriending the otherness and being alert to the alien, being drawn to the familiar and resisting the strangeness, and being attracted to work satisfaction that is optimally balanced with family investments. We might manage better with the inevitable misunderstandings and conflicts of interest with our dearest ones, so often based on divergences from the sense of the familiar self. The emergence of positive self-assets and emotional forces may thus rekindle hope and renew our motivation to deepen communication with others, to reconcile with the imperfections of true self-familiarity and with the otherness of our loved ones. Thus we might rehabilitate and nurture our self-esteem despite our various handicaps.

Finally, we might recognise that good and evil are embedded in all of us and need to be regulated and acknowledged, that we crave intimacy and tenderness and may join together eagerly and contentedly in order to overcome separateness, loneliness and various injuries.

Even if only a segment of the above is achieved, it might enable us to better manage our lives and, mainly, our destructive impulses, and to release expressions of love that are usually held in check and yet remain so crucial for our sense of happiness. Free from some of the shackles of the past we may enjoy our work and pursue the art of couplehood concealed within the mystery of childhood.

I wish to conclude with what Freud so importantly states in *Civilization and its Discontents*:

> Professional activity is a source of special satisfaction if it is a freely chosen one—if, that is to say, by means of sublimation it makes possible the use of existing inclinations, of persisting or constitutionally reinforced instinctual impulses. And yet, as a path to happiness, work is not highly prized by men. They do not strive after it as they do after other possibilities of satisfaction (Freud, 1930a, p. 80).

> Exploiting love [is] for the benefit of an inner feeling of happiness. (ibid., p. 102)

Love, as well as work or any creative enterprise may underlie the secret of our happiness.

# GLOSSARY

*Accommodation*: An ego adaptation mechanism enabling the infant to reorganise cognitive (Piaget, 1936) or emotional structures, making room for new information, so it can be processed and adjusted accordingly (assimilated) within the old elements. Involves structural change.

*Adaptation mechanisms*: We assume that adaptation mechanisms are stimulated by the energy of the life instinct. Through adaptation mechanisms (e.g., internalisation and transference) the individual's ego manages to connect the emerging stimulus to the object that may bring satisfaction/pleasure, improving its efficiency and benefits. Adaptation mechanisms emerge and evolve each from its previous function and may regress or reverse to their preceding functions. An example: the progression achieved from incorporation via introjection, to internalisation, identification etc. This progress reflects the individual's increasing cognitive abilities and emotional intelligence.

*Affect*: A complex psychophysiological chain of events that includes both a subjective experience and physiological and cognitive components. (Compare feeling, emotions, and mood.)

*Affect theory*: For modern affect theory, an affect is the purely biological aspect of emotion: when a stimulus activates a mechanism that releases a known pattern of biological events, an affect has been triggered.

*All-or-nothing principle*: The id may be regarded as an archaic agency of self-regulation that is activated to regulate inborn instinctual tension according to the all-or-nothing principle, similar to the nature of the activation of the nervous system. This implies that when tension reaches a certain threshold, the instinctual response is total and compulsive (all), and that when it is below that threshold, no stimulus response will occur (nothing).

*Anal stage*: Represents the second stage of emotional-psychosexual development, from one year up to three years of age. Due to physical maturation and the ability to master the sphincters, the toddler's awareness is involved with the anal zone. It provides further sources for libidinal satisfaction (anal eroticism) and aggressive satisfaction (anal sadism), and for gaining mastery gratification (libido fused with aggression). The development of this emotional stage stimulates new inner conflict, as well as conflicts between the caregivers and the toddler in relation to the weaning process (toilet training and cleanliness training). The process may "imprint" recurrent behavioural characterisations, such as excessive restraining, retention, obstinacy and orderliness, or messiness, as well as ambivalence, activity/passivity, mastery, separation, and individuation. (Compare oral.)

*Animism*: The belief that inanimate objects are alive and as such have lifelike qualities, such as feelings and intentions.

*Annihilation*: One of the primal anxieties, indicating an intense emotional experience of danger to one's existence.

*Anxiety*: An intense emotional state with attendant physiological arousal characterised by feelings of unpleasant anticipation of impending danger.

*Association*: A *bond* between two or more psychical elements that form an "associative chain". Associations appear also through reverberation of memory traces from past experiences in present occurrences.

*Attachment*: A bonding between two individuals, where each gains a sense of security or a secure attachment from the emotional relationship. Children may be involved in different patterns of attachment relationships in early life.

*Attachment theory*: The human infant's predisposition to participate in social interaction.

*Awareness*: The ability to notice and become conscious of, feel, or perceive something hitherto ignored.

*Body image*: The subjective experience of one's body as a whole.

*Boundaries*: Individual and societal guidelines, rules or limits for behaviour, including permissible or impermissible actions; indicate the perceived or represented frame of separateness and the capacity for bodily and emotional control.

*Cathexis*: Interest, attention, or emotional investment in a specific person or thing. It can be conceptualised also as investing values, feelings, or drives in another person.

*Cognition*: A transformational process of sensory input from the senses that is mentally stored as data, whether encoded, abstracted or elaborated, adaptively assimilated and accommodated, or recovered and exercised as knowledge. The stored knowledge may appear in present experiences as sensations, perceptions, memories, representations, imagination, behaviour, affective scripts, learning and remembering via conceptualising, reasoning, thinking, mentalizing, and judging.

*Compulsion*: An irresistible impulse to act, regardless of whether or not one's motive is rational or appropriate given the interpersonal context.

*Conflict*: Inner conflict refers to incompatible forces or structures within the mind (such as retaining/liberating), whereas external conflict is a struggle between the individual and attributes of his outside world (such as needing to consider both the object's demands and the self's needs).

*Death instinct*: Death instincts are regulated by the id and aspire to reduce the tension to an optimal level, or back toward an inorganic state. Unregulated death versus life instincts may be directed toward the destruction of the self. (Compare life instinct.)

*Decision-making*: The process of choosing between alternatives; selecting or rejecting available options regarding short- or long-term intentions.

*Defence mechanism*: We may assume that defence mechanisms are stimulated by the energy of the death instinct. Through defence mechanisms (such as denial and repression) the individual's ego manages to disconnect the emerging response from the object (stimulus) that evokes anxiety. Thus, the ego manages to preserve the self from being flooded by anxiety and its attendant dangers (e.g., annihilation, object loss, loss of love, loss of control). (Compare adaptation mechanism.)

*Denial*: One of the primitive defence mechanisms by which an individual unconsciously refuses to recognise some painful attribute or perception of his inner or outer reality. Thus, the ego defends the self from being flooded by anxiety and/or by other unpleasurable affects or concerns.

*Developmental stages*: Periods of life initiated by significant transitions or changes in physiological, or psychological functioning. Pre-genital stages: oral and anal. Genital stages: oedipal, latency, puberty, and adulthood.

*Drives*: There is often confusion between instincts (life and death) and drives (libido and aggression). Instincts seem to be regulated by the id (see id and instincts). Drives seem to be regulated by the ego, which manages to invest the instinctual energy in an object so as to gain satisfaction/pleasure.

*Ego*: (Latin for 'I'). One of the original three major agencies of the personality—*id, ego, superego*, to which have been added the *ego ideals* and *innate narcissism*. Since the ego is understood as having developed from the id, it is seen as relatively more coherent and organised. The ego's main function in self-preservation is the regulation of drives and emotions and mediation of the demands of the external world, their channelling toward appropriate object relations, and their expression. This occurs essentially through adaptation and defence mechanisms.

*Ego ideals*: Initially used interchangeably with superego, an ego ideal has come to mean a project of the ego to be achieved. It may arouse a fantasy (such as an inner imagining of play), evoking motivation to realise these goals.

*Emotion*: Psychic subjective experience (e.g., happiness, distress, fear, or rage) of an intense physiological arousal that produces changes in the psychic situation, cognitive processes, and behavioural reactions as described in subjective terms. When an affect resonates with memories of that same affect and the affects they trigger, it is said to be an emotion. (Compare affect, feeling, and mood).

*Emotional resonance*: Empathic attunement to another's facial expressions and body language, sensations, and feelings. Makes possible meaningful communion and communication with another, even without sharing a common language, as between different species. Crucial for the survival of the human infant and parent–child relationship.

*Empathy*: A mode of perceiving or "feeling into" another person by vicariously experiencing (in a limited way) their psychological state. A key concept in both affect theory and self-psychology. Helps understand another individual and bridge the otherness between people.

*Envy and Jealousy*: The desire or greed to own another's possessions (as in "all-or-nothing"). Envy is generally linked with the anxiety of annihilation (having nothing) or object loss.

*Erotogenic zones and psychosexual stages of development*: The pre-genital (oral and anal) and genital (oedipal) stages represent the predominant body zone intensely susceptible to stimulation, triggering sensual excitement. During these developmental stages the infant focuses his pleasurable/erotic and motivational/interpretative activity (first experienced with the mother in infancy), around the relevant erotogenic zone, such as the mouth and skin or the anus, as he or she develops emotional, psychomotor and cognitive intelligence. Erotic pleasure (from the Greek word *Eros* or sexual love/God of Love) is accompanied by psychophysiological changes, such as heartbeat, blood pressure, and hormonal secretion; the excitement spreads to other systems, both biological and mental.

*False self*: The concept of the false self describes the individual's need to falsify his true self in order to satisfy his caretakers' expectations and maintain their love. To the extent that a false self is assumed, it means the individual is relinquishing the expression of his or her true self.

*Familiarity principle*: Innate narcissism is activated to immunise the baby's self-cohesiveness according to the familiarity principle as it alternates between two poles: attraction to the familiar and resistance to that which evokes strangeness.

*Fantasy (or phantasy)*: This concept may be considered as "playing" in imagination. An important adaptation mechanism that allows the individual to cope with reality and communicate with others. In his imagination, he plays with and finds an outlet for the drives and emotions he was unable to express overtly, given the love relations with his objects and their expectations.

*Fixation*: During the normal psychic development elaborated in this book, the infant experiences occurrences or relations with particular objects that satisfy him excessively, and he or she may become addicted to this mode of gratification. Alternately, the infant may undergo frustrating traumatic experiences that he or she is unable to integrate at the time, if at all. Both these poles may serve as points of fixation. Under the impact of stress or anxiety, the individual is unable to cope or function according to his capabilities or developmental level, and tends to regress to these earlier fixation points (e.g., an infant who is already weaned from sucking his pacifier or from diapers may suddenly regress to sucking, or become encopretic).

*Frustration*: Frustration occurs when the individual invests his drives and emotions in particular objects or areas in order to gain satisfaction, yet fails or is deprived or otherwise barred from gaining this need gratification.

*Fusion/Defusion*: Usually, life and death instincts are processed and co-exist in fusion—unless defused as a consequence of frustration or trauma. Fusion may also occur between the self and its object, and is manifested when each component significantly impacts the whole. May be represented in variable forms, provided a balance is obtained between the components. Defusion signifies that each of the components operates separately according to its own aim and characteristics, imbalanced and independently of the other. This imbalance may assume powerful proportions.

*Good object/bad object*: An object (or part of an object) that provides satisfaction or satisfactory interactions in response to the individual's ego investment of drives and emotions is experienced as good object, whereas an object that fails or frustrates the ego's investment is experienced as a bad object.

*Habituation*: Like the organism, the psychic process tends to adjust to repeated stimuli, which, no longer novel, attract less attention.

*Hallucination*: An appearance (involving any of the five senses) of a sensory stimulus or perception of an external object, which, although absent in the proximate environment, is nevertheless experienced as real.

*Healthy narcissism*: I define healthy narcissism as an innate emotional immune system for safeguarding the familiarity and the well-being of the individual against invasion of the self by foreign sensations. The narcissism processes information according to the familiarity principle, involving attraction to the familiar and the resisting of the alien. There is a sense of well-being in the presence of the familiar and alertness and vulnerability upon facing that which is strange. Since childhood, the familiar is tempting, and strangeness, whether from within (illness) or from outside (otherness), evokes awareness or even intolerance. The process of narcissistic immunisation may be compared to the activity of the biological immunological system, which identifies the familiar protein of the cell and rejects the foreign protein (bacteria, virus). (Compare, pathological narcissism.)

*Id*: The id represents one of the three agencies of Freud's structural model of the personality (id, ego and superego). From the economic point of view, the id is comprised of the energy reservoir of the life and death instincts. It represents the basic, discharge/satisfaction-seeking motives of human psychic life. Dynamically, the id is in conflict with the ego and the superego.

*Idealisation*: One of the ego's adaptation mechanisms in the oral stage, idealisation enables the baby to preserve the good object by elevating him to the level of perfection, thereby safeguarding it from aggression.

*Immune system*: The biological immune system safeguards the code of the human cell's protein as familiar and constant, identifies foreign invaders with a different protein code that may endanger the integrity of body cells, and blocks them. My concept of healthy narcissism as providing an emotional immune system reveals some similarities between the emotional and biological immune processes. We may also recognise a common denominator between biological autoimmune disease and the pathological characteristics of the narcissistic immune system.

*Imprinting*: May be considered a primitive form of survival learning, similar to introjection. Experiences leave imprints of memory traces on the narcissistic neural network, which serve as "anchoring" comparison data for recognising the familiar and resisting strangeness.

*Incorporation*: Represents one of the ego's most primitive adaptation mechanisms in the oral stage, providing the baby a corporal model of absorption of the object (such as suckling) throughout his instinctual discharge. (Compare introjection internalisation, idealisation.)

*Insight*: The capacity to apprehend or recognise a hidden narrative or script that unconsciously influenced the individual's experience and interpretation of daily occurrences. Insight is experienced as an enlightenment of an emotional state, now viewed from a different perspective. It may be achieved through attentiveness to free associations and how they are experienced in the body, the differentiation between past and present, and their reintegration through different associative links and pathways.

*Instinct*: An inherent urge by a living entity to restore an earlier state of things it was obliged to abandon. In addition to the conservative instincts that impel toward repetition, others push toward the production of new forms. The id represents the reservoir of life and death instincts, which are "everything that is inherited, that is present at birth, that is laid down in the constitution" (Freud, 1940a [1938], p. 145).

*Intelligence*: An innate psychic potential, which throughout development, provides the individual with the skill of adaptation to reality and environment, and allows him (or her) to utilise his psychomotor, cognitive, and affective capabilities efficiently.

*Internalisation*: One of the important adaptation mechanisms from the anal stage. May be conceived as the ego's psychological absorption, digestion, and integration of inputs from the outside inside, providing "building blocks" for the rudimentary ego and the foundation of the ego's consolidation. The process of internalisation requires the complementary processes of assimilation (absorption and digestion) and accommodation (integration). These building blocks refer as well to internalisation of the interpersonal field of relationship and object relations.

*Interpretation*: One of the most important guidelines, tools, and techniques of psychoanalysis and dynamic psychotherapy; aims to shed light on the patient's unconscious or hidden narratives and conflicts. The analyst provides meaning to his (or her) patient's associations, feelings and anxieties, sensory input and physical sensations, memories, and dreams by linking them to the patient's narratives in a manner that enables him to make new connections. During this "working through" process of both partners, the patient is able to mentalize and acknowledge a new perspective or understanding of the latent meaning of his communications. This hopefully will enable the patient to become more present and fully alive in his dealings with both his inner and outer daily life.

*Introjection*: One of the baby's primitive (oral stage) adaptation mechanisms (following incorporation) that operates by absorbing the objects' sensory characteristics from the outside inward, similar to the physical activity of swallowing. It is as if the baby is swallowing parental sensual characteristics—such as voices, reaction tones, warmness, and rhythms—without digesting them. The introjections facilitate recognition of the objects by the five senses and enable the baby to familiarise himself with the sensory uniqueness of each of his parents and to preserve their characteristics exactly as *he* senses them. (Compare incorporation, internalisation.)

*Intuition*: A process based on innate narcissistic "gut feelings" which allow the individual to perceive, sense, and observe his surroundings.

*Isolation*: A defence mechanism operating from the anal stage onward against the anxiety of loss of control over emotions. Isolating the emotion or experience from the event blocks the feared outburst of affect. (Compare rationalisation.)

*Jealousy*: An emotional reaction of stress, jealousy appears with the possessive need emerging in the anal stage. The toddler is threatened by a sibling-rival who might "kidnap" his parents' love; this arouses his unconscious wish for the exclusion of the rival.

*Jointness-separateness object relations*: Jointness-separateness is a relatively new term I use to describe the pattern of normal object relations occurring following the birth of the baby. Jointness-separateness is defined as a dynamic process, representing an emotional system for attachment and for communication between separate individuals who jointly approach each other, meeting in a shared virtual space. Jointness-separateness represents *triadic* relations between two individuals (separate self-spaces)—the baby's self-space and the parent's self-space—relations that take place in a virtual third shared "space", where they come together temporarily. A momentary sense of blurring of the boundaries between them may ensue. I visualise self-space as a shell symbolising one's fortress of separateness. Via his senses, the baby/adult recognises the boundaries of his own shell and detects the non-self around him (or her). From the self-space of *separateness* the individual can emerge partially, and be in touch with what he experiences as a non-self, that is, another individual also partially outside his shell. In these moments, each senses the presence of the other in the shared space and thus communication (both verbal and non-verbal) can take place. The individual always preserves his separateness and his inner sense of freedom to either join the object in intimacy in the shared space or alternatively withdraw from this non-self, remaining ensconced in his self-familiar space until ready to venture out again. Thus, from infancy to adulthood, getting hurt emotionally is inevitable because the other, even if he is a familiar person and dear to us, is still a separate individual who asserts his otherness. Jointness-separateness object relations indicate a healthy development that relies on healthy narcissism and generates separation-individuation, communication, and relationship. Jointness represents an encounter between mother and infant, psychotherapist and patient, or any partners simultaneously experiencing mutual intimacy while concomitantly safeguarding separateness.

*Libido theory*: The libido is understood as psychic energy comparable to physical energy, which the ego may invest in his objects. The libidinal investment is referred to as "cathexis". The ego invests the libidinal energy in the object so as to repeat pleasurable experiences and regain familiar satisfactions, well-being, and pleasure with this particular libidinal object.

*Love*: Affects or emotions associated with the libidinal cathexis experienced with the object. This affect emerges out of the experience of the ego's libidinal energy successfully invested in the libidinal object. The individual's investment or the "re-finding of the object" may be experienced as satisfaction, pleasure, a blissful state, elation, or euphoria. The affect of love is one of the most important emotions for the consolidation of self-esteem, self-confidence, and object relations. Love is enriched through the relations of intimacy that the infant experiences with his parents and is intensified with the perception of object constancy, separateness, and jointness.

*Memory Traces*: The way in which events are thought to be "inscribed" upon the memory and assist as traces of the original episodes linked to similar traces. A memory may be re-actualised in one associative context while remaining inaccessible to consciousness in another. I suggest that abstracted sensory characteristics and affective data are imprinted and stored in the narcissistic network as a basis for recognising the familiar and resisting strangeness. Similarities between resonances and reverberations of memory traces from the past and current experiences evoke the sense of familiarity. Strangeness is generally experienced whenever the resonation of memory traces does *not* correspond to what is currently experienced. Throughout the day, mostly unconscious memory traces reverberate within us, influencing the way in which we perceive ourselves and reality, the other, and our relationships. Moreover, they affect how others relate to us.

*Monologue and Dialogue*: Maintaining a monologue indicates that the individual is speaking without taking into consideration the presence of another, whereas maintaining a dialogue indicates the individual is taking the presence of another into consideration. Here, each senses if he or she is liable to listen and be listened to, communicate and be understood. This is accompanied by the wish to be recognised and held in a communication and relationship with this other.

*Mourning*: Any loss of a meaningful or loved object (e.g., a person, animal, or transitional object) undermines the cohesiveness of self-familiarity due to the emergence of painful feelings. One may come to feel as if part of the self is lost, much like the faeces and teeth of childhood. Feelings of strangeness regarding the missing object or part may emerge. A healthy narcissistic immune process, mourning occurs mainly from the anal stage onward and tends to preserve the significant loss as part of the self-assets and possessions, and to restore the self-familiarity as a familiar wholeness that includes representations of the lost one. The mourning process may be brief or prolonged, involving a withdrawal from outside interests or investments. When the mourning process is accomplished, the individual feels stronger, and more resilient—as if he managed to hold or internalise his possessions, including the loss of his significant object or significant ideals—while creating a new coherent self-image, with its attendant limits, capacities, and relationships.

*Narcissism*: The term "narcissism" emerged from the myth of Narcissus, who fell in love with his own image and loved his self. Freud's concepts of primary and secondary narcissism are related to three phenomena: choice of an object, relationship pattern, and ego ideal (from which the concept of self-esteem has evolved as being virtually synonymous with narcissism). Libidinal investment directed solely to the ego/self or the object may evoke a supreme experience of elation, in the realm between idealisation, omnipotence, and infatuation. It may also arouse the blissful state (defined as happiness) when there is ostensibly no longer a need for external objects. While we are unwilling to forgo the narcissistic perfection of childhood, conditions of organic pain and illness nonetheless tend to lead to a withdrawal of interest in the external world, regained upon recovery.

We may differentiate normal from pathological narcissism: Healthy narcissism activates an immunologic process of restoring the stabilisation of cohesiveness, integrity, and vigorousness of the self, following injuries, and the restoration of the relationship with the other, despite its otherness. Healthy narcissism contributes to improving love relationships, the tolerance of separateness, otherness, and withdrawal, and jointness via intimacy. Moreover, it sustains emotional intelligence as part of the process of adapting to change, and intensifies curiosity and the investigation of the environment. It also supports relating to otherness and enhances one's "joie de vivre".

In contrast, pathologic narcissism indicates an excessive vulnerability and anxiety, a lack of self-cohesion and self-confidence, and intolerance for otherness and for separation. This is accompanied by (and in part due to) a dependence on the other for need satisfaction (self-object) or alternatively by idealising the self as a grandiose self. Both cases lead to fragile, primitive, or impaired object relations. In my view, pathological narcissism implies an emotional autoimmune system that may attack the self. This may betray the relentless pursuit of self-perfection, which may variously alternate with feelings of entitlement, eruptions of rage or destructive power against the self, and the risk of producing mental pathological symptoms.

*Nirvana principle*: Refers to the psychic effort to reduce and keep constant the threshold of tension accompanying archaic demands on the self—as manifested by withdrawal, seclusion, or deep sleep.

*Non-self*: Anything that evokes a sense of strangeness to the familiar sense of self.

*Object*: Initially understood as the medium through which instinctual energy may be satisfied, I define the object as the target of the ego's drives for a satisfying emotional investment: The individual's ego invests drives and emotion in a specified or named object that might bring about the wished-for satisfaction, whether a live object such as the caregiver, or a lifeless one like one of the person's transitional objects. The object must be both differentiated from and significant to the self.

Along with the consolidation of the perception of object constancy (from approximately seven months), the external object may come to be perceived, represented, or imagined within the mind. It may be an internal image of the object, one that generally but not exactly corresponds to the external one, as it includes the various subjective experiences of the self, related to the relations with this external object. A *libidinal object* is one toward whom there is an attraction, mainly for an intimacy that might satisfy the individual's needs for love relations.

*Object constancy*: This is one of primary adaptation mechanisms that enable the baby to attach to his object despite its frequent disappearances. Until the age of five to six months, the object exists for the baby only when visible and "need-satisfying." From about seven months onwards, the baby preserves the object and/or its representation/ image even in its absence: the perception of the object is constant. The baby searches for the disappearing object if the relations with it are continuous, constant, stable, and permanent. The odour, voice, and touch represent the object as a stable wholeness.

*Object relations theory*: The terms *object relations* and *object relationships* may be used to designate the attitudes and behaviour of someone toward his or her object, whether an actual person or mental image. Object relations theory encompasses: (1) the development from early relatedness in the infant to complex mental functioning and mature adult relationships; (2) the motivations for relationships; and (3) the enduring and distinctive relationship patterns that characterise individuals.

*Oral stage*: Represents the first stage of emotional-psychosexual development, which takes place from birth to eighteen months. In this stage, the primary source of pleasure, gratification, familiarisation, and relations is linked to the stimulation of the mouth, lips, and skin.

*Otherness*: Represents the sense of strangeness that emanates from the familiar object, evoking a sense that the other is not recognised as familiar.

*Perception*: The ego functions by mobilising adaptation mechanisms to scan and convert incoming sensory stimuli into mental messages.

A necessary process for registering and recognising the experience of both inner sensation and external reality, perception has both conscious and unconscious aspects.

*Phenomenon*: A familiar sensual occurrence that can be experienced alone or via sharing the experience in intimacy with another person. It can be sensed as a transitional phenomenon that emotionally bonds separate individuals together.

*Pleasure principle*: The first economic principle of ego regulation is the pleasure principle: the individual is attracted or motivated to repeat, recreate, or reproduce immediate and maximum satisfaction and pleasurable experiences with the object and to avoid unpleasure. Pleasure or unpleasure are experiences linked to familiar or unfamiliar levels of tension. (Compare reality principle.)

*Projection*: One of the primitive defence mechanisms mobilised by the ego in order to protect the self from being flooded by the anxiety of strangeness or annihilation. The individual rejects and expels (as if spitting out or vomiting) unbearable emotions, feelings, or wishes that otherwise would provoke these anxieties. As we expel these intolerable sensations from the self, we tend to locate them outside, in another person.

*Proprioception*: Stems from the Latin word *proprius* (one's own, proper), combined with "perception". The ability to perceive and sense the position, location, orientation, and movement of the body and its parts in relation to each other and in extrapersonal space, that is, outside the body. Proprioceptors are sensory nerve terminals (e.g., in the muscles, tendons, and the labyrinth) which provide information concerning body movements and position.

*Protective shield*: The need of the organism (or of the self) to be protected against stimuli by protective layers that filter out those stimuli or excitations that threaten its stability. In my view, narcissism serves as a protective immunising shield for the self.

*Rationalisation*: A defence mechanism mobilised by ego regulation, functioning from the anal stage onwards against the anxiety of uncontrolled occurrences or the unknown, and against strangeness. The toddler/adult tries to give himself subjective reasons or explanations for behaviour (his or that of others), and produces excuses and rational justifications for his acts and thoughts (according to his reality principle. This should enable him to alleviate his anxiety and his intolerable sense of the unknown and maintain or regain control. Adults often use rationalisation under the guise of ideology and principles.

*Reaction formation*: From the anal stage onwards, defence mechanisms are mobilised against the anxiety of loss of control. The awareness and outburst of emotions is blocked by a reaction formation that converts the emotion into its diametrical opposite, for example, from attraction to repulsion.

*Reality principle*: The second economic principle of the ego's regulation is the reality principle, which emerges during the anal stage. This implies that the individual is attracted to or motivated to repeat, recreate, or otherwise reproduce long-term satisfaction in accordance with the rules imposed by the object/family/society/reality. The individual is willing to postpone immediate satisfaction in order to obtain gratification for his behaviour in the form of a sense of belonging with his objects, as well as to avoid anger and punishment. (Compare pleasure principle.)

*Recognition*: The inborn, unconscious capability of the individual's narcissism to resonate the relevant memory traces, enabling the identification of the person or the occurrence as familiar.

*Regression*: The ego mobilises this defence mechanism against the anxiety of annihilation which may overwhelm the self when the individual cannot cope efficiently with present conflicts, and in his efforts to manage better, returns to an earlier fixation mode of mental functioning. For example, compulsive outbursts may indicate a regression from a psychological ego regulation of restraint to a physiological id regulation of the compulsive discharging of instinctual tension that remains unconnected to any object. A toddler experiences a state of stress or a traumatic event related to an acute sense of jealousy, betrayal, or loss of security, and reacts by vomiting, as he used to when he was eight months old. One may distinguish between three forms of regression: (1) a regression concerning the object; (2) a regression related to the libidinal stage (such as in the previous example); and (3) a regression to a previous position in the advancement of ego regulation functioning, such as in the first example above (regression to physiological id regulation).

*Repetition compulsion*: The archaic default mode of the id's regulation of instinctual discharge of excitation—unrelated to the object and uninfluenced by the ego's regulation in accordance to the pleasure principle.

*Representation*: An adaptation mechanism via which the individual's ego manages to recognise experiences and objects as familiar. The ego condenses and combines a wide range of subjective data into schematic reproductions of significant objects, relations, sense of the self, or occurrences. Narcissistic resonances of these reproductions in present experiences (e.g., in the form of sensations and associations) enable the individual to cope by recognising them as familiar and by differentiating among them in varying occurrences. Hence, these representations are always personal and subjective.

*Repression*: A defence mechanism from the oral stage, mobilised by the ego against the anxiety of annihilation. Unconsciously activated to disconnect the instincts and drives, or emotional stimuli from the object of satisfaction, who may trigger reverberations of unbearable frustration, trauma, and the anxiety of annihilation. Repression attempts to hide from awareness these painful resonances. Notwithstanding, the repressed instinct and drives often resurface and reappear in consciousness and are then repetitively repressed by the ego to avoid anxiety.

*Resistance*: A defence mechanism mobilised by the ego from the oral stage, which operates in combination with the narcissistic immune agency that stimulates attraction to the familiar and resistance to strangeness. The combined defence protects the self against the anxiety of strangeness or annihilation erupting from the inner or outside world.

*Self*: An agglomeration of sensations and memory traces of numerous personal experiences is organised subjectively into a coherent and enduring configuration of the sense of a familiar self that resists everything that is a non-self. Gradually, from birth, the baby's sense of his familiar self begins to crystallise, and he can identify himself as familiar in his changing environment, and recognise and be attracted to a familiar non-self while differentiating himself from anything that is strange to him. Along with the baby's interaction with the non-self, his inborn narcissism is constantly triggered to preserve the sense of a familiar self as wholeness, a process enhancing self-esteem.

*Self-flooding*: The self is exposed to emotional states of uncontrolled and unbalanced explosions of drives and emotions, leading to anxiety, which the ego has to manage via defence mechanisms. The anxiety may take various forms linked to development. In addition, self-flooding may be understood as the physiological activation of an individual's autonomic nervous system in response to a traumatic event at a certain point in time.

*Self-object*: The term refers to the baby's (or child/adult's) experience of the other as being need-satisfying—in the service of his self yet undifferentiated from the self (not a distinct non-self).

*Separateness*: Represents the capacity to sense and detect any alien sensation to the familiar self, and experience it as non-self. Gradually the infant is also capable of sensing his personal "shell-space" as distinct from other non-selves, recognising his object as separate from his self and not only as a familiar non-self. The capacity to acknowledge separateness and otherness depends on the consolidation of healthy narcissism. One of our major difficulties is to relate to the separateness and otherness of the other, always a non-self, an unknown, a stranger to one's self-familiarity. An impassable boundary separates between people and despite one's emotional resonance and empathic attunement, one cannot really recognise the "within" of this other personal shell, its self-space.

*Separation*: This term refers to the need for withdrawal, present already from birth, whenever the sense of strangeness or of non-self occurs. It may represent a physical act or a psychic act disconnecting narcissistic attraction or drive investments from outside objects and diverting them toward the inside. It also refers to the dynamic process of separation-individuation (see below). However, throughout their object relations, both infant and caregiver experience and reproduce rituals of separation that prepare them to free each other from the jointness bonding. Otherwise, a sudden or unprepared separation might be experienced as an abandonment, rejection, trauma, or anxiety.

*Separation-individuation*: A process consolidating a sense of the self as a distinct entity functioning separately from the object, shaping one's individuation and tolerating the separateness of the object. Mahler's theory of the four sub-phases (differentiation, practicing, rapprochement, on the way to object constancy) comprising the process of separation-individuation, signifies the infant's gradual emergence from the symbiotic dual unity with the mother as he distinguishes his self from the object and develops his own individual characteristics and self-representations.

*Shame*: The opposite of pride, this family of affects refers to a broad spectrum of painful affects sometimes referred to as shame-humiliation. Shame includes feelings of embarrassment, mortification, unworthiness, and disgrace, which may accompany a sense of being rejected, ridiculed, exposed, or of otherwise losing the respect of self and others. While early experiences of being seen, looked at, exposed, and scorned are significant in producing shame, shame may be more widely understood as emerging whenever there is an impediment to expressing a continued interest-excitement or other positive affects, (such as enjoyment-joy) but may also emerge in relation to the experiencing of negative affects (e.g., revenge or disgust). Precursors of shame anxiety may be seen in the early patterns of gaze aversion and later stranger anxiety. Shame may be assembled with an infinite variety of combinations of sensations, affects, images, and memories, thus providing each person with a unique experiential/affective script (Tomkins, 1987). As a character trait, it protects against disgraceful exposure, so as to maintain self-esteem. Moreover, it preserves values and ideals on both an individual and cultural level.

*Somatisation*: Appears to be a primitive mechanism, mobilised from early babyhood against any strangeness. The influence of the psyche on the soma (psycho-somatisation) includes the tendency of the individual's ego regulation to mobilise primitive defence mechanisms against the flooding of the self by excessive anxiety. The individual responds to the stimuli and to his distress with physiological and somatic symptom expression rather than by psychic emotional regulation. We note that disease and/or self-destructiveness are frequently associated with aggression, the anxiety of the loss of a meaningful object, or that of strangeness/annihilation. It is also noted that mental representation and symbolisation are needed to regulate emotions through adaptation mechanisms, and thus integrate psyche and soma.

*Splitting*: A primitive defence mechanism mobilised by the ego regulation available at the oral stage, against the anxiety of annihilation and object loss. The ego mobilises splitting, in my view, on the basis of the narcissistic principle—attraction to the familiar and the resistance to strangeness. Whenever the primary caretaker offers familiar pleasurable satisfaction and responds immediately and totally to the baby's emerging needs, he is experienced by the baby as a good object, triggering attraction toward him (or her). Whenever the caregiver frustrates or arouses sensations of strangeness or unpleasure, he is experienced by the baby as a bad object, triggering resistance to him. Thus, the same parent-object is experienced alternately as familiar, good, and ideal, or as bad, evil, and a stranger. From eight months onward, the ego manages to preserve the good and familiar satisfying object as a whole entity. It integrates (integration = adaptation mechanisms) the split-off good and bad objects into a single, constant, good-enough parental figure, while aggression toward the frustrating good object is projected or displaced (projection and displacement = defence mechanisms) on to the figure of a stranger. Hence, now the actual object is cathected as a good object, despite the inevitable frustrations, while the unfamiliar is experienced as an evil stranger (split between the "good and bad guys"). In certain exceptional cases of extreme trauma or anxiety, the ego may *split its own self* instead of the object (borderline personality or psychosis; dissociative identity disorder ("multiple personality").

*Stranger anxiety*: An affective reaction of resistance toward the unknown or a stranger, often referred to as eight-month anxiety. The baby might react with apprehension or distress and withdraw, refusing to make contact (especially eye contact), crying, or even screaming.

*Structural Theory*: Freud's attempt to explain the enduring, organised, and interrelated aspects of mental functioning whereby the mind (psychic apparatus) is divided into three "structures" of relatively enduring motivational configurations called the id, ego and superego (see definitions). Ego ideals was added later (Chasseguet-Smirgel, 1975) and, in my view, innate healthy narcissism may also be included.

*Sublimation*: One of the more sophisticated adaptation mechanisms from the anal stage, motivating creativity, dreams, work, and art. It is manifest when intolerable impulses or conflict of any kind—in the context of familial/social relations—are expressed in an acceptable form such as feelings, ideas, and creativity and characterised by a converted regulated psychic aim. The power of the sexual instinct, stressed Freud, is placed at the disposal of civilised activity, and diverted toward a valued non-sexual aim. Sublimation comprises the sense of "sublime". Freud thus explained the source and underpinnings of socially valuable, apparently non-sexual and conflict-free activities.

*Superego*: The superego is considered to be differentiated from the earlier ego. Representing an internalisation of parental attitudes, reactions, and values, so as to master the sexual and aggressive instincts of the oedipal phase, it is seen as the moral aspect of the personality. It contains the conscience, which may evoke a sense of guilt for the individual's wishes.

*Symbiosis*: The concept of symbiosis represents the mother–infant relation of dependency on each other as a need-satisfying object, whereby the self is undifferentiated from the object. Baby and mother perceive their duality as an omnipotent unity within one common boundary. Symbiosis may represent a mental state of the baby and his mother, as if they were one dual unity with a barrier between them and the rest of the world. Symbiosis may be considered as a defence mechanism against the anxiety of annihilation, which risks flooding the self of each partner when hints of separateness appear between them.

*Symbolisation and symbolism*: Both concepts use symbols, that is, a sign or character used as a conventional, albeit frequently unconscious representation of an object, function, or process. In the process, one mental representation may stand for another via vague suggestion, convention, or accidental relation. From the anal stage, symbolisation is considered an important adaptation mechanism, enabling the improvement of psychic regulation, communication, and dreams.

*Symptom formation*: The neurotic symptom formation represents the defence mechanisms that the ego mobilises against anxiety, particularly when the primal defences do not suffice to soothe and contain the anxiety, and a redoubling of defensive operations is needed. The symptom is a compromise formation the ego uses to impede the repressed drives, wishes, fantasies, memories, sensations, affects, or conflicts from reappearing into consciousness. This allows partial satisfaction to be experienced, generally as secondary gain. Instead of keeping the object "online" in intimacy via libidinal drive expression, the individual manages to elicit and maintain his object's attention and ministrations through the symptom.

*Threshold level*: A physiological level of sensory reaction to the stimulus, producing an emotional experience accompanied by motor manifestations. In the oral stage, the threshold level is low and functions according to the all-or-nothing principle, manifesting excessive vulnerability toward inevitable frustrations and injury.

*Transference*: Represents one of the significant adaptation mechanisms allowing the individual to experience familiarity with unknown people or situations. In each meaningful relationship, the individual spontaneously re-experiences and re-manages his first childhood attachments. Transference allows a sort of re-actualisation of past infantile prototypes of experiences with primal objects. Transference emerges not only in everyday life but also especially during psychoanalysis, for example, as in a transference neurosis. It thus serves the analyst as a major portal of encounter with his patient's past unconscious emotional experiences, that is, with various significant objects in different periods of his life, or as I would put it, with the childhood layers hidden in the individual. At times, transference risks evoking resistance to the analysis or the analyst, as well as to leadership figures, yet more generally it provokes attraction to the re-familiar object.

*Transitional phenomenon, transitional object, transitional space*: Winnicott (1953) introduced these terms to designate a phenomenon or object of significant value to the child that is placed in between the inner world and the perception of the reality principle and external world. Transitional phenomena are thought to represent the source of creativity. The transitional object represents the infant's first "not-me" possession; it may be a toy or parts of the child's or mother's body, through which the child finds consolation. Transitional phenomena represent, to my view, a very important adaptation mechanism, experienced by both child and caregiver within the "intermediate area" as transitional phenomena (object, phenomenon, and space) that bridge their separateness, and mediate between separate individuals, such as baby and parent.

*Trauma*: A trauma may be considered as a breach or shock that provokes injury to the self and can affect the sense of self-familiarity. In these moments of disruption or breakdown, the narcissistic immunisation and the stimulus barrier or protective shield are violated, including those optimally provided by the parent. The ego in such circumstances is overwhelmed and obliged to mobilise excessive protective defence mechanisms. It is important to stress, however that acute trauma symptoms may be followed by restoration of self-familiarity and a strengthening of the ego and its resiliency, and may involve mobilisation of adaptation mechanisms and accelerated reorganisation, particularly when the healthy narcissism and the ego can function together. In addition, trauma may be understood as an encounter of an event with a specific nervous system at a particular time. Traumatic symptoms are seen as both physiological and psychological.

*Triadic object relation*: I view object relations from birth as triadic relations (from the word "three"), among the parent's space, the baby's space (each senses the non-self of the other), and a virtual transitional space. The boundaries between baby and parent may be blurred temporarily in the transitional shared space under the impact of moments of intimacy between them. In contrast, Mahler and others consider object relations from birth as dyadic.

*True self, False self*: The true self develops in an atmosphere of acceptance and care by the *good-enough mother* who appreciates the child's spontaneous gestures. Interference with this process may result in the child's withdrawal from authenticity and spontaneity, and result in a nuanced response to a hostile world, with a false self that passes for real. The false self represents a defence mechanism through which the self is protected by the ego against the anxieties of abandonment and strangeness: the true self is hidden, replaced by a false self, resulting in the inhibition of the child's individuation.

*Uncanny*: Describes the sense of unease and fear experienced when something happens that seems to confirm an early-surmounted belief in the omnipotence of thought and/or to reactivate an animistic mode of thinking. Examples: seeing one's "double", déjà vu, and feeling that someone who is dead is among the living.

*Unconscious: Adjective*: Describes mental content not available to conscious awareness at a given time, but manifested, among other things, by slips of the tongue, dreams, and disconnected thoughts and associations, as well as bodily sensations, affects, and behaviour. Affective dispositions related to instincts and drives give rise to wishes and motivations that strive for conscious expression but are opposed by other forces (now conceptualised as the ego and superego).

*Noun*: the unconscious (UC) relates to one of the dynamic systems described by Freud in his early *topographic* theory of the psychic apparatus. He believed that a portion of the mental contents and activities representative of the instincts had never been conscious (primal repression), and were denied access to consciousness by an exacting censorship imposed on the UC by the preconscious (PC). Other contents eventually gained consciousness but were then repressed (repression proper). The repression was maintained by means of a special energy—an anti-cathexis. This concept of the distribution and interplay of psychic energies constitutes the economic viewpoint of Freud's meta-psychology.

*Undoing*: Represents a defence mechanism dating from the anal stage against the anxiety of losing control and experiencing guilt. The individual, through a magical thought, tries to believe, and make the other believe, that certain thoughts, words, gestures, actions, or behaviours never occurred.

*Weaning*: Refers to the gradual process of separation-individuation-socialisation. Both baby and mother have to separate from their common intimacy and ultimate satisfaction of breastfeeding in order to allow the infant the autonomy to eat various kinds of food by himself. However, nobody is willing to forgo the blissful moments and satisfaction he has, unless encouraged and gratified by other satisfactions.

These represent mainly the consolidation of individuation, during which intimacy and satisfaction can be safeguarded as transitional phenomena (see definition). Throughout the lifespan, the individual experiences different forms of weaning from his tendency to become addicted to his pleasures, and this weaning process always arouses inner conflicts or conflicts with external demands. The first weaning process is that of the infant from the oral pleasures of suckling and taking in the mother's breast and milk (and milk substitutes), while encouraging him to find satisfaction and pleasure in eating according to family and social mores. The second refers to diaper weaning in the anal stage. The weaning practice of liberating a toddler from diapers encourages him to manifest his body mastery of retaining and expelling according to family and social manners. The weaning process affects the baby's relationship with his caretaker and touches upon many issues, such as befriending other sources of satisfaction and generally expanding one's familiarity as well as interpersonal boundaries between self and non-self, emotional proximity and closeness, and, particularly, with respect to issues of control and power within relationships and in the family.

*Withdrawal*: Represents the need to flee within oneself and to seclude oneself from outside threats following the arousal of feelings such as pain, discomfort, or distress. It may also represent an intense craving for being held (contained), for example, by an internalised representation of a comforting image or resource.

# REFERENCES

Adler, B. (2003). Psychoanalysis and female sexuality. In: Y. Hatab (Ed.), *Psychoanalysis in Theory and Practice*. Tel Aviv: Dyonon Publishers. (Hebrew).

Amital-Teplizki, H., & Shoenfeld, Y. (1991). Has schizophrenia an immunologic basis. *Harefuah, 120*: 392–394. (Hebrew).

Anderson, J., & Szuchman, P. (2011). *Spousonomics: Using Economics to Master Love, Marriage, and Dirty Dishes*. New York, NY: Random House.

Anzieu, D. (1985). *Le Moi-Peau*. Paris: Dunod.

Anzieu, D. (1987). Formal signifiers and the ego-skin. In: D. Anzieu (Ed.), *Psychic Envelopes* (pp. 11–16). London: Karnac, 1990.

Aron, L. (1993). Working toward operational thought: Piagetian theory and psychoanalytic method. *Contemporary Psychoanalysis, 29*: 289–313.

Basch, M. F. (1983). Empathic understanding: A review of the concept and some theoretical considerations. *Journal of the American Psychoanalytic Association, 31*: 101–126.

Baumeister, R., Vohs, K. D., & Tice, D. M. (2007). The strength model of self-control. *A Journal of the Association of Psychological Science, 16(6)*: 351–355.

Bellak, L., Hurvich, M., & Crawford, P. (1969). Psychotic egos. *Psychoanalytic Review, 56*: 525–542.

359

Ben-Artsy Solan, A. (11 September 2014). *The unique importance of the clinical psychologist in the evaluation of ADHD: Executive functioning as reflected in the WISC IV and Bender-Gestalt II.* Presented at the Professional Committee for Clinical Psychology, Ministry of Health, Tel-Aviv, Israel.

Bick, E. (1968). The experience of the skin in early object relations. *International Journal of Psycho-Analysis, 49:* 484–486.

Bion, W. R. (1962). *Learning from Experience.* London: Tavistock.

Blatt, S. J. (1974). Levels of object representation in anaclitic and introjective depression. *Psychoanalytic Study of the Child, 29:* 107–157.

Bloom, P. (2010). *How Pleasure Works: The New Science of Why We Like What We Like.* New York, NY: Norton.

Bollas, C. (1992). *Being a Character: Psychoanalysis and Self Experience.* London: Routledge.

Bowlby, J. (1988). *A Secure Base: Parent–Child Attachment and Healthy Human Development.* New York, NY: Basic Books.

Britton, R. (1989). The missing link: Parental sexuality in the Oedipus complex. In: *The Oedipus Complex Today: Clinical Implications* (pp. 83–101). London: Karnac.

Britton, R. (2004). Subjectivity, objectivity and triangular space. *Psychoanalytic Quarterly, 73:* 47–61.

Buber, M. (1947). *Between Man and Man.* London: Routledge, 2002.

Chasseguet-Smirgel, J. (1975). L'Ideal du Moi. *Revue Française de Psychoanalyse, 37:* 709–929. (French)

Chasseguet-Smirgel, J. (1976). Some thoughts on the ego ideal: A contribution to the study of the "illness of ideality". *Psychoanalytic Quarterly, 45:* 345–373.

Chomsky, N. (1985). *The Logical Structure of Linguistic Theory.* Chicago, IL: University of Chicago Press.

Colomobelli-Negrel, D., Hauber, M. E., Robertson, J., Sulloway, F. J., Hoi, H., Griggio, M., & Kleindorfer, S. (2012). Embryonic learning of vocal passwords in superb fairy-wrens reveals intruder cuckoo nestlings. *Current Biology, 22:* 2155–2160.

Corbyn, Z. (8 November 2012). *Wrens teach their eggs to sing.* Nature. Retrieved from www.nature.com/news/wrens-teach-their-eggs-to-sing-1.11779, October 2013.

Damasio, A. (1999). *The Feeling of What Happens.* London: Heinemann.

Dannenberg, Gh. D., & Shoenfeld, Y. (1991). Stress reaction and the immune system. *Harefuah, 120:* 455–459. (Hebrew)

DeHart, G. B., Sroufe, L. A., & Cooper, R. G. (1996). *Child Development: Its Nature and Course.* New York, NY: Basic Books.

de M'Uzan, M. (2006). Invite à la fréquentation des ombres. *Bulletin of the European Psychoanalytical Federation, 60:* 14–28. (French)

Durban, J. (2011). Shadows, ghosts and chimaeras: On some early modes of handling psycho-genetic heritage. *International Journal of Psycho-Analysis, 92(4)*: 903–924.

Duruz, N. (1981). The psychoanalytic concept of narcissism. Part II: Toward a structural definition. *Psychoanalytic Contemporary Thought, 4*: 35–67.

Ellis, H. (1898). Critical Notices. *Mind, 7(26)*: 249–255.

Emde, R. N. (1988a). Development terminable and interminable: I. Innate and motivational factors from infancy. *International Journal of Psycho-Analysis, 69(1)*: 23–42.

Emde, R. N. (1988b). Development terminable and interminable: II. Recent psychoanalytic theory and therapeutic considerations. *International Journal of Psycho-Analysis, 69(2)*: 283–296.

Erikson, E. H. (1950). *Childhood and Society*. New York, NY: Norton.

Esman, A. H. (1983). The "stimulus barrier": A review and reconsideration. *Psychoanalytic Study of the Child, 38*: 193–207.

Fisher, P. (2011). *MS2. Immunology Module: Prologue*. Retrieved from http://missinglink.ucsf.edu/lm/immunology_module/prologue/about-themodule.html, 22 September 2013.

Flavell, J. H. (1963). *The Developmental Psychology of Jean Piaget*. Princeton, NJ: Van Nostrand.

Fonagy, P., & Target, M. (1997). Attachment and reflective function: Their role in self-organization. *Development and Psychopathology, 9*: 679–700.

Fonagy, P., & Target, M. (2002). Early intervention and the development of self-regulation. *Psychoanalytic Inquiry, 22*: 307–335.

Fonagy, P., & Target, M. (2007). Playing with reality: IV. A theory of external reality rooted in intersubjectivity. *International Journal of Psycho-Analysis, 88*: 917–937.

Freud, A. (1936). *The Ego and the Mechanisms of Defense*. London: Hogarth Press.

Freud, S. (1894a). *The Neuro-Psychoses of Defense. S. E., 3*: 45–61. London: Hogarth.

Freud, S. (1900a). *The Interpretation of Dreams. S. E., 4–5*. London: Hogarth.

Freud, S. (1905c). *Jokes and Their Relation to the Unconscious. S. E., 8*: 117–181. London: Hogarth.

Freud, S. (1905d). *Three Essays on the Theory of Sexuality. S. E., 7*: 125–243. London: Hogarth.

Freud, S. (1908b). Character and Anal Eroticism. *S. E., 9*: 169–175. London: Hogarth.

Freud, S. (1911b). Formulations on the Two Principles of Mental Functioning. *S. E., 12*: 218–226. London: Hogarth.

Freud, S. (1911c). Psycho-Analytic Notes on an Auto-Biographical Account of a Case of Paranoia. *S. E., 12*: 3–82. London: Hogarth.

Freud, S. (1912b). The Dynamics of Transference. *S. E.*, *12*: 99–108. London: Hogarth.

Freud, S. (1912–1913). Totem and Taboo. *S. E.*, *13*: 75–99. London: Hogarth.

Freud, S. (1914c). On Narcissism: an Introduction. *S. E.*, *14*: 69–101. London: Hogarth.

Freud, S. (1914d). On the History of the Psycho-Analytic Movement. *S. E.*, *14*: 3–71. London: Hogarth.

Freud, S. (1914g). Remembering, Repeating and Working Through. *S. E.*, *12*: 147–156. London: Hogarth.

Freud, S. (1915a). Observations on Transference-Love. *S. E.*, *12*: 159–171. London: Hogarth.

Freud, S. (1915c). Instincts and their Vicissitudes. *S. E.*, *14*: 111–140. London: Hogarth.

Freud, S. (1915d). Repression. *S. E.*, *14*: 143–158. London: Hogarth.

Freud, S. (1915e). The Unconscious. *S. E.*, *14*: 161–171. London: Hogarth.

Freud, S. (1916–1917). *Introductory Lectures on Psycho-Analysis. S. E.*, *15–16*: 303–319. London: Hogarth.

Freud, S. (1917e). Mourning and Melancholia. *S. E.*, *14*: 239–245. London: Hogarth.

Freud, S. (1918a). The Taboo of Virginity (contributions to the psychology of love III). *S. E.*, *11*: 193–208. London: Hogarth.

Freud, S. (1919h). The Uncanny. *S. E.*, *17*: 219–253. London: Hogarth.

Freud, S. (1920g). *Beyond the Pleasure Principle. S. E.*, *18*: 7–64. London: Hogarth.

Freud, S. (1921c). Further problems and lines of work. In: *Group Psychology and the Analysis of the Ego. S. E.*, *18*: 100–104. London: Hogarth.

Freud, S. (1921c). Being in Love and Hypnosis. In: *Group Psychology and the Analysis of the Ego. S. E.*, *18*: 111–116. London: Hogarth.

Freud, S. (1923b). *The Ego and the Id. S. E.*, *19*: 3–27. London: Hogarth.

Freud, S. (1926d) *Inhibitions, Symptoms and Anxiety. S. E.*, *20*: 77–174. London: Hogarth.

Freud, S. (1927c). *The Future of an Illusion. S. E.*, *21*: 3–56. London: Hogarth.

Freud, S. (1930a). *Civilization and its Discontents. S. E.*, *21*: 59–145. London: Hogarth.

Freud, S. (1933a). The dissection of the psychical personality. In: *New Introductory Lectures on Psycho-Analysis S. E.*, *22*: 57–81. London: Hogarth.

Freud, S. (1933a). Anxiety and instinctual life. In: *New Introductory Lectures on Psycho-Analysis S. E.*, *22*: 81–111. London: Hogarth.

Freud, S. (1933b). *Why War? S. E.*, *22*: 197–215. London: Hogarth.

Freud, S. (1937c). Analysis Terminable and Interminable. *S. E.*, *23*: 211–254. London: Hogarth.

Freud, S. (1940a). *An Outline of Psychoanalysis. S. E., 23*: 141–207. London: Hogarth.

Freud, S. (1950). A Project for a Scientific Psychology. *S. E., 1*: 175–391. London: Hogarth.

Gabbard, G. O. (1993). On hate in love relationships: The narcissism of minor differences revisited. *Psychoanalytic Quarterly, 62*: 229–238.

Gendlin, E. T. (1982). *Focusing.* New York, NY: Bantam.

George, J., Levy, Y., & Shoenfeld, Y. (1996). Immune network and autoimmunity. *Internal Medicine, 35(1)*: 3–9.

Gerzi, S. (2005). Trauma, narcissism and the two attractors in trauma. *International Journal of Psycho-Analysis, 86*: 1033–1050.

Goodkin, K., & Visser, A. P. (Eds.) (2000). *Psychoneuroimmunology: Stress, Mental Disorders and Health.* Washington, DC: American Psychiatric Press.

Green, A. (1999). The dead mother: The work of Andre Green. In: G. Kohon (Ed.), *The New Library of Psycho-Analysis.* London: Routledge.

Green, A. H. (1978). Self-destructive behavior in battered children. *American Journal of Psychiatry, 135(5)*: 579–581.

Greenspan, S. I. (1979). Intelligence and adaptation: An integration of psychoanalytic and Piagetian developmental psychology. *Psychological Issues, XII(3–4)*: Monograph 47/48. New York, NY: International Universities Press.

Grunberger, B. (1971). *Narcissism: Psychoanalytic Essays.* Madison, CT: International Universities Press.

Harlow, H. (1959). Love in infant monkeys. *Scientific American, 200*: 68–74.

Hartmann, H. (1939). *Ego Psychology and the Problem of Adaptation.* New York, NY: International Universities Press, 1958.

Hartmann, H. (1950). Comments on the psychoanalytic theory of the ego. *Psychoanalytic Study of the Child, 5*: 74–96.

Hartmann, H. (1952). The mutual influences in the development of ego and id. *Psychoanalytic Study of the Child, 7*: 9–30.

Hefner, A. G., & Guimaraes, V. (2011). *Animism.* Retrieved from www.themystica.com/mystica/articles/a/animism.html on 27 October 2003.

Houzel, D. (1990). The concept of psychic envelope. In: D. Anzieu (Ed.), *Psychic Envelopes* (pp. 27–58). London: Karnac.

Houzel, D. (1996). The family envelope and what happens when it is torn. *International Journal of Psycho-Analysis, 77*: 901–912.

Isaacs, S. (1948). The nature and function of phantasy. *International Journal of Psycho-Analysis, 29*: 73–97.

Jacobson, E. (1953). The affects and their pleasure-unpleasure qualities in relation to the psychic discharge processes. In: R. M. Loewenstein (Ed.), *Drives, Affects, Behavior, Vol. 1.* New York, NY: International Universities Press.

Jacobson, E. (1964). *The Self and the Object World*. New York, NY: International Universities Press.

Jones, E. (1908). Rationalisation in everyday life. In: *Papers on Psychoanalysis Fifth Edition* (pp. 1–9). London: Karnac, 1977.

Kahneman, D. (2009). Questioning a chastened priesthood. *Finance & Development, 46(3)*: 4.

Kahneman, D., & Tversky, A. (1979). Prospect theory: An analysis of decisions under risk. *Econometrica, 47*: 263–292.

Kandel, E. R. (2006). *In Search of Memory: The Emergence of a New Science of Mind*. New York, NY: W. W. Norton & Company.

Kandel, E. R., Siegelbaum, S., & Schwartz, J. H. (1991). Synaptic transmission. In: E. R. Kandel, J. H. Schwartz, & T. M. Jessell (Eds.), *Principles of Neural Science (Third Edition)* (pp. 123–134). New York, NY: Elsevier.

Kelly, V. C. (1996). Affect and the redefinition of intimacy. In: D. L. Nathanson (Ed.), *Knowing Feeling: Affect, Script, and Psychotherapy* (pp. 55–104). New York, NY: W. W. Norton.

Kelly, V. C. (2009). *A Primer of Affect Psychology*. Retrieved from www. tomkins.org/what.../vernon-kelly-a-primer-of-affect-psychology,    21 December 2014. Also reprinted in *The Art of Intimacy and the Hidden Challenge of Shame* (see below) as Appendix I.

Kelly, V. C. (2012). *The Art of Intimacy and the Hidden Challenge of Shame*. Rockland, ME: Maine Authors Publishing.

Kernberg, O. F. (1975). *Borderline Conditions and Pathological Narcissism*. New York, NY: Jason Aronson.

Kernberg, O. F. (1980). *Internal World and External Reality*. New York, NY: Jason Aronson.

Kernberg, O. F. (1984). *Severe Personality Disorders: Psychotherapeutic Strategies*. New Haven, CT: Yale University Press.

Khan, M. R. (1963). The concept of cumulative trauma. *Psychoanalytic Study of the Child, 18*: 286–306.

Klein, M. (1957). Envy and gratitude. In: *The Writings of Melanie Klein, Vol. 3* (pp. 176–235). London: Hogarth Press, 1975.

Klein, M. (1959). On the sense of loneliness. In: *Envy and Gratitude and Other Works 1946–1963* (pp. 300–313). New York, NY: The Free Press.

Kohut, H. (1966). Forms and Transformations of Narcissism. *Journal of the American Psychoanalytic Association, 14*: 243–272.

Kohut, H. (1971). *The Analysis of the Self*. New York, NY: International Universities Press.

Kohut, H. (1972). Thoughts on narcissism and narcissistic rage. *Psychoanalytic Study of the Child, 27*: 360–400.

Kohut, H. (1977). *The Restoration of the Self*. New York, NY: International Universities Press.

Laor, N. (1990). Seduction in tongues: Reconstructing the field of metaphor in the treatment of schizophrenia. In: G. L. Ormiston & R. Sossower (Eds.), *The Discrimination of Medical Authority: Contributions to Medical Studies, No. 27* (pp. 141–175). New York, NY: Greenwood.

Laplanche, J., & Pontalis, J. B. (1973). *The Language of Psychoanalysis* (D. Nicholson-Smith, Trans.). London: Karnac Books and The Institute of Psychoanalysis, 1988.

Levinas, E. (1969). *Totality and infinity* (A. Linguis, Trans.). Pennsylvania: Duquesne University Press.

Levine, P. (2010). *In an Unspoken Voice: How the Body Releases Trauma and Restores Goodness.* Berkeley, CA: North Atlantic Books & ERGOS Institute Press.

Maiello, S. (1995). The sound object: A hypothesis about pre-natal auditory experience and memory. *Journal of Child Psychotherapy, 21*: 23–41.

McClelland, R. T. (2004). Normal narcissism and the need for theodicity. In: P. Van Inwagen (Ed.), *Christian Faith and the Problem of Evil* (pp. 185–206). Grand Rapids, MI: W. B. Eerdmans.

McCloskey, G., & Perkins, L. A. (2013). *Essentials of Executive Functions Assessment.* Hoboken, NJ: Wiley.

McClure, S. M., Laibson, D. I., Loewenstein, G., & Cohen, J. D. (2004). Separate neural systems value immediate and delayed monetary rewards. *Science, 306*: 340–370.

McKechnie, J. (1983). *Webster's New Universal Unabridged Dictionary: Deluxe Second Edition.* New York, NY: Simon & Schuster.

Mahler, M. S. (1968). On human symbiosis and the vicissitudes of individuation. In: P. Buckley (Ed.), *Essential Papers on Object Relations* (pp. 200–221). New York, NY: New York University Press, 1986.

Mahler, M. S. (1972a). On the first three subphases of the separation individuation process. *International Journal of Psycho-Analysis, 53*: 333–338.

Mahler, M. S. (1972b). Rapprochement subphase of the separation individuation process. *Psychoanalytic Quarterly, 41*: 487–506.

Mahler, M. S., & McDevitt, J. B. (1968). Observations on adaptation and defence in statu nascendi. *Psychoanalytic Quarterly, 37*: 1–21.

Mahler, M. S., Pine, F., & Bergman, A. (1975). *The Psychological Birth of the Human Infant: Symbiosis and Individuation.* New York, NY: Basic Books.

Martin, E. A. (Ed.) (2007). *Oxford Concise Medical Dictionary.* Oxford: Oxford University Press.

Martin, J. H. (1991). Coding and processing of sensory information. In: E. R. Kandel, J. H. Schwartz & T. M. Jessell (Eds.), *Principles of Neural Science* (pp. 777–791). New York, NY: Elsevier.

Matthew, T. G., Baumeister, R. F., DeWall, C. N., Maner, J. K., Plant E. A., Tice, D. M., Brewer L. E., & Schmeichel, B. J. (2007). Self-control relies on glucose as a limited energy source: Willpower is more than a metaphor. *Journal of Personality & Social Psychology, 92*: 325–336.

Modell, A. H. (1993). *The Private Self.* Cambridge, MA: Harvard University Press.

Moore, B. E., & Fine, B. D. (1990). *Psychoanalytic Terms & Concepts.* London and New Haven, CT: The American Psychoanalytic Association and Yale University Press

Nacke, P. (1899). Kritisches zum Kapitel der normalen und pathologischen Sexualitaet. *Arch. Psychiat. Berlin, 32*: 356–386. (German)

Nathanson, D. L. (1992). *Shame and Pride: Affect, Sex and the Birth of the Self.* New York, NY: Norton.

National Institute of Health (NIH) (2008). *Immune System Self and Nonself.* National Institute of Allergy and Infectious Diseases. Retrieved from www.niaid.nih.gov/topics/immuneSystem/pages/selfnonself.aspx, 10 October 2014.

Neukom, M., Corti, V., Boothe, B., Boehler, A., & Goetzmann, L. (2012). Fantasized recipient-donor relationships following lung transplantations: A qualitative case analysis based on patient narratives. *International Journal of Psycho-Analysis, 93*: 117–137.

Nunberg, H. (1931). The synthetic action of the ego. *International Journal of Psycho-Analysis, 12*: 123–140.

Ogden, T. H. (1989). *The Primitive Edge of Experience.* London: Karnac, 1992.

Orbach, I. (1996). The role of the body experience in self-destruction: Early attachment and suicidal tendencies. *Clinical Child Psychology and Psychiatry, 1*: 607–619.

Orbach, I. (2007). From abandonment to symbiosis: A developmental reversal in suicidal adolescents. *Psychoanalytic Psychology, 24*: 150–166.

Ortega-Hernandez, O. -D., Kivity, S., & Shoenfeld, Y. (2009). Olfaction, psychiatric disorders and autoimmunity: Is there a common genetic association? *Autoimmunity, 42(1)*: 80–88.

Pally, R. (1997a). I. How the brain actively constructs perceptions. *International Journal of Psycho-Analysis, 78*: 587–593.

Pally, R. (1997b). II. How the brain actively constructs perceptions. *International Journal of Psycho-Analysis, 78*: 1021–1030.

Pally, R. (1997c). III. Memory: Brain systems that link past, present and future. *International Journal of Psycho-Analysis, 78*: 1223–1234.

Piaget, J. (1936). *The Origins of Intelligence in Children.* New York, NY: International Universities Press, 1952.

Piaget, J. (1977). *The Essential Piaget* (H. E. Gruber & J. J. Voneche (Eds.)). New York, NY: Basic Books.

Pine, F. (2004). Mahler's concepts of "symbiosis" and separation-individuation: Revisited, reevaluated, refined. *Journal of the American Psychoanalytic Association, 52*: 511–533.

Piontelli, A. (1987). Infant observation from before birth. *International Journal of Psycho-Analysis, 68*: 453–463.

Piontelli, A. (1989). A study on twins before and after birth. *International Review of Psycho-Analysis, 16*: 413–426.

Proust, M. (1913). *Remembrance of Things Past, Vol. I.* (C. K. Moncrieff, Trans.) Ware, Hertfordshire: Wordsworth Edition, 2006.

Quinodoz, D. (1990). Vertigo and object relationship. *International Journal of Psycho-Analysis, 71*: 53–63.

Quinodoz, D. (2003). Words that touch. *International Journal of Psycho-Anaysis, 84*: 1469–1485.

Quinodoz, J. -M. (1993). *The Taming of Solitude: Separation Anxiety in Psychoanalysis.* (P. Slotkin, Trans.) London: Routledge.

Quinodoz, J. -M. (1996). The sense of solitude in the psychoanalytic encounter. *International Journal of Psycho-Analysis, 77*: 481–496.

Racker, H. (1968). *Transference and Countertransference.* London: Karnac, 1988.

Rank, O. (1911). Ein Beitrag zum Narzissismus. *Jb. psychoan. Psychopath. Forsch., 3*: 401–426.

Reich, A. (1953). Narcissistic object choice in women. *Journal of the American Psychoanalytic Association, 1*: 22–44.

Reich, A. (1960). Pathologic forms of self-esteem regulation. *Psychoanalytic Study of the Child, 15*: 215–232.

Rizzolatti, G. (2004). The mirror-neuron system. *Annual Review of Neuroscience, 27*: 169–192.

Rizzolatti, G., & Fabbri-Destro, M. (2010). Mirror neurons: From discovery to autism. *Annual Review of Neuroscience, Experimental Brain Research, 200(3–4)*: 223–237.

Rolnik, E. J. (2012). *Freud in Zion: Psychoanalysis and the Making of Modern Jewish Identity.* London: Karnac.

Rosenfeld, H. (1971). A clinical approach to the psychoanalytic theory of the life and death instincts: An investigation into the aggressive aspects of narcissism. *International Journal of Psycho-Analysis, 52*: 169–178.

Rosenfield, I. (1992). *The Strange, Familiar and Forgotten: An Anatomy of Consciousness.* London: Picador/Macmillan General, 1995.

Ross, G. (2008). *Beyond the Trauma Vortex into the Healing Vortex. A Guide for Psychology & Education.* Los Angeles, CA: International Trauma-Healing Institute.

Routledge, C., Arndt, J., Wildschut, T., Sedikides, C., Hart, M., Juhl, J., Vingerhoets, A. J., & Schlotz, W. (2011). The past makes the present meaningful: Nostalgia as an existential resource. *Journal of Personality & Social Psychology, 101(3)*: 638–652.

Routledge, C., Wildschut, T., Sedikides, C., Juhl, J., & Arndt, J. (2012). The power of the past: Nostalgia as a meaning-making resource. *Memory, 20(5)*: 452–460.

Rutter, M., & Rutter, M. (1993). *Developing Minds Across the Life Span*. Harmondsworth: Penguin.

Sacks, O. (1985). The president's speech. In: *The Man Who Mistook His Wife For A Hat and Other Clinical Tales* (pp. 76–80). New York, NY: Summit.

Sacks, O. (1987). *A Leg to Stand On*. New York, NY: Harper & Row.

Saint-Exupery, A. de (2000). *The Little Prince*. (R. Howard, Trans.) New York, NY: A Harvest Book, Harcourt Inc.

Sandler, A. M. (1977). Beyond eight-month anxiety. *International Journal of Psycho-Analysis, 58*: 195–207.

Sandler, J. (1960). The background of safety. *International Journal of Psycho-Analysis, 41*: 352–356.

Sandler, J. (1985). Towards a reconsideration of the psychoanalytic theory of motivation. *Bulletin of the Anna Freud Centre, 8*: 223–264.

Sandler, J. (1987). *From Safety to Superego*. London: Karnac.

Sandler, J. (1988). Psychoanalytic technique and 'Analysis Terminable and Interminable'. *International Journal of Psycho-Analysis, 69*: 335–345.

Sandler, J. (1990). On internal object relations. *Journal of the American Psychoanalytic Association, 38*: 859–880.

Sandler, J., & Sandler, A. M. (1998). *Internal Objects Revisited*. London: Karnac.

Schafer, R. (1954). *Psychoanalytic Interpretation in Rorschach Testing: Theory and Application*. New York, NY: Grune & Stratton.

Schafer, R. (1968). *Aspects of Internalization*. New York, NY: International Universities Press.

Schindler, L. W. (1991). *Understanding the Immune System*. Darby, PA: Diane Publishing Company.

Segal, H. (1983). Some clinical implications of Melanie Klein's work—Emergence from narcissism. *International Journal of Psycho-Analysis, 64*: 269–276.

Shidlo, R. (1985). The relationship in normal adults between depression and self and object representation (Doctoral Dissertation, The California School of Professional Psychology, San Diego, 1985). *Dissertation Abstracts International*. No. 8517940. Ann Arbor: University Microfilms International.

Shidlo, R. (2012). *The Rosebush Murders: A Helen Mirkin Novel*. Los Altos, CA: Hoopoe Publishing.

Skelton, R. (Ed.) (2006). *The Edinburgh International Encyclopedia of Psychoanalysis*. Edinburgh: Edinburgh University Press.

Slutzky, R. (1966). La personnalité de l'éducateur d'enfant inadapté. *Médecine et Hygiène, Geneve*, 234 S. (French)

Smith, S. (1977). The golden fantasy: A regressive reaction to separation anxiety. *International Journal of Psycho-Analysis, 58*: 311–324.

Solan, M. (2002). *Attachment styles and exercising authority while performing a role*. Unpublished Masters thesis, Bar-Ilan University, Ramat-Gan, Israel. Retrieved from NNL National Library (Publication Number 004405276).

Solan, M., & Mikulincer, M. (2003). Patterns of communication and exercise of authority in fulfilling a task. *Kav Ofek, 4*: 9–24. (Hebrew)

Solan, R. (1973). Constipation in childhood. *Harefuah, 84*: 9. (Hebrew)

Solan, R. (1986). Refoulement—deni—sublimation. *Revue Française de Psychanalyse, 50*: 533–538. (French)

Solan, R. (1989a). Objet transitionnel-symbolisation-sublimation. *Revue Française de Psychanalyse, 53*: 1843–1845. (French)

Solan, R. (1989b). Idealization and de-idealization. *Sichot, 3*: 17–24. (Hebrew)

Solan, R. (1991). "Jointness" as integration of merging and separateness in object relations and narcissism. *Psychoanalytic Study of the Child, 46*: 337–352.

Solan, R. (1996). The leader and the led—their mutual needs. In: L. Rangell & R. Moses-Hrushovski (Eds.), *Psychoanalysis at the Political Border* (pp. 237–255). Madison, CT: International Universities Press.

Solan, R. (1998a). Narcissistic fragility in the process of befriending the unfamiliar. *American Journal of Psycho-Analysis, 58*: 163–186.

Solan, R. (1998b). The narcissistic vulnerability to change in object relation. In: *Psychoanalyse in Israel Theoriebildung und therapeutische Praxis*. Rafael Moses (Hg.) Series: *Psychoanalytische Blätter, Bd. 9*, pp. 30–56. Göttingen: Vandenhoeck & Ruprecht, 1998.

Solan, R. (1999). The interaction between self and others: A different perspective on narcissism. *Psychoanalytic Study of the Child, 54*: 193–215.

Solan, Z., Horn, D., Ruppin, E., & Edelman, S. (2005). Unsupervised learning of natural languages. *Proceedings of the National Academy of Sciences of the United States of America, 102*: 11629–11634.

Solms, M. (2004). Freud returns. *Scientific American, 290(5)*: 83–89.

Solnit, A. J. (1982). Developmental perspectives on self and object constancy. *Psychoanalytic Study of the Child, 37*: 201–218.

Spero, M. H. (2009). The joke envelope: A neglected precursor of the psychic envelope. *Psychoanalytic Study of the Child, 64*: 193–226.

Spitz, R. (1945). Hospitalism. *Psychoanalytic Study of the Child, 1*: 53–74.

Spitz, R. (1962). Autoerotism reexamined. *Psychoanalytic Study of the Child, 17*: 283–315.

Spitz, R. (1965a). *The First Year of Life*. New York, NY: International Universities Press.

Spitz, R. (1965b). The evolution of dialogue. In: M. Schur (Ed.), *Drives, Affects, Behavior, Volume 2* (pp. 170–192). New York, NY: International Universities Press.

Stern, D. N. (1984). Affect attunement. In: J. D. Call, E. Galenson, & R. L. Tyson (Eds.), *Frontiers of Infant Psychiatry, Volume 2*. New York, NY: Basic Books.

Stern, D. N. (1985). *The Interpersonal World of the Infant*. New York, NY: Basic Books.

Stern, D. N. (1992). The "pre-narrative envelope": An alternative view of "unconscious phantasy" in infancy. *Bulletin of the Anna Freud Centre, 15*: 291–318.

Stern, D. N. (2004). *The Present Moment in Psychotherapy and Everyday Life*. New York, NY: W. W. Norton.

Stojanovich, L., & Marisavljevich, D. (2007). Stress as a trigger of autoimmune disease. *Autoimmune Review, 7(3)*: 209–213.

Stolorow, R. D. (1975). Toward a functional definition of narcissism. *International Journal of Psycho-Analysis, 56*: 179–185.

Strous, R. D., & Shoenfeld, Y. (2006). Schizophrenia, autoimmunity and immune system dysregulation: A comprehensive model updated and revisited. *Journal of Autoimmunology, 27(2)*: 71–80.

Symington, N. (1993). *Narcissism: A New Theory*. London: Karnac.

Tomkins, S. (1962). *Affect imagery consciousness: (Vol. I) The Complete Edition*. New York, NY: Springer, 2008.

Tomkins, S. (1963). *Affect imagery consciousness: (Vol. II) The Complete Edition*. New York, NY: Springer, 2008.

Tomkins, S. (1979). Script theory: Differential magnification of affects. In: H. E. Howe, Jr. & R. A. Deinstbier (Eds.), *Nebraska Symposium on Motivation* (pp. 201–236). Lincoln, NE: University of Nebraska Press.

Tomkins, S. (1987). Script Theory. In: J. Arnoff, A. I. Rabin, & R. A. Zucker (Eds.), *The Emergence of Personality* (pp. 147–216). New York, NY: Springer.

Tuckett, D. (2011). *Minding the Markets: An Emotional Finance View of Financial Instability*. Basingstoke: Palgrave Macmillan.

Tulving, E., & Thomson, D. M. (1973). Encoding specificity and retrieval processes in episodic memory. *Science, 277*: 374–380.

Tustin, F. (1981). *Autistic States in Children*. London: Routledge and Kegan Paul.

Tustin, F. (1990). *The Protective Shell in Children and Adults*. London: Karnac.

Tyson, P., & Tyson, R. (1990). *Psychoanalytic theories of development: An Integration*. New Haven, CT: Yale University Press.

Ulman, R. B., & Brothers, D. (1988). *The Shattered Self: A Psychoanalytic Study of Trauma*. New York, NY: Routledge, 1993.

Van der Waals, H. G. (1965) Problems of narcissism. *Bulletin of the Menninger Clinic, 29*: 293–311.

Vygotsky, L. S. (1962). *Thought and Language.* (E. Hanfmann & G. Vakar, Trans.) Cambridge, MA: MIT Press, 1975.

Wild, R. (2009). *Index Investing for Dummies.* Indianapolis, IN: Wiley.

Winnicott, D. W. (1951). Transitional objects and transitional phenomena. In: P. Buckley (Ed.), *Essential Papers on Object Relations* (pp. 254–271). New York, NY: New York University Press, 1986.

Winnicott, D. W. (1952a). Anxiety associated with insecurity. In: *Through Paediatrics to Psycho-Analysis* (pp. 97–100). New York, NY: Routledge, 2014.

Winnicott, D. W. (1952b). Primary Maternal Preoccupation. In: *Through Paediatrics to Psycho-Analysis* (pp. 300–305). New York, NY: Routledge, 2014.

Winnicott, D. W. (1953). Transitional objects and transitional phenomena— A study of the first not-me possession. *International Journal of Psycho-Analysis, 34*: 89–97.

Winnicott, D. W. (1958). The capacity to be alone. *International Journal of Psycho-Analysis, 39*: 416–420.

Winnicott, D. W. (1960). Ego distortion in terms of true and false self. In: *The Maturational Processes and the Facilitating Environment* (pp. 140–152). New York, NY: International Universities Press, 1965.

Winnicott, D. W. (1962). The theory of the parent–infant relationship. In: *The Maturational Processes and the Facilitating Environment* (pp. 37–55). New York, NY: International Universities Press, 1965.

Winnicott, D. W. (1971). *Playing and Reality.* London: Tavistock Publications.

## Website Resources

Note. These references lack page numbers, since none are provided online.

Ellis, K. (30 December 2011). *Stop the propellers.* She Knows. Retrieved from www.sheknows.com/parenting/articles/849023/good-or-bad-parenting-helicoptering-parenting, 23 September 2013.

Fragment 93: *The Fragments of Heraclitus*, with translation and notes, maintained by Randy Hoyt. Retrieved from www.heraclitusfragments.com, 12 October 2014.

Kahneman, D. (2009a). *Bank managers receive incentives that are unrelated to the public interest.* (Interview by G. Rolnik). The Marker Week. Retrieved from www.themarker.com/1.529515, 13 January 2015. (Hebrew).

Rettner, R. (3 June 2010). *"Helicopter" parents have neurotic kids, study suggests.* Live Science. Retrieved from www.livescience.com/10663-

helicopter-parents-neurotic-kids-study-suggests.html,    23    September 2013.

Tuckett, D., & Levinson, N. A. (Eds.) (2010). *PEP Consolidated Psychoanalytic Glossary*. Retrieved from www.pep-web.org, 14 December 2014.

# INDEX